Crisis and Disaster
COUNSELING

10/6/09

To

Lucy + Jeremy

for your kindness + generosity
but especially for friendship.

With Much Love,
Priscilla

*This book is dedicated to all the people whose lives touched mine
in the first week after Hurricane Katrina at the Cajun Dome in Lafayette, LA.*

Crisis and Disaster
COUNSELING

Lessons Learned From Hurricane Katrina and Other Disasters

Priscilla Dass-Brailsford, Editor

Lesley University

Los Angeles | London | New Delhi
Singapore | Washington DC

For information:

SAGE Publications, Inc.
2455 Teller Road
Thousand Oaks, California 91320
E-mail: order@sagepub.com

SAGE Publications Ltd.
1 Oliver's Yard
55 City Road
London EC1Y 1SP
United Kingdom

SAGE Publications India Pvt. Ltd.
B 1/I 1 Mohan Cooperative Industrial Area
Mathura Road, New Delhi 110 044
India

SAGE Publications Asia-Pacific Pte. Ltd.
33 Pekin Street #02-01
Far East Square
Singapore 048763

Printed in the United States of America.

Library of Congress Cataloging-in-Publication Data

Crisis and disaster counseling: Lessons learned from hurricane Katrina and other disasters/edited by Priscilla Dass-Brailsford.

    p. cm.

Includes bibliographical references and index.

ISBN 978-1-4129-6508-8 (pbk.: alk. paper)

   1. Disaster victims—Counseling of—United States—Case studies. 2. Crisis intervention (Mental health services)—United States—Case studies. 3. Emergency management—United States—Case studies. I. Dass-Brailsford, Priscilla.

HV555.U6D56 2010
363.34'86—dc22   2009008631

This book is printed on acid-free paper.

09   10   11   12   13   10 9   8   7   6   5   4   3   2   1

Acquisitions Editor:	Kassie Graves
Editorial Assistant:	Veronica Novak
Production Editor:	Karen Wiley
Copy Editor:	Jennifer Stallard
Typesetter:	C&M Digitals (P) Ltd.
Proofreader:	Andrea Martin
Indexer:	Julie Grayson
Cover Designer:	Janet Foulger
Marketing Manager:	Stephanie Adams

Contents

Preface

Since August 29, 2005, for people in the Gulf Coast region and for most Americans, Katrina epitomizes not only a woman's name but also the stark images of pain, suffering, and devastation caused by the storm. Hurricane Katrina did not just affect New Orleans. Many other towns along the Mississippi–Alabama Gulf Coast such as Bay St. Louis and Waveland also bore the brunt of this catastrophic storm. But when the 17th Street Canal, London Avenue Canal, and Industrial Canal levees breached in New Orleans, the disaster escalated in unimaginable ways, and the Crescent City captured the attention of the national and international community.

It certainly captured my attention, so much so that I could not shake off the images of the crying faces and victims pleading for help, all of which was aired repeatedly by the media. As a trained crisis responder, I knew I had to go down to New Orleans to help. That opportunity came on Labor Day, a week after the storm had struck, when I was deployed to Baton Rouge, LA.

The following 2 weeks were spent at the Cajun Dome in Lafayette, a small town outside Baton Rouge that sheltered more than 2,000 men, women, and children, many of them recently rescued by the National Guard from the torrid waters of Katrina. This experience was unlike any past crisis intervention that I had conducted. As I watched my peers on the mental health team work tirelessly through it all, I realized that we were all participating in an event of historical significance; as an academic, I knew that this point in time had to be documented for future generations. Thus, the idea for this book germinated on one of those hurricane-humid days in Louisiana.

At the outset, an apology must be made: The magnitude of Hurricane Katrina was so great and its effect on New Orleans so massive that I have chosen to focus mostly on Hurricane Katrina and New Orleans in this book. This in no way diminishes the effects of Hurricane Rita that soon followed Katrina, nor does it minimize the challenges faced by people in other towns along the Gulf Coast affected by the storms.

In recent years, there has been an increase in natural disasters, nationally and globally. The earthquakes in Kashmir (October 2005) on the heels of the tsunami in Southeast Asia (December 2004) are examples of disasters that significantly changed the field of disaster studies. After the catastrophic consequences of Hurricane Katrina in 2005, there was a keen and vital interest in understanding how to work with survivors of disasters over the short and long term.

In conceptualizing how to present this book, I decided to initially provide an overview of the field before inviting authors to focus on specific areas and population groups. Thus, Chapter 1 provides a background on the disaster field by looking back at several large-scale disasters that occurred in the United States after the middle of the 20th century: Hurricane Betsy in New

Orleans in 1965, Hurricane Camille in Mississippi in 1969, an earthquake in northern California in 1971, and Hurricane Agnes in the Mid-Atlantic states and New England in 1972.

Many questions have emerged since Hurricane Katrina barraged the Gulf Coast in 2005: Was the disaster a natural one and thus unavoidable? Could it have been less lethal if the weakened levees had been effectively repaired? Would restoration of the damaged swamps, marshes, and barrier islands have buffered New Orleans against the wrath of Hurricane Katrina? Chapter 2 explores these questions.

One of the distinguishing aspects of New Orleans culture is the jazz funeral, which is a major celebration that draws big crowds. However, relocation and the sheer number of victims affected this tradition and complicated the grief for thousands of survivors. Chapter 3 reviews funerals and burial practices and the symbolic meaning they hold for survivor families while Chapter 4, on effective interventions, provides readers with concrete and useful skills that can be used in disaster situations. It is a practical and resource filled chapter.

In Chapter 5, on African American families, Boyd-Franklin explores the multiple ways that families adapt in the aftermath of a disaster, by first discussing their expressions of grief and loss, followed by how these memories are held within the family and passed on to future generations. In Chapter 6, Knapp offers insights into working with children in disasters and crises; the chapter prepares the reader to recognize the signs of crisis, methods of treatment, particular developmental concerns, as well as protective factors that reduce the impact of the traumatic event(s) for children.

In Chapter 7, Houston, Reyes, Pfefferbaum, and Wyche describe a study that focused on identifying the challenges to adaptational resilience among displaced survivors of Hurricane Katrina from the vantage point of service providers who worked with them in the greater Houston metropolitan area. They identify the most common problems and needs encountered by service providers and the types of services and solutions that were found to be effective in disaster recovery.

Cherry, Allen, and Galea explore several themes in Chapter 8 on older adults, including the heterogeneity of the older adult age group, their special needs, the influence of pre-existing mental conditions, the role of prior hurricane experiences, and the effects of ageism and ageist attitudes on disaster planning, response, and recovery.

During disasters, spiritual needs often go unrecognized and unaddressed, yet they should be included in response efforts. McCombs, in Chapter 9 on spiritual dimensions after disasters, explores the following spiritual themes: sense of direction, meaning, and purpose in life; and feelings of connectedness with oneself, with others, and with God.

In Chapter 10, on working with rural and diverse communities, Boyd, Quevillon, and Engdahl examine important issues in responding to disasters at the community level, with specific attention to rural and ethnic minority communities and the issues that affect disaster response services in diverse communities.

In Chapter 11, Marotta includes the voices of survivors as she describes 10 lessons learned while working with the Red Cross as part of a Disaster Mental Health Team in the Washington, DC, metropolitan area. Using case examples, the author discusses matters of safety and the ecology of disasters. In Chapter 12, on the federal role in disasters, Dodgen and Meed examine how the mental health needs of survivors fit into the National Response Framework. In Chapter 13, Carr focuses on the challenges faced by cross-cultural workers using community-based approaches in an international setting on the African continent. Finally, responding to the endless needs of a large number of severely traumatized individuals at disaster sites can take its toll on first responders; organizations that are responsible for deploying volunteers into the field must be attentive to the high risk their volunteers face in developing secondary trauma. Chapter 14 addresses these concerns.

The audience for this book includes mental health, social service, and human service professionals (e.g., psychologists, social workers, school psychologists, mental health and pastoral counselors). In addition, policy makers at the local, state, and national levels will benefit from the information provided here, while the skill-building focus will make it useful for human services training programs. The perspective taken throughout this book is that psychological and behavioral adaptations to trauma are expressions of pain and efforts to cope with unacceptable environmental demands and stressors. These adaptations should be perceived not as pathological but as grounded in cultural systems of meaning making. First responders and the organizations they represent are responsible for locating and using the strength inherent within traumatized individuals, families, and communities—an approach that can effectively assist survivors of disasters toward healing, recovery, and resilience.

Hurricane Katrina was a recent disaster, described as the deadliest and most expensive natural disaster in U.S. history, and incalculable in terms of loss of life, destruction to property, and economic hardship. The massive displacement, homelessness, and overall trauma experienced by survivors of Hurricane Katrina will require mental health monitoring for years to come. This book serves as a record of a momentous event in this nation's history. Most important, it serves as a testimony to those who lost their lives in the tragedy.

Acknowledgments

Hurricane Katrina changed many lives, and it certainly changed mine in the 2 short but intense weeks I spent at the Cajun Dome in Lafayette, LA, a town that I did not even know existed before September 6, 2005. First, my heartfelt gratitude goes to the many survivors I worked with in the first weeks after the storm. Amid the stories of pain and suffering, their resiliency and unflappable spirit shone through. It is a spirit that will always hold a special place in my heart, and it is their stories and culture that became the inspiration to write this book.

There were many others whose dedication and sacrifice were inspiring: my peers on the mental health team and members of the National Guard who worked tirelessly late into the night and the early hours of the morning to comfort those who were terrified and to support others who were in pain.

Thousands of volunteers throughout and outside the United States assisted in making life a little more bearable for the survivors of the storm. Some of the authors in this book had a direct or indirect role in providing valuable assistance or psychological first aid to the victims of Hurricane Katrina. I feel honored and grateful to have amassed such a strong and engaging group of authors. Their descriptive recollections, intense research, and sound practical recommendations make this book an important contribution to the disaster field.

During the many times I have returned to New Orleans, I have met hundreds of mental health workers, clergy, and professionals who continue the daunting task of rebuilding and recovery. These professionals deserve high praise and acknowledgment as well. Their endless work is important to the recovery of New Orleans and the return of its citizenry, and their persistence amid many challenges has motivated me to document an important time in the history of our country.

Throughout the writing, editing, and preparation of this book, I have been guided by a strong and dependable team at SAGE Publications: First, my sincere thanks go to my acquisitions editor, Kassie Graves, for believing in me once again by providing an opportunity to write this second book. I have valued Kassie as a thoughtful, dependable, and supportive presence during the past few years of writing. Veronica Novak, senior editorial assistant, has always been just a telephone call away and available to answer questions and guide me along the path of publishing. Karen Wiley, my production editor at SAGE, has guided me through the daunting task of bringing this book to production. As a highly capable production editor, she quickly made me feel at ease about the production process, listened attentively when necessary, made the process transparent, and managed the project with flexibility. Jennifer Stallard, manager of editorial freelancers at SAGE, was indispensable during the copyediting process; her patience, expertise, and commitment to producing a polished product within a short timeframe were much appreciated. We were indeed a good team, and it was a pleasure working with all of you!

I would also like to acknowledge Lesley University for the time provided during my sabbatical year to work on this book project. My research assistant Acey Neel helped in the early stages of this project in researching and reading relevant articles; I appreciated her tenacity in taking courses, working full-time, and helping me with the research all at the same time. Doug DiMartile, another research assistant, and my son Juden Dass really helped me out in a crunch whenever necessary; thank you both for your support. As a visiting professor at Georgetown University's School of Medicine during my sabbatical, I am grateful to my new colleagues in the Center for Trauma and the Community for their friendship and providing me with a comfortable space to complete my writing. Finally, my endless gratitude and appreciation goes to my family, especially my husband, Keith W. Brailsford, for his unwavering support and patience as I worked late into the night and most weekends to meet writing and editing deadlines. He is the wind beneath my wings. This book would not have been possible without the love and strength I have felt from him.

A Historical Overview of Disasters and the Crisis Field

Priscilla Dass-Brailsford

Hurricane Katrina cut a wide swath of destruction across the Gulf Coast at the end of August 2005. In the span of 5 hours, the storm devastated approximately 90,000 square miles in the Gulf Coast areas (Alabama, Louisiana, and Mississippi) and displaced hundreds of thousands of people, leaving much of New Orleans under water for several weeks. The reconstruction process has taken several years at an estimated cost of $81.2 billion (U.S.), making Hurricane Katrina one of the costliest natural disasters in U.S. history. However, U.S. cities have arisen from massive devastation before; the Great San Francisco Earthquake of 1906 and Hurricane Andrew in 1992 are a few examples of events that have challenged the resources of other cities in the past. In this chapter, several major disasters are discussed to provide a historical backdrop to the crisis and disaster field. These disasters offer important lessons that future disaster responders are urged to heed. Finally, this chapter provides an overview of the major agencies involved in disaster planning, management, and response.

CHAPTER HIGHLIGHTS

✦ Provides a history of the evolution of the crisis and disaster field;

✦ Reviews in depth some of the worst disasters, both nationally and internationally in terms of the contributions made to the disaster field; and

✦ Describes the development of major disaster and crisis response organizations (e.g., American Red Cross, Federal Emergency Management Agency).

BACKGROUND

Disasters have occurred long before recorded history. For example, in approximately 1500 B.C., the Mediterranean Stroggli island blew up after a tsunami nearly eradicated the Minoan civilization. The area is now called Santorini, and Plato referred to it as the site where the city of Atlantis disappeared under the waves (Crossley, 2005). In 3000 B.C., a major global paleo-climate event, of which little is known, appears to have affected sea-level vegetation and surface chemistry. It is speculated that this disaster may have been the flood recorded in the Old Testament of the Bible. About 65 million years ago, a space rock hit the Earth and wiped out dinosaurs and countless other animal species. Many other natural disasters occurred globally prior to Hurricane Katrina. Similar to Hurricane Katrina, they were cataclysmic events that reshaped government policy and captured the nation's empathy for generations.

The disaster timeline lists some of the significant disasters that occurred in the world over the past century (see below). The lessons learned paved the way for major changes in the delivery of disaster and crisis services as we know it today.

These disasters are reviewed because of the impact they had in terms of loss of life and property damages, as well as the contribution they made in the development of the crisis and disaster field.

Disaster Timeline

Date	1889	1900	1906	1925	1930s	1931	1935	1938	1942	1965	1969
Event	Johnstown Flood	Galveston Hurricane	San Francisco Earthquake	Tri-State Tornado	Dust Storms	Yellow River Floods	Labor Day Hurricane	Great New England Hurricane	Cocoanut Grove Nightclub Fire	Hurricane Betsy	Hurricane Camille
Affected Area	U.S. (PA)	U.S. (TX)	U.S. (CA)	U.S. (MS, IL, ID)	U.S. (OK, TX)	China	U.S. (FL)	U.S. (NY, RI, CT, MA, NH)	U.S. (MA)	Bahamas, U.S. (FL, LA)	U.S. (LA, MS, VA)
Number of People Killed	2,200	6,000	3,000+	695	65	1 to 4 million	405	720	492	75	250
Property Damage	$10 million	$30 million	$400 million	$1.4 billion	N/A	$81.2 billion	$6 million	$4.7 billion	$122,500	$1 billion	$1.12 billion
What Did We Learn?	Recovery time needed, especially for low-income communities	Improvement in disaster management necessary	Stricter building standards and codes necessary	Improvement in warning systems necessary	Importance of taking care of the land	Better construction of dykes, levees, and dams to prevent flooding of river	Improvement in communication needed	Improvement in dyke system necessary	Changes in fire codes needed; crisis services launched	Federal government became involved in levee construction	Improvement in hurricane readiness and interagency communication required

The Great San Francisco Earthquake (1906)

On April 18, 1906, residents of San Francisco were awakened by an earthquake that would later devastate their city. The magnitude of the main tremor extended from 7.7 to 7.9 on the Richter scale, the result of a 296-mile rupture along the 800-mile San Andreas fault line that lies on the boundary between the Pacific and North American plates. During the earthquake, the ground west of the fault line moved northward. The point where the most extreme shift occurred measured 21 feet across. Seismologists estimated the speed of this rupture to have been 8,300 mph northwards and 6,300 mph southwards. Residents from Los Angeles to central Nevada reported feeling the effects of the earthquake, which was later rated 8.3 on the Richter scale, developed in 1935 to measure the magnitude of earthquakes.

The earthquake lasted approximately 1 minute but was a secondary concern to the destructive 4-day fire that followed. Broken water hydrants made fighting the fires a challenge, and the fire resulted in the destruction of almost 500 city blocks. Damages were estimated at $400 million at the time; more than 225,000 people were left homeless, and the death toll was approximately 3,000. Scientists predict a 62% probability of a larger earthquake (6.7 or more in magnitude) occurring in the Bay Area in the next 30 years.

Many new developments in the disaster field occurred as a result of the San Francisco earthquake and efforts by the Californian governor George Pardee, who put

1970	1972	1972	1980	1987	1989	1992	1995	2001	2004	2005
Bhola cyclone	Hurricane Agnes	Buffalo Creek Disaster	Mt. St. Helens Volcano	Texas Tornado	Exxon Valdez Oil Spill	Hurricane Andrew	Kobe Earthquake	9/11 Terrorist Attacks	Indian Ocean Tsunami	Hurricane Katrina
Pakistan, Bangladesh, and India	U.S. (FL, PA)	U.S. (VA)	U.S. (WA)	U.S. (TX)	U.S. (AK)	U.S. (FL, LA)	Japan	U.S. (NY, D.C., PA)	Indonesia	U.S. (LA, MS)
500,000	48	125	57	30	500,000 seabirds and other animals	26	6,279	3,000+	126,000	1,800+
$1.5 billion	$3.1 billion	$50 million	$1.1 billion	$1.3 million	$5 billion punitive damages	$25 billion	$100 billion	$38 billion	Unknown	$80 billion
Improvement in early warning systems needed	Improvement in early warning system needed; media coverage helpful	Need to address delayed onset of posttraumatic stress disorder	Relocation of population to safer areas necessary	Multilanguage warning systems necessary	Attention to loss of natural resources and economic and cultural loss	More advanced warning systems	Disaster preparation and response strategies lacking	Better airport security	Improved agency coordination beneficial	Restore wetlands and improve levees

together a task force of renowned scientists to investigate the causes of the earthquake. Four years after the disaster, the Lawson (1908/1969) report, which laid the foundation for what we know about earthquakes today, was produced. The exhaustive report was favorably received upon its publication and continues to be highly regarded by seismologists, geologists, and engineers concerned with earthquake damage to buildings; the report stands as a milestone in the development of understanding earthquake mode of action and origin.

Thus, the study of seismology grew rapidly after the San Francisco earthquake and the data collected after the catastrophe transformed the field into a respected science that would prove invaluable in predicting future earthquakes and understanding their impact; the 1906 disaster marked the birth of earthquake science in the United States.

Given the exorbitant financial costs incurred after the disaster, earthquake preparedness became a major priority for city officials and local businesses throughout the city of San Francisco. Unfortunately, in their haste to restore economic and pre-disaster functioning, more emphasis was placed on rebuilding quickly rather than securely. As a result, building codes were not modified to accommodate the possibility of a similar or worse earthquake occurring. Despite the Bay Area's vulnerability to earthquakes, thousands of homes today do not meet current earthquake safety standards, making the city no less safe today than it was in 1906. In fact, its vulnerability is greater for several reasons: It is situated in the proximity of two active fault systems, its population has doubled to almost 800,000, and its economy ranks as the 21st largest in the world. As a result, if a major earthquake occurred today, a larger number of structures would collapse rather than sustain damage; this would increase the potential human death toll tremendously.

Hurricane Betsy (1965)

Hurricane Betsy was the first hurricane in the United States to cost a billion dollars in estimated damages, earning it the infamous title "Billion Dollar Betsy." The hurricane gained momentum as it came over the Florida Keys on September 7, 1965, emerging as a Category 3 storm after crossing Florida Bay and entering the Gulf of Mexico. It came ashore at Grand Isle, south of New Orleans, where it caused immense property damage before traveling upriver, triggering a 10-foot rise in the Mississippi River. The hurricane continued to move in a northwesterly direction, grew into a Category 4 storm with 155 mph winds, and caused major storm surges in Lake Pontchartrain, north of the city of New Orleans. These high storm surges caused an overtopping of the levee system so that water reached the eaves of several houses in the Crescent City. Hurricane Betsy was the first hurricane to directly hit New Orleans. The hurricane killed 76 residents in New Orleans, most of whom lived in the Ninth Ward area where water reached the highest level. Extreme flooding also occurred in the St. Bernard's Parish neighborhood of New Orleans. Sadly, history repeated itself many years later in 2005, when Hurricane Katrina wreaked similar devastation in both these neighborhoods of New Orleans.

At the time of the disaster, the federal government was minimally involved in the construction of levees and floodwalls; this responsibility fell within the purview of local government agencies. However, the devastation caused by Hurricane Betsy prompted the federal government to become more actively involved in disaster management. The U.S. Army Corp of Engineers was authorized to build 16-foot-high levees to protect New Orleans from future disasters, even though it was not clear whether such levees would sufficiently protect the city. That question was answered with alarming clarity when Hurricane Katrina washed ashore in 2005.

Although the U.S. Army Corp of Engineers has overseen the construction of millions of dollars of federal hurricane protection projects in New Orleans, parts of the metropolitan areas of New Orleans do not meet federal flood protection standards. Budgetary constraints have limited the Corp's ability to construct and repair constantly sinking levees, while the city's vulnerability to flooding has dramatically increased in recent years. The construction of 120 miles of levees and floodwalls, initiated before Hurricane Katrina and costing approximately $740 million were predicted to provide more than $11 billion in storm damage reduction benefits. Since Hurricane Katrina, the cost of this project has risen to $2 billion.

Hurricane Camille (1969)

As a Category 5 hurricane, Camille was recorded as one of the strongest and most intense storms to make landfall in the United States. Unlike most hurricanes, it struck at its greatest intensity after entering the Gulf Coast from the Caribbean Sea on August 16, 1969. Hurricane Camille first made landfall at the mouth of the Mississippi River on August 17, accompanied by 200-mph winds. The devastation in the southern Mississippi region was astounding; property and other building structures from Ansley to Biloxi completely disappeared under the storm's wrath, and only foundation slabs remained as reminders of where buildings had once existed.

Hurricane Camille's 22.6-foot tidal surges were the highest recorded in U.S. history by the Army Corp of Engineers. As the hurricane moved inland into the southeastern states, the intensity of the storm weakened, but flooding increased and roads, bridges, and buildings were washed away. Devastating flash floods and landslides along the Blue Ridge Mountains destroyed many small communities and caused more than 100 deaths in the states of Virginia and Tennessee. Overall, the best estimate of the number killed by the hurricane was 255 persons. About 50 to 75 people were never found, and the total damages from the storm were estimated at $4.2 billion.

Pielke and Pielke (1997) present two important lessons that Hurricane Camille delivered in terms of testing the nation's level of disaster preparedness and identifying areas for improvement. First, they indicate that hurricane preparedness should be viewed as the "cost of doing business." Waiting for a storm to occur to demonstrate a city's level of preparedness is futile. When a hurricane makes landfall, it results in extreme disruption; communication, power, transportation, and other necessary infrastructures are destroyed or malfunction. Second, decisions made under disaster conditions have to be made quickly; therefore, advanced planning is critical and establishing relationships and other important linkages prior to the disaster supports this goal. Decisions can then be made quickly, based on prior discussions and long-standing relationships. With Camille, coordination between government agencies and state and local officials was enhanced because of such pre-existing plans.

Hurricane Agnes (1972)

Hurricane Agnes blew across the Florida panhandle on June 19, 1972, and scurried up the Atlantic coast into Pennsylvania on June 22, 1972. Although only a Category 1 hurricane when it hit Florida, the rainfall produced by the storm made it more destructive than previous hurricanes. At the time, it was identified as the costliest disaster in U.S. history. Twelve states were devastated before the hurricane made landfall in Pennsylvania, where it became known as Pennsylvania's worst disaster: Forty-eight deaths occurred in the state; 222,000 residents became homeless; and damages were estimated at $2.1 billion. The overall estimated damages from the storm were $3.1 billion and 117 people were killed.

The hurricane produced 18 inches of rain over 2 days, and the subsequent flooding caused the evacuation of entire towns. A bold prediction by the National Weather Service in Harrisburg, Pennsylvania, that floodwaters would overtop the 3-foot-high levees that were built in 1936 around Wilkes-Barre and Scranton, resulted in an orderly evacuation of 100,000 people; this ultimately saved many lives. There were many similarities between Hurricanes Agnes and Katrina: The rushing waters of Agnes tore out a section of a cemetery near Wilkes-Barre, causing 2,000 caskets to be washed away and leaving body parts strewn in residential areas. Returning residents found 5-foot-high watermarks above the first-floor windows of their homes. Cars had floated away and garbage and debris littered the streets. Although advanced, early warning systems were not available at the time, extensive media coverage played a major and supportive role in preparing the public for an effective evacuation.

When Vice President Agnew visited the hurricane-affected area 10 days after the storm had made landfall, disaster victims were still waiting in line for temporary housing at Red Cross shelters. Thousands of disaster victims continued to live in federal trailers a year later. In addition, there were major communication gaps between state and federal agencies of government about which expenses would be reimbursed by the federal government (Miskel, 2006). First responders and Red Cross volunteers reported a similar situation developing in the Gulf Coast after Hurricane Katrina. Much blame was placed on people who did not evacuate fast enough, although they had just a few hours of advance warning. Today, improved technology in advance disaster warning systems provides at least 12 hours' notice. However, despite this advanced warning capability, 33 years later, survivors of Hurricane Katrina faced a similar situation to the survivors of Hurricane Agnes.

The Texas Tornado (1987)

On May 22, 1987, a violent, multiple-vortex tornado, with winds of 207 to 260 miles per hour devastated Saragosa, Texas, a community of approximately 5,200 people in southwest Texas. The tornado inflicted widespread damage throughout the town. The worst damage occurred in residential and business areas where property and other building structures were completely destroyed. Thirty people were killed and 131 injured. Among the destroyed buildings was a community hall in which about 80 people had gathered for a preschool graduation ceremony; the disaster took 22 lives, and approximately 60 people were injured inside the hall (Centers for Disease Control and Prevention, 1988).

This tornado disaster raised several important issues about general tornado and disaster preparedness (National Academy of Sciences, 1987). First, providing a warning message is an integral part of overall disaster preparedness; such warnings should be broadcast in languages that can be understood by all the residents who live in high-risk areas. For example, because Saratoga, Texas, had a large bilingual Latino population at the time of the disaster, warnings would have ideally been broadcast in both English and Spanish. Second, appropriate actions should include plans for coordination with the news media and local officials, training storm spotters and developing public awareness efforts. Third, groups with mobile communications capability, such as the police and fire departments, highway patrols, and amateur radio operators, play a crucial role in disaster management and should be involved as early as possible. Fourth, establishing surveillance systems to assess and improve preparedness efficiency is fundamental to disaster preparedness. Fifth, potential shelters should be identified and evaluated for capacity and the services that they can provide prior to a disaster. Finally, follow-up investigations conducted in the aftermath of natural disasters are invaluable in the information they can provide to improve future disaster preparation.

In addition, the Texas Tornado provided significant lessons on the importance of cultural competency when responding to disasters. For example, a study conducted among African American and White elderly survivors in the affected area found that both groups showed psychosocial improvement sooner than younger survivors of the disaster (Bolin & Klenow, 1988). However, there was a large discrepancy between the recovery rates of elderly African American and White residents, which the researchers attributed to social class differences. The African American elderly occupied a lower socioeconomic status than the White elderly, and a lack of resources prevented some of them from evacuating quickly, maintaining a pre-disaster level of functioning and making it difficult, if not impossible, to repair or rebuild their homes after the disaster.

Moreover, African American residents were most vulnerable to repeated dislocation, and multiple moves to temporary housing predicted lower recovery rates. In contrast familial factors did not play a major role nor did they affect the recovery of elderly Whites, because most of them lived on their own, but were important for older African Americans, especially those who lived with their children or extended family; separation from family members thus became an additional hardship. Clearly, the Texas Tornado provided valuable insight on how to best support the African American elderly in the aftermath of disasters. Sadly, these lessons were not heeded after Hurricane Katrina as African American elderly were separated from their families and dispersed to different states. It would take months before they were finally reunited with their families.

Buffalo Creek Disaster (1972)

On February 26, 1972, a rain-soaked impoundment dam of the Buffalo Creek Coal Company collapsed in Logan County, Virginia, pouring 138 million gallons of black wastewater down the narrow hollow. By the time the water subsided at the Guyandotte River, 125 persons were dead, 1,000 were injured, and 500 homes were completely demolished. Property damage exceeded $50 million, and the catastrophe caused immense human suffering.

Two years after the dam collapsed, 381 plaintiffs who were involved in a lawsuit participated in a study that produced interesting findings; African Americans who experienced fewer stressors, less property damage, and no fatalities had less disaster-related impairment (Gleser, Green, & Winger, 1981). In addition, African American men fared psychologically and emotionally better than their White counterparts; this was attributed to the leading role they played in organizing lawsuits and other community activities following the disaster. However, a follow-up study 14 years later showed a remarkable change in the original findings (Green et al., 1990). Most specifically, 11% of the participants who did not have posttraumatic stress disorder (PTSD) in the initial study were showing PTSD symptoms 2 years later; the only variable that accounted for the delayed onset of these symptoms was race. The researchers concluded that as time passed, prejudicial attitudes toward African Americans re-emerged and their risk for PTSD reappeared. This study demonstrates the importance of being attentive to social and ecological factors when formulating support services and understanding how to best help in a culturally competent manner after disasters.

Exxon Valdez Oil Spill (1989)

On March 24, 1989, the oil tanker Exxon Valdez departed Alaska for the state of Washington. At about midnight, it struck a reef and became grounded. According to official reports, the ship that was carrying 53.1 million gallons of oil spilled 10.8 million gallons of its contents in Prince William Sound, Alaska. It is considered one of the most devastating man-made environmental disasters to occur at sea.

A study conducted among 600 community residents (both native and nonnative participants) found that exposure to the disaster resulted in a decline in social relationships; an increase in health problems, substance abuse, and domestic violence; and a decline in subsistence activities (Palinkas, Downs, Patterson, & Russell, 1993). However, Alaskan Natives had a higher risk (two or three times higher) for PTSD and generalized anxiety disorders because, for them, the loss of natural resources was not only economic but also cultural. As a result of the environmental damage, they lost an important mechanism to transmit traditional values and culture, the core of Native identity, ideology, and social organization to the next generation (Green, 1996). Similarly, many families affected by Hurricane Katrina had lived in the Crescent City for multiple generations and many survivors reported that Hurricane Katrina did not destroy their homes but their cultural and historical roots. An awareness of the cultural meaning that losses may hold for survivors is integral to helping and supporting their recovery.

Disasters Beyond U.S. Shores

The Kobe Earthquake Disaster (1995)

The Kobe earthquake, which occurred on January 17, 1995, was the most devastating natural disaster to strike Japan in 72 years. The earthquake measured 7.0 on the Japanese scale and killed 6,279 people. The earthquake occurred in an area where seismic hazards were not of major concern; disaster preparedness was thus not a high priority for residents in the area. Nearly 90% of the deaths occurred as a result of collapsed buildings. Direct physical damage from the earthquake exceeded $100 billion (Chang, 1996). The number of persons killed and the lack of preparedness daunted first responders.

Many deaths and business disruption could have been reduced if the threat had been recognized earlier and adequate preparations made. The Kobe disaster brought businesses to a standstill; all steel mills, the area's leading industry, were temporarily shut down. Seven months after the earthquake, a Kobe Chamber of Commerce survey revealed that 40% of small shops that closed due to the earthquake remained closed because many business owners could not afford to repair their buildings. Several lessons can be inferred from this disaster and applied to U.S. disaster preparedness efforts. First, the disaster underscored the importance of disaster preparedness and response planning. Second, linkages among agencies at the federal, state, and local levels are salient and should be established in advance of disasters. Third, preparedness strategies such as comprehensive community response plans, mutual aid agreements, and memoranda of understanding should be developed in advance. Drills and exercises should be conducted on a regular basis. Fourth, public–private sector collaboration, particularly with key crisis-relevant organizations such as lifeline service providers, should be established as early as possible. Fifth, developing strategies that allow for the restoration of transportation system, manufacturing, and other commercial and economic activities to reduce social and economic challenges is critical. Sixth, devising plans for providing short-term, long-term, and permanent housing for large numbers of displaced residents is useful in reducing individual and family stress. Finally, preparedness initiatives should be attentive to the unique challenges that each catastrophic event presents.

The Indian Ocean Tsunami (2004)

An earthquake measuring 9.0 on the Richter scale arose out of the Indian Ocean to strike the northwest coast of Indonesia on December 26, 2004. The earthquake's seismic shock generated a tsunami that rushed onto the shores of surrounding countries. The path of destruction wreaked by the tsunami resembled a nuclear disaster. Banda Aceh (Indonesia) was the hardest hit. In a matter of minutes, 126,000 people were killed and 93,000 were reported missing. This disaster required an international response and ranks globally among the most destructive disasters in terms of financial aid and humanitarian assistance provided.

A UNICEF (2007) report provides several guidelines on improving humanitarian efforts after disasters. The report indicated that several activities initiated at the time of the tsunami resulted in lasting improvements and provided a model for future interventions: Partnerships were expanded between UN agencies, the private sector, and the military; funding was timely and abundant; the global corporate trigger mechanism allowed for sufficient supplies, fundraising, and deployment of staff; and administratively, efficient monthly tracking and twice-yearly reports generated a rigorous schedule of audits and evaluations. Information was widely shared through reports to donors, public UNICEF reports, and the posting of evaluations and information on the UNICEF Web site.

However, the report also identified several shortcomings. These included more effective coordination and partnership to reach all who were affected by disasters; communication of the knowledge and skills needed to identify warning signs so that people can better prepare and cope with disasters; expansion of emergency surge capacity, including strengthening of staff capacity and overall preparedness; delivery of appropriate supplies in a more timely fashion; improvement in emergency supplies and reliable information to target the most vulnerable people; greater accountability to stakeholders; and adequate funding and adaptable financial and administrative procedures to allow for rapid response to emergencies.

In addition, a report by *Science & Technology* (2004) outlined several important guidelines to prepare for future tsunamis. First, there is a need for effective tsunami detection, forecasting and warning, advanced sensing equipment, rapid data analysis, and effective warning broadcast systems that provide clear instruction and reach everyone at risk. Second, there should be emergency communication systems and programs to educate and inform the public of the threat of tsunami hazards for all at-risk communities, not just those that have experienced tsunami threats in the past. Third, it is important to develop and adopt a comprehensive all-hazards plan that is integrated, action based, and capable of addressing all types of hazards and vulnerabilities. Finally, international efforts to reduce the threat of tsunamis and other hazards should strive to address both national and regional challenges. Thus, all systems and infrastructures designed to help in the detection, warning, and response to tsunamis and other hazards should promote international, national, and regional cooperation and collaboration.

As a result of the number of catastrophes that people all over the world have faced through the years, the crisis and disaster field has grown and organizations have been developed to provide assistance in the aftermath of crises and disasters. The next section addresses the evolution of the disaster field and the organizations that provide support. Except for the Federal Emergency Management Agency (FEMA), which is a federal organization, most disaster organizations depend on public support and the goodwill of their volunteers.

HISTORY AND EVOLUTION OF CRISIS AND DISASTER RESPONSE SERVICES

At the turn of the 20th century, formal mental health services and crisis services were nonexistent. The first crisis service was a suicide hotline that was established in San Francisco in 1902 and a suicide prevention program (National Save a Life League) that began in New York City in 1906. The formal beginnings of crisis and disaster responding in the United States have often been attributed to the Cocoanut Grove fire and the work of Lindemann (1944) who treated many of the survivors of the fire.

In November 1942, a huge fire occurred at the Cocoanut Grove Night Club in Boston, a building with a licensed capacity of 500 people, but which held about 1,000 people on the night of the fire. It took about 15 minutes for the fire to turn the Cocoanut Grove nightclub into an inferno. With many of the 1,000 partygoers trapped inside, the death toll quickly reached 492 while another 166 were injured, making it the worst nightclub fire in history. The devastating fire prompted the strengthening of fire code regulations.

Lindemann (1944), from his work with survivors, identified common emotional reactions that he called "normal grief reactions." These reactions included a preoccupation with victims killed in the fire, identification with the deceased, strong feelings of guilt and anger, and various other somatic complaints. At about the same time, Caplan, who had also treated many of the survivors of the Cocoanut Grove fire, became interested in what constituted a crisis event. Parad and Caplan (1960) defined a crisis as occurring when individuals face insurmountable obstacles that overwhelm their usual and customary methods of problem solving; these challenges contribute to feelings of helplessness, and as psychological resources are quickly depleted, tensions mount and unresolved past issues are triggered and become prominent. Caplan is credited with the development of crisis theory as we know it today.

The follow-up services provided to survivors of the Cocoanut Grove fire were a catalyst in shifting popular thinking from long-term care to the benefits of short-term interventions. Caplan (1964) found that early and short-term interventions were most beneficial to disaster survivors. Such interventions helped survivors resolve the crisis and sometimes even helped them function at higher levels than before the crisis occurred.

In addition, Lindemann (1944) proposed that clergy and other professionals should offer grief services after a disaster; prior to this, only psychiatrists provided services to those suffering from anxiety and depression. Later, both Caplan and Lindemann collaborated to establish the Wellesley Project in Massachusetts, a community mental health program for individuals suffering from traumatic events. The precursor to using volunteers in crisis intervention and disaster services was a result of their inclusion of paraprofessionals in the Wellesley Project.

Another important change that shaped crisis interventions as practiced in the United States was the passing of the Community Mental Health Centers Act in 1963, which led to the establishment of community mental health centers that were more accessible to residents. A major result of this legislation was the development of the 24-hour emergency service that still exists today. Volunteering in a crisis has become the norm for mental health professionals and others interested in humanitarian assistance. This involves affiliation with private or federal organizations that play a leading role in providing immediate and effective services to people who are affected by a disaster.

HISTORY AND EVOLUTION OF THE AMERICAN RED CROSS

The founding of the American Red Cross in 1881 is attributed to Clara Barton, who earned the nickname "Angel of the Battlefield" during the American Civil War when, as a nurse, she rendered support to wounded soldiers. After the war, she lobbied for the successful establishment of the American Red Cross, modeled after the International Red Cross, which was founded in Switzerland in 1863.

In 1900, the American Red Cross obtained a congressional charter that mandated the organization to fulfill the provisions of the Geneva Convention: aiding the wounded during war, providing communication between family members and members of the U.S. military, and administering relief to those affected by disasters. The Red Cross emblem (a red cross on a white background) has become representative of help and relief in times of crisis. However, the Red Cross is not federally funded but an independent charitable organization that acts at both national and international levels and is supported through public funding. Nonetheless, when disasters occur, the Red Cross is given the responsibility of receiving and dispersing federal funds to disaster survivors.

In the decade following its inception, the American Red Cross responded to several national disasters. It was severely tested in World War I when excessive demands for its services caused an increase in the number of Red Cross chapters and volunteers. The

American Red Cross sent thousands of nurses overseas and helped on the home front by establishing hospitals for veterans, delivering care packages, organizing ambulances, and training dogs to search for the wounded. In World War II, it played a similar role and developed a blood collection service to aid the wounded, a legacy that flourishes today as the Red Cross Blood Bank.

The American Red Cross continues to be an important organization that offers aid to millions of people affected by crises and disasters. It played a key role in providing food and shelter for survivors of Hurricane Katrina. By working with local medical facilities in areas unaffected by the disaster, the Red Cross supported the needs of those requiring medical assistance. Another important responsibility of the Red Cross was the distribution of FEMA checks to individuals and families affected by Hurricane Katrina.

HISTORY AND EVOLUTION OF THE SALVATION ARMY

The Salvation Army, which was chartered in the United States in 1899, is an organization that provides emergency services to individuals and communities affected by disasters and other catastrophic events. The Galveston Hurricane of 1900 was the first major disaster that the Salvation Army responded to in the United States. The Salvation Army has since responded to thousands of disasters across the United States, honoring a century-old commitment to serving those in need. Similarly, in 1906, when the San Francisco earthquake struck, the Salvation Army played a prominent role in setting up feeding and sheltering stations.

In 2001, the Salvation Army, with its mobile canteens, counselors, and thousands of volunteers, played a major role in providing food services at Ground Zero in New York after the 9/11 terrorist attacks on the World Trade Center. The Salvation Army's efforts at Ground Zero focused on the provision of mobile canteens (feeding units). In addition, Salvation Army counselors provided support and comfort to rescue and recovery personnel who worked under challenging and painful conditions and chaplains prayed for firefighters and other responders as they recovered the bodies of victims. By December 2001, the entire feeding operation at Ground Zero was turned over to the Salvation Army; their operations moved into a 35,000-square-foot tent owned by the Environmental Protection Agency, and it earned the nickname "The Taj Mahal" because of its imposing presence. It was a sanctuary for workers, a place where they could get hot meals and temporarily escape the anxiety and challenges of recovery work. Volunteers and Salvation Army personnel from around the country helped make the "tent" a place of comfort and consolation for rescue personnel and first responders.

THE NATIONAL ORGANIZATION FOR VICTIM ASSISTANCE (NOVA)

NOVA was founded in 1975 as a nonprofit organization working on behalf of victims of crime and disaster, guided by four purposes: to serve as a national advocate for victim rights and services, to provide direct services to victims, to provide educational resources, and to support both victims and victim assistance professionals. NOVA is the umbrella organization to more than 8,000 victim service-providing agencies in the United States and its National Crisis Response Team of trained crisis responders that responds rapidly to disasters. In addition, NOVA's specialized group of trainers and crisis interveners is always available to provide crisis training to communities in need.

HISTORY AND EVOLUTION OF FEMA

As a federal organization, FEMA is mandated to coordinate the federal government's efforts in preparing, preventing, mitigating, responding, and recovering from all domestic disasters. The Congressional Act of 1803, besides being the first disaster legislation, led to the formation of FEMA after a New Hampshire town was affected by an extensive fire.

A flurry of disasters in the 1960s and 1970s (Hurricane Carla in 1962, Hurricane Betsy in 1965, Hurricane Camille in 1969, Hurricane Agnes in 1972, the Alaskan Earthquake of 1964, and the San Fernando Earthquake in Southern California in 1971) prompted legislation that required greater cooperation between federal agencies through the Disaster Relief Act that was passed in 1974. The legislation authorized the sitting president to declare a disaster and coordinate activities. Through an executive order in 1979, President Carter merged many of the separate disaster-related responsibilities of the federal government into FEMA. The new agency was faced with many unusual challenges in its first years: the contamination of Love Canal, the Cuban refugee crisis, and the accident at the Three Mile Island nuclear power plant. Later, the Loma Prieta Earthquake (1989) and Hurricane Andrew (1992) drew public attention to the role of FEMA.

As a result of the terrorist attacks on September 11th, national preparedness and homeland security became a primary focus for FEMA. The Office of Homeland Security was established to coordinate activities with the Office of National Preparedness so that the nation's first responders were trained and equipped to deal with weapons of mass destruction. In addition, FEMA dispersed funds to help communities establish disaster and crisis protocols.

In 2003, FEMA, together with 22 other federal agencies, became a part of the Department of Homeland Security. The new department was established to provide a coordinated approach to national security in the aftermath of emergencies and disasters, primarily to prepare the nation should disasters occur, and to effectively manage recovery efforts. FEMA's mandate is to work in partnership with other organizations that are part of the national emergency management system, including state and local emergency management agencies, other federal agencies, and the American Red Cross.

Typically FEMA's involvement in a disaster begins after a presidential declaration of a major disaster and at the request of a state governor. Four years after the traumatic consequences of September 11, 2001, Hurricane Katrina in 2005 delivered an unwelcome aftershock to U.S. citizens and tested FEMA's role in unprecedented ways. At a time when homeland security was at the forefront of political dialogue, the federal government's inability to provide timely humanitarian assistance to the citizens of New Orleans and the Gulf Coast raised doubts about the strength and reliability of U.S. disaster readiness (Mohr & Powell, 2007). This was deeply unsettling to both the American public and the displaced residents of Hurricane Katrina, calling into question the commitment to collective responsibility.

It came as no surprise when President Bush changed the directorship of the agency as the disaster unfolded in the Gulf Coast. On October 4, 2006, the Post-Katrina Emergency Reform Act was signed into law; this legislation significantly reorganized FEMA, providing it with a new authority and a more vigorous preparedness mission.

PRACTICAL IMPLICATIONS

- Coordination, collaboration, and partnership between local, state, and federal organizations should be established before disasters.
- Hurricane preparedness should be viewed as integral; drills and other disaster exercises should be practiced with regularity.
- Reconstruction and restoration efforts should be attentive to reducing future catastrophes.
- Warning messages are a critical part of disaster preparedness and should be broadcast in languages that can be understood by all residents.
- Cultural competency is an important aspect in first responder training.
- The role of cultural, contextual, and ecological factors cannot be minimized in recovery efforts.
- Preparedness initiatives should be attentive to the unique challenges of each catastrophic event.
- Disaster plans should include the provision of short-term, long-term, and permanent housing for displaced residents.
- Potential shelters should be identified and evaluated prior to disasters.
- Family integrity should always be considered in relocation plans.

CONCLUSION

Disasters often strike with little or no warning, but are capable of major death and destruction. They often have long-lasting and large-scale economic, political, and psychological consequences and become an entrenched part of the history of affected areas (e.g., we cannot think about New Orleans without remembering the hurricane that damaged the city in 2005). Although disasters are in many ways unpredictable, modern technology and advanced tracking systems can reduce their unpredictability. In addition, learning lessons from past disasters can help in managing and reducing the detrimental effects of future disasters.

This chapter outlined several disasters and the lessons that each of them offered. The hope is that those involved in crisis and disaster response work will learn from the past. Disasters are inevitable; it is therefore important to turn the knowledge that has been gained from research and experience into practical action. Crisis and disaster studies is a new area of research and teaching, and very few academic programs offer courses in this important field of study. One way to practically apply what has been learned is by preparing future generations; devoting increased academic attention in research and training in the field of disaster studies is a mechanism through which this can be achieved.

REFERENCES

Bolin, R., & Klenow, D. J. (1988). Older people in disaster: A comparison of Black and White victims. *International Journal on Aging and Human Development, 26*, 29–43.

Caplan, G. (1964). *Principles of preventative psychiatry.* New York: Basic Books.

Centers for Disease Control and Prevention. (1988). Tornado disaster: Texas. *Morbidity and Mortality Weekly Report, 37*(30), 454–456.

Chang, S. E. (1996, November). *Regional economic impact of the January 17, 1995 Kobe, Japan earthquake.* Paper presented at the 43rd North American meeting of the Regional Science Association International, Washington, DC.

Crossley, D. (2005). *10 worst natural disasters.* Retrieved December 2, 2008, from http://www.eas.slu.edu/hazards.html

Gleser, G., Green, B., & Winger, C. (1981). *Prolonged psychosocial effects of disaster.* New York: Academic Press.

Green, B. L. (1996). Cross-national and ethnocultural issues in disaster research. In A. J. Marsella (Ed.), *Ethnocultural aspects of posttraumatic stress disorder: Issues, research, and clinical applications* (pp. 341–361). Washington, DC: American Psychological Association.

Green, B. L., Lindy, J., Grace, M., Gleser, G., Leonard, A., Korol, M., et al. (1990). Buffalo Creek survivors in the second decade: Stability of stress symptoms. *American Journal of Orthopsychiatry, 60*, 43–54.

Lawson, A. C. (1969). *The California Earthquake of April 18, 1906* (Report of the State Earthquake Investigation Commission). Washington, DC: Carnegie Institution. (Original work published 1908)

Lindemann, E. (1944). Symptomatology and management of acute grief. *American Journal of Psychiatry, 101*, 141–148.

Miskel, J. F. (2006). *Disaster response and homeland security: What works, what doesn't.* Westport, CT: Praeger Security International.

Mohr, C. L., & Powell, L. N. (2007). Through the eye of Katrina: The past as prologue? *The Journal of American History, 94*, 692–695.

National Academy of Sciences. (1987). *Saragosa, Texas, Tornado May 22, 1987: An evaluation of the warning system.* Washington, DC: National Academy Press.

Palinkas, L., Downs, M., Patterson, J., & Russell, J. (1993). Social, cultural and psychological impacts of the Exxon Valdez oil spill. *Human Organization, 52*, 1–13.

Parad, H. J., & Caplan, G. (1960). A framework for studying families in crisis. *Social Work, 5*(3), 3–15.

Pielke, R. A., Jr., & Pielke, R. A., Sr. (1997). *Hurricanes: Their nature and impacts on society.* New York: John Wiley.

Science & Technology. (2004). *Lessons learned from the December 26, 2004 Indian Ocean disaster.* Retrieved August 12, 2008, from http://www.sdr.gov/Tsunami%20Science%20and%20Technology%20Lessons%20Learned%202005–1130%20FINAL.pdf

UNICEF. (2007). *Humanitarian action report 2008—Tsunami response 2004 Indian Ocean earthquake and tsunami: Lessons learned.* Retrieved August 20, 2008, from http://www.unicef.org/har08/index_tsunami.html

CHAPTER 2

Hurricane Katrina

What Went Wrong?

Priscilla Dass-Brailsford

Several different explanations about the causes and consequences of Hurricane Katrina have surfaced since it barraged the Gulf Coast and New Orleans in particular in August 2005. Some people consider the disaster a natural one and therefore unavoidable. Others believe that the disaster was caused through human error; it could have been less fatal if the faulty and weakened levees surrounding the city of New Orleans had been repaired and evacuation orders mandated before the storm made landfall.

Another explanation attributes the consequences of the storm to progressive and cumulative environmental neglect and/or not restoring and appropriately protecting the swamps, marshes, and barrier islands along the Gulf Coast with vegetation that could have buffered the vulnerable coastline against the wrath of Hurricane Katrina (Brinkley, 2006; van Heerden & Bryan, 2006). This chapter provides a review and discussion of the different explanations that have evolved after the storm and the rationale that underlies each of them. A multitude of issues around personal and government responsibility emerged when local officials failed to provide clear and timely evacuation orders and federal officials failed to provide immediate disaster assistance. A critical analysis of the results can shed light on lessons learned and help formulate strategies and ideas for well-timed targeted interventions in future disasters. Although New Orleans was not the only city affected by Hurricane Katrina, the focus of this chapter is on the Crescent City of New Orleans.

CHAPTER HIGHLIGHTS

✦ Provides a background on Hurricane Katrina and the factors that contributed to its destructive consequences;

✦ Discusses the role of institutional prejudice, cultural mistrust, and socioeconomic factors in the challenges faced by many African American survivors of Hurricane Katrina;

✦ Describes the philanthropy and willingness to help fellow citizens that emerged among residents in the surrounding towns of disaster-affected areas;

✦ Reviews some of the challenges in reconstruction and rebuilding after the storm; and

✦ Outlines past federal programs that have helped other communities in crisis overcome similar challenges.

BACKGROUND

Hurricane Katrina was one of the worst natural disasters in American history. A year after the storm struck, the Louisiana Department of Health and Hospitals (2006) confirmed more than 1,600 deaths and over 1,000 people missing. Hurricane Katrina alone accounted for more than $80 billion in damages (U.S. Department of Transportation, 2006). The levees in New Orleans broke in 53 places, and federal officials—the Army Corps of Engineers in particular—blamed their own flawed designs for the inability of the levees to hold back the torrid waters of Katrina. Approximately 80% of the city was flooded, and hospitals, nursing homes, police departments, and other institutions were understaffed and overburdened. The basic infrastructure of the city was incapacitated. The slow response by the U.S. government, which is often emulated by the global community, was criticized nationally and internationally. In addition, both the media and survivors of the hurricane leveled heavy criticism against the Federal Emergency Management Agency (FEMA), the federal office responsible for disasters, which had clearly failed in carrying out its national obligations.

Americans watched in horror as media coverage in the last days of August 2005 showed storm surges increase in the Gulf Coast and threaten southern states situated close to its shores (Louisiana and Mississippi in particular). The hurricane made landfall at the small town of Buras in the farthest reach of the Mississippi Delta at 6:10 a.m. on August 29, 2005. But this was only the beginning. Forty miles north of Buras, flooding of residential areas in New Orleans had already begun. By 8:30 a.m. breached levees obliterated entire neighborhoods such as the Ninth Ward in New Orleans and Biloxi in Mississippi. Pictures of stranded survivors in New Orleans drew national and international outrage. The survivors were waving sheets from their rooftops to attract the attention of passing helicopters, walking knee-deep in murky water, and pleading for fresh water outside the Superdome while bloated corpses bobbed in the flooded main streets of New Orleans. The Superdome and the Convention Center in downtown New Orleans were bursting with destitute evacuees. The American public was appalled to hear media reports of police pointing their weapons at desperate survivors. Veteran newscasters were visibly shaken as they reported on the grim and distressing situation evolving in the Gulf Coast. Their comments forced local and federal authorities to quickly attend to the crisis that had developed in New Orleans and the surrounding areas.

What became fairly clear in the days after Hurricane Katrina was that the United States was a country divided by both race and class. The pleading, anguished, and tear-filled faces frequently portrayed on television were predominantly Black. Although the racial and socioeconomic divisions that exist in this country are sometimes not evident, for those who have lived privileged and sheltered lives, the vast chasm between the rich and poor, the haves and the have-nots, and its intersection with race was a shocking revalation. As these blatant class distinctions that fell along racial lines were repeatedly broadcast on every channel on television, public attention on developments in the Gulf Coast grew and remained focused on the area for several weeks and months after the storm. How could something like this happen in the United States? How did a natural disaster with predictable destructive consequences become a human-made disaster with unpredictable and catastrophic consequences? We first examine the environmental factors that contributed to the devastating consequences of Hurricane Katrina.

ENVIRONMENTAL FACTORS

Shore erosion had been progressively occurring in the Gulf Coast. Rising sea levels slowly tore away at the edges of the coastline, causing marshlands and wetlands to disappear as nature redesigned the coastal landscape. Evidence of the ongoing loss of wetlands in the United States was first documented at the turn of the 20th century, although it likely took place long before. Besides the naturally occurring erosion of land, other significant changes had been taking place along the Mississippi Gulf Coast since the 1950s (van Heerden & Bryan, 2006). Land usage along the coastline had increased through urban developments, which tripled between 1950 and 1992. Nearly 40% of marsh loss has been attributed to this environmental change as urban development displaced ecologically valuable marshland that served as an invaluable protection against storm surges (Brinkley, 2006).

Marshlands, or wetlands, are one of nature's most valuable ecosystems. They are responsible for cleansing polluted water, recharging groundwater, and acting as a buffer by absorbing and deflecting storm surges. In the coastal towns of Gulfport and Biloxi, where dredge-and-fill commercial, industrial, and residential properties have been extensively developed, there have been especially high rates of marsh loss and wetland atrophy (van Heerden & Bryan, 2006). The effects of this depletion were first evident when Hurricane Camille made landfall in Mississippi in August 1969. At the time, the prolific coastal development of the 1950s had already begun to deplete the wetlands. With less available marshland, storm wave energy caused 210 miles per hour winds and battered the Gulf Coast shoreline. Thus, storm surges rose 25 feet above normal sea levels to completely destroy properties along beachfront areas. Hurricane Camille clearly offered lessons on the devastating consequences of neglecting the marshlands and a need to view them as a valuable resource. But because it was a lesson that was not heeded, it had similar catastrophic consequences in 2005. Hurricane Katrina may not have been as calamitous had appropriate attention been paid to the preservation of marshland along the Gulf Coast. However, besides the neglect of marshlands, an added stressor to the shoreline of the Gulf Coast was the development of the casino industry.

THE CASINO INDUSTRY

The casinos and gambling industry have been blamed for an acceleration of the Gulf Coast's environmental degradation. Major development projects can be seen in the concrete structures that proliferate along the coastline. Since 1992, this historic landscape has been transformed into a myriad of blinking neon lights, symbolic of casinos and the gambling industry. Prior to Hurricane Katrina, the Mississippi Department of Marine Resources documented the direct and indirect detrimental consequences of dockside gaming on coastal areas (Hollomon, 1998). This was evident in the dredging that occurred for barge placement, water bottom and wetland fill, shoreline alteration, increased surface water runoff in impervious areas, and degraded water quality that was easily visible in the pollutants that washed ashore. By 1998, dead fish and debris were frequently seen along the coastal shores. The story of the Gulf Coast has been one of urban development motivated by economic factors and a blatant disregard for the negative environmental effects.

The Mardi Gras tradition in New Orleans and the French Quarter that draws millions of tourists every year has earned New Orleans a reputation as the nation's party city and pleasure destination. Visitors escape the confines of their regular lives and let go of their inhibitions as they revel in the music, food, liquor, and sex that is so freely available on Bourbon Street, the location of the French Quarter (Stanonis, 2008). Many public and media statements criticized the city as corrupt and sinful and its citizens too absorbed in pleasurable activities to prepare adequately for the storm. Bibler (2008) condemns such statements as erroneous and a cover-up by an incompetent government that did not respond quickly enough and had planned poorly for a hurricane of Katrina's magnitude; thus, New Orleans became a scapegoat for the nation's guilty conscience. The levees constructed by the Army Corps of Engineers were inadequate and unable to withstand the fury of Hurricane Katrina.

POORLY CONSTRUCTED LEVEES

The inadequate and poor construction of the floodwalls and levee system in Louisiana has been identified as one of the onerous factors that contributed to the disastrous consequences. Because federal flood control policy did not hold public safety as a priority, plans for a nationally comprehensive system for river and harbor projects in the Gulf Coast were never supported. Instead, federal policy appeared to favor piecemeal projects across the Gulf Coast, mostly in response to political pressures by local residents. In addition, there has been a lack of a long-term vision, specifically in terms of setting priorities on public safety after disasters and in key areas of inexpensive transportation, swamp drainage, and sheltering. As a result, the pumps, canals, and levees that were constructed to protect the lower Mississippi from floods and hurricanes were installed piecemeal and lacked proper planning. Under these circumstances, it is not surprising that the levees around New Orleans, which were intended to withhold a Category 3 storm, failed when Katrina roared ashore as a Category 4–level hurricane. The flooding of the city began the night before the hurricane made landfall, when the water surges forced Lake Pontchartrain to burst and flood the city of New Orleans, while most people slept.

ARE THERE NATURAL DISASTERS?

Some social scientists studying disasters question whether disasters are natural occurrences or socially constructed events influenced by demographic and socioeconomic character-istics, prejudices, and values that society may hold as important at a certain point in time (Hartman & Squires, 2006). They argue that social factors such as class, race, ethnicity, gen-der, and other factors play a major role on the impact and outcomes of disasters; low-income individuals, minorities, women, the elderly, and other disenfranchised groups are disproportionately affected by disasters.

Examples of how chronic and endemic social realities have contributed to the negative consequences of disasters are illustrated in some of the disasters that have befallen impov-erished global communities. The Indian Ocean Tsunami (2005), the Kashmir Earthquake (2005), and Hurricane Jeanne in Haiti (2004) are some examples of communities that have been severely affected by disasters because of a lack of resources. All these disasters were illustrative of how decades of socioeconomic inequality, social stratification, and extreme poverty heightened the disastrous consequences of a catastrophic event. It was the poor and disenfranchised who inhabited the most disaster prone areas; many had no other choice, and even when the disasters were forecasted, they lacked the resources to evacuate to safety and became helpless victims. Once things settled down, many survivors returned to these high-risk areas; they could not envision any alternative. Similarly, the disastrous conse-quences of Hurricane Katrina can be understood in the context of socioeconomic inequal-ity, with its historical roots in slavery, which was prevalent in Louisiana long before the storm.

INSTITUTIONAL PREJUDICE AND CULTURAL MISTRUST

The history of African Americans in the United States has been marked by both oppression and the quest for freedom and dignity; many African Americans have struggled and con-tinue to struggle with overcoming institutionalized racism and racial oppression. Similarly, a history of racism and White dominance has resulted in a mistrust of many institutions that have treated Black people unfairly: the criminal justice system, educational institutions, and other government agencies (Terrell & Terrell, 1984). Similar views are held of helping agen-cies such as FEMA, the American Red Cross, and other mental health institutions. It is not surprising, therefore, that these feelings of mistrust led African Americans to question the help offered by such agencies after the storm.

The slow and delayed governmental response was therefore perceived as an example of prejudice and racial discrimination that was still evident in the United States nearly 40 years after the civil rights movement. Race has often been used as a framework for explaining what happened in New Orleans. Moreover, New Orleans has always been viewed as backward, foreign, corrupt, and decadent, because of its mixed heritage and unique history of racial and cultural mixing (Bibler, 2008). Approximately 98% of the low socioeconomic communities of the Ninth Ward were obliterated; it was where most African Americans lived and where the levees flooded or broke. Thus, Hurricane Katrina did not destroy New Orleans but significantly reduced its African American population.

The hurricane highlighted the systemic and institutional failures in disaster preparedness, response, and recovery; despite decades of warnings regarding the potential catastrophic consequences of an event of this nature in New Orleans, local, state, and federal governments were ill prepared to respond. Hurricane Katrina exposed the results of decades of institutional discrimination and inequality that resulted in a pervasive struggle for survival among individuals and families on the lower rungs of the socioeconomic ladder. A pattern of blame, civic mistrust, and neglect permeated this state in the Deep South for many years. African Americans in the region were viewed as a source of the city's problems so much so that "the predominantly black New Orleans was conceptualized as a lynched body strapped to the nation" (Bibler, 2008, p. 19).

The media played a significant role in promoting the negative stereotype of the Black residents of New Orleans in the aftermath of the storm. Instead of engendering sympathy and support, some portrayals of stranded communities, mostly Black, pleading for help, generated fear among the rest of the U.S. citizenry—a fear that New Orleans was too messy to clean up, too many tax dollars would have to be expended to restore the city, and that it would be a financial burden that the rest of the nation would have to carry. A rapid decline in public goodwill toward survivors of the disaster resulted.

An example of this self-protective behavior was evident when the police, in Gretna, a largely White community in the west bank of New Orleans, threatened to shoot the large crowds of Black New Orleanians who tried to cross the bridge to the West Bank in search of dry land, fresh water, and shelter from the blistering sun. They were perceived as ill intentioned intruders at a time when resources were not so plentiful.

Furthermore, public doubts about the integrity of the stranded survivors were heightened by the broadcasting of two pictures that were repeatedly aired on television: one was of a Black man supposedly "looting" a grocery store and another of a White couple supposedly "finding food" in a similar store. The looter image promoted the stereotype of the untrustworthiness and predisposition of some African Americans toward criminal behavior. This depiction was in sharp contrast to that of an older White woman filling her cart with plants in another store, which, she informed the reporter, would die if she did not take care of them.

Comments that Hurricane Katrina had cleansed New Orleans of the working poor, who were overwhelmingly African American, and the criminals that the city would rather not see return, emerged after the hurricane (Long, 2007). It seemed like the heavy winds and waters of Hurricane Katrina had erased their very existence. A look at the nearly barren coastline where the eye of the storm passed over conjures up the metaphor that the slate has been wiped clean—almost believable. In this unsupportive environment, thoughts circulated that the city, because of its topography, would always be vulnerable to flooding and other natural disasters and therefore should be completely bulldozed and left to nature.

However, using race as a primary lens to explain the effects of Hurricane Katrina can cause one to miss the insidious role played by socioeconomic factors; poverty was prevalent in New Orleans before the storm, and it is a factor that prevented many former residents from returning to their homes.

SOCIOECONOMIC FACTORS

Many questions and accusations about the city's local and state officials and their perceived inertia circulated in the aftermath of the storm: Why did the mayor delay the evacuation orders? Why did the governor delay a declaration of a state of emergency which delayed the federal government from helping sooner? Why didn't the city build stronger levees? Why were people living below sea level and in such a perilous area in the first place? Why didn't they just relocate to a safer place? There are reasonable answers to some of these questions.

First, the federal government had been reducing funding for levee projects and wetlands conservation for years, placing the city in a precarious position. Most of the people who were unable to evacuate were socioeconomically indigent; they simply did not have the resources to leave. Thus, socioeconomic inequities played an integral factor in why they did not evacuate. These inequities were prevalent before the storm but simply became more prominent after it; the curtain was lifted on the huge divide between the rich and the poor, which, in New Orleans, fell along racial lines.

Much blame for an ineffective evacuation of the city pointed to the mayor, governor, and local government officials; although some attributions of blame are legitimate, the socioeconomic reasons that prevented many residents from evacuating should not be obscured. Although a few people refused to evacuate because of past false alarms, many simply lacked the resources to do so. Public assistance checks were expected to arrive around the time of the storm, and those who depended on them hoped to leave once they had the money. Many poor people do not have credit cards or savings accounts that are popular in middle-class communities. State and federal authorities had for years ignored the trajectory of deprivation and exclusion that had developed as a result of poverty. Germany (2007) points out some alarming data indicating that the tragic conditions exposed by Hurricane Katrina were long in the making. It took the disaster of Hurricane Katrina to reveal the pervasive socioeconomic stress that was always prevalent in New Orleans.

In the mid-1960s, New Orleans, a city of nearly 650,000 residents, was one of the most impoverished, most unequal, most violent, and least educated places in the United States. Three of every four Black residents lived near the poverty line; one of every two lived below it. Almost 50% of the city's income went to the top fifth of the population, while the bottom fifth survived on about 4%. Furthermore, only 3 of every 10 Black men aged 25 to 44 had education beyond middle school. The city's traditionally all-Black public schools were oppressively overcrowded, and over the next decade and a half, White residents abandoned all but a few public schools (Germany, 2007).

The local murder rate was almost twice the national average. The incidence of infant mortality, diphtheria, and tuberculosis rivaled any in the nation. Physical infrastructure was not much better. In the predominantly Black Lower Ninth Ward, nearly 90% of the roads lacked adequate paving and drainage. Approximately one fourth of the city's 202,643 public housing units were considered to be dilapidated or deteriorating.

According to the Brookings Institution (2005), not much had changed in 45 years, by the time Hurricane Katrina made landfall. Instead, the city of New Orleans had grown increasingly segregated by both race and income and had developed high concentrations of poverty. Blacks and Whites were living in literally different worlds before the storm hit. In 2000, the Black median household income in the city was half that of Whites: $21,461 as opposed to $40,390. The Black poverty rate was three times higher than the White poverty rate: 35% compared to 11%. Poor Blacks were five times as likely to live in areas with extreme poverty rates—43% of poor Blacks lived in concentrated poverty, compared to 11% of poor Whites. The Black college attainment rate was about four times lower than the White college attainment rate; 13% of Black adults had a college degree or higher, compared to 48% of White adults. Only two thirds of Black adults had at least a high school diploma, compared to 89% of White adults.

Hurricane Katrina has been described as a profoundly southern tragedy (Watson, 2008). The storm struck at one of the South's economically poorest regions where historic poverty intensified the devastation and destruction of the storm. In contrast, the cultural richness of the area magnified the loss for both residents and the nation as a whole.

PHILANTHROPY AND CHANGES IN THE SURROUNDING AREAS

Although many things went wrong after Hurricane Katrina, many positive things also occurred. Crises often offer opportunities for philanthropic actions. Despite the underlying challenges wreaked by the storm, Hurricane Katrina brought out the best in people. Residents struggled to help each other, and some risked their lives to save those who were stranded. For example, private boat owners did not hesitate to rescue survivors from attics, trees, and roofs of buildings. Across the country, volunteers scurried to collect and send water and supplies to New Orleans. Many people were willing to shelter evacuees for indeterminate periods of time. Compelled by the distraught faces of the survivors of the storm portrayed in the media, even global help became prolific and Red Cross volunteers from Europe descended on the Gulf Coast.

Churches and other civic groups provided help immediately; many still continue to support survivors to return to their former lives. These humane, heroic, and noble acts of compassion by concerned citizens were a sharp contrast to the delayed response by federal and state institutions. The rapid evacuation of New Orleans changed the landscape of the towns surrounding New Orleans. Hotels were soon filled to capacity, forcing many residents to open their homes to family and friends fleeing the storm. Because storm damage to their homes prevented many New Orleanians from returning to the area for a long period of time, the result was a dramatic population shift and demographic change in the surrounding cities. The scheduled academic school year was unable to begin because of severe storm damage; thus, some families were forced to make a temporary move to a surrounding town that ultimately became a more permanent one.

In addition to those survivors who evacuated after the storm, thousands of first responders descended on the cities in the Gulf Coast to help in the recovery and reconstruction efforts. In most neighborhoods of New Orleans, houses bore the markings of volunteer officials who checked dwellings in hurricane-affected areas in search of victims. Their markings appear on the doors of many storm damaged homes as odd hieroglyphics, a large X with symbols in each quadrant. One of the quadrants has a notation of the first responder's home state (e.g., PA, NY, VA). However, those who visited or returned to New Orleans after the storm were primarily focused on the number at the bottom of the quadrant, which indicated how many were found dead in a particular dwelling or building. Most of the homes with a number of fatalities were completely obliterated so few doors showed annotations with human death. Sometimes records of dead pets (goldfish, cats, dogs, etc.) are marked in the quadrant—a sad reminder of the tangible losses that survivors faced.

Large regional distribution centers for items such as gasoline, produce, and groceries located in and around New Orleans were damaged or destroyed at a time when the demand for these items was huge. As a result, goods disappeared as soon as they were put on store shelves. Lines outside supply stores grew rapidly; there were similar lines at gas stations, which resorted to rationing because of delays in delivery. As businesses began to reopen, they faced major challenges. Customers, many seeking to use FEMA or Red Cross funds to replace clothing and property lost in the hurricane, clamored for goods and services. In contrast, companies struggled to meet the increased demand; many employees who had evacuated before the hurricane hit were unable to return to their former employment. As a result of staff shortages, many businesses dramatically reduced their hours of operation and hired untrained or unqualified employees.

Communication was also a major problem after the storm. Telephone communication, both landlines and cell phones, was unavailable and provided only intermittent access for a long time. Toll-free calling, which is most often used for customer service during recovery periods, was inaccessible. Another significant communications mechanism, the U.S. Postal Service, suffered serious setbacks after Hurricane Katrina. Although mail in the Gulf Coast was delayed for months, some mail never made it to its destination or was completely lost and unrecoverable due to the flooding.

Metropolitan New Orleans was without power for periods of time that extended from a few days to more than 2 weeks. Major television and radio networks in New Orleans were either damaged or destroyed. Communication thus became a challenge, even when residential power was restored. Two primary New Orleans–based radio stations collaborated in establishing their base of operations in Baton Rouge. For months after Hurricane Katrina, these radio stations served as a major source of public information and provided resources for both residents and businesses; radio broadcasts quickly became a reliable way for city, parish, and state government officials to disseminate information.

Although the circumstances of the disaster created a chaotic situation in the area—handicapping recovery and rebuilding efforts and forcing many individuals, businesses, and government entities to exist in this antiquated existence for a significant period of time—it was collaboration and goodwill that made an unbearable situation manageable.

RECOVERY AND REBUILDING

Reconstruction efforts in New Orleans and surrounding areas have been impeded by both physical realities and rigid bureaucracy. These impediments extend from a lack of money, to a lack of vision, from racial undercurrents to political inaction, making the future of

New Orleans and the lives of many of its former residents uncertain. Rebuilding and restoration of the infrastructure was initially limited to areas that remained fairly intact after the storm. These were areas with predominantly White and middle-class residents. The heavily damaged neighborhoods such as the Ninth Ward with primarily Black residents remained deserted. Observers have described it as resembling an area in which a nuclear bomb had exploded. Because the area is identified as vulnerable to future flooding, little or nothing is being done to protect or rebuild it.

Further along the Gulf Coast, debris littered the ground more than 2 years after the storm, with crumbled buildings, great piles of concrete and metal twisted into strange shapes, and bridges that lead to nowhere. Nature, however, has not been as patient as the former residents of New Orleans. It has begun its own rebuilding by re-establishing the greenery; concrete slabs have been overtaken by grass and weeds. In some ways, this has been a mixed blessing, because it has covered up the distressing sights that may otherwise be evident.

A United Nations High Commissioner for Refugees (2000) report considers it a human rights violation when displaced victims cannot return to their homes or find new homes after a natural disaster and that discrimination and violations of economic, social, and cultural rights become more entrenched as the displacement lingers on. As of 2008, experts project that by the end of 2008, only about 55% of the former residents of New Orleans will have returned to their former homes. The main impediments to their return are a lack of affordable housing and public services.

Hurricane Katrina and its aftermath have also taken a psychological toll on its victims. For example, Kessler et al. (2008) conducted a large-scale study investigating the psychological effects on survivors immediately after Hurricane Katrina made landfall. A follow-up study was conducted 3 years later and showed no reduction in the levels of trauma. In some cases, an actual increase occurred. According to Kessler et al., this finding is an unexpected one for which there is no precedent. The conclusion was that the devastation and displacement have not ended for many survivors of Hurricane Katrina, thus prolonging their psychological distress. In addition, the availability of mental health services has also been severely reduced and the number of psychologists in the New Orleans area dropped by 35% between 2005 and 2007 (Wang et al., 2008).

The natural support system provided by families and friends that is so much a part of the New Orleans culture became deeply fragmented after the storm. Many individuals who had never left their neighborhoods prior to the hurricane were completely dispersed geographically or living in trailers under cramped conditions. Many of these trailers were found to have toxic levels of formaldehyde, but the renovation plans on the subsidized housing developments in which many people lived before the storm appeared to be severely delayed or cancelled. The slow recovery has also been attributed to these findings. Thousands of homes have neither been rebuilt nor torn down. As a result, New Orleanians, surrounded by daily reminders of the disaster, are unable to escape the devastating images of 2005 and begin the process of recovery.

Hurricanes Katrina and Rita and the accompanying levee failures displaced more than a half million people. Today, more than 200,000 people remain displaced. Many people trusted that they would return to their homes soon after the storm and that the initial evacuation was temporary. Instead of being supported in their desire to return to their former homes, survivors have instead been burdened with additional obstacles. For example, city ordinances in New Orleans mandated homeowners to repair their homes before they even received their insurance checks. Thus, in an attempt to clean up the city after the storm, many homes were bulldozed without the permission of their owners. There are, however, historical examples of governmental support of its citizenry during challenging times; the New Deal was one such program.

The New Deal and the Work Projects Administration

During the Great Depression (1933-1937), President Franklin D. Roosevelt implemented the New Deal, a series of programs, with the goal of relief, recovery, and reform of the U.S. economy. Shortly after the Great Depression, in the fall of 1933, Roosevelt enacted the first government jobs program, the Civil Works Administration, and then in the spring of 1935, he enacted the Work Projects Administration (WPA).

The WPA was the largest and most comprehensive New Deal agency. This "make-work" program provided jobs and income to the unemployed during the Great Depression by primarily employing unskilled blue-collar workers in construction projects across the nation. In addition, the government jobs program strove to give people equal pay based on their skill level. The parks along the Chicago Lakefront district and the Golden State Bridge in San Francisco are examples of WPA projects that changed the lives of poor people. These federal programs revitalized the economy and restored faith in the government. Through the WPA program, workers developed infrastructure by building roads, bridges, parks, schools, hospitals, and levees, which corresponded to an increase in educational programs, child care, job training, and medical care. WPA workers performed plays, took photographs, wrote poetry and books, taught art classes, and painted murals. The program made unemployed individuals upwardly mobile so that they could attain middle-class standards.

The Fair Housing Act is another example of a federal intervention that allowed many working-class White families to become upwardly mobile. It took political will to make programs like the WPA possible; a similar will is needed to reconstruct the Gulf Coast. A motivated and engaged government can provide financial resources for the masses through long-term employment, fair wages, and housing incentives that help people reconstruct their lives. A federal jobs program will revitalize the Gulf region and will be indicative of the federal government's commitment to advancing the interests of those in need of resources.

Endemic poverty had pervaded the Gulf region prior to the hurricanes due to decades of institutional neglect. Such a reconstruction project will not only address the problems related to inadequate levees and destroyed homes but also respond to the much deeper problems of urban poverty that have surfaced since the collapse of the inner cities in the late 1960s and early 1970s. The urban centers have been in a long, steady decline, and revitalization programs have failed to address poverty. Instead, they have been pushed aside by gentrification plans that cater to the needs of wealthier residents; unfortunately, a similar gentrification plan appears to be emerging in New Orleans. It is a model that does nothing to address the systemic economic and racial inequalities in society. One of the key elements of rebuilding urban infrastructures is for a reconstruction program to go beyond housing with the obligation to build high-quality public schools which are filled with top-quality teachers and teaching materials. An additional obligation is to build high-quality public housing, with adequate community services such as child care centers and medical facilities.

A government jobs program in the Gulf region has the potential to become a broader social template to salvage failing cities and rebuild the nation. The federal government's slow action during the hurricanes and its continued failure to address the problems caused by the storm as they persist in the Gulf Coast hangs like a shadow over the United States.

Gabriel (2008) suggests that a solution for the displaced survivors of Hurricane Katrina does not lie in limited aid packages from Congress to private foundations that will distribute the money at their own discretion without public oversight but rather lies in a government jobs program. It will be a solution that future generations will point to as an exemplar for progress. A 21st-century WPA will be symbolic of the generosity and goodwill of the American people; most important, it will allow the indigent and economically distressed evacuees to return home.

IMPLICATIONS AND FUTURE DIRECTIONS

An overview of what went wrong before, during, and after Hurricane Katrina made landfall in the Gulf Coast raises a few important issues. First, is the importance of securing the physical safety of areas that are vulnerable to disasters and flooding. The External Review Panel of the American Society for Civil Engineers constructed after Hurricane Katrina concluded that despite continuing improvements to the hurricane protection system and attempts to secure the levees and decrease New Orleans' hurricane vulnerability, the danger that residents face from a hurricane similar in size and strength to Katrina "remains unacceptable." It has also urged the U.S. Army Corps of Engineers to convey this level of risk to both the residents of the city and the federal government.

The External Review Panel recommended that the Corps formulate an effective evacuation and emergency management plan for the region, continue to upgrade the level of protection, and work with the city of New Orleans and other organizations to develop a strategy for a comprehensive, systematic plan to manage flood risks, by including the development and implementation of effective warning and evacuation plans (Shuster, 2008).

Additional issues that need to be addressed include the training of civilian physicians and others in disaster or battlefield triage; education of the public and medical personnel regarding military evacuation protocols; hospital owners (corporations) and administrators would need to have a feasible and tested plan that is actually followed at the time of crisis. They should predict the possibility of a total hospital evacuation; the protection of doctors and nurses from criminal charges and civil suits when they are providing services during a federally declared emergency (amendment of the Good Samaritan statute); and finally, have medical and ethical guidelines for disaster care (Pou, 2008). Federal, state, and local governments should strive to plan, test, and coordinate response efforts in order to respond effectively during disasters.

Second, an awareness of historical and contextual factors and the role they play in the manifestation of difficulties that survivors experience is crucial in disaster recovery response and planning. This awareness has to be considered in conceptualizing the healing and recovery of disaster survivors (Burstow, 2003; Cross, 1998; Danieli, 1998). Mental health professionals who fail to incorporate salient factors such as an individual's personal and group identity, socioeconomic status, and cultural norms have a limited understanding of their potential strengths and the barriers that impede functioning (Waller, 2001).

An individual's identity, whether related to gender, age, sexual orientation, geographical location, or vocation, influences perceptions of available choices (Halpern & Tramontin, 2007). It is incumbent on helping professionals to be aware of the different ways in which individuals of ethnic minority groups experience psychological distress subsequent to exposure to a disaster. For example, Perilla, Norris, and Lavizzo (2002) strongly recommend that "symptomatology should be viewed in its totality, taking into consideration the historical, social, economic, and political factors in which individuals from these groups find themselves" (p. 41). Given the demographic profile of the city of New Orleans, counselors working with survivors of Hurricane Katrina need to consider the impact of intergenerational trauma caused by slavery. The legacy of racism and discrimination in the United States has led to healthy cultural mistrust among African Americans (Grier & Cobbs, 1968). This general distrust, self-protection, and reluctance to seek help is likely to permeate interactions with all institutions, including helping agencies during disasters.

Nobles (1986) encourages the use of culture-centered counseling interventions that emphasize collective understanding through a family support group format when working with African American clients. Central to this approach is collaboration between client and counselor wherein they identify issues and explore alternative perspectives and behaviors collaboratively. In addition, Nobles encourages both clients and counselors to move beyond the traditional boundaries of the presenting problem in order to change and grow; this will allow for the creation of new possibilities and the discovery of new discourses.

Third, the importance of community-based interventions should be emphasized. As a result of a disaster, not only individuals but also entire communities are likely to experience trauma (Cross, 1998; Halpern & Tramontin, 2007). These individuals and communities may also have developed culturally relevant and community-based coping skills through their previous experiences with disasters. Using community-based interventions that enable residents to offer support to one another can be an effective means of helping individuals and developing community-wide resilience (Levine, 1997).

PRACTICAL IMPLICATIONS

- A plan for the effective evacuation and emergency management of the Gulf Coast region should be formulated and upgraded on a regular basis.
- A strategy for a comprehensive, systematic plan to manage flood risks, which includes the development and implementation of effective warning and evacuation plans, should be developed for the high-risk areas.
- Efforts to protect the marshlands and wetlands in the Gulf Coast region should be initiated.

- Those in the helping professions should be aware of the historical and contextual factors and the role they may play in the manifestation of difficulties that some survivors experience after a disaster.
- Disaster responders should be aware of the role that institutional prejudice and cultural mistrust play in the lives of ethnic minority groups; in providing services to African American survivors of a disaster, they must be willing to examine the effects of institutionalized racism and the role of power and oppression in the lives of their clients.
- The use of culture-centered counseling interventions that emphasize collective understanding, collaboration between client and counselor, and exploration of alternative perspectives is necessary in order to effectively help ethnic minority communities.

CONCLUSION

Hurricane Katrina was one of the most devastating hurricanes in U.S. history, resulting in more than 1,600 deaths and displacing hundreds of thousands of people (Louisiana Department of Health and Hospitals, 2006). African Americans and the socioeconomically distressed people living in areas that were supposedly protected by the failed levee system were particularly hard hit by the disaster. New Orleans lost almost half its population to other parts of the country, where many survivors of the storm were initially evacuated.

For years, Category 4 or 5 storms had threatened the Gulf Coast. Predictions were made that the bowl New Orleans occupies would become completely awash with water and chemical products, making it a massive tomb and potentially killing tens of thousands of people. The disaster of Hurricane Katrina took Americans by surprise; yet in many ways, it was not a surprise at all. It almost appeared straight from the textbooks in terms of its impact and effect on vulnerable groups. Besides dispossessing many communities, Hurricane Katrina exposed bureaucratic mismanagement as well.

The hurricane wreaked chaos up and down the Gulf Coast and deep into the interior. It affected several states in its path, but its destructive impact on New Orleans was of epic proportions. There are multiple reasons for this: the city's people suffered grievously, its physical damage was enormous, and the storm's ability to dislocate hundreds of thousands of people was unparalleled, injecting misery not only into New Orleans but also into the country as a whole. New Orleans has always held a special place in American culture that made its ordeal especially significant.

There have been several analyses of the storm and what went wrong. All of the explanations appear to be plausible, but the question of whether the consequences of the storm were preventable still remains. What is certain is that as of 2009 (nearly 4 years after the storm), many residents of New Orleans are still scattered, and it is not certain whether they will return to their storm ravaged homes. In 2007, 2 years after the storm, the estimated population of New Orleans was only at 70% of its pre-storm level and the proportion for neighboring St. Bernard's Parish had not reached 40% (Kaiser Family Foundation, 2008). Much has been learned from the Hurricane Katrina experience, but unless the government and medical and legal communities heed the valuable lessons offered by the disaster, we will miss one of the greatest opportunities for improving how we manage national disasters, and that would be the greatest tragedy of all.

REFERENCES

Bibler, M. P. (2008). Always the tragic Jezebel: New Orleans, Katrina, and the layered discourse of a doomed southern city. *Southern Cultures, 14*(2), 6–27.

Brinkley, D. (2006). *The great deluge.* New York: HarperCollins.

Brookings Institution. (2005). *Special analysis: New Orleans after the storm: Lessons from the past, a plan for the future.* Washington, DC: Author.

Burstow, B. (2003). Toward a racial understanding of trauma and trauma work. *Violence Against Women, 9,* 1293–1317.

Cross, W. E. (1998). Black psychological functioning and the legacy of slavery. In Y. Danieli (Ed.), *International handbook of multigenerational legacies of trauma* (pp. 387–400). New York: Plenum.

Danieli, Y. (1998). Introduction: History and conceptual foundations. In Y. Danieli (Ed.), *International handbook of multigenerational legacies of trauma* (pp. 1–20). New York: Plenum.

Gabriel, J. (2008). A twenty-first century WPA labor policies for a federal government jobs program. *Social Policy, 1*(1), 38–43.

Germany, K. B. (2007). The politics of poverty and history: Racial inequality and the long prelude to Katrina. *Journal of American History, 94*(3), 743–751.

Grier, W., & Cobbs, P. (1968). *Black rage.* New York: Bantam Books.

Halpern, J., & Tramontin, M. (2007). *Disaster mental health: Theory and practice.* Belmont, CA: Brooks/Cole.

Hartman, C., & Squires, G. D. (2006). *There is no such thing as a natural disaster: Race, class and Hurricane Katrina.* New York: Routledge.

Hollomon, C. Z. (1998). Environmental effects of dockside gaming in coastal Mississippi. In *Marine resources and history of the Mississippi Gulf Coast* (Vol. 3, pp. 309–311). Biloxi: Mississippi Department of Marine Resources.

Kaiser Family Foundation. (2008). *New Orleans three years after the storm: The second Kaiser post-Katrina survey, 2008.* Retrieved February 9, 2009, from http://www.kff.org/kaiserpolls/upload/7789ES.pdf

Kessler, R. C., Galea, S., Gruber, M. J., Sampson, N. A., Ursano, R. J., & Wessely, S. (2008). Trends in mental illness and suicidality after Hurricane Katrina. *Molecular Psychiatry, 13*(4), 374–384.

Levine, P. A. (1997). *Walking the tiger: Healing trauma.* Berkeley, CA: North Atlantic Books.

Long, A. P. (2007). Poverty is the new prostitution: Race, poverty, and public housing in Post-Katrina New Orleans. *Journal of American History, 94*(3), 795–803.

Louisiana Department of Health and Hospitals. (2006). *Reports of missing and deceased.* Retrieved February 4, 2009, from http://www.dhh.louisiana.gov/offices/page.asp?ID=192&Detail=5248

Nobles, W. W. (1986). Ancient Egyptian thought and the development of African (Black) psychology. In M. Karenga & J. H. Carruthers (Eds.), *Kemet and the African worldview: Research, rescue and restoration* (pp. 100–118). Los Angeles: University of Sankore Press.

Perilla, J. L., Norris, F. H., & Lavizzo, E. A. (2002). Ethnicity, culture, and disaster response: Identifying and explaining ethnic differences in PTSD six months after Hurricane Andrew. *Journal of Social and Clinical Psychology, 21,* 20–45.

Pou, A. (2008). Hurricane Katrina and disaster preparedness. *New England Journal of Medicine, 358*(14), 1524.

Shuster, L. A. (2008). Risk analysis: ASCE panel finds risk level in New Orleans "unacceptable." *Civil Engineering, 78*(6), 15–16.

Stanonis, A. J. (2008). Through a purple (green and gold) haze: New Orleans Mardi Gras in the American imagination. *Southern Cultures, 14*(2), 109–131.

Terrell, F., & Terrell, S. (1984). Race of counselor, client sex, cultural mistrust level, and premature termination from counseling among Black clients. *Journal of Counseling Psychology, 31,* 371–375.

United Nations High Commissioner for Refugees. (2000). *Handbook for emergencies.* Retrieved February 11, 2009, from http://www.unhcr.org/cgi-bin/texis/vtx/publ/opendoc.pdf?tbl=PUBL&id=3bb2fa26b

U.S. Department of Transportation. (2006). *Catastrophic hurricane evacuation plan: A report to Congress.* Retrieved May 29, 2008, from http://www.fhwa.dot.gov/reports/hurricanevacuation/chapter1.htm#ch103

van Heerden, I., & Bryan, M. (2006). *The storm.* New York: Viking.

Waller, M. A. (2001). Resilience in ecosystemic context: Evolution of the concept. *American Journal of Orthopsychiatry, 71,* 290–297.

Wang, P. S., Gruber, M. J., Powers, R. E., Schoenbaum, M., Speier, A. H., Wells, K. B., et al. (2008). Disruption of existing mental health treatments and failure to initiate new treatment after Hurricane Katrina. *American Journal of Psychiatry, 165*(1), 34–41.

Watson, H. (2008). Front porch. *Southern Cultures, 14*(2), 1–5.

CHAPTER 3

Ignore the Dead

We Want the Living

Priscilla Dass-Brailsford

> *Oh, freedom! Oh, freedom!*
> *Oh, freedom over me!*
> *And before I'd be a slave,*
> *I'll be buried in my grave,*
> *And go home to my Lord and be free.*
>
> —Traditional Spiritual

One of the distinguishing aspects of New Orleans culture is the jazz funeral. Few cities bury their dead in the high style of this southern city, where a funeral can last a week and feature jazz bands and parades, which draw bigger crowds than weddings. The funeral is a major celebration with roots that have been passed down from Africa. After Africans were brought to America as slaves, providing a proper burial for those who passed away was important for surviving family members and friends who mourned their loss; it fulfilled a cultural tradition of properly honoring the dead. The brass bands that initially accompanied the dead on their way to the cemetery increased in popularity in New Orleans during the early 18th century and were frequently requested to play processional music at funerals. The practice of including music during funeral processions was derived from African cultural patterns of celebrating the diverse aspects of life; death was thus viewed as an important aspect of life.

However, this tradition was interrupted when Hurricane Katrina scattered the communities that made New Orleans funerals so extraordinary. The floods that took so many lives in New Orleans also forced the city's institutions of death (funeral homes, churches, and cemeteries) to shut down. Although holding crypts and refrigeration could preserve the dead, they could not do the same for the traditional New Orleans funeral, because family members, close friends, and neighbors were dispersed all over the country. The sheer number of fatalities made the task of providing each deceased individual with a

New Orleans style burial almost impossible. For thousands of survivors, the inability to provide loved ones with a traditional funeral filled them with guilt and complicated their grieving process. Many were unable to set aside thoughts of those who had died so tragically.

Thus, survivors viewed the statement made by FEMA director Michael Brown, "Ignore the dead we want the living," as lacking in compassion and culturally insensitive; it clearly failed to understand and appreciate the significance of a long-standing funeral tradition practiced by the residents of the Gulf Coast. Instead of focusing on their own survival, the dead and missing absorbed the attention of many survivors who were temporarily housed in shelters. As one survivor appropriately commented, "Those that are living can take care of themselves now . . . the dead cannot; we have to do our duty to those who have passed."

This chapter provides an overview of funeral and burial practices, the symbolic and ritualistic meaning that these practices hold for bereaved families, and coping and recovery after the loss of a loved one. This introduction is followed by a discussion of the different stages of grieving and mourning and a review of some diverse burial practices and the New Orleans jazz funeral in particular. The chapter ends with a discussion of different practices to memorialize the dead and celebrate anniversaries.

CHAPTER HIGHLIGHTS

+ Discusses the ritualistic aspects of funerals;

+ Outlines strategies to help bereaved individuals overcome loss;

+ Describes the stages of mourning and grieving;

+ Outlines some diverse funeral practices, specifically the jazz funeral; and

+ Discusses the significance of anniversaries and memorials.

THE FUNERAL AS A RITUAL

Funerals are ritualized life events that give survivors opportunities to celebrate the lives of those who have died and an opportunity for mourners to receive support from others. Research evidence suggests that funeral rituals help in the adjustment of bereaved persons (Bolton & Camp, 1986, 1989). These rituals represent both psychosocial and therapeutic benefits for adults and children (Fulton, 1995; Irion, 1990; Marrone, 1997). Thus, ignoring the dead after a major disaster is not wise; it does not support the healing and recovery of survivors.

Bereaved individuals derive many benefits from funeral services or similar rites of passage when a loved one dies. First, the funeral ritual enhances mourners' recovery after the death of a loved one by facilitating and/or renewing the social support of friends and family members whom they may have not seen for a long time but who may attend the funeral. Second, the ritual of the funeral helps bereaved individuals to establish a deeper connection with the deceased so that the loss experience can be meaningfully contextualized and better understood (Gamino, Easterling, & Stirman, 2000).

According to Fulton (1995), funerals serve important psychological functions of separation and integration. Separation functions are those that acknowledge that a death has occurred; by disposing of human remains through a burial or cremation, there is a symbolic acceptance of the finality of death. The process allows mourners to come to terms with the fact that the deceased will no longer be around. Thus, an initial step toward healing is taken by the ritual of the funeral ceremony.

In addition, funerals give bereaved individuals the opportunity to express their grief publicly while surrounded by family, friends, and other community members. It symbolically acknowledges their loss. This acknowledgment plays a central role in the recovery of survivors, especially those who experience a loss as traumatic. Moreover, the religious rituals that are sometimes conducted at funerals provide survivors with opportunities for spiritual and psychological closure.

Integration functions, according to Fulton (1995), are those functions that support the social order by encouraging survivors to integrate the loss experience into their lives. Funerals provide opportunities to eulogize and pay tribute to the deceased and to socially support the bereaved through fellowship and communal togetherness, and funerals can enhance integration by contextualizing the loss in a religious or philosophical framework of afterlife and continuity.

According to Irion (1990), funerals are human rituals in which bereaved individuals seek a connection with the dead and find meaning in it. In addition, the ritual of the funeral ceremony provides mourners with opportunities to express their feelings of grief and to affirm that life is valuable and something to be celebrated even in the face of death. Thus, funerals are often conducted for the living and not the dead.

Participation in funerals can help the bereaved individual gain "symbolic mastery" over death (Doka, 1984). For example, the bereaved can actively participate in the planning of the funeral ceremony itself, which provides symbolic mastery and imbues survivors with a sense of control and empowerment. In addition, participation in preparing and planning how the funeral will be conducted can aid in the survivor's adjustment after the loss of a loved one. In a study conducted among 74 mourners, active participation in planning funeral services was found to be highly correlated with the subsequent grief adjustment of participants (Gamino et al., 2000). Those who found the funeral "comforting" and/or who participated in planning the funeral reported fewer grief reactions. They also fared better psychologically at a follow-up assessment that was conducted. The benefits of participating in funeral ceremonies included receiving and providing support and comfort as well as allowing for public expressions of grief (Lemming & Dickson, 1994; Welford, 1992).

In another study, Bolton and Camp (1986, 1989) found that grief adjustment among widowed individuals correlated positively with their level of participation in rituals prior to, during, and following funeral rites. Acknowledging gifts or sympathy cards, sorting and disposing of the personal effects of the deceased, and visiting the burial site of the deceased were reported as activities that integrated loss and improved the adjustment of the bereaved. Similarly, the simple act of attending a funeral and/or burial service was found to enhance recovery. In contrast, bereaved individuals who did not attend a funeral displayed significantly greater emotional distress (Faschingbauer, 1981).

Hayslip, Booher, Riddle, and Guarnaccia (2005), in a study that examined participants' attitudes toward funerals, found that the funeral was a much-needed opportunity for bereaved individuals to express their grief in a public arena while receiving emotional support from family and friends. They concluded that the funeral itself can thus be conceptualized as a form of intervention.

The nature of funerals has changed in recent years and currently better reflects the psychosocial needs of bereaved persons and communities (Irion, 1990). Indeed, there is evidence that the funeral is generally positively viewed by the public (Fulton, 1995). Middle-aged and older adults find the traditional funeral ritual to be more valuable than younger adults do. Given the therapeutic value of funerals, it behooves grief counselors and other professionals in the helping field to encourage bereaved clients to participate in appropriate and culturally relevant funeral practices (Bowen, 1991). In situations where funeral participation may not be possible (e.g., travel to the funeral is prohibitive or no formal services are held), mourners should be encouraged to construct a personally meaningful bereavement ceremony to acknowledge their loss, facilitate their healing, and support their recovery (Bosley & Cook, 1993; Rando, 1988).

HELPING THE BEREAVED

In a study conducted among bereaved individuals, Cook and Bosley (2001) found that participants viewed the opportunity to express sad emotions and discuss the loss of a loved one as helpful. However, they perceived helpers who focused on giving advice and who were hasty in promoting recovery to be insensitive and disregarding of their feelings of sadness and not providing them with enough opportunities to share their concerns.

Similarly, Balk (1997) found that bereaved families that reminisced about loved ones, shared pleasant memories, and discussed death openly recovered sooner. Crying, engaging in rituals, and focusing on the present were actions that improved coping abilities and helped bereaved individuals adapt to their losses. In addition, such individuals believed in the importance of resuming their normal routines as soon as possible; staying busy was perceived as one way of coping. They also believed that their loved ones were better off in death, especially if intense pain and suffering preceded their passing. Bereaved individuals valued receiving acknowledgment about their loss and the significance of the deceased individual in their lives. Establishing and maintaining connections with other bereaved individuals, especially those who were going through similar experiences of loss and grief, was perceived as valuable.

Similar findings were reported in a study conducted by Castle and Phillips (2003), who also found that adjustment after the loss of a loved one was facilitated by participation in appropriate funeral rituals. In addition, study participants reported that reminiscing about a deceased individual was often experienced as more therapeutic than professional counseling.

An increasing number of professionals in the helping field are beginning to recognize rituals as powerful tools in managing death. When mourners participate in grief rituals with others who are supportive and empathic, their coping abilities are vastly improved (Klass, 2001; Romanoff & Terenzio, 1998).

Bereaved individuals who experience the sudden death of a loved one interact with many professionals in the immediate aftermath of their loss. The way they are treated by professionals during this critical period shapes the grieving process and how they later manage and cope with their loss. When support is not perceived as helpful, it may prolong and complicate the grieving process. The personal and social costs that can occur from inept or inadequate professional interventions can be quite steep (Janzen, Cadell, & Westhues, 2003). Providing bereaved individuals with appropriate information about their loss may be a core contributing factor to helping them make sense of what has happened; those who are adequately informed about the details of their loss usually adjust better and improve more quickly (Winje, 1998).

Losing someone intiates a period of crisis for most people and thus calls for the development and restoration of coping mechanisms. Crisis theory has much to offer in terms of informing mental health professionals on how to help survivors regain a sense of control and make appropriate choices as they move toward a resolution of the crisis (Golan, 1979). In this way, the manner in which the crisis is dealt with can positively influence the grieving process (Wheeler, 1994). Briefly, the principles of crisis theory encourage helping professionals to observe the following guidelines when working with those who experience a loss:

a. Normalize and validate feelings and experiences

b. Provide information about grief (reactions and phases to expect)

c. Provide referral and resources to help during the grieving process (e.g., support and grief group)

d. Offer immediate assistance in problem solving, perhaps involving advocacy on behalf of the client

e. Listen intently and empathically so that nothing is missed

f. Facilitate the acquisition of basic needs (food, shelter, etc.)

Those that want to help in crisis situations should be skilled in these principles. In addition, knowledge of the stages of mourning and the process that bereaved individuals can expect in both the short and long term is necessary.

Stages of Mourning and Loss

One of the greatest challenges that people face is the death of a loved one. Freud (1959) defined *mourning* as the gradual withdrawal of libido from the loved object that results in dejection, disinterest, and detachment from others and the environment. Recovery from loss occurs when the libido is no longer invested in the person who has passed but is reinvested in a new object (Leick & Davidson-Nielsen, 1991).

Bereavement often results when a loved one dies and grief is the affective expression of bereavement, expressed in feelings of sorrow, guilt, and confusion. Grief comes from the Latin word *grevis* (meaning "something grave and serious"), implying that when we grieve, we are gravely and seriously affected by sorrow (Coryell, 1998). Some people may experience bereavement for a long time without the accompanying reactions of grief. However, at some point, the affective experience of grief has to occur for full recovery from a loss to take place.

Mourning is the physical expression of grief and often influenced by cultural factors. For example, wearing black, crying, praying, and removing oneself from others may be part of a cultural tradition. Worden (1991) describes the four tasks of mourning as follows:

a. Accepting the reality of the loss by coming to terms with the fact that the loved one will no longer be physically around: This acceptance results in a reduction of denial.

b. Grieving and its physical expressions (crying, yelling, or ruminating): This allows for a full expression of loss.

c. Adjusting to an environment in which the deceased is missing can be challenging for survivors: The survivor has to find new ways of coping and adopt new roles in the absence of a loved one.

d. Withdrawing emotional energy from the deceased and reinvesting it in new relationships is necessary: This can be experienced as a betrayal by some survivors, but those in the helping professions can help survivors to deal with the guilt that may be generated by helping them acknowledge and accept that although the loved one may not be around, he or she will not be forgotten.

Several models of grief and loss have been proposed. For example, Bowlby (1980) described the four phases of mourning as progressing along the following lines: numbing, yearning, and searching for the loved one; and disorganization, despair, and reorganization. However, a widely accepted model on loss and grief was developed by Elizabeth Kubler-Ross (1969), who did extensive work with terminally ill patients. The model identifies five stages of death and dying. It has universal applicability and is useful for people who are dying as well as those emotionally close to them. The different stages are descriptive of the antici-pated grieving process. Not every individual goes through each stage, and the stages do not necessarily occur in a predictable sequence:

a. Denial and isolation describes the initial reaction to loss; shock and numbness become pervasive and mourners report feelings of disbelief.

b. Anger follows as the reality of having lost someone sinks in. Rage, envy, resentment, and bitterness may surface as bereaved individuals ask: Why me? How could this happen? Why is life so unfair? Sometimes the anger is directed toward the person who has died, and some survivors may criticize the deceased for not having taken better precautions to maintain their health and well-being, while others may blame the deceased for contributing to their death (e.g., by driving too fast). Feelings of abandonment may become strong at this stage, and sometimes feelings of anger and disappointment may be directed toward institutions and the circumstances that surround a disaster. For example, after Hurricane Katrina, many survivors felt deep resentment toward state and federal institutions for an inadequate response and the hurricane itself for wreaking the havoc it did.

c. Bargaining occurs as individuals begin to make pacts or promises, hoping that this will obviate an impending loss. For example, survivors may make promises to go to church more regularly or donate money to a charity if a loved one heals or recovers from an illness.

d. Depression results as the reality of the loss is slowly accepted. Sadness, guilt, pessimism, and a sense of worthlessness become pervasive at this stage.

e. Acceptance is initiated as mourners disengage from the loss, and the working-through phase of recovery begins at this point.

Mourning is a long-term process and people have different ways of dealing with it. Holidays, anniversaries, and family events may interrupt and complicate the process. Although mourning takes a long time, when the bereaved individual is able to think and talk about a loved one without feeling overwhelming sadness and pain, mourning is considered over.

DIVERSE FUNERAL PRACTICES

The literature on crisis intervention increasingly calls attention to cultural sensitivity when working with diverse communities (Brock, Lazarus, & Jimerson, 2002; Heath & Sheen, 2005; Rabalais, Ruggiero, & Scotti, 2002; Sandoval & Lewis, 2002). However, practical application lags behind what is proposed in the research literature. Cultural sensitivity and understanding, and knowing how to appropriately meet the needs of individuals and families from diverse backgrounds, continue to present challenges to many mental health professionals (Pedersen, 2003; Sue & Sue, 2003). These skills will be more severely tested as U.S. society becomes increasingly diverse.

Recognizing the challenges of providing effective crisis intervention to people of diverse backgrounds, James and Gilliland (2001) state that "although crisis intervention is never easy, cultural insensitivity may make it even more difficult" (p. 26). Communities most in need of crisis and trauma-focused services tend to be ethnically and culturally diverse; as a result, when providing appropriate crisis services to such communities, people in the helping professions must strive to offer culturally appropriate interventions that are reflective of the cultural needs of diverse populations (Romualdi & Sandoval, 1995). For example, to appropriately minister to Asian Americans who experience the loss of a loved one, cultural awareness and an understanding of their perceptions of death is of paramount importance; knowing that their thanatology (interpretation of death) is a part of their ontology (how they exist), from generation to generation, is indispensable (Kwon, 2006).

Another group that may need culturally specific interventions after death are Southeast Asians. An example of an intervention that was initially conducted with a lack of cultural sensitivity was the Stockton schoolyard shooting, a tragic event that occurred in Stockton, California, in 1989, when a man randomly fired shots from his AK-47 rifle across a school's playground. Five students were killed in the incident, and a teacher and 29 students were wounded. The school served approximately 70% students of Southeast Asian descent (Armstrong, 1991). Because most of the parents did not speak English, communication became a major barrier between the parents and school authorities. Although mental health professionals tried to assist families in the grieving process, these professionals were English speaking and therefore experienced major challenges in supporting the traumatized school community. Following the shooting, many students and their parents avoided returning to school because they believed that ghosts and evil spirits lurked in the hallways. After consultation with parents and community members, a Buddhist monk was invited into the school to perform exorcisms to rid the school of these spirits. This action was perceived as helpful by the parents and helped make the school environment more comfortable. Although not a typical intervention provided by mental health professionals, this was a culturally appropriate and unique intervention that met the needs of this particular community.

Although the fear of death is a universal phenomenon, people in different cultures have different ways of dealing with it. For example, in most of North America, mourning is viewed as a private matter. A 2-hour visiting period with the deceased occurs during the wake, which typically takes place in a funeral home. Mourners are encouraged to control their grief and return to their normal routine as quickly as possible. In contrast, the Black church plays a significant role in the funeral traditions of many African American communities (Holloway, 2002). Such communities hold long funeral services and tributes, which are perceived to honor the dead and testify to the great impact of their lives on the living. Opportunities to process the loss are often restricted to interactions with those in the mental health field through participation in grief groups rather than individual therapy. In some cultures, mourners are encouraged to publicly display their grief. For example, in Arab countries, women commonly ululate (a loud cry) to express their grief at funerals. Haitian women overtly display feelings of sadness and loss by beating their breasts as they wail loudly.

Sometimes there are cultural norms that structure the expression of loss after a funeral ceremony. For example, it is common for some members of Middle Eastern and Catholic cultures to wear black for a year after the loss of a loved one to symbolize a state of mourning. Similarly in South Asia, widows are required to wear white clothing for a year after the death of a spouse. Until recently, *sati* was commonly practiced among Hindu communities in India; widows were expected to immolate themselves on a husband's funeral pyre when he passed away.

Funerals and burial practices are a universal human social experience, and every society has a unique pattern of dealing with the death of its members. The Amish community offers a case in point; their mourning practices follow a defined structure that captures the simplicity and isolation of the Amish culture. After five schoolchildren were slain in Pennsylvania in 2006, the Amish showed quiet faith and strong communal bonds that helped them face a major tragedy and the media attention that the incident generated (Hampson, 2006). Amish funerals are held on the family property because they have no churches. The service, which is more than 2 hours long, is simple. There is no singing or eulogizing of the deceased; nor is there communion or flowers. Scripture is read in an old German dialect and sermons are delivered in the local Pennsylvanian Dutch dialect. Afterward, the casket is taken to a small Amish cemetery in a black horse-drawn hearse, followed by a long procession of horse-drawn carriages. At the grave, which is dug by hand, prayers are recited with perhaps a German hymn sung a cappella style (without any instruments). The casket is lowered into the ground and covered with soil. Later, the grave is marked with a simple tombstone, the same size and shape as others, as a reminder that in death, everyone becomes equal. Mourners head back to the family farm for a hearty Amish meal of meat, potatoes, vegetables, and pies prepared and served by volunteers. Underscoring the whole process is a strong belief in a close, living God, an unseen actor who controls every aspect of life according to a script that is beyond the understanding of human beings.

Many non-Western cultures perceive death as the passage of the deceased from the world of the living to the world of the dead. A great majority of cultures talk of a destiny beyond that of a single lifetime, and funeral rituals are structured to convey the deceased from the land of the living to whatever world they believe lies ahead. Death ceremonies in many non-Western cultures occur over a longer period of time, primarily because there is an expectation that many family members and friends will attend the funeral. Because they may have traveled long distances to pay their respects to the dead, there is an expectation that they will spend an extended period of time in the home of the deceased. For example, in Korean communities, family and friends come to the home of the deceased as soon as they hear about the death of a family member to offer their condolences. This visit lasts at least 70 hours or 3 days; visitors spend the time talking about the deceased, eating, drinking, and sometimes playing cards.

In most African countries, family and friends gather to sing, play the drum, and prepare the body for burial. African funeral processions are fairly common aspect of a ceremony, because the living are expected to support the dead on her or his way to the afterlife. Mourners value the structure of the death ritual to affirm their interconnectedness to their community. In addition, ceremonies for the deceased offer opportunities to re-evaluate and redefine social relationships, as loyalties shift from the person who has passed to those who are living (Hunter, 2007).

In Haitian culture, when a death is impending, the entire family gathers to pray and cry around the bed of the ill individual. Religious medallions and other spiritual artifacts are used in the prayer ceremonies. Once the person dies, the entire extended family becomes involved in the funeral ceremony. The oldest family member makes all the funeral arrangements and notifies family members, and the funeral is not held until it is convenient for all family members to attend. Mourning practices include *veye*, *dernier priye*, and *prise de deuil*. *Veye* are preburial activities. *Dernier priye* is a home-based ritual that consists of 7 days of continuous prayer and is believed to support the soul as it passes into the next world. *Prise de deuil*, which takes place on the 7th day, is similar to a funeral and begins the official mourning period (Colin & Paperwalla, 2003).

All cultures have a period of bereavement for those left behind, and all bereaved individuals experience a redefinition of roles that is the inevitable result of the absence of the deceased. Funerals fulfill many social and psychological functions, and the funeral ceremony is significant in commemorating the completion of human existence.

The Jazz Funeral

African Americans have maintained distinctly African funeral and memorial traditions based on the African belief that death is not the end of life but rather a transition into the spirit world. The majority of African belief systems are monotheistic and based on a hierarchical pattern, with God at the highest point, followed by spirits, human beings, animals, and plants. When people die, they are elevated to the status of a spirit. In this form, they are capable of exercising control or authority over the living. Thus, proper burial practices are viewed as important, and there is a strong belief that the dead should be respected and revered.

The New Orleans jazz funeral procession is a tradition derived from West Africa, a place where many African people were captured and brought over to the New World to serve as slaves. The joyful music and exuberant dancing that accompany the funeral reflect the belief that the deceased is about to enter the domain of the spirit world and it is a moment to be celebrated. Rejoicing over death was also a symbolic response to a life of enslavement and oppression. Death became a triumph of redemption, an entry to freedom, and an escape from the oppression of slavery. According to historian Sybil Kein (2000), most slaves believed that when they died, their spirits would go back to the ancestral land of Africa. Death was therefore not a time for mourning but a celebration, because they believed it gave them a passage to the homeland. It was a belief that sustained them through difficult times and instilled them with hope. These African rituals, ways of thinking, and worldviews became a powerful part of the cultural memory of slaves in Louisiana. It is this idea of celebration that is epitomized in the jazz funeral, which is constructed as a tribute to life rather than a concession to death. Often, the funerals are arranged according to the wishes of the deceased who will sometimes choose the music and even the musicians who will play at their funerals.

The jazz funeral follows a detailed structure. A typical jazz funeral begins with a march by the family, friends, and a brass band to the cemetery from the home of the deceased, the funeral home, or the church. Throughout the march, the band plays somber dirges and hymns. A change in the tenor of the ceremony takes place after the deceased is buried, when the hearse leaves the procession and members of the procession say their final farewell. The body is considered to be "cut loose" at this point. Then the music becomes more upbeat, often starting with a hymn or spiritual music played in a swinging fashion and continuing with more popular, upbeat tunes. This is followed by raucous music and cathartic dancing; onlookers can join the procession at this point to celebrate the life of the deceased. Those who follow the band just to enjoy the music are called the "second line." They sometimes twirl a parasol or handkerchief in the air as they walk or dance.

The grave is a powerful point of contact between the world of the living and the dead. In the American South, for example, the burial traditions of the Bakonga African culture have persisted. Mourners who follow this cultural tradition place a variety of objects on graves to assist the deceased in their spirit journey home and to discourage spirits from haunting the living in search of their belongings. Thus, objects placed on graves include those owned by the deceased, such as clocks, dishes, and other objects that are broken to free the spirit. White objects, especially shells, are common grave decorations, because the world of the dead is considered to be "white and watery." There is evidence that some of these practices were taken to the American North, where non-Christian burial traditions have persisted. The recent excavation of a 19th-century African American cemetery in Philadelphia revealed that shoes, coins, and plates had been placed on some burial sites, reflecting the African belief in the use of such items by the deceased on their journey to the spirit world.

Unfortunately, most people whose lives were abruptly taken by Hurricane Katrina were not honored with the traditional jazz funeral. Instead, they remained unidentified, stored in warehouses with a simple toe tag, until they were found by family members several days, weeks, and months after the storm. This anonymity in death was perceived as disrespectful of the deceased. Mourning for many survivors became complicated by the fact that they were not able to give their loved ones a proper burial, which highlighted the multiple losses they already experienced by the storm.

MEMORIALIZING THE DEAD

Creating a memorial to remember a loved one is important in preserving the memory of the deceased person; in this way, it establishes a new relationship with the deceased. Mental health professionals can contribute to this process by helping bereaved individuals explore ways they may want to memorialize the dead. One of the central goals of the grieving process is incorporating memories of the deceased into the bereaved individual's life in a different way; it involves planning and preparing for a new life without the deceased person (Rando, 1993).

Rituals and other forms of memorializing surged after the 9/11 terrorist attacks; they were public expressions of grieving that held important meaning for mourners (Lawrence, 2005). According to *U.S. News & World Report* (Schulte, 2005), the first homage after the Oklahoma City bombing appeared on the sidewalks and fences near the Alfred P. Murrah Federal Building, just hours after the explosion. Many other commemorative acts soon followed. For example, the simple flowers that were painted by the hands of children to acknowledge the passing of their peers marked the beginning of a remarkable flood of tributes from the people of Oklahoma City—a Vietnam veteran who donated his Purple Heart, requesting that it be given to the parents of a murdered child, and children who donated their special toys to survivors of the bombing.

There are many diverse ways to memorialize the dead. Traditionally, members of the Catholic faith hold a special mass after the death of a loved one. Jewish families may conduct an unveiling ceremony a year after the death of a loved one when a marker or a monument is placed on the grave and unveiled for family and friends; the widow or widower is not allowed to remarry until this ceremony is conducted. Other Jewish families continue to remember the deceased on special anniversaries through the lighting of candles, special prayers, and commemorative plaques.

Perhaps no disaster saw more memorials than those that were created after the World Trade Center bombing on September 11, 2001, when family and friends peppered New York City with shrines and pictures of missing victims. Messages, personal possessions, and poems that expressed their lamentations were placed on any available space. In Manhattan parks, miniature reconstructions of the Twin Towers surrounded by candles were commonplace. New Yorkers chose to publicly express their loss through memorials; their sense of community often transcended their religious beliefs and any prior differences they may have had. The entire nation joined them in their grieving. National and global sympathy was manifested through the organizing of church services, candlelight prayer vigils, and other community gatherings to symbolically express feelings of compassion and support for survivors.

Condolence books, in both electronic and paper formats, are ubiquitous features of funerals that can serve as a special memorial to the passing of an individual (Brennan, 2007). Providing mourners with an opportunity to record and express their grief in a socially appropriate manner, such as condolence books, bridges the gap between the living and the dead and connects acutely affected communities with the wider society. It helps the bereaved to begin to come to terms with their loss. An initial step in the recovery process is to allow family, friends, and acquaintances to share their personal grief with others through statements in a condolence book. Several researchers have reported on the benefits of writing to access and articulate feelings of loss; the act of writing becomes a vehicle that leads toward greater inner understanding (Houlbrooke, 1998; Pennebaker, 1997; Smythe & Pennebaker, 1999).

Two significant and traumatic events that occurred late in the 20th century in the United Kingdom are testaments to the revival of the forgotten tradition of condolence books and their inherent value: the 1989 Hillsborough soccer stadium disaster that occurred in the United Kingdom when soccer fans were crushed to death after a game, and the death of Princess Diana in 1997 in a car crash in Paris. There was a widespread resurgence in the use of condolence books to record and express feelings of loss and grief, and the condolence book served an important purpose in that it was able to reach a large group of people. Such condolence books then became a historical record of the way society mourned and helped make meaning of their loss at a particular point in time. Condolence books thus provide a social forum, a thanatological resource for the public expression of personal grieving (Sofka, 1997). As a therapeutic outlet, it can support mourners toward an eventual resolution of their grief.

Traumatic Anniversaries

Recognizing and acknowledging feelings that may surface around the anniversary of the death of a loved one is a crucial part of the recovery process. It is therefore important for people in the helping profession to remind bereaved individuals not to ignore this special time and to find a way to acknowledge the significance of anniversaries. At the same time, survivors should be directed to seek healthy ways to cope with the distress that may emerge during this critical time by spending time with family and friends or sharing memories and feelings with trusted others. Contemplative practices such as walking, meditating, praying, journaling, and scrapbooking may also offer bereaved individuals much-needed solace during a challenging time.

The anniversary of the September 11th terrorist attacks on New York and the Pentagon is an example of a remembrance ceremony acknowledging those who were tragically killed in 2001. Every year at the exact time that the disaster occurred, family and friends of deceased individuals and other New Yorkers gather at the site of the World Trade Center to faithfully remember those whose lives were taken in the attack. In what has become a traditional ceremony at the site of the bombings in New York, the names of the 2,972 individuals who died or went missing are read aloud. The commemoration is carried out at the same time that the tragic events occurred in 2001; the accompanying bell ringing is a reminder of a somber and significant moment in the lives of the mourners.

Some people find other ways to honor the passing of a loved one. For example, many African American communities have a tradition of hosting a barbecue around the time when a loved one passed away, family and friends drop in whenever they can to pay their respect to the mourning family, and T-shirts are made to commemorate the anniversary. Families also visit the graveside of the deceased, place flowers, or simply stand around reminiscing about the individual who died. Some families volunteer at soup kitchens or homeless shelters as symbolic reminders of their loss and a way of helping others who are less fortunate. Most important, survivors should be encouraged to reach out to others and not isolate themselves during this challenging time. The connection between the dead and living is probably best exemplified in the Hispanic cultural practice of celebrating the Day of the Dead.

The Day of the Dead

The Day of the Dead is a special day designated to remember loved ones who have died. Many people of Hispanic descent believe that on this day, the dead visit the earth and it is easier for departed souls to visit the living. Altars with candles, photos, memorabilia of the departed, and their favorite foods are displayed to welcome the spirits, and people go to cemeteries to communicate with the souls of dead relatives. The intent is to encourage visits from departed souls so that they will hear the prayers and comments of the living.

Celebrations sometimes take on a humorous tone, as family and friends recall pleasant memories and share anecdotes about the departed. Plans for the festival are made throughout the year as family members gather special objects that are later offered to the dead. During the dates of November 1 and 2, families visit the cemeteries where their loved ones are buried. The graves are cleaned and decorated with *ofrendas*, or offerings, which often include orange marigold flowers, also known as the "Flower of the Dead."

These flowers are thought to attract the souls of the dead to the graveside. Families also place trinkets or the deceased's favorite candies on the grave as an enticement to the departed souls to "visit" the living. *Ofrendas* are also put in homes, usually in the form of foods such as candied pumpkin, "bread of the dead," or "sugar skulls" as a welcoming gesture for the deceased. Some people believe that the spirits of the dead eat the "spiritual essence" of the *ofrenda* food, so even though family members may eat the food after the festivities, they believe it lacks nutritional value. Pillows and blankets are also taken out so that the deceased can rest after their long journey. In some parts of Mexico, people spend all night beside the graves of family members. Thus, the separation between the living and the dead is viewed as almost nonexistent and the dead are treated as if they are a living part of the family.

PRACTICAL IMPLICATIONS

- The funeral is a significant ritual in many cultures, and serves several functions: specifically as an expression of public grieving and an opportunity to generate support and establish a new relationship with the deceased.
- Crisis theory provides several principles to help bereaved individuals.

- Several stages of mourning and grief (denial, anger, bargaining, depression, and acceptance) have universal applicability and help those who are dying and those close to them (Kubler-Ross, 1969).
- Anniversaries and memorials are an acknowledgment of loss and are positive mechanisms to honor the dead and to help survivors manage their loss.

CONCLUSION

Remembering the dead and honoring their passing is important for bereaved individuals and families. Funerals and other burial practices are rituals that have become traditionally entrenched. Reeves and Boersma (1989) outline some advantages of using rituals as a psychotherapeutic technique in dealing with maladaptive grief. They point out that it provides a sense of structure and stability, increases feelings of personal power and control, and adds meaning to the experience of loss. In addition, a ritual motivates mourners to change and grow, creates a sense of community, and allows bereaved individuals to integrate their loss as they receive acknowledgment, support, and acceptance from caring others. Given the psychosocial and therapeutic benefits of funerals, ignoring the dead after a major disaster is not wise; it does not promote the healing of survivors.

REFERENCES

Armstrong, M. (1991). Cross-cultural issues in responding to a tragedy: The Stockton schoolyard shootings. In J. Sandoval (Ed.), *Resources in crisis intervention: School, family, and community applications* (pp. 97–99). Silver Spring, MD: National Association of School Psychologists.

Balk, D. E. (1997). Death bereavement and college students: A descriptive analysis. *Mortality, 2,* 207–221.

Bolton, C., & Camp, D. J. (1986). Funeral rituals and the facilitation of grief work. *Omega, 17*(4), 343–352.

Bolton, C., & Camp, D. J. (1989). The post-funeral ritual in bereavement counseling. *Journal of Gerontological Social Work, 13*(3–4), 49–59.

Bosley, G. M., & Cook, A. S. (1993). Therapeutic aspects of funeral ritual: A thematic analysis. *Journal of Family Psychotherapy, 4*(4), 69–83.

Bowen, M. (1991). Family reaction to death. In F. Walsh & M. McGoldrick (Eds.), *Living beyond loss: Death in the family* (pp. 79–92). New York: Norton.

Bowlby, J. (1980). Loss: Sadness and depression. In *Attachment and loss* (Vol. 3). New York: Basic Books.

Brennan, M. (2007). Condolence books: Language and meaning in the mourning for Hillsborough and Diana. *Death Studies, 32*(4), 326–351.

Brock, S. E., Lazarus, P. J., & Jimerson, S. R. (Eds.). (2002). *Best practices in school crisis prevention and intervention.* Bethesda, MD: National Association of School Psychologists.

Castle, J., & Phillips, W. L. (2003). Grief rituals, aspects that facilitate adjustment to bereavement. *Journal of Loss and Trauma, 8,* 41–71.

Colin, J. M., & Paperwalla, G. (2003). People of Haitian heritage. In L. D. Purnell & B. J. Paulanka (Eds.), *Transcultural health care: A culturally competent approach* (pp. 70–84). Philadelphia: F. A. Davis.

Cook, A. S., & Bosley, G. (2001). The experience of participating in bereavement research: Stressful or therapeutic? *Death Studies, 19,* 157–170.

Coryell, D. M. (1998). *Good grief: Healing through the shadow of loss*. Santa Fe, NM: Shiva Foundation.

Doka, K. J. (1984). Expectation of death, participation in funeral arrangements, and grief adjustment. *Omega, 15*(2), 119–129.

Faschingbauer, T. R. (1981). *Texas Revised Inventory of Grief manual*. Houston, TX: Honeycomb.

Freud, S. (1959). Mourning and melancholia. *Collected Papers* (Vol. 4). New York: Basic Books.

Fulton, R. (1995). The contemporary funeral: Functional or dysfunctional? In H. Wass & R. A. Neimeyer (Eds.), *Dying: Facing the facts* (3rd ed., pp. 185–209). Philadelphia: Taylor & Francis.

Gamino, L. A., Easterling, L. W., & Stirman, L. S. (2000). Grief adjustment as influenced by funeral participation and occurrence of adverse funeral events. *Omega, 41*(2), 79–92.

Golan, N. (1979). Crisis theory. In F. J. Turner (Ed.), *Social work treatment: Interlocking theoretical approaches* (2nd ed., pp. 499–533). New York: Free Press.

Hampson, R. (2006, October 5). Amish community unites to mourn slain schoolgirls. *USA Today*. Retrieved February 13, 2008, from http://www.usatoday.com/news/nation/2006-10-04-amish-shooting_x.htm

Hayslip, B., Booher, S., Riddle, R., & Guarnaccia, C. A. (2005). Proximal and distal antecedents of funeral attitudes: A multidimensional analysis. *Omega, 52*(2), 121–142.

Heath, M. A., & Sheen, D. (Eds.). (2005). *School-based crisis intervention: Preparing all personnel to assist*. New York: Guilford.

Holloway, K. F. C. (2002). *Passed on: African American mourning stories: A memorial*. Durham, NC: Duke University Press.

Houlbrooke, R. (1998). *Death, religion and the family in England, 1480–1750*. Oxford, UK: Clarendon.

Hunter, J. (2007). Bereavement: An incomplete rite of passage. *Omega, 56*(2), 153–173.

Irion, P. E. (1990). Changing patterns of ritual response to death. *Omega, 22*(3), 159–172.

James, R. K., & Gilliland, B. E. (2001). *Crisis intervention strategies* (4th ed.). Pacific Grove, CA: Brooks/Cole.

Janzen, L., Cadell, S., & Westhues, A. (2003). From death notification through the funeral: Bereaved parents' experiences and their advice to professionals. *Omega, 48*(2), 149–164.

Kein, S. (Ed.). (2000). *Creole: The history and legacy of Louisiana's free people of color*. Baton Rouge, LA: LSU Press.

Klass, D. (2001). Continuing bonds in the resolution of grief in Japan and North America. *American Behavioral Scientist, 44*, 742–764.

Kubler-Ross, E. (1969). *On death and dying*. New York: Macmillan.

Kwon, S. (2006). Grief ministry as homecoming: Framing death from a Korean-American perspective. *Pastoral Psychology, 54*(4), 313–323.

Lawrence, J. S. (2005). Rituals of mourning and national innocence. *The Journal of American Culture, 28*(1), 35–48.

Leick, N., & Davidson-Nielsen, M. (1991). *Healing pain, attachment, loss and grief therapy*. London: Routledge.

Lemming, M., & Dickson, G. (1994). *Understanding death, dying and bereavement*. New York: Harcourt Brace.

Marrone, R. (1997). *Death, mourning and caring*. Pacific Grove, CA: Brooks/Cole.

Pedersen, P. B. (2003). Multicultural training in schools as an expansion of the counselor's role. In P. B. Pedersen & J. C. Carey (Eds.), *Multicultural counseling in schools: A practical handbook* (2nd ed., pp. 190–210). Needham Heights, MA: Allyn & Bacon.

Pennebaker, J. W. (1997). Writing about emotional experiences as a therapeutic process. *Psychological Science, 8*, 162–166.

Rabalais, A. E., Ruggiero, K. J., & Scotti, J. R. (2002). Multicultural issues in the response of children to disasters. In A. M. La Greca, W. K. Silverman, E. M. Vernberg, & M. C. Roberts (Eds.), *Helping children cope with disasters and terrorism* (pp. 73–99). Washington, DC: American Psychological Association.

Rando, T. A. (1988). *How to go on living when someone you love dies.* New York: Bantam.

Rando, T. A. (1993). *Treatment of complicated mourning.* Champaign, IL: Research Press.

Reeves, N., & Boersma, F. (1989). The therapeutic use of ritual in maladaptive grieving. *Omega, 20,* 281–291.

Romanoff, B. D., & Terenzio, M. (1998). Rituals and the grieving process. *Death Studies, 22,* 697–712.

Romualdi, V., & Sandoval, J. (1995). Comprehensive school-linked services: Implications for school psychologists. *Psychology in the Schools, 12,* 306–317.

Sandoval, J., & Lewis, S. (2002). Cultural considerations in crisis intervention. In S. E. Brock, P. J. Lazarus, & S. R. Jimerson (Eds.), *Best practices in school crisis prevention and intervention* (pp. 293–308). Bethesda, MD: National Association of School Psychologists.

Schulte, B. (2005, April 10). Moving on, looking back. *U.S. News & World Report.* Retrieved on February 18, 2009, from http://www.usnews.com/usnews/news/articles/050418/18oklahoma.htm

Smythe, J. M., & Pennebaker, J. W. (1999). Sharing one's story: Translating emotional experiences into words as a coping tool. In C. R. Snyder (Ed.), *Coping: The psychology of what works* (pp. 70–89). New York: Oxford University Press.

Sofka, C. J. (1997). Social support "internetworks," caskets for sale and more: Thanatology and the information superhighway. *Death Studies, 27,* 553–574.

Sue, D. W., & Sue, D. (2003). *Counseling the culturally different: Theory and practice* (4th ed.). New York: John Wiley and Sons.

Welford, J. (1992). American death and burial custom deviation from medieval European cultures. *Forum,* 6–9.

Wheeler, I. (1994). The role of meaning and purpose in life in bereaved parents associated with a self help group. *Omega, 28*(4), 261–271.

Winje, D. (1998). Cognitive coping: The psychological significance of knowing what happened in the traumatic event. *Journal of Traumatic Stress, 11,* 617–643.

Worden, J.W. (1991). *Grief counseling and grief therapy: A handbook for the mental health practitioner.* New York: Springer.

CHAPTER 4

Effective Disaster and Crisis Interventions

Priscilla Dass-Brailsford

The primary objective of disaster interventions is the stabilization of injury and illness and the preservation of life. The priority of those responding to a disaster is attention to the physical and psychological needs of survivors. Mental health professionals who provide psychological first aid in the aftermath of natural disasters must be adequately prepared.

CHAPTER HIGHLIGHTS

+ Defines a crisis and discusses its expectable phases and reactions;

+ Discusses effective disaster interventions and important ecological and cultural considerations for disaster responders;

+ Reviews important principles and guidelines that address the psychological needs of survivors; and

+ Outlines specific interventions and the appropriate steps in disaster counseling.

DEFINING A CRISIS

Caplan's (1964) conceptualization of "psychological disequilibrium" and an individual's inability to escape its debilitating consequences is frequently cited in the crisis literature as a definition of a crisis (p. 53). Similarly, Slaikeu (1990) defined *crisis* as "a temporary state of upset and disorganization, characterized chiefly by an individual's inability to cope with a particular situation using customary methods of problem solving" (p. 15). Thus, a crisis typically results in an increase in tension, anxiety, and emotional unrest, and an inability to maintain daily functioning.

James and Gilliland (2005) define *crises* as events or situations that are perceived as unbearably difficult and exceed an individual's available resources and ability to cope. In a crisis, an adverse force disrupts normal patterns and structured communities so that normal functioning is suspended. Hurricanes, tornadoes, fires, mudslides, cyclones, tsunamis, chemical explosions, terrorist attacks, war, and shootings in communities are examples of adverse force and crisis events.

The event itself, its level of threat and danger, and the individual's relationship to the crisis characterize crisis events. It is not surprising that the closer the individual is to the crisis event, the more debilitating the consequences. For example, in the aftermath of Hurricane Katrina, those who lived in the hardest hit areas of the Ninth Ward, St. Bernard's Parish, and New Orleans East were more affected than those who resided in surrounding areas. In addition, when a crisis is caused by man-made errors, survivors have greater difficulty in accepting the consequences; they also find it harder to forgive those who caused the disaster.

The duration and intensity of the crisis influence individuals' responses to the event. Hurricane Katrina is a good example of a storm that was of a long duration. Although the hurricane itself lasted just a few hours, the subsequent severe flooding and breaching of the levees in New Orleans and surrounding areas brought fresh stressors and new dangers that lasted for a longer period of time. Normalcy and daily functioning took months and years to re-establish. Initially, floodwaters prevented people from returning to their homes. Thus, many family members who were dispersed during the storm were not able to see each other for an extended period of time. In addition, because the infrastructure in storm-devastated areas was completely destroyed, normal lines of communication (e.g., cellular phones and landlines) were unavailable. In contrast, after the terrorist attacks on New York and the Pentagon on September 11, 2001, survivors were able to return home. Most of them were reunited with their families and able to sleep in their own beds on the night of the attack. Engaging in these familiar activities was comforting and facilitated their recovery efforts. The likelihood of a similar disaster occurring delays recovery and increases hypervigilance among survivors. It leads to an inability to adjust and adapt to changed circumstances, which increases the impact of stressful events. Fear, tension, and/or confusion and a high level of subjective discomfort thus dominate the thoughts and actions of survivors. The threat of Hurricane Rita that followed rapidly on the heels of Katrina interrupted the recovery of many survivors who had to quickly transition from a state of disequilibrium to a reactivated state of acute crisis. Many had to evacuate their temporary homes and seek new shelter.

Finally, although most traumas begin as a crisis, not all crises develop into traumas (Dass-Brailsford, 2007). Socioeconomic status and the availability of emotional and other protective factors, such as family and adequate economic support, determine whether a disaster remains a crisis or develops into a traumatic experience. The length of time it takes to resolve the crisis, an individual's coping abilities, and past functioning are other contributing factors that determine when and whether regular functioning will resume.

PHASES OF A DISASTER

There are several phases of a disaster, and because each disaster is unique, some phases are more prominent than others and may therefore last longer.

a. *Threat and warning phase*: During this phase, warnings are posted or communicated via the media to residents who live in potentially affected areas so that they can make necessary preparations and mobilize their evacuation plans. It is important that relevant authorities are not only explicit in their communication about the impending disaster but also that relevant information is conveyed to all affected parties in a language that they can understand. Clear and direct communication reduces confusion, removes any doubts, and leaves individuals with a solid plan of action. It is important that everyone understand the level of threat and what actions he or she will need to take to maintain physical and psychological safety. For example, in an impending hurricane, individuals should know whether simply boarding up their houses will be sufficient or whether they need to evacuate to ensure survival. If evacuation becomes necessary, it is important to preserve the integrity of the family by keeping its members together. This reduces unnecessary emotional turmoil and the pain of loss and separation.

b. *Impact phase*: This phase begins when the disaster actually occurs. Panic and confusion usually result, no matter how well prepared individuals are. In the face of a disaster, a range of reactions emerge, and it may not be surprising to observe some individuals reacting with calmness and control while others become helpless and overwhelmed.

   The impact phase is also characterized by fragmentation as an inventory of fatalities and injuries is made. Property losses and damage can be massive, and some people may struggle to comprehend how they were able to survive such a major catastrophe. The role of some family members becomes severely tested in disasters. For example, women may find themselves burdened by their roles as mothers, spouses, and/or daughters. On the other hand, family loyalty becomes especially strong during this phase; it can define and guide individual behavior and actions.

c. *Rescue phase*: This phase begins in the immediate aftermath of a disaster when rescue operations are mobilized. Weaver (1995) describes it as the heroic phase of a disaster. A shared sense of loss emerges and capable individuals engage in activities that help others; such actions often contribute to a reduction in the loss of lives. Family members are reunited, shelters arranged, supplies distributed, sanitation provided, and debris cleaned up. The slightly injured should be treated first in this phase of a disaster so that they can then assist with the rescue and management of those who are more seriously injured. Those who have strong leadership characteristics and are willing to help can play a pivotal role in disasters.

   Despite much devastation, strong community morale may coalescence into effective working groups. The barriers of social class are lowered as strangers share resources and help each other. During this time, those who reside outside the affected areas often send supplies and other basic goods. When outside help pours into affected areas, this phase may be perceived as a honeymoon period (Weaver, 1995). However, similar to a honeymoon, the good times come to an end as the media focus on the disaster diminishes or shifts to other events. This can cause survivors to feel abandoned and forgotten.

    d. *Reconstruction*: This phase occurs after the disaster when reconstruction and recovery efforts are initiated. Survivors begin to adjust to a new equilibrium as they begin to accept their changed status. For some, it is a phase that is filled with disillusionment and disappointment, as the promises made during the rescue phase are not fulfilled. This distressing period is sometimes perceived by survivors as a second disaster.

The extent of damage to social institutions (schools, churches, hospitals, department stores, etc.) determines the shape and progress of recovery and reconstruction in disaster-affected areas. If these institutions are restored quickly, people can resume some of their functioning by returning to their former homes. The severity of the disaster influences how quickly people stabilize; for some people, it may be a matter of weeks, whereas for others, it may take months or years before normalcy returns. Many survivors of Hurricane Katrina were not able to return to their homes until a few years after the storm. Others who relocated to other states waited for the infrastructure in their towns to be repaired. Those whose homes were completely destroyed had nothing to return to and had to make the hard choice of establishing a new home outside the state in which they lived for many years.

EXPECTABLE REACTIONS TO DISASTERS AND CRISES

A wide range of responses and reactions usually accompanies a crisis and varies greatly depending on several contextual factors that are related to the individual, the environment he or she inhabits, and the event itself. People react differently to stress and crises based on their own skills or behaviors, abilities to cope, maturation levels, and personalities. Extreme situations tend to magnify some personality characteristics and minimize others. The reactions that survivors experience in response to a disaster vary based on socioeconomic circumstances, race and ethnicity, and geographic location. The event itself—its causes, severity, duration, and the individual's proximity to it—determines the reactions that develop.

Expectable reactions can be categorized as emotional, cognitive, behavioral, and physical. These reactions are not necessarily unhealthy or maladaptive, but rather normal responses to abnormal events. Although most people recover within a few weeks, for some individuals, these responses may persist for a longer period of time. If any of these reactions continue to present challenges beyond a month after the disaster has occurred and the reactions impair daily functioning, the individual may have developed posttraumatic stress disorder. It is important that such individuals receive professional help. Over time, it is common for symptoms to vary in intensity. Some individuals may not experience any significant reactions for a long time but will relapse quickly when faced with a similar life stressor in the future. On rare occasions, symptoms may have a delayed onset and appear months or years later. The reactions that survivors commonly report are further described:

Shock and numbness: These reactions emerge very soon after a disaster occurs. It is not surprising to see survivors with a blank expression, sitting or standing in almost immobile positions and not knowing what to do next. Although some individuals may be in a stunned or dazed condition, others may engage in aimless wandering and undirected pacing in an attempt to reduce their level of stress. Passivity and docility are common and contrasting reactions.

The sense of shock can render some individuals helpless and hopeless. Others may report denial, disbelief, and an inability to cope. When there is little or no warning before a disaster, disbelief, bewilderment, and a refusal to accept the reality of the situation become prominent.

Guilt: In the aftermath of a disaster, especially one in which many lives have been lost, those who survive may experience immense guilt. They may feel that they do not deserve or have a right to live; sometimes feelings of guilt or self-blame are legitimate (e.g., when parents feel that they could have taken better precautions after a child is killed in an automobile crash or a house fire).

Anger: When aid and support by local and federal authorities is not forthcoming, feelings of anger and rage surface quickly. Survivors may feel angry at the disaster itself for taking the life of a loved one. When a disaster is man-made or caused through human negligence, survivors struggle to maintain neutrality, and feelings of anger and blame are hard to squelch.

Crying: Although some people are not able to physically express their feelings of loss, others cry profusely and find that they are unable to stop their tears. Crying is also culturally related; some survivors appear to be stoic and in control, almost presenting a mask of control, because it is perceived as inappropriate to express their emotions in public. For others, crying, screaming, and lamenting their loss in a visible manner, especially in the company of others, is culturally appropriate; pain that is shared may be perceived as pain that is spared. In addition, expressions of pain may be an appropriate way to solicit support from community members.

Anxiety and fear: Feelings of anxiety and fear are commonly expressed emotions after a disaster. Survivors may hold the irrational thought that the disaster will happen again, and such thinking can trigger extreme anxiety. However, as we have seen in the aftermath of Hurricane Katrina, these thoughts were not irrational after all. Hurricane Rita became a realistic fear as it swiftly followed on the heels of Hurricane Katrina, forcing many evacuees from New Orleans who had relocated to Baton Rouge and surrounding towns to relocate once again.

Usually parents and other adults can placate their children by informing them that hurricanes are unusual occurrences that occur once in several years. In the case of Hurricane Katrina, however, such explanations did not hold true, and it became a challenge to explain to children that they had to deal with another hurricane less than a month later.

Concentration and attention: In the immediate aftermath of a disaster, survivors may experience difficulties in focusing their attention and concentrating on tasks due to their inability to stop thinking about the recent disaster. Unfortunately, helping agencies are often inattentive to this reaction to disasters and give survivors lengthy forms to fill out at a time when their ability to concentrate is impaired.

Perseveration: In an attempt to accept the reality of the disaster, some individuals may have a need to recount and replay the event repeatedly; the same thoughts are turned over in their minds incessantly as they try to come to terms with the crisis. Similarly, retelling the story to a first responder several times is expectable, as survivors struggle to cognitively integrate the reality of the situation.

Fluctuations in appetite and sleep: Sleep and appetite disturbances are physical reactions that usually appear early after a disaster. Many individuals may find it difficult to sleep, and even if they are able to fall asleep, they may be troubled by vivid dreams and nightmares. Some people may not be able to fall asleep at all, and when they do, it may be only for a short time, induced more by exhaustion than a desire to sleep. A lack of sleep increases feelings of irritability and frustration and can become a vicious cycle for many people. Others may find that they want to sleep all the time. Sleeping becomes a way to cope with the unreality of the situation with individuals having hope that things will be normal again when they awaken.

Disturbances in appetite are also commonly reported by survivors. Some individuals lack an appetite and may not want to eat at all, no matter how attractive a meal. Even when they are able to eat, they may experience nausea or an upset stomach; as a result, they may go without eating for several days. Such individuals risk developing serious health and other medical conditions and should be carefully monitored for dehydration.

Others may develop a voracious appetite, especially for foods high in fats and carbohydrates. They may report feelings of hunger and emptiness no matter how much they eat. This is also a situation that should be carefully monitored, especially if the individual suffers from diabetes, hypertension, high cholesterol, and other medical problems.

Behavioral: Traumatic exposure manifests itself behaviorally in symptoms of withdrawal, increased or decreased talking, and erratic or repetitive movements. Some survivors may pace interminably with a sense of aimlessness in their movements; others may display exaggerated startle responses or may become irritable and impatient and show an increase in antisocial, impulsive, and high-risk behaviors.

Physiological: Physiological reactions may include an elevated heart rate and blood pressure, difficulty breathing, hyperventilation, chest pains, muscle tension, fatigue, excessive perspiration, dizziness, headaches, and stomachaches. Some people also report physical exhaustion and weakness.

Group cohesiveness: One positive reaction to disasters and crises is the cohesiveness that can develop among survivor groups. As similar problems of finding shelter and food present themselves, it is common for individuals to develop a shared sense of community and connectedness. Similarly, family members may express a need to be with each other all the time, even though prior to the disaster, these relationships may have been tenuous. People tend to be more open to forgiving each other and forgetting about past conflicts in the aftermath of a disaster. Funerals, for example, often bring estranged families together.

Leadership: Those with leadership potential and those who held a leadership position prior to a crisis quickly ascend to taking on leadership roles in a crisis. Philanthropy and feelings of goodwill become pervasive. Such leaders often think of others before themselves. There have been many stories, in the aftermath of Hurricane Katrina, of neighbors helping each other and sharing limited resources.

Grief: Those who have lost a loved one often become preoccupied with thoughts about the dead person. They have feelings of guilt for having survived and go through their daily activities with a diminished sense of enthusiasm and motivation. Grief reactions depend on the intensity and strength of the relationship (e.g., losing a child or a partner can be emotionally more difficult). Both overreaction and underresponding by bereaved survivors should be closely monitored and given equal attention. Those who are able to express their feelings of loss openly tend to heal more quickly than those who are preoccupied with their loss and unable or unwilling to discuss it.

Individuals affected by traumatic events may experience some or several of these reactions. It is common for individuals to feel as if they are on a roller coaster. Reactions may temporarily abate or suddenly increase in intensity as time passes. Survivors should be reassured that these reactions are expected and understandable; an affirmation that other traumatized individuals have reported experiencing similar reactions can be validating. Traumatic experiences have long-term effects, which may be detrimental for the stable functioning of the brain and the body. Finally, not everyone experiences acute reactions after a disaster. As time goes by, the enormity of the crisis will begin to sink in and symptoms may become manifest in some people for the first time. It is not surprising that the suicide rate increased tremendously in New Orleans a year after Katrina occurred (Kessler et al., 2008).

CHARACTERISTICS AND PRINCIPLES OF EFFECTIVE DISASTER INTERVENTIONS

The following factors play an important role in the execution of effective crisis and disaster interventions.

Characteristics of the First Responder

The ability to think and act quickly and creatively is crucial. People who are affected by a crisis sometimes develop tunnel vision; they are unable to see the alternatives and options available to them. The crisis responder may have to be the one who proposes solutions. Thus, the crisis responder has to maintain an open mind to solve problems creatively and explore the best options with survivors. People in crisis often feel out of control; when opportunities to empower and restore control to affected individuals present themselves, the crisis responder should quickly take advantage of them. Crisis work is not for everyone. The crisis responder must be able to stay calm and collected. In addition, the ability to maintain empathy while avoiding subjective involvement in the crisis and maintaining healthy boundaries is an important skill to develop.

Mental health professionals providing services in disaster settings should be trained in empathic listening; those who listen attentively give survivors an opportunity to express their emotions and receive appropriate emotional validation. Sandoval (1985) has written about the need to adequately reflect a victim's feelings after a disaster, and Dyregrov (1999) has noted the importance of validating a survivor's thoughts, feelings, and impressions through effective listening. Active reflective listening is a core competency in psychological first aid (Parker, Everly, Barnett, & Links, 2006). Besides these important characteristics, crisis responders who are familiar with the principles of short-term interventions are well equipped to help after disasters.

Short-Term Interventions

Crisis interventions are always short term and involve establishing specific goals that are achievable within a short period of time. For example, in response to a suicidal client, a crisis counselor may increase the frequency of sessions with the client until the client's suicidal ideation subsides. Because management, rather than resolution, is the objective of crisis interventions, crisis responses are often described as emotional first aid (Rosenbluh, 1981).

Crisis interventions are not process focused but action-oriented and situation-focused interventions (Aguilera, 1998; Pollin, 1995). Such interventions prepare clients to manage the sequelae of a traumatic event. Crisis counselors help their clients to recognize and understand the impact of a crisis and anticipate its emotional and behavioral consequences. They help their clients in developing coping skills and identifying appropriate resources and support. With the assistance of the first responder, clients can then formulate a safety plan to cope with current and anticipated challenges related to the crisis.

In the immediate aftermath of a disaster, seeking counseling may not be a high priority for affected people. They may be involved in processing the necessary paperwork to obtain financial assistance; trying to get in contact with family members or friends who are dislocated; obtaining clothing, food, or medical care; and generally trying to rebuild their lives. Although they may experience emotional pain, ensuring that basic needs are met takes precedence. It is for this reason that the initial focus of psychological first aid is on providing basic needs (Everly, Phillips, Kane, & Feldman, 2006; Parker et al., 2006).

Restoration of Power and Control

A crisis is often characterized by loss of safety and control. It is therefore incumbent on professionals in human services to focus on the restoration of power and control in the client's internal and external environments (Yassen & Harvey, 1998). The goal is not to ask probing and exploratory questions but rather to focus on the "here and now." The crisis responder merely acts as an emotional crutch at a time when self-direction is impossible (Greenstone & Leviton, 2002). Crisis responders do not attempt to make major changes in their clients; instead, they serve as catalysts for clients to discover their own internal and external resources, which can then be used to enhance their recovery (Saleebey, 1997).

Because a crisis intervention is the first and possibly the only intervention that some clients may encounter after a calamity, the goal is always to mobilize coping skills, provide support, and restore pre-crisis functioning. Crisis interventions require that responders possess some familiarity with the setting in which they will be working. The ability to direct people to local shelters and other safe places and to offer help in finding loved ones is crucial in disaster settings.

Multicultural Competency

Understanding and attending to the diverse cultural needs of individuals and communities in crisis is crucial in the aftermath of a disaster, because it has implications for how an intervention is perceived and received by survivor communities (Pedersen & Carey, 2003). Disaster contexts provide a rich opportunity for understanding the confluence of ethnicity and traumatic experience as people begin to share their stories of survival.

To respond effectively to the mental health needs of disaster survivors, responders—regardless of their racial, ethnic, or cultural background—must first be sensitive to the unique experiences, beliefs, norms, values, traditions, customs, and language of survivors, (Athey & Moody-Williams, 2003). Crisis interventions are challenging and can become more difficult or have disastrous consequences when the first responder is culturally insensitive (James & Gilliland, 2005). Although there has been an increase in the literature on cultural competence among mental health providers (Sue & Sue, 2003), practical application of this knowledge remains in its infancy.

For example, following Hurricane Katrina, many African American citizens living in the Gulf Coast region experienced challenges in receiving appropriate help; a cultural breakdown between those designated to receive aid after the storm and those delivering it was apparent. The lack of competence by service providers mobilized the American Psychological Association (2006) to examine the training of volunteers who offered disaster mental health assistance to victims and relief workers through national humanitarian organizations and governmental agencies. The major finding that emerged was a clear need to improve the training of mental health providers so that they could be more prepared to work with diverse populations in the aftermath of disasters.

Ecological and Community Aspects

All people belong to communities, whether they experience them as supportive or not. Individuals are an integral part of the communities in which they live (Magnavita, 2006). The interrelationship between people and their environment is a dynamic and complex ecosystem (Callenbach, 1998). Religious groups, health clubs, the workplace, families, and a close-knit group of friends are examples of community groups.

Network therapy has capitalized on the beneficial aspects of community support in supporting healthy functioning, and an important component of this intervention is developing a network of caring people to support a person's recovery (Galanter, 1993). Similarly, the role of the community in enhancing recovery and restoring much-needed social support has been well documented (Norris, Perilla, & Murphy, 2001; Norris & Stevens, 2007).

Interventions that encourage survivors to give back by supporting others who are less fortunate in their community improve their self-esteem and overall recovery. Such actions also enhance social connectedness and improve the community as a whole.

Training in Disaster Response

A solid training in crisis intervention (with a focus on identifying suicidal and homicidal ideation) as well as experience in counseling is indispensable for working in the field of crisis intervention. Trained professionals already experienced in handling emergencies will likely perform best under disaster conditions. Because every disaster is unique and survivors experience a diversity of traumatic responses, first responders who have experience in applying a number of different interventions available to them are most effective. A disaster site should not be the place where helping professionals test their skills for the first time (Dass-Brailsford, 2008). The American Red Cross requires that those who volunteer on disaster mental health teams be trained and certified according to designated standards. Other organizations that offer disaster mental health training are as follows:

Community Emergency Response Teams

International Critical Incident Stress Foundation

Department of Homeland Security Trauma Response Teams

Medical Reserve Corps

National Disaster Medical System Teams

National Organization for Victim Assistance

Disaster work is challenging and has the potential to become even more challenging if a responder does not have the requisite skills. An inevitable consequence of being a first responder in a disaster situation is exposure to many physical and emotional stressors. It is not known whether certain occupations are intrinsically associated with higher risk for psychological distress or whether the risk is a result of working outside one's area of training and expertise (Guo et al., 2004). However, Perrin et al. (2007) found that those who had responded to the September 11th disaster with less experience and training had a greater risk of developing posttraumatic stress disorder. Thus, adequate training should be a priority for first responders.

THEORETICAL APPROACHES AND INTERVENTION MODELS

The Chinese translation of the word *crisis* consists of two separate characters, exemplifying danger and opportunity (Greene, Lee, Trask, & Rheinscheld, 2000). Although crises may be perceived as negative events, crisis interventions provide opportunities for clients to learn new coping skills while identifying, mobilizing, and enhancing those they may already possess. Disaster mental health services must be executed in a manner that recognizes, respects, and builds on the strengths and resources of survivors and their communities (Athey & Moody-Williams, 2003). A strength-based approach is most appropriate, because it makes use of the resources that survivors already possess.

Everly and Flynn (2006) describe psychological first aid as providing compassionate support during a crisis. It is designed to reduce acute psychological distress and facilitate support. The goal is to assist with current needs and promote adaptive functioning rather than to elicit details of traumatic experiences and losses. Applying the concepts of brevity, immediacy, contact, expectancy, proximity, and simplicity (BICEPS) underlies their model of psychological first aid.

Immediate crisis intervention or psychological first aid involves establishing rapport with the survivor, gathering information to make a short-term assessment, and providing immediate services to avert future crises. Psychological first aid entails the facilitation of the "trauma story" by allowing survivors to vent their feelings in an appropriate manner so that intense and negative emotions are released (Raphael, Wilson, Meldrum, & McFarlane, 1996).

Although this intervention is an important element of the healing process for victims, many victims are initially resistant to receiving crisis intervention services, because they often associate such services with mental health counseling and are afraid to be diagnosed with a mental health disorder. This resistance is fairly common after a crisis; the first responder should anticipate this happening and figure out ways to work around it. Crises require an immediate response, which is critical to ensure the safety of victims and their families, especially if there is impending danger to victims. Waiting hours or days to talk to a crisis intervention counselor is not practical; in that time, the need for such services usually diminishes.

Crisis intervention should not be assigned to one specific agency or organization but rather be a collaborative effort in which multiple agencies or organizations participate. This includes victim advocacy organizations, private agencies or organizations (such as hospitals or schools), social service agencies, law enforcement, and corrections. For the crisis intervention to be effective, it must be provided in an orderly, structured, humanistic manner, and must focus on the individuality of each survivor. It involves caring for the medical, physical, psychological, and other uniquely personal needs of the survivor by providing information about local resources or services and making referrals to other agencies for ongoing services. This may include working with other agencies to reduce the additional trauma imposed by going through complex and often frustrating bureaucratic systems.

Besides reducing risk factors for survivors, the focus is on maximizing social support systems, improving coping skills, and helping survivors attain greater self-esteem and self-worth. Because this is the initial period of recovery, it may take considerable time, effort, and resources before the survivor resolves long-term issues associated with the crisis (Roberts, 1990). Recovery interventions help survivors restabilize their lives and become healthy again. It involves helping them avoid further victimization.

The model described next encapsulates many of the principles of effective crisis intervention strategies.

An Empowering Model of Crisis Intervention

In *A Practical Approach to Trauma: Empowering Interventions,* Dass-Brailsford (2007) introduces an empowering model of crisis intervention that is based on important principles taken from community psychology, strength-based and solution-focused therapies. The model has three basic steps: pre-intervention, assessment, and disposition.

Pre-intervention

Before responding to a community or an individual in crisis, first responders should find out as much as possible ahead of time about the host community or individuals with whom they will be working. The responder can expect that as a result of a crisis event, survivors may have difficulties with attention, focusing, and memory. Asking survivors questions they may have difficulty answering can be perceived as disempowering. Getting as much background information before initiating a crisis intervention circumvents this from occurring. In addition, first responders should prepare themselves by engaging in stress-reduction procedures as early as possible and alerting their support system (supervisors, family, and colleagues) about an impending disaster deployment. This preliminary action helps responders maintain stability as they prepare to support distressed individuals or communities.

Assessment

The assessment step involves identifying the needs of distressed individuals or communities in order to provide them with appropriate emotional support, services, and other resources. The primary goal is to assess how the crisis is affecting individuals so that plans for recovery can be developed and healing can begin. The three objectives of assessment are as follows:

- medical and health functioning (e.g., diabetes, hypertension, physical injuries);
- psychological functioning conducted through a quick mental status evaluation (e.g., level of risk to self and others and other behaviors); and
- an assessment of a survivor's support and belief system, the acculturation level of those new to the country, and the availability of economic resources.

In addition, current concerns and precipitants to the crisis are identified. Gathering information about how an individual handled similar crises in the past helps in problem solving and planning for the future. Making an accurate assessment is critical, because it guides the overall intervention and a wrong decision can lead to lethal consequences. Although situations may be similar, each person is unique; therefore, the first responder should avoid overgeneralizing from one client to another.

An ecological chart is a useful mechanism for identifying resources and areas of future support. Figure 4.1 is constructed with the affected individual or community in the middle, encircled by significant groups, identified as important by the client or the client community. Once the responder constructs this chart, he or she can proceed to explore with the survivor those people who can provide ongoing support. This assists in the later disposition and transition of the survivor.

Those with acute psychiatric concerns will need hospitalization or a psychopharmacology assessment, whereas the physically injured will need immediate medical help. Individuals who present with numbness and shock may not have fully absorbed the impact of the disaster. They may actually be in a pre-crisis state and the first responder will have to assess how the person will react when this realization is made. There are also vulnerable groups that have no prior experience of a trauma and therefore lack coping skills. These survivors will have to be closely monitored before a disposition is made, because there is no way of knowing how they will handle their losses.

The responder will have to prioritize those who need attention first. Obviously, the physically injured and those experiencing severe psychological symptoms such as suicidal and homicidal ideation will be high on the list, whereas those with mood disturbances and minimal resources and support networks will need to be monitored for a longer time.

FIGURE 4.1   Ecological Chart

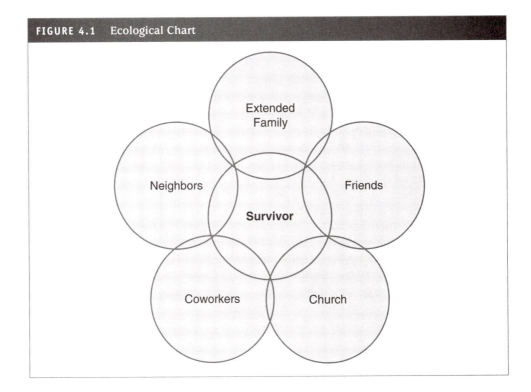

Disposition

The first responder should allow survivors to talk as little or as much as they feel necessary about the crisis event or other concerns. The telling and retelling of a traumatic event assists in the healing process as it becomes a vehicle for increasing integration and understanding (Houlbrooke, 1998; Pennebaker, 1997; Smythe & Pennebaker, 1999).

Psycho-educational information on what actions can be taken to maintain safety and stabilization are valuable steps in helping clients toward assuming control of their lives. This information provides them with knowledge and prepares them to anticipate the process of recovery so that there will be no surprises. For example, giving survivors a handout that outlines the stages of grief and loss and common expectable reactions reduces unnecessary stress and normalizes the process for them.

Decisions on how to handle the crisis are always made by exploring options with the survivor. This is an action that restores control and supports the empowerment of survivors. In addition, decisions, which actively include the participation of survivors, promote compliance, while thinking creatively usually resolves most problems. Finally, because crisis intervention requires short-term involvement, it is important to refer the individuals to other helping resources as soon as stability is established.

Referral and Resource List

A referral and resource list is an indispensable asset when conducting crisis interventions. The effective crisis responder keeps updated information about helping agencies in a client's community. Once a referral and resource list has been developed, making sure that phone numbers, addresses, and names of contact persons are constantly updated is critical. It can be frustrating for a client in crisis to call a disconnected number for help. In addition, it may be useful to have some knowledge about the process that a client may have to go through to receive services to inform him or her about this process. If time allows, it is useful to visit these agencies ahead of time. Such visits increase the responders' familiarity with the services they can later offer to clients. Knowing whether they have a waiting list, sliding scale of payment, or if priority is given to those in crisis is important information that can be communicated to clients.

Information about available resources should be clearly printed on a card and carefully reviewed with a client before termination. Because one of the challenges people in crisis often face is the ability to remember mundane information, the crisis responder should have clients clearly review the next steps before they leave. Getting permission to call them a few days later to get an update on how they are doing will be perceived as supportive. The next section details several other interventions that are often conducted after a crisis or traumatic event.

Other Interventions

Debriefings

Debriefings, first developed in the U.S. military, are often conducted within 24 to 72 hours after a traumatic event. The immediacy of this intervention is intended to help affected individuals "get over" negative reactions and resume normal functioning. Mitchell (1983) developed the critical incident stress debriefing to help emergency service personnel manage the trauma reactions that may be triggered in the performance of their vocation. Although these debriefings were originally developed for specific populations, they are now used with civilian groups affected by traumatic events.

A debriefing is a single-session, semi-structured crisis intervention designed to minimize the negative consequences of a traumatic event and serves several purposes: to review reactions, process the experience, and discuss coping skills. It prepares group participants to begin to deal with the stress of their current experience and help them with incidents that may occur in the future. The important role of positive attachments in supporting resilience among victims of disasters has been documented (Chemtob, 2005; Everly, Flannery, & Mitchell, 2000). Some researchers have theorized that one of the most efficacious elements of debriefings is the social support that people obtain from being part of a group (Busutill, 1995; Flannery, 1990; Wollman, 1993).

However, the efficacy of debriefings as an effective form of crisis intervention has been controversial. Critics argue that debriefings offer no opportunity for follow-up treatment and may cause individuals unnecessary distress by exposing those who may not have symptoms to the negative reactions of others who may be symptomatic. Several studies show that debriefings have no effect in preventing the psychological sequelae that follow a traumatic event. In contrast, other studies (Irving & Long, 2001; Matthews, 1998; Richards, 2001), conducted mostly with homogeneous groups, indicate that psychological debriefings are beneficial.

In light of these findings, debriefings should be used with caution. Until researchers can provide more definitive data on their efficacy, debriefings should not be discounted. It is important for the responder to first carefully assess the cultural needs and ecological resources of the community before evaluating whether a debriefing is the most appropriate intervention.

Group Interventions

Trauma-focused group interventions are useful in educating participants about the process of recovery, reviewing crisis reactions, and considering coping responses. To create a feeling of safety among group members, it is important to begin with a discussion of confidentiality and a respect for each other's responses. According to Herman (1997), the solidarity of a group provides the strongest protection against terror and despair and the strongest antidote to traumatic experiences. The group format and the presence of others who have experienced the same event creates a sense of community; it also provides each person with opportunities to express emotions and receive appropriate validation.

The group leader prepares participants by making predictions about what to expect in the short and long term. Outlining the stages of recovery from a disaster reduces unnecessary anxiety and prepares group members to face the future. Group leaders should be able to listen intently, monitor all group members at the same time, normalize reactions, and slow the process down if things get too emotional. When dealing with panic and dissociative symptoms, the leader provides group members with support and later makes a referral for a higher level of care.

The leader strives to foster natural group resilience by focusing on effective coping skills that have been used in both the past and present. Group members explore other potential support systems. Individual coping skills can be facilitated by using the group as a model. Group members are encouraged to share their difficulties as a way of dividing their pain.

When a group is large, it may be more appropriate to conduct a group meeting to provide information and reduce chaos. When appropriately done, community meetings can enhance coping, restore morale, engender cohesion, and provide opportunities to screen those who may be at increased risk for psychological problems.

PRACTICAL IMPLICATIONS

- Disaster responders should be skilled in the principles of crisis intervention.
- The principles of psychological first aid guide effective crisis interventions.
- The empowering model of crisis intervention identifies and uses the strengths and resources of clients so that they can be empowered toward recovery.
- Debriefings, although often used in crisis situations, should be conducted with caution.
- Trauma focused group interventions have psycho-educational benefits that enhance the coping behaviors of survivors.

CONCLUSION

Responding in the aftermath of a disaster requires specialized skills and training. The disaster mental health responder usually interacts with individuals in their most vulnerable moment. To provide effective interventions, helping professionals should be adequately trained and prepared to work efficiently and skillfully. The principles of psychological first aid guide effective crisis interventions. The empowering model of crisis intervention is described as an appropriate intervention that acknowledges clients' strengths, restores control, and empowers them to take charge of their lives. Most importantly, individual psychological interventions should be culturally and ecologically appropriate and include a full consideration of the family, community, and other systems that surround survivors. Several organizations that provide disaster training have been outlined. It is incumbent on mental health professionals who wish to perform the services of first responders after disasters to seek the appropriate training offered by these organizations.

REFERENCES

Aguilera, D. (1998). *Crisis intervention: Theory and methodology* (8th ed.). St. Louis, MO: Mosby.

American Psychological Association. (2006). APA's response to international and national disasters and crises: Addressing diverse needs. *American Psychologist, 61*(5), 513–521.

Athey, J., & Moody-Williams, J. (2003). *Developing cultural competence in disaster mental health programs: Guiding principles and recommendations*. Rockville, MD: U.S. Department of Health and Human Services.

Busutill, A. (1995). Psychological debriefing. *British Journal of Psychiatry, 166*, 676–681.

Callenbach, E. (1998). *Ecology: A pocket guide*. Berkeley: University of California Press.

Caplan, G. (1964). *Principles of preventive psychiatry*. New York: Basic Books.

Chemtob, C. M. (2005). Finding the gift in the horror: Toward developing a national psychosocial security policy. *Journal of Aggression, Maltreatment, & Trauma, 10*, 721–727.

Dass-Brailsford, P. (2007). *A practical approach to trauma: Empowering interventions*. Thousand Oaks, CA: Sage.

Dass-Brailsford, P. (2008). After the storm: Recognition, recovery and reconstruction. *Journal of Professional Psychology: Research & Practice, 39*(1), 24–30.

Dyregrov, A. (1999). Helpful and hurtful aspects of psychological debriefing groups. *International Journal of Emergency Mental Health, 3*, 175–181.

Everly, G. S., Flannery, R. B., & Mitchell, J. T. (2000). Critical incident stress management (CISM): A review of the literature. *Aggression and Violent Behavior, 5*, 23–40.

Everly, G. S., & Flynn, B. W. (2006). Principles and practical procedures for acute psychological first aid training for personnel without mental health experience. *Preview International Journal of Emergency Mental Health, 8*(2), 93–100.

Everly, G. S., Phillips, S. B., Kane, D. K., & Feldman, D. (2006). Introduction to and overview of group psychological first aid. *Brief Treatment and Crisis Intervention, 6*, 130–136.

Flannery, R. D. (1990). Social support and psychological trauma: A methodological review. *Journal of Traumatic Stress, 3*, 593–611.

Galanter, M. (1993). *Network therapy for alcohol and drug abuse*. New York: Guilford.

Greene, G. J., Lee, M., Trask, R., & Rheinscheld, J. (2000). How to work with clients' strengths in crisis intervention. In A. R. Roberts (Ed.), *Crisis intervention handbook: Assessment, treatment and research* (pp. 31–55). Oxford, UK: Oxford University Press.

Greenstone, J. L., & Leviton, S. C. (2002). *Elements of crisis intervention: Crises and how to respond to them.* Pacific Grove, CA: Brooks/Cole.

Guo, Y., Chen, C., Lu, M., Tan, H. K., Lee, H., Wen, W., et al. (2004). Posttraumatic stress disorder among professional and non-professional rescuers involved in an earthquake in Taiwan. *Psychiatry Research, 127*(1–2), 35–41.

Herman, J. L. (1997). *Trauma and recovery.* New York: Basic Books.

Houlbrooke, R. (1998). *Death, religion and the family in England, 1480–1750.* Oxford, UK: Clarendon.

Irving, P., & Long, A. (2001). Critical Incident Stress Debriefing following traumatic life experiences. *Journal of Psychiatric & Mental Health Nursing, 8*(4), 307–314.

James, R. K., & Gilliland, B. E. (2005). *Crisis intervention strategies* (4th ed.). Belmont, CA: Thomson.

Kessler, R. C., Galea, S., Gruber, M. J., Sampson, N. A., Ursano, R. J., & Wesseley, S. (2008). Trends in mental illness and suicidality after Hurricane Katrina. *Molecular Psychiatry, 13*(4), 374–384.

Magnavita, J. J. (2006). In search of the unifying principles of psychotherapy: Conceptual, empirical, and clinical convergence. *American Psychologist, 61*, 882–892.

Matthews, L. R. (1998). Effect of staff debriefing on posttraumatic stress symptoms after assaults by community housing residents. *Psychiatric Services, 49*, 207–212.

Mitchell, J. T. (1983). When disaster strikes: The critical incident debriefing process. *Journal of Emergency Medical Services, 8*, 36–39.

Norris, F. H., Perilla, J. L., & Murphy, A. D. (2001). Postdisaster stress in the United States and Mexico: A cross-cultural test of the multicriterion conceptual model of posttraumatic stress disorder. *Journal of Abnormal Psychology, 110*(4), 553–563.

Norris, F. H., & Stevens, S. P. (2007). Community resilience as a metaphor and the principles of mass trauma intervention. *Psychiatry: Interpersonal and Biological Processes, 70*(4), 320–328.

Parker, C. L., Everly, G. S., Barnett, D. J., & Links, J. M. (2006). Establishing evidence-informed core competencies in psychological first aid for public health personnel. *International Journal of Emergency Mental Health, 8*, 83–92.

Pedersen, P. B., & Carey, J. C. (2003). *Multicultural counseling in schools: A practical handbook* (2nd ed.). Needham Heights, MA: Allyn & Bacon.

Pennebaker, J. W. (1997). Writing about emotional experiences as a therapeutic process. *Psychological Science, 8*, 162–166.

Perrin, M. A., DiGrande, L., Wheeler, K., Thorpe, L., Farfel, M., & Brackbill, R. (2007). Differences in PTSD prevalence and associated risk factors among World Trade Center disaster rescue and recovery workers. *American Journal of Psychiatry, 164*(9), 1385–1394.

Pollin, I. (1995). *Medical crisis counseling: Short-term therapy for long-term illness.* New York: Norton.

Raphael, B., Wilson, J., Meldrum, L., & McFarlane, A. C. (1996). Acute preventive interventions. In B. A. van der Kolk, A. C. McFarlane, & L. Weisaeth (Eds.), *Traumatic stress: The effects of overwhelming experience on mind, body, and society* (pp. 463–479). New York: Guilford.

Richards, D. (2001). A field study of critical incident stress debriefing versus critical incident stress management. *Journal of Mental Health, 10*(3), 351–362.

Roberts, A. R. (Ed.). (1990). *Crisis intervention handbook: Assessment, treatment and research.* Belmont, CA: Wadsworth.

Rosenbluh, E. S. (1981). *Emotional first aid.* Louisville, KY: American Academy of Crisis Interveners.

Saleebey, D. (Ed.). (1997). *The strengths perspective in social work practice* (2nd ed.). Boston: Allyn & Bacon.

Sandoval, J. (1985). Crisis counseling: Conceptualizations and general principles. *School Psychology Review, 14*, 257–265.

Slaikeu, K. A. (1990). *Crisis intervention: A handbook for practice and research* (2nd ed.). Needham Heights, MA: Allyn & Bacon.

Smythe, J. M., & Pennebaker, J. W. (1999). Sharing one's story: Translating emotional experiences into words as a coping tool. In C. R. Snyder (Ed.), *Coping: The psychology of what works* (pp. 70–89). New York: Oxford University Press.

Sue, D. W., & Sue, D. (2003). *Counseling the culturally different, theory and practice* (4th ed.). New York: John Wiley.

Weaver, J. (1995). *Disasters: Mental health interventions.* Sarasota, FL: Professional Resources Press.

Wollman, D. (1993). Critical incident stress debriefing and crisis groups: A review of the literature. *Group, 17,* 70–83.

Yassen, J., & Harvey, M. R. (1998). Crisis assessment and interventions with victims of violence. In P. M. Kleespies (Ed.), *Emergencies in mental health practice.* New York: Guilford.

Families Affected by Hurricane Katrina and Other Disasters

Learning From the Experiences of African American Survivors

Nancy Boyd-Franklin

This chapter explores the multiple ways in which families adapt in the aftermath of a disaster. It focuses primarily on African Americans and uses Hurricane Katrina as a learning opportunity to inform future responses to African Americans and other ethnic minority families affected by disaster. To contextualize the experiences of African Americans, the chapter begins with an exploration of the role of race and racism in previous disaster responses and its impact on intervention and treatment strategies. Cultural mistrust and healthy cultural suspicion resulting from such experiences are discussed as they relate to the responses of African Americans to treatment interventions in disaster situations.

CHAPTER HIGHLIGHTS

+ Discusses ways to sensitize responders and clinicians to the special needs of children, adolescents, older adults, and extended family members during disasters;

+ Highlights ways in which cultural strengths such as spirituality and religious orientation may be engaged when working with African Americans; and

+ Supports responders and mental health providers in using family systems and multisystems models to design culturally sensitive trauma interventions for African American and other ethnic minority families in future disasters.

DOUBLE PSYCHOLOGICAL TRAUMA: THE DISASTER AND EXPERIENCES OF RACISM

To fully comprehend the responses of African American clients and families, it is important to understand that the trauma of any disaster can be exacerbated by the trauma of racism (Boyd-Franklin, 2008, in press). Culturally insensitive and disrespectful treatment during and after the disaster may be experienced as racism (Dass-Brailsford, 2006, 2007; Law, 2006); yet such manifestations of racism are often denied by others. This denial can lead to further trauma and severe emotional consequences for some African Americans. It is important for mental health practitioners to understand that African Americans often view situations related to race very differently from White Americans and those from other cultural and racial groups. The aftermath of Hurricane Katrina is an excellent example of these differences in perception (Boyd-Franklin, 2008, in press).

Television images of the aftermath of Hurricane Katrina shocked viewers across America. Many watched in horror as families were left in deplorable conditions with no food or water for as long as 5 days (Boyd-Franklin, in press). Dyson (2006) and Troutt (2006) have shown that the overwhelming majority of those who suffered grievously were Black and poor. Thus, in addition to the profound tragedy of the loss of so many lives, the displacement of families, and the utter devastation of homes and other property in the area, this disaster exposed a reality that is frequently denied (i.e., that poor Black people are often forgotten or invisible Americans)—their needs as well as their existence are often disregarded in disaster planning and relief efforts (Dyson, 2006; Troutt, 2006).

The experience of Hurricane Katrina challenged the denial of racism and classism in America, although reactions were split along racial lines. A CNN/USA Today Gallup poll conducted approximately 2 weeks after the storm asked respondents whether the race of the victims contributed to the slow response of the government. Sixty percent of Black interviewees viewed race as a factor, whereas only 12% of Whites gave a similar response (Boyd-Franklin, 2008, in press; CNN, 2005). Many in the African American community questioned whether the government's response would have been as slow if those most affected by the storm had been affluent Whites. On the other hand, the denial of the role of race and racism was clear in the responses of White Americans.

This difference in perspective is not unusual. Studies of Black and White individuals' responses to major events in America have often documented significantly divergent perspectives (Dyson, 2006; Troutt, 2006). In many instances, White Americans have given a "class, not race" response, attributing the differences in treatment to the poverty or lower socioeconomic status of the victims (Boyd-Franklin, 1989). In the instance of Hurricane Katrina, however, even the default rationale of classism was denied. Respondents to the poll were asked whether the slow response of the government was due to the poverty of the victims. The results were similar to the question on race—whereas 63% of the Blacks viewed poverty as a factor, only 21% of Whites did (CNN, 2005). These responses are striking in their own right and can greatly affect the reactions of African Americans to the trauma of disaster experiences.

THE PSYCHOLOGICAL TRAUMA OF PERCEIVED RACISM

For many years, there has been a debate in the mental health field about the psychological impact of perceived racism (Blitz & Pender Greene, 2006; Carter, 2007; Franklin, Boyd-Franklin, & Kelly, 2006; Utsey, Chae, Brown, & Kelly, 2002). Consequently, many therapists and disaster responders questioned African Americans' characterization of certain acts as racist, arguing that the alleged perpetrators may not have committed such acts intentionally. These clinicians did not realize that African Americans are vulnerable to the trauma of perceived racism, even if the intent of the perpetrator remained uncertain. Research documenting the psychological trauma created by experiences of perceived racism has created a paradigm shift in the field (Utsey et al., 2002).

One aspect of the psychological trauma of perceived racism is that it causes intense anger and rage among those who experience it—reactions common among African American survivors of the storm. In addition, many survivors remain angry about the treatment they continue to receive (Dyson, 2006). It is important that clinicians and other responders do not automatically perceive anger as a negative response. Anger can play a positive role in coping for African Americans who have experienced the psychological trauma of racism. Some forms of anger can mobilize disenfranchised individuals and families and therefore act as a healthy response to racism among oppressed groups.

Similarly, mental health providers and other responders must be trained to recognize that there are many different kinds of racism. Peggy McIntosh (1998), a noted White feminist scholar, reported that she, like many other White Americans, had been taught to view racism as "individual acts of meanness." She acknowledges that although all forms of racism are problematic, it is the more subtle forms of institutional racism—often invisible to those not directly affected by them—that are most psychologically damaging. For example, many African American scholars have argued that generations of institutional racism have helped to create the poverty in the African American communities in Louisiana, Mississippi, and Alabama (Boyd-Franklin, in press; Dyson, 2006; Troutt, 2006). They have also argued that the geographic concentration of poor, Black residents in the area of New Orleans most vulnerable to flooding and inferior levees was also related to generations of institutional racism (Dyson, 2006).

CULTURAL MISTRUST, HEALTHY CULTURAL SUSPICION, AND RESPONSES TO TREATMENT AMONG AFRICAN AMERICANS

One common response to the anger caused by the psychological trauma of perceived racism among African Americans has been a protective coping mechanism that has been termed *cultural mistrust* or *healthy cultural suspicion* (Boyd-Franklin, 2003). Because of multigenerational experiences with the psychological trauma of racism, many African Americans have learned to be suspicious of the intentions of others, especially those in positions of power.

Such suspicions can increase the difficulty of establishing therapeutic rapport with African American clients and families, especially in cross-racial contexts. In addition, there remains a great deal of stigma attached to therapy in the African American community (Boyd-Franklin, 2003). It is often viewed as only appropriate for mentally sick, weak, or crazy people.

Mental health providers of all ethnic backgrounds must be trained to allow African Americans in psychotherapy and counseling sessions the opportunity to express anger at racist treatment, especially in the aftermath of disasters (Boyd-Franklin, 2008; Dass-Brailsford, 2006; Law, 2006). Cokley, Cooke, & Nobles (2006) issued a publication, *Association of Black Psychologists: Guidelines for Providing Culturally Appropriate Services for People of African Ancestry Exposed to the Trauma of Hurricane Katrina*, which addressed these concerns:

> Providers must be willing to honestly discuss the roles of institutionalized racism (and classism) in the woefully inadequate response of the federal and state governments. The African American survivors need an outlet to vent their frustrations with governmental bureaucracy that was appallingly slow in responding to a crisis situation involving a predominately poor and Black population. (p. xxxiv)

In disaster situations such as Hurricane Katrina and its aftermath, African Americans are vulnerable to the double trauma of the disaster as well as the experience of perceived racism, a situation likely to exacerbate the cultural mistrust and healthy cultural suspicion among many African Americans. There is considerable diversity, however, in African American communities, and not all Black clients or families will present with anger or healthy cultural suspicion. Responders should therefore not assume that all Black people would report perceived racism in given situations. Similarly, first responders should not assume that Black survivors would be comfortable in talking about racism, particularly in cross-racial situations. It is essential, however, for disaster responders and mental health providers to anticipate and understand these responses when they occur so that they can avoid the tendency to "take it personally" and to respond in negative ways. These potential reactions make it particularly important that responders and mental health providers take the time to join and establish therapeutic rapport with traumatized African Americans in disaster situations and address their needs in a respectful and warm manner before a survivor may be ready to explore the psychological trauma of racism.

EXTENDED FAMILIES AND INFORMAL KINSHIP NETWORKS

Many African Americans exist in a collectivistic cultural context in which contact with extended family members are the norm (Boyd-Franklin, 2003). In addition to mothers, fathers, brothers, sisters, aunts, uncles, cousins, grandparents, and so forth, these families often have a close informal kinship network composed of non-blood friends and supporters who are considered a part of the "family." These individuals might include friends, neighbors, babysitters, "play mamas," godparents, and church family members (including the minister, the minister's wife, deacons, deaconesses, Sunday school teachers, and other close members of the congregation).

Many of the African American families in the Gulf Coast region had lived in their communities for generations. Children were often raised with multiple blood and non-blood caregivers in close proximity, and they and their families had a sense of security connected to their experience of living in a familiar community. Hurricane Katrina disrupted this sense of security and communal care, as many children and families experienced the total loss and devastation of their homes and communities in addition to the loss of life.

Misconceptions and stereotypes about African American families abound and contributed to many of the culturally insensitive responses in the rescue efforts after Hurricane Katrina (Boyd-Franklin, in press; Dyson, 2006). Because of the stereotype of households in low-income African American communities as single parent and female-headed, African American fathers—particularly those who were not married to the mothers—were treated as if they were invisible (Franklin et al., 2006). As a consequence, rescue efforts after Hurricane Katrina, designed to attend to the needs of women and children, often left fathers behind and contributed to the further fragmentation of many of these families. In addition, as many family members were displaced, the diaspora of African Americans in this country became even more pronounced. Many families have yet to be reunited, and the devastation of their homes and communities makes it starkly evident that there is no end in sight to their separation. Families that have remained intact confront other overwhelming challenges. For example, families living in FEMA trailers face constant threats of eviction, often live in unsafe trailer parks where the social ills of drugs and violence threaten the well-being of their children (Ruscher, 2006), and are exposed to environmental hazards, such as toxic levels of the carcinogen formaldehyde confirmed by FEMA to be present in the trailers (Skipp, 2008).

Considerations Regarding Extended Family Members During a Disaster

It is important that disaster planning, particularly for ethnic minority individuals from collectivistic cultures (e.g., African American, Caribbean, African, Latino, Asian, Native American, etc.), uses a family systems model that considers connections to extended family and informal kinship networks. In such families, extended family is often deeply involved in these children's lives and children may be cared for by many different members of the network. Given these realities, it behooves first responders to ensure that families are kept together and that interventions include the whole family system, not just individuals. Attempts should always be made to work as quickly as possible to reunite children with their families or familiar adults.

Many African Americans and others from close, extended families are often in frequent contact with their family members. Thus, for many of these families, the concern and anxiety felt for missing extended family members, close friends, and neighbors added to the trauma already experienced after Hurricane Katrina. One of the most important interventions developed informally by the Red Cross and other first responders during this period was a database that provided families with information regarding displaced family members. A lesson for future disasters would be the development of a comprehensive national online locator database that can track family members and significant others in a reliable fashion. Access to such information should also be available by telephone for those without Internet service or computer skills so that all concerned individuals can locate family members as quickly as possible in the immediate aftermath of a disaster.

For generations, African American families have had a tradition of "taking in" extended family members in times of trouble. After Hurricane Katrina, many Black families throughout the country opened their homes to family members displaced by the storm, which highlights the strength of Black families. It was not unusual for three families (consisting of 10 to 15 members) to live together in a one- or two-bedroom home or apartment, sharing one bathroom. Many of the welcoming families were already living in meager socioeconomic circumstances and receiving no aid or financial support. As time progressed, this situation became increasingly burdensome for some families and added to their emotional distress. It is important for FEMA and other governmental agencies to learn from this experience and anticipate the needs of families so that relatives do not have to bear this burden. Although the priority of FEMA in the aftermath of the storm to find homes for those who were homeless and living in shelters was necessary and understandable, consideration should have been given to those who took on the responsibility of sheltering family members and significant others. Early financial aid would have eased the stress on supportive extended family networks that opened their homes to survivors, although many of these needs were not apparent until months later.

TRAUMA EXPERIENCES OF AFRICAN AMERICAN CHILDREN AND ADOLESCENTS

Many of the children and adolescents affected by Hurricane Katrina experienced the loss of their homes and communities, separation from their families and extended family members, and the loss of all that was familiar to them (Dass-Brailsford, 2007). Some experienced the death of close family members and subsequent feelings of grief and loss. Many people spent days abandoned without food or water in locations such as the Convention Center and the Superdome in New Orleans (Gheytanchi et al., 2007). For African American children and adolescents, the trauma of the hurricane was frequently exacerbated by the trauma caused by discrimination. In addition, many African American youth witnessed their parents and other adult extended family members being treated disrespectfully by those in authority designated with the task of evacuating New Orleans after the hurricane. Observing adults they trust treated in this way is particularly traumatic for children and adolescents, because it can increase their sense of insecurity, feelings of being unprotected, fears of abandonment, and loss of a sense of safety.

In addition to these traumas, it is also important for disaster responders to recognize that many African American children and adolescents often function as "parental children" (Boyd-Franklin, 2003). This role is particularly common in poor and working-class families in which parents have jobs but are unable to afford child care. These children, some as young as 9 or 10 years old, often serve as caregivers for younger children, older adults, and even their overwhelmed parents. Unlike in Latino culture whereby the parental child is often female, in African American culture, both older boys and girls serve in this role. After Hurricane Katrina, young parental children undertook the care for younger siblings and cousins during periods of separation from extended family members. In addition, there were many situations in which parental children rescued other family members. Some of these valiant youth experienced trauma related to the extreme guilt that they felt over their inability to prevent injury or death of family members.

The Trauma of Relocation and Dislocation for African American Children and Adolescents

It was traumatic for children and adolescents of all cultures to be uprooted from their families and familiar surroundings following Hurricane Katrina. There were, however, a number of important additional considerations for the African American youth as they entered new, unfamiliar communities. The trauma of being uprooted combined with their intense anger about the disrespect and racism that they and their families had experienced contributed to increased behavioral and conduct problems among some of these children and adolescents. Many service providers and school personnel did not understand that such behaviors were a manifestation of a traumatic response. In addition, as many of these young people found themselves in predominantly White communities and school systems for the first time, they often experienced racism. Some communities that had initially been welcoming in the immediate aftermath of the storm became less so as the months went by. There was a sense that the newcomers had overstayed their visit and problems developed, such as an acute need for mental health services for African American youth who found themselves resettled in unwelcoming communities in states throughout the country. It is uncertain whether this need was met adequately, given that some states were homogeneously populated and such a need had not been presented in the past.

For many African American adolescents, it was particularly difficult to establish a new peer group. Many felt very isolated and struggled for the first time with being the only one or one of few Black youth in their new schools and communities. This type of experience can lead to confusion about cultural or racial identity. Some children and adolescents felt ashamed about their homelessness, the low-income status of their families, and their dependency on the charity of others.

For those in predominantly White communities, stereotypes led, in some instances, to fears and racial profiling, particularly of African American males by the police. Some of these adolescents banded together to protect themselves. This was misinterpreted as gang behavior and sometimes led to turf and gang issues in some communities.

ISSUES FOR ELDERLY AFRICAN AMERICANS IN DISASTER SITUATIONS

The welfare of older adults is an important consideration in any disaster (see Chapter 8 in this book). Failure to understand the central role of the elderly in African American families accounted for many misunderstandings and lack of cultural sensitivity in the post-Katrina response. To avoid future problems, it is crucial that disaster responders understand the beliefs in many African American families regarding the role and care of older adults.

Older adults in African American families often serve as the family leader or switchboard through whom all communications are made (Boyd-Franklin, 2003). Often, grandmothers, grandfathers, and great aunts or uncles may also serve as a family caregiver. This is particularly (but not exclusively) true among older women. Such individuals may be referred to as the "heart and soul of the family." As the movie *Soul Food* so graphically depicts, these individuals often cook and host family gatherings in their homes. Some families experience a crisis when the core person who holds the family together dies, which is what occurred after Hurricane Katrina.

Kinship care is a cultural tradition in many African American families. With both parents working, grandmothers, and even great grandmothers, may provide care for children. In addition, some families have parents who are unable to care for their children due to drug or alcohol abuse, mental illness, incarceration, or medical concerns. In these situations, grandparents or other older adults in the family may be assigned the task of raising children. Even when these older adults are living in poverty, they are not given the level of financial support provided to nonfamily, foster parents (Boyd-Franklin, 2003). Many multigenerational families who were made homeless during Hurricane Katrina lived with older relatives in cramped conditions.

During and after Hurricane Katrina, older adults caring for or raising their grandchildren often found themselves in very precarious situations. Many had medical concerns that were exacerbated by the stress of being trapped on rooftops or being forced to live without food, water, or medicine for days. It is important for disaster responders to understand the cultural beliefs about the care of the elderly in African American families. Many African American families do not believe in placing elderly relatives in nursing homes. (It should also be noted that Black families that are forced to place an older family member in a nursing home might experience a great deal of guilt, particularly if such a family member is injured or killed during a disaster.)

As a result, older individuals are often cared for by family, friends, and neighbors in the community. During and after Hurricane Katrina, many media reports repeatedly raised the question of why families did not evacuate and placed blame on the victims. Clearly, there were many reasons, including the lack of transportation, money, or other financial means (e.g., credit cards). However, many older adults refused to leave their homes and communities in which their families had lived for generations. Many adult children made a decision to remain in their homes despite the hurricane threat, because older relatives refused to leave. These responses must be considered in future disaster planning. Outreach to families before, during, and after this type of disaster might help to prevent unnecessary traumatic losses.

FAMILY SYSTEMS APPROACHES TO DISASTER INTERVENTIONS

It is important that mental health providers move beyond the emphasis on individual children and adults and adopt a family systems approach in designing disaster and trauma interventions for African American and other clients and families from collectivistic, ethnic minority cultures. Family therapy is a culturally compatible approach, because it allows us to involve the strengths of the family and extended family members in the treatment process.

Given the cultural mistrust and healthy cultural suspicion discussed previously, it is essential that clinicians and disaster responders focus first on joining and establishing therapeutic rapport with African Americans in disaster situations. Listening to their pressing immediate concerns for their close family members is a crucial part of building therapeutic rapport. Helping families to connect with lost family members will build credibility and further the therapeutic alliance. In addition, helping families navigate the burdensome bureaucratic hurdles that they face in obtaining aid from the Red Cross, FEMA, and other relief organizations can be a tremendous service. Many clinicians, however, do not consider providing this type of concrete assistance to be part of their job and are hesitant to become involved. In disaster and post-disaster situations, such interventions can be more help than any other in relieving emotional and psychological distress.

In the process of connecting with African Americans, it is very important for responders to be respectful. Many older Black Americans consider it very disrespectful for young people to call them by their first names, so the responder should ask older adults how they would like to be addressed (Boyd-Franklin, 2003). It is also important to introduce oneself to all members of the family, because many African American families are alienated by a formal, rigid, professional manner and will be relieved if responders are warm and welcoming and connect with them in a "down-to-earth" way.

GUIDELINES FOR FAMILY THERAPISTS WORKING WITH AFRICAN AMERICAN FAMILIES DURING DISASTERS

Disaster responders must also remember that parents and caregivers are very stressed in these situations, fearful for themselves and for the safety of their children. Initially, they may be angry about the way in which they and their family members have been treated but the responder must remember not to take these responses personally. Instead, the responder should acknowledge their anger and the reasons for it and recognize and reframe for the family that they are all doing the best that they can in very difficult circumstances. This is especially relevant for African American parents who often feel judged by others in crisis situations. In shelters, for example, parents and other caregivers may encounter criticism of their parenting practices, particularly if resorting to physical punishment with a misbehaving child. In addition, many African American parents may feel disrespected in front of their children in these stressful post-disaster periods. Many mental health workers are child advocates and can become angry with parents if the parents' behavior is not consistent with what they have been trained to consider healthy for children. It is crucial that responders remember the enormous stress that these parents are experiencing and resist the urge to rescue children from their parents. Remember that parents who are blaming their children for acting out may have felt blamed by others.

It is particularly important that all interventions during these periods be strength based and focus on the family members' resilience. As Boyd-Franklin and Bry (2000) have indicated, "never underestimate the power of praise" (p. 40). Therapists should praise parents and other caregivers for their attempts to protect their children and other family members during the crisis period, recognize the love and the concern that family members have for each other, focus the family members on pulling together during this time of crisis, and acknowledge their concern and their efforts to reunite the family if members are separated. It is essential that disaster responders maintain a focus on the positive points, because families under extreme stress do not present with their strengths but rather are more likely to attract attention because of their problems. Therapists and disaster responders must focus on empowering the parents to help their children. This requires working with the parents in family sessions and not taking over and talking only to the children. When something traumatic occurs, it is necessary to help all family members to understand that it is normal to feel upset in these disaster situations (Dass-Brailsford, 2007).

Families are often overwhelmed with survival needs in disasters. Many feel isolated and are stranded because of lack of transportation. During these times, responders and therapists need to reach out to these families in homes, trailers, or shelters. In the book *Reaching Out in Family Therapy*, Boyd-Franklin and Bry (2000) have emphasized the importance of this reaching out process, because it allows the therapist the opportunity to experience the family's current reality. It also allows mental health responders to offer crisis intervention and provide prevention services that may minimize the impact of the disaster and help mobilize the resilience of all family members.

THE MULTISYSTEMS MODEL AND GROUP INTERVENTIONS

The multisystems model (Boyd-Franklin, 2003) reminds us that many individuals and families are deeply embedded in a contextual reality that may include poverty and experiences with racism. These individuals and families, who may have many needs for concrete services—especially if they are poor and/or homeless—may feel particularly vulnerable to the intrusions of multisystemic bureaucracies such as FEMA, the Red Cross, other disaster relief organizations, social service agencies, police, the courts, child protective services, schools, mental health services, hospitals, welfare departments, housing programs, and so forth. As indicated previously, many families during Hurricane Katrina did not have cars or other transportation, financial resources or credit cards, or a place to go after losing their homes. Mental health providers must recognize that many clients and families, especially indigent ones, need concrete services and that assisting with these needs can provide a means for joining and establishing therapeutic rapport, particularly with individuals and families who may have a great deal of mistrust because of the treatment they have received during the disaster.

Another aspect of the multisystems model is often the need for interventions through multiple treatment modalities (Boyd-Franklin & Bry, 2000). This might involve advocacy and empowerment of the family to present their concerns to the many agencies that may have some power (i.e., be able to effect change) over their lives. In addition to the family therapy interventions, individual therapy, group therapy, and multiple family groups can be very helpful for individuals who have been dislocated from their families and communities. For example, groups involving extended family members and adults and children from multiple families can be provided by first responders in shelters, trailer parks, and later in communities to which these families have been relocated (Boyd-Franklin & Bry, 2000).

Group treatment can be particularly helpful for children, adolescents, and adults who feel isolated and alone. For example, groups can be established by age for children and adolescents in shelters during and after a disaster. Schools can become an excellent resource for gathering groups of children or adolescents who have been traumatized by a disaster experience (Boyd-Franklin & Bry, 2000). These groups can also be helpful in situations when all of the children have experienced the same traumatic event.

Parents are often deeply traumatized during disasters by their grief and loss. In addition to family treatment, groups for parents can allow them a safe place in which to discuss their own fears and fears for their children. Many of the African American survivors of Hurricane Katrina had to deal with the trauma of their loss of family members, their homes and communities, and the feelings of their children, in addition to the need to cope with their anger at the racism and disrespect with which they were treated in the aftermath. Group interventions can help to validate their experiences and emotions in these situations.

THE ROLE OF SPIRITUALITY AND RELIGION IN THE LIVES OF AFRICAN AMERICANS

Spirituality and religion are important aspects of the cultural tradition of many African Americans (Boyd-Franklin, 2003). Spirituality refers to a belief in or a relationship with God or with a higher power. Religion is the formal practice of one's spiritual beliefs, and some practice it through church involvement. Christian churches with significant African American presence include Baptist, African Methodist Episcopal, Church of God in Christ, Methodist, Episcopal, Roman Catholic, Presbyterian, Lutheran, Seventh Day Adventists, and many Pentecostal Churches. There are now many large nondenominational churches in African American communities. Jehovah's Witnesses are a growing presence. Religious diversity also includes Muslim groups such as Nation of Islam and Sunni Muslim, and there are also growing numbers of African Americans who practice African religions such as the Ifa religion originating with the Yoruba tribe from Nigeria, the Akan from Ghana, and Kemet (which had its origins in ancient Egypt). Some African Americans do not believe in God or have spiritual or religious beliefs. There are also many African Americans who are deeply spiritual but are not involved in any formal religion or house of worship.

The awareness of many diverse religious traditions in the African American community can serve as a resource for training disaster responders and mental health clinicians (see Boyd-Franklin, 2003, for descriptions of these traditions). It is very important for mental health providers and disaster responders to not make assumptions but to recognize the diversity within the African American community and ask African Americans about their spiritual or religious beliefs.

Many Christian African Americans who are involved in church refer to their churches as "church homes" or "church families" (Boyd-Franklin, 2003). It is common in the Gulf Coast region for membership in a church family to extend for generations. Thus, for many survivors, Hurricane Katrina destroyed not only their home and community but also their church homes. The sense of church as family and home is so strong that during my visits to Louisiana and Mississippi, I was impressed by the number of African American ministers who traveled to areas such as Atlanta, Georgia, and Houston, Texas, to minister to members of their congregation scattered after the storm.

Role of Spirituality in the Resilience of African Americans in Disaster Situations

Research studies have documented the important role of religious beliefs and spirituality in the lives of African Americans during and after Hurricane Katrina. Elliott and Pais (2006) studied the emotional supports and coping skills used by more than 1,200 Black and White survivors of the hurricane. The results revealed "strong racial, but not class differences. In general whites are much more likely to report relying on families and friends to get through these difficult emotional times, whereas blacks are much more likely to report relying on religious faith" (p. 313). Ironically, this strong emphasis on the first priority of religious faith was high even among those Blacks who reported a great deal of support from family, extended family, and friends. Elliott and Pais (2006), in their discussion of this result, emphasized the following:

> Among blacks in the region, religious faith seems to be part of the communal glue that individuals and families use to cement social relationships and to ensure the emotional support that such relationships provide. So even when helping one another to cope, African Americans from the area are likely to report that it is God that has made this type of network assistance possible, not family or friends themselves. (p. 315)

Having an understanding of this difference in coping is particularly important for first responders in disaster situations. Many in the mental health field have been trained not to inquire about spiritual and religious coping strategies in psychological assessments and interventions. Others ask very limited questions such as "Are you a member of a church?" but will not inquire in any depth about the spiritual beliefs that contribute to the resilience of African American survivors. This is very unfortunate, because in designing disaster interventions for African Americans and other groups with strong religious and spiritual beliefs, the spiritual emphasis is essential (see Chapter 9 in this book for a discussion of the role of spirituality in disaster responses).

The Role of African American Churches in Disaster Situations

Black churches are a natural base for disaster interventions in African American communities. They have often earned the trust of community members, even those who are not members of the congregation. One of the lessons of Hurricane Katrina has been the importance of reaching out and establishing partnerships with Black churches before a disaster. It is also essential that churches are involved in disaster planning. Many first responders, both in the states affected by the disaster and those who responded to the call in relocation shelters in other states, found Black churches tremendously helpful in creating supports for distressed families (Billingsley & Motes, 2007; T. Davis, personal communication, December 1, 2005). Generally, personal introductions by members of the congregation are the most effective way to connect with Black pastors or churches. For those of other ethnic and racial backgrounds, it is helpful to identify African Americans who can introduce you to their ministers and church families. Many church families in states where survivors of Katrina were relocated adopted displaced families and provided them with housing, food, counseling, financial assistance, and spiritual help in this traumatic time (Billingsley & Motes, 2007; T. Davis, personal communication, December 1, 2005).

As the loss of a close church family can be an additional traumatic experience for an African American family, culturally and spiritually familiar surroundings can help promote healing. It is very important to help displaced families find Black churches in their new locations that are of the same denomination, although denomination alone is not sufficient for the healing process. For example, many African Americans who were members of Roman Catholic churches in Louisiana were deeply distressed when they were relocated to other areas of the country where it was often difficult or impossible to find a Black Roman Catholic church.

Spirituality and Religion in Healing Trauma, Death, Grief, and Loss

Many African Americans believe in the power of prayer to heal trauma, particularly when it is related to death, grief, disaster, and loss. Disaster responders and mental health providers should not be surprised that some African Americans might ask you to pray with them during such times. It is important to follow the client's or the family's lead. Usually a family member will step forward to lead the prayer. The clinician can simply be with the family and join hands during this important ritual. Mental health providers are cautioned not to impose their own spiritual practice or beliefs on the family (also see ch. 9 in this book for a further discussion of the role of spirituality in providing meaning and comfort to victims of disasters).

Spiritual metaphors are a part of African American culture, and many African Americans, even those who are not religious, use these metaphors to find comfort in times of trauma, death, grief, and loss. Boyd-Franklin (2003) and Mitchell and Lewter (1986) have described these core spiritual beliefs and metaphors. For example, in troubled times, African Americans may say, "God will hold your hand as you run this race." The message is that you will never be alone with the pain of this world. Others will say, "God is in charge" or "God is in control," with the message that it is important to surrender to the will of God. Words from hymns, gospel songs, and spirituals can also provide comfort. For example, gospel songs often have words that encourage persistence and perseverance: "I'm so glad trouble don't last always"; or "After you've done all you can, you just stand and let God see you through." Similarly, there are a number of traditional hymns that are sung at funerals and wakes and other times of loss, such as "Precious Lord, Take My Hand" and "Amazing Grace."

African Americans will sometimes quote familiar biblical sayings in the midst of a disaster experience, for example, "Weeping may endure for a night, but joy cometh in the morning" (Psalms 30:5); "I can do all things through Christ who strengthens me" (Philippians 4:13); "Though I walk through the valley of the shadow of death, I will fear no evil for thou art with me" (Psalms 23). For more than 400 years, through the experiences of slavery, discrimination, and racism, African Americans have learned to rely on their spiritual beliefs to help them get through life's journey (Boyd-Franklin, 2003).

Funerals are an extremely important part of African American culture. African Americans have survived and been resilient during periods of slavery, oppression, discrimination, and racism, because they held onto the belief that they might suffer in this world but that death led to release or freedom to go home to God in heaven. A very old African American spiritual, "Oh Freedom," captures this concept:

Oh Freedom, Oh Freedom,
Oh Freedom over me.

And before I'd be a slave,
I'd be buried in my grave,
And go home to my God
And be free.

Thus, for African Americans, the funeral is a rite of passage to heaven. In African American churches, printed funeral brochures are titled, "A Celebration of the Life" or "Homegoing Service." Typically, African American families will wait a week or more for all family members to assemble for the funeral. Dass-Brailsford in Chapter 4 of this book discusses the cultural obliviousness of FEMA director Michael Brown, who commented in the aftermath of Hurricane Katrina, "Ignore the dead; we want the living." He was totally unaware of the importance of the tradition of the jazz funeral to the African American community in New Orleans, which is a communal celebration of the life of the deceased individual and the homegoing to heaven.

For many African Americans, one of the most painful and traumatic experiences in the aftermath of the storm was their inability to locate the bodies of the deceased and provide them with a respectful funeral (Dass-Brailsford, 2006). In future disasters, it is very important for responders to recognize this need for closure. Even if the body is never found, the family may draw spiritual, emotional, and psychological comfort and closure from a memorial service that allows family members to come together and mourn the loss of their loved one.

Mental health first responders working with African American survivors can help to facilitate this healing process. Many mental health providers have been taught to keep strict boundaries in their relationships with clients. In many disaster situations or periods of loss, they debate the appropriateness of attendance at the funeral of a client or a member of a family with whom they have worked. Therapists should certainly ask the family's permission, particularly in cross-racial situations, but African American families are often very touched by the fact that a therapist or responder would demonstrate this level of caring for the family and respect for the deceased by attending the funeral. In many cases, this deepens the therapeutic alliance with family members and the acceptance of therapy within the community (Boyd-Franklin, 2003).

Akinyela (2007) has developed an approach called "Testimony Therapy" that builds on Africentric concepts and an African American spiritual tradition in which a person gives testimony about a trauma that he or she has been through and survived. It is a testimony to the spiritual resilience of the human spirit. In many Black churches, prayer meetings may end with the testimony of members who give examples of traumatic life experiences and give testimony that "God saw me through." Boyd-Franklin (2008) describes the ways in which this tradition of giving testimony can be incorporated into the treatment of African American disaster and trauma survivors.

Mental health providers can use the reframe, "You are a survivor," or say "You have a very important testimony to give about all that you have suffered and the fact that God brought you through and helped you to survive." It is very important, however, that providers in disaster situations remember that there is tremendous diversity in the African American community and they should not assume that all Black people share these beliefs. Spiritual metaphors should be used only in circumstances in which an individual has already indicated that he or she embraces this spiritual or religious belief system.

PRACTICAL IMPLICATIONS

There are many lessons that can be learned from Hurricane Katrina that can enable first responders and crisis counselors to offer culturally sensitive treatment to African Americans in disaster situations (Dass-Brailsford, 2006):

- The psychological trauma of perceived racism may exacerbate the effects of any disaster for African Americans. Therefore, responders and counselors must be open to discussing clients' feelings about racism in a nondefensive manner.
- It is extremely important to recognize the role of extended family members in this culture and the first priority after safety should be to help locate missing family members.
- Responders should understand and inquire about the importance of religion and spirituality for African Americans and reach out to local Black churches.
- Responders should use a family systems and multisystems model when developing trauma interventions for African American and other extended family cultures. These approaches can provide a collective, communal approach to healing.

CONCLUSION

This chapter has discussed the cultural strengths in the African American community as a prototype for the development of culturally sensitive disaster interventions. It has addressed the psychological trauma associated with the loss of life, home, and community in disasters. In addition, it has used the response to Hurricane Katrina as an example of the ways in which experiences with racism and classism can exacerbate the trauma of these disasters. This strength-based model will allow responders and counselors to build on the resilience of African American families in times of trouble. Finally, the incorporation of the spirituality and religious orientation of African Americans and other communities of color as a component of psychological interventions for trauma survivors can tap a wellspring of spiritual power that can help facilitate the healing process.

REFERENCES

Akinyela, M. (2007, April). *Everything is everything: Africentric approaches to healing and self-healing.* Paper presented at the Culture Conference of the Multicultural Family Institute in Highland Park, NJ.

Billingsley, A., & Motes, P. S. (2007). *The role of the African American church in promoting post-catastrophic resilience.* Retrieved December 28, 2007, from http://www.sc.edu/katrinacrisis/ billingsley_ motes.shtml

Blitz, L., & Pender Greene, M. (Eds.). (2006). *Racism and racial identity: Reflections on urban practice in mental health and social services.* Binghamton, NY: Haworth.

Boyd-Franklin, N. (1989). *Black families in therapy: A multisystems approach.* New York: Guilford.

Boyd-Franklin, N. (2003). *Black families in therapy: Understanding the African American experience* (2nd ed.). New York: Guilford.

Boyd-Franklin, N. (2008). Working with African Americans and trauma: Lessons for clinicians from Hurricane Katrina. In M. McGoldrick & K. Hardy (Eds.), *Re-visioning family therapy* (2nd ed.). New York: Guilford.

Boyd-Franklin, N. (in press). Racism, trauma and resilience: The psychological impact of Hurricane Katrina. In K. Wailoo, R. Anglin, & K. O'Neill (Eds.), *Katrina's imprint: Race and vulnerability in America.* New Brunswick, NJ: Rutgers University Press.

Boyd-Franklin, N., & Bry, B. H. (2000). *Reaching out in family therapy: Home-based, school, and community interventions.* New York: Guilford.

Carter, R. T. (2007). Racism and psychological and emotional injury: Recognizing and assessing race-based traumatic stress. *Counseling Psychologist, 35*(1), 13–105.

CNN. (2005). *Reaction to Katrina split along racial lines.* Retrieved September 13, 2005, from http://www.cnn.com/2005/US/09/12/katrina.race.poll/index.html

Cokley, K., Cooke, B., & Nobles, W. (2006, March). Association of Black Psychologists: Guidelines for the treatment of African American Hurricane Katrina survivors. *Communique,* xxxii–xxxiv.

Dass-Brailsford, P. (2006, March). Eye witness report: Ignore the dead; we want the living! Helping after the storm. *Communique,* vi-viii.

Dass-Brailsford, P. (2007). *A practical approach to trauma: Empowering interventions.* Thousand Oaks, CA: Sage.

Dyson, M. E. (2006). *Come hell or high water: Hurricane Katrina and the color of disaster.* New York: Basic Books.

Elliott, J. R., & Pais, J. (2006). Race, class, and Hurricane Katrina: Social differences in human responses to disaster. *Social Science Research, 35,* 295–321.

Franklin, A. J., Boyd-Franklin, N., & Kelly, S. (2006). Racism and invisibility: Race-related stress, emotional abuse, and psychological trauma for people of color. *Journal of Emotional Abuse, 6*(2/3), 9–30.

Gheytanchi, A., Joseph, L., Gierlach, E., Kimpara, S., Housley, J., Franco, Z. E., et al. (2007). The dirty dozen: Twelve failures of the Hurricane Katrina response and how psychology can help. *American Psychologist, 62*(2), 118–130.

Law, B. M. (2006). The hard work of healing: Katrina's cultural lessons. *APA Monitor on Psychology, 27*(9), 40–42.

McIntosh, P. (1998). White privilege: Unpacking the invisible knapsack. In M. McGoldrick (Ed.), *Re-visioning family therapy: Race, class, and gender in clinical practice* (pp. 147–152). New York: Guilford.

Mitchell, H., & Lewter, N. (1986). *Soul theology: The heart of American Black culture.* San Francisco: Harper & Row.

Ruscher, J. B. (2006). Stranded by Katrina: Past and present. *Analyses of Social Issues Public Policy, 6*(1), 33–38.

Skipp, C. (2008). Toxic trailers. *Newsweek.* Retrieved February 16, 2008, from http://www.newsweek.com/id/11828

Troutt, D. D. (2006). *After the storm: Black intellectuals explore the meaning of Hurricane Katrina.* New York: The New Press.

Utsey, S. O., Chae, M. H., Brown, C. F., & Kelly, D. (2002). Effect of ethnic group membership on ethnic identity, race-related stress, and quality of life. *Cultural Diversity and Ethnic Minority Psychology, 8,* 366–377.

CHAPTER 6

Children and Crises

Kenyon C. Knapp

Crises have been a part of the human experience since the beginning of recorded history. However, in recent years, crisis incidents have become increasingly more violent and intentional, while natural disasters have also increased. "The frequency of recorded natural disasters has been rising rapidly," according to the International Council for Science (Agence France-Presse, 2005, p. 1), but so have terrorism, arson, school-related violence (increases internationally, decreases nationally; National School Safety Center, n.d.), and workplace violence. Children are frequently caught in the crossfire of these events and due to their developmental level are often less equipped to cope with the negative consequences that these incidents generate.

The goal of this chapter is to increase recognition of crisis signs, methods of treatment, particular developmental concerns, as well as factors that may be protective and thus reduce the impact of the traumatic event(s) among children. It should be noted that Hurricanes Katrina and Rita are discussed as examples of events that necessitated crisis interventions, though other types of disasters are also examined.

BACKGROUND

The author was privileged to travel to the Gulf Coast following Hurricane Katrina, as well as prior to and after Hurricane Rita, and was able to invest a significant amount of time working with people who were struggling with the effects of those disasters. Being a first responder in a crisis of the magnitude of Hurricane Katrina had a significant impact on the author. Clinical training does not adequately prepare an individual for the immediacy and short-term nature of crisis work. Many crisis workers reported similar experiences—regardless of whether they were counselors, social workers, marriage and family therapists, psychologists, or psychiatrists—and they had to adapt past therapeutic techniques to the unstructured, brief, short-term, and often intense disaster environment.

CHAPTER HIGHLIGHTS

+ Provides guidelines on working with children in crisis;

+ Reviews developmental concerns that should be borne in mind when working with children;

+ Describes typical attributions of child survivors of disasters;

+ Outlines the role of protective and risk factors in shaping health outcomes; and

+ Discusses interventions that have demonstrated efficacy with children.

GOALS OF DISASTER WORK

The goal of disaster work is to help individuals develop strategies to improve their circumstances in the short term and thus rapidly bring some stability into their lives. Crisis work involves doing psychological triage work, in which quick assessments are made so that referrals can follow.

An initial mistake of many crisis workers is to assume that everyone involved in a crisis will have posttraumatic stress disorder (PTSD), yet Ruzek et al. (2007) note that "most psychological responses to trauma are relatively immediate, mild, and transient" (p. 17). Gaffney (2006) stated, "After September 11, 2001, some experts warned that there would be an entire nation suffering from posttraumatic stress disorder" (p. 1002). However, Fletcher (1996, as cited in Dyregrov & Yule, 2005) noted that in a "meta-analysis of 34 samples that included 2,697 children who had experienced trauma, 36% of children (comparable to the rate of 24% in adults) met criteria for PTSD following a range of traumas" (p. 179). The truth of the matter about how many people develop PTSD after a traumatic event is not a simple equation but rather a combination of exposure to the event and previous risk factors, which is discussed in detail later in this chapter. Frequently following a traumatic event, public figures will suggest that large numbers of people will immediately experience PTSD, yet it is not that simple. First of all, people must have the PTSD symptoms for at least 4 weeks to qualify for that diagnosis, whereas severe stress symptoms for 2 days to 4 weeks would qualify the person for the 308.3 Acute Stress Disorder (American Psychiatric Association, 2000).

Another word of caution is that we should not assume that counseling is the best strategy for all traumatized children. Part of being a counselor is the ethical mandate to respect the client's right to "self-determination" (American Counseling Association, 2005), and that includes respecting the counseling choices of the client. Often the best thing a crisis counselor can do is connect a child with a supportive system rather than attempt to develop a counseling relationship. The support systems that people are familiar with are usually the most comforting to them. Therefore, it behooves crisis counselors to help traumatized children connect with their family, friends, religious community, neighbors, or other supports that may be specific to a particular child. Immediately after Hurricane Katrina, the author worked with several children in the Gulf Coast and noted that many of them exhibited clinical levels of anxiety and distress, yet quickly returned to a calm state once they were reunited with their families and friends.

A crucial way to begin any therapeutic service with children in crisis is to verbally and mentally frame the crisis in a way that creates and sustains hope for them. As Dyregrov and Yule (2005) state, "Children are very sensitive to their parents' reactions both to the event itself and to talking about it afterwards" (p. 176). The well-intentioned but naive crisis worker might say to a child after hearing his or her heart-wrenching story, "Oh my goodness, that's just horrible! You must really miss . . ." The empathy displayed in the previous response may be perceived as appropriate at the time, yet the crisis worker might inadvertently be creating a sense of helplessness in the child rather than focusing on his or her strengths and resources. A more helpful response might be, "So after it happened, you helped your family and friends, and comforted them. That sounds like you were a real support and encouragement! And now you're able to help . . ." Crisis workers should not ignore or minimize the grief and loss a child may experience but at the same time they should focus on positive aspects of the child's behavior. By focusing on these positive aspects, crisis workers help children feel empowered and goal oriented so that they become more functional in the present, while reducing their posttraumatic stress reactions.

DEVELOPMENTAL CONCERNS

Highly publicized national and international disasters in recent years have caught the world's attention of the need to help survivors of trauma. However, there is a dearth of literature related to helping children in crisis, and little systematic attention has been paid to the mental health needs of children who have been survivors of crises and disasters (Minkowski et al., 1993). Gaffney (2006) noted that "few studies have explicitly studied children's memories of traumatic events" (p. 1005). Certainly more research is needed on how disasters affect children.

However, Pynoos, Steinberg, and Goenjian (1996) found that children who experience trauma tend to have problems with "narrative coherence"—the ability to organize material coherently so that the narrative has a beginning, middle, and end. The trauma seems to have a disruptive influence on the child's ability to think in a linear way, thus raising concerns about other educational abilities that may be negatively affected such as reading, writing, or math. The primary reason that traumas are challenging for children to deal with is that the trauma forces a child or adolescent to address issues that he or she is developmentally ill prepared to do (Kraybill-Greggo, Kraybill-Greggo, & Collins, 2005).

The two most common reactions of children to crisis are changes in their behavior or behavioral regression (University of the State of New York, n.d.). Preschool-age children (1 to 5 years) most often react with regressive behavior when faced with crisis. For example, they will often revert to bed-wetting, clinging to parents, crying, and trembling with fear; as well, they are more likely to have nightmares. School-age children (5 to 11 years) also tend to display regressive behaviors such as thumb sucking, whining, and/or clinging to parents.

They may avoid school, become depressed, and develop fears about the weather or their physical safety.

In a study on the psychosocial effects of a disaster after the Andaman and Nicobar Islands were hit by a tsunami on December 26, 2004, the majority of the children had nonspecific symptoms such as clinging behavior, insomnia, decreased appetite, bed-wetting, nonspecific anxiety symptoms, PTSD symptoms, excessive crying, poor socialization, and nonspecific somatic symptoms (Math, Girimaji, Benegal, Kumar, Uday, & Nagaraja, 2006). Despite these prolific reactions, the researchers reported little evidence of diagnosable illnesses.

Preadolescents (11 to 14 years) often experience sleep and appetite disturbances, problems at school, psychosomatic complaints (headaches, vague pains, bowel problems), rebellion, and loss of interest in social activities (University of the State of New York, n.d.). Adolescents (14 to 18 years) often have poor concentration or confusion, headaches or other physical complaints, aggressive behaviors, withdrawal and isolation, indifference, irresponsible or delinquent behavior, and agitation or decrease in energy level. Encouraging teenagers to participate in the rehabilitation of their community provides them with a sense of being part of the solution and it gives them a job to do each day during chaotic times. Teenagers and younger children benefit from resuming their social activities and participating in athletics.

Typical Attributions of Children Affected by Disasters

The word *disaster* is derived from the Latin *dis* ("against") and *astrum* ("stars")—hence, "the stars are against us" (Miller, 1999, p. 24). This attribution for disaster victims is common in both children and adults; they may feel like the whole world is conspiring against them and that they cannot win. Although much of crisis counseling is focused on helping clients cope better in the immediate moment, a fatalistic view of life can be a great impediment to progress. The task of the crisis counselor is to bring perspective to the lives of those they counsel so that they do not lose all hope.

Children draw most of their cues about how to react to crisis from their parents, and "if parents respond in a calm manner, the child can feel protected and secure" (Dyregrov & Yule, 2005, p. 180). This is not to suggest that parents can always give their children detailed and accurate reasons for why various crises occur, but they can convey experientially that even if the larger world does not seem to make sense, there can be stability and security in that family. This explanation can be calming for children. After a crisis, children are likely to feel confused and sad and may lose their vision of life's purpose. Children exposed to chronic and repeated stressors—such as victims of physical and sexual abuse, war, or harassment—may develop personality changes, various self-injurious behaviors, and suicidal behaviors.

An unfortunate but all-too-common attribution in children is for them to blame themselves, because they cannot understand why the traumatic event took place. They revert to the simple conclusion that they must have somehow caused it to happen (Patten, Gatz, Jones, & Thomas, 1989). Although there is some variation from culture to culture in how children perceive the causes of crises, many children blame themselves (Elsass, 2001). Therapeutic goals in helping children should strive to rectify these negative attributions and reduce unnecessary guilt and shame.

PROTECTIVE AND RISK FACTORS

Worden (1996), in his research, found that children or adolescents who have a caring adult in their life are likely to embrace the positive aspects of the grief process. As children go through the grief and loss process, they experience sadness, anger, anxiety, and guilt, similar to adults. However, they process these feelings differently based on their developmental level. Mostly, they look at things from their own perspective. For example, children may feel angry after a parent dies, because in their egocentric mind, the parent did this to them.

Children may also feel guilty over losses that they had absolutely no control over. Because children cannot understand why something has occurred, they resolve the confusion by blaming themselves. Counselors who work with children whose parents are in the middle of a divorce often observe this behavior; children usually cannot understand the ambivalent and confusing information that their parents convey to them. Parents and counselors need to probe the attributions that children arrive at after a crisis and educate them in a nurturing and warm way that the crisis event was not their fault. This often leads children to ask numerous "why" questions that adults often cannot answer, but this is preferable to the children blaming themselves.

People often question why some children seem to bounce back resiliently while others are left with long-term consequences after a devastating upheaval in their lives (Gaffney, 2006). Hamblen (1998) found the following:

> There are three factors that have been shown to increase the likelihood that children will develop PTSD. These factors include the severity of the traumatic event, the parental reaction to the traumatic event, and the physical proximity to the traumatic event. (para. 5)

Pynoos, Frederick, and Nader (1987) found a positive correlation between proximity to the traumatic event and the risk of developing PTSD, yet following deeper investigation, they found that proximity is more than just physical closeness to the danger zone. They found that the physical distance between the child and the traumatic event may not be as important; with technological advances (e.g., digital cameras, television, and cell phones), they are able to get a complete understanding of the traumatizing event. The media exacerbate the traumatizing impact of an event by replaying it repeatedly. Some examples are the planes flying into the World Trade Center buildings in New York, the bloody student falling from the library window at Columbine High School in Colorado, or the tsunami waves crashing ashore in Indonesia (and nearby) in 2004 and killing 230,000 people.

As academia and the media have realized the impact of broadcasting traumatic material, a heated debate has developed over issues such as freedom of speech and the press versus responsible reporting without sensationalizing the gory details. The resolution of this debate does not seem imminent, and we continue to "rubberneck" at car accidents on our highways and traumatic events aired on our television sets. A professional and healthy balance between information and inundation of news of crises needs to be found, and more research in this area is warranted.

Dyregrov and Yule (2005) found that a "lack of social support, problems in family cohesion, the female gender, prior exposure to trauma, prior psychiatric problems, and a strong acute response have all been associated with later posttraumatic problems" (p. 178). Husain and Nair (1998) found that "the impact of trauma has been found to be mediated by loss of relatives and support networks, lack of basic health needs, internal displacement or immigration, parental psychopathology, and socioeconomic adversity" (p. 262).

Protective factors help children cope better with given stressors and decrease the severity of the symptoms related to the traumatic event. Tolan and Dodge (2005) found that the family was a central factor in children's mental health well-being and a protection against risk. The speed with which interventions are delivered to traumatized children can be either a risk or protective factor, as "early psychosocial interventions after a traumatic event" have been shown to help people cope much better than a delayed intervention (Purtscher, 2005, p. 121). Figley's (2007) research on protective factors for soldiers can also be used with children, as he noted that training, trust, unit cohesion, and a sense of humor were all helpful. If children have done drills to prepare for a traumatic event, trust their parent(s), feel a sense of belonging, and can notice the humor in things even during hard times, they will fare much better.

The use of memorials and rituals to process grief and loss has also been shown to play a protective role in the lives of children. When there is a loss at a school, having a specific location where children can bring cards and/or flowers, being able to engage in writing assignments about the event, or using artwork to express their grief and loss can soften the blow of the trauma (National Association of School Psychologists, 2002). If children are familiar with rituals such as these prior to a trauma, then they have a socially sanctioned way to deal with their grief and loss; this can be quite helpful in their long-term recovery.

Traumatic events in the lives of children usually leave behind negative residual effects, but the effects can be worse for children with pre-crisis risk factors. Steinhausen, Mas, Ledermann, and Metzke (2006) list the following as risk factors:

- Parents who are substance users
- Low socioeconomic status
- Limited social support
- Residential placement or foster care
- Parents with mental disorders
- History of physical abuse

Berkowitz (2003) states that exposure to community violence may predispose some children to cope poorly with future crises. In addition, Bokszczanin (2008) notes that frequent exposure to a traumatic event, family conflict, and overprotectiveness by parents can lead to an increase in negative consequences following a crisis adolescents who face these risk factors. Alisic, Van Der Schoot, Van Ginkel, and Kleber (2008) found that age alone can be a significant risk factor, because younger age usually entails limited coping strategies.

Vijayakumar, Kannan, and Daniel (2006) found that the severity of children's exposure to the traumatic events of the Asian tsunami in 2004 was significantly related to the anxiety and somatic symptoms that they experienced. In addition, they found that pre-existing vulnerability worsened these symptoms. There was a high correlation between both the severity of exposure and pre-existing vulnerability with PTSD symptoms. The researchers concluded that children who experienced the death or injury of parents or siblings in the disaster were more likely to develop an anxiety disorder, whereas those with a pre-existing vulnerability were more likely to develop an affective disorder. Counselors and other crisis workers should be aware of these identified risk factors and anticipate that survivors will have a greater need for mental health services in the future.

For example, the author worked with one family in Louisiana where there were four children, both biological parents, and a grandmother who escaped the Gulf Coast as Hurricane Rita was about to make landfall. The family loaded themselves and a few belongings into a sedan and tried to drive away, but their car broke down along the side of the road, not far from the coastline. They walked up the deserted road together in hurricane force winds until a policeman saw them and gave them a ride to the shelter. Two of the children had a history of mental illness, the family was from a lower socioeconomic status, and they had experienced significant fear for their safety during the storm, yet they were a very close and supportive family. One of the children with a history of mental illness had severe anxiety reactions that required immediate treatment, but the others coped much better, thus illustrating how protective factors can outweigh and sometimes counteract risk factors leading to positive outcomes in most cases.

INTERVENTIONS

The need for evidence-based interventions in postcrisis areas has been staggering in recent years. Abramson's study (2006, as cited in Burton, 2006) found that in some Gulf Coast areas of Louisiana, nearly 50% of the parents reported that at least one of their children had emotional or behavioral problems they did not have before they became displaced. Following the September 11, 2001, attacks, it was estimated that more than 10,000 children lost their parents or loved ones as a result of that day's terrorist attack on the World Trade Center and the Pentagon (Cohen, Goodman, Brown, & Mannarino, 2004). Similar incidents can be listed from disasters and crises that have occurred globally, illustrating the need for the counseling field to address interventions in this area.

The American Academy of Child and Adolescent Psychiatry (2003) gives the following guidelines regarding how to respond to the questions of children:

- Use words and concepts your child can understand. Make your explanation appropriate to your child's age and level of understanding. Don't overload a child with too much information.
- Give children honest answers and information. Children will usually know if you're not being honest.
- Be prepared to repeat explanations or have several conversations. Some information may be hard to accept or understand. Asking the same question over and over may be your child's way of asking for reassurance.
- Acknowledge and support your child's thoughts, feelings, and reactions. Let your child know that you think his or her questions and concerns are important.
- Be consistent and reassuring, but don't make unrealistic promises.
- Avoid stereotyping groups of people by race, nationality, or religion. Use the opportunity to teach tolerance and explain prejudice.

- Remember that children learn from watching their parents and teachers. They are very interested in how you respond to events. They learn from listening to conversations with other adults.
- Let children know how you are feeling. It's OK for them to know if you are anxious or worried about events. However, don't burden them with your concerns.
- Don't confront your child's way of handling events. If a child feels reassured by saying that things are happening very far away, it's usually best not to disagree. The child may need to think about events this way in order to feel safe.

PLAY THERAPY

A common treatment modality for children with psychological concerns is play therapy, because their verbal and cognitive abilities have not yet reached the level of development needed for most therapies that involve talking. Axline (1969) stated that play is the natural medium of self-expression for children to express fears, frustration, and aggression and make sense of and feel in control of their environment. Carter (1987) described a nondirective form of play therapy with puppets, whereby a little boy who saw his father murdered acted out his family issues and his feelings with the puppets. The boy was allegedly able to work through much of his grief, with the counselor providing a safe environment for therapeutic play. In contrast other crisis counseling experts such as Terr (1981, as cited in James & Gilliland, 2005) suggest that a nondirective approach "may be ill advised, because restitutive play becomes increasingly destructive and serves only to increase anxieties" (p. 134).

James and Gilliland (2005) recommend guided imagery (Sluckin, Weller, & Highton, 1989), a variety of play therapy techniques (Landreth, 1987), artwork (Drucker, 2001), puppets (Carter, 1987; James & Myer, 1987), sand tray (Allan & Berry, 1987; Vinturella & James, 1987), dance (D. R. Johnson, 2000), poetry (Gladding, 1987), writing (Brand, 1987), music (Bowman, 1987), computer art (R. G. Johnson, 1987), drama (Irwin, 1987), as well as drawing and role playing traumatic events (Eth & Pynoos, 1985, p. 37; James, 2003), as "these techniques may be controlled and paced by the therapist in consideration of the psychological safety of the child" (p. 134). There is a growing body of research showing the efficacy of directed play therapy with children who have experienced crisis.

There are many reasons why play therapy is helpful for children who have experienced crisis. One reason is that it provides a safe environment for the child to express his or her thoughts and feelings through activities. It is important for children to have the opportunity to express their grief, shock, or sense of loss in noncritical environments, as "criticisms for not mourning correctly may be supported by parental and family reactions to the child's lack of emotional response or may develop within the child's thinking without parental assistance" (Fogarty, 2000, p. 8). Most children do not have a well-defined script of how to act after a traumatic event, much less how to handle themselves when they feel emotionally numb after a tragedy.

Landreth (2002) states that for a therapeutic relationship to develop in play therapy, the therapist has to strive to care for the child and experience "a genuine prizing of the person of the child, so what occurs is an absence of evaluation or judgement" (p. 73). This person-centered style of play therapy proposed by Landreth is essentially derived from

Carl Rogers' humanistic theory but applied to children in the form of play therapy. Webb (1999) expanded on the application methods of play therapy by including art, storytelling, group art activities, games, and doll play.

However, counselors must be cautious in how they conduct play therapy with children following a trauma; children will sometimes re-enact their trauma in what Dripchak (2007) calls "posttraumatic play." Dripchak suggests using Ericksonian principles so that resolution and acceptance are achieved with the children, rather than having them engage in a potentially harmful pattern of simply replaying the trauma through play therapy. The reader may notice the differences here between Landreth's (2002) and Dripchak's approaches and assumptions, notably Landreth's assumption is that play is inherently healing, whereas others believe that a directive approach is more beneficial.

SPIRITUALITY

Spiritual and religious beliefs can be a great source of strength and stability for people in crisis, although nonreligious therapists may miss, neglect, or ignore this coping mechanism. Gunn (2007), who worked in the Gulf Coast following Hurricane Katrina, states that "spiritual beliefs or faith may be one of the only things that help people survive and find strength and hope" (p. 936). The author found a similar dynamic, in which a displaced minister and his wife who were in the shelter held impromptu church services with singing and praying that had a very calming and peaceful effect on the sometimes chaotic environment of the shelter. In one situation in a shelter, the author was sent to assess and treat an elderly woman who seemed to be mentally unstable. Upon meeting the lady and establishing some rapport, the author found out that the older lady was scheduled for a hip replacement surgery just a few days before Hurricane Katrina approached, her surgery was cancelled, and in the chaos, she lost her pain medications. Upon quickly procuring the needed pain medications for her, the lady was quite relieved and asked the author to read to her from the book of Psalms in her Bible. As the author read to her "the days of the blameless are known to the Lord, and their inheritance will endure forever" (Psalms 37:18, New International Version), an almost palpable peace came over her. Holtz (1998) and Hoovey (2000) also found that involvement in faith was a strong protective factor against distress. One area of caution that counselors should consider when they encounter people who are strongly affiliated with religious beliefs is the possibility that there is "toxic faith," where survivors obsess over shaming themselves or becoming codependent in their relationship with God (Arterburn & Felton, 2001). Overall, though, increased examination and utilization of the spiritual and religious resources of clients (including children) should be considered for ways in which they help clients cope.

COGNITIVE BEHAVIORAL INTERVENTIONS

Traumatic grief cognitive-behavioral therapy is a developing therapy for treating PTSD and other grief-related difficulties that has demonstrated efficacy (Cohen, Berliner, & March, 2000). This treatment modality includes several components: affective identification and modulation skills; stress-management techniques; the cognitive triad (learning the connections between thoughts, feelings, and behaviors); creation of the child's trauma narrative; cognitive processing of the events leading up to death; effective parenting techniques provided individually to parents; psychoeducation about trauma and safety planning; and joint parent–child sessions.

The psychoeducation portion of cognitive-behavioral therapy involves education about death, grief, recognition of loss, ambivalent feelings about the deceased, remembrance of the relationship, preservation of positive memories of the deceased, preparation for reminders of the trauma and loss, and parent–child grief sessions (Cohen et al., 2004). This intervention was used in New York following the September 11th terrorist attacks and reported positive results; the research is ongoing.

CRISIS INTERVENTIONS

In a crisis situation, crisis counselors should adhere to the following suggestions for assisting children after a tragedy (The American Academy of Experts in Traumatic Stress, 2003):

1. Be aware of your own reactions to the event.

2. Keep yourself available for providing extra attention to your child.

3. Be mindful of the child's cognitive and emotional functioning level.

4. Use empathetic communication by acknowledging, understanding, and expressing an appreciation of your child's experience.

5. Do not speculate and give false information about what has taken place.

6. Monitor exposure to media.

7. Realistically provide reassurance about the child's safety.

8. Consider the reactions of children with histories of past traumatic experiences, losses, or emotional disturbance (e.g., depression, anxiety).

9. Make an effort to maintain a "normal" routine.

10. Monitor your own emotional status.

The U.S. Department of Health and Human Services, Substance Abuse and Mental Health Services Administration (2005), outlines developmentally appropriate responses to crisis events, which include the following:

For elementary-age children

- Provide extra attention and consideration.
- Set gentle but firm limits for acting-out behavior.
- Listen to a child's repeated telling of his or her trauma experience.
- Encourage expression of feelings through conversation and play.
- Provide home chores and rehabilitation activities that are structured but not too demanding.

- Rehearse safety measures for future incidents.
- Point out kind deeds and the ways in which people helped each other during the traumatic event.

For preadolescents and adolescents

- Provide extra attention and consideration.
- Be there to listen, but don't force them to talk (they'll likely talk more this way!).
- Encourage discussion of trauma experiences among peers.
- Promote involvement in community recovery work.
- Urge participation in physical activities (sitting around a shelter is not good).
- Encourage resumption of regular social and recreational activities as soon as possible.
- Rehearse family safety measures for future incidents.

As many children following a crisis will still be attending school, critical incident stress debriefing was adapted with a school-based approach (K. Johnson, 1989). Miller (1999) states that this approach incorporates an introductory phase, in which the goals and purposes of the group are spelled out; a fact phase, in which the children each describe what happened to them in the disaster; a feeling phase, in which the children may express the emotions and reactions they had to the crisis; a teaching phase, in which the group leader educates the children to the nature of stress symptoms and the course of recovery; and a closure phase, in which the children are encouraged to develop some plan of action to facilitate improved coping in the future.

Although the majority of children are likely to improve with group sessions on relaxation and other activities, those with a family history of psychopathology may need further assessments and individual intervention. Unexplained symptoms in a child after a disaster may indicate the need for psychiatric evaluation.

Assessments

The Impact of Event Scale, the most commonly used adult scale, was adapted for use with children and adolescents (Dyregrov & Yule, 2005). The adaptation for children is one of the better assessments available and can be found at the referenced locations (Children and War Foundation, n.d.).

A commonly used instrument is the Child Posttraumatic Stress Reaction Index, which "has been modified to be a self-report instrument" (Dyregrov & Yule, 2005, p. 178). Another option is the Child PTSD Symptom Scale, which is a 17-item scale that can be used to make an initial diagnosis and monitor progress (Foa, Johnson, Feeny, & Treadwell, 2001).

Another way to assess trauma and the functioning level of children and adolescents is with structured interviews. The Clinician Administered PTSD Scale for Children is regarded as the gold standard to diagnose PTSD in children (Dyregrov & Yule, 2005). Another helpful structured interview assessment is the Anxiety and Depression Interview Schedule for Children PTSD Module. This assessment has modules not only for PTSD but also for anxiety disorders and depression (Silverman & Albano, 1996). The use of assessments such as these gives clinicians a wealth of information that will help them make better decisions in the treatment process. As symptoms can sometimes be identified more quickly with assessment instruments, treatment interventions can be applied sooner, thus increasing the chances of a better outcome.

PRACTICAL IMPLICATIONS

- Children are the most vulnerable when disasters occur.
- Children will display a myriad of reactions, which fluctuate based on a child's developmental age.
- Mental health support for children should be immediate and ongoing to prevent future problems.
- The family is a major protective factor for children who experience disasters.
- Several assessment instruments have been recently developed and adapted for use with children.

CONCLUSION

In a world torn by wars, natural disasters, abuse, and terrorist attacks, the most vulnerable members of society are often the children. Lee (2006) documented the great need to construct new schools in Louisiana following Hurricane Katrina as well as provide increased emotional support to help children overcome challenges. Lamberg (2008) reported that physicians, psychiatrists, mental health workers, and others are increasingly making well-coordinated efforts to assist children who are dealing with grief and loss. Yet for those who do crisis counseling with children, these efforts rarely seem to be enough.

Berkowitz (2003) documented how early intervention strategies are most effective in reducing long-term psychological damage in children, and this chapter adds to that effort. Kruczek and Salsman (2006) noted that recovering from a traumatic event is not always a linear process, as PTSD symptoms may go into remission or reoccur depending on future events in the child's life, which may ease or aggravate anxiety.

Assessment instruments specifically designed for traumatized children are increasing, as are versions of adult tests that are being adapted for use with children. Jones (2008) also outlines the need for culturally valid assessment instruments that are becoming increasingly necessary as crisis counseling efforts are becoming international; the recent Asian tsunami of 2004 provided an example of crisis counseling at a global level.

Crisis counselors must keep developmental considerations in mind as they work with children; varying responses are appropriate and expected among children. Counselors must also prepare themselves emotionally for the disturbing stories that they will be told as they work with traumatized people. Yet they should remember that it is an honor to serve, support, and encourage people, especially children, during very difficult times in their lives.

REFERENCES

Agence France-Presse. (2005, October 19). *Scientists warn of growing natural disasters.* Retrieved November 21, 2007, from http://www.abc.net.au/news/newsitems/200510/s1486219.htm

Alisic, E., Van Der Schoot, T., Van Ginkel, J., & Kleber, R. (2008). Trauma exposure in primary school children: Who is at risk? *Journal of Child & Adolescent Trauma, 1*(3), 263–269.

Allan, J., & Berry, P. (1987). Sandplay. *Elementary School Guidance & Counseling, 21,* 300–306.

American Academy of Child and Adolescent Psychiatry. (2003). *Talking to children about terrorism and war.* Retrieved December 29, 2008, from http://www.aacap.org/cs/root/facts_for_families/talking_to_children_about_terrorism_and_war

American Academy of Experts in Traumatic Stress. (2003). *Practical suggestions for assisting children in the aftermath of a tragedy.* Retrieved January 8, 2008, from http://www.aaets.org

American Counseling Association. (2005). *Code of ethics.* Alexandria, VA: Author.

American Psychiatric Association. (2000). *Diagnostic and statistical manual of mental disorders* (4th ed., Text rev.). Washington, DC: Author.

Arterburn, S., & Felton, J. (2001). *Toxic faith.* Colorado Springs, CO: Shaw Books.

Axline, V. (1969). *Play therapy.* New York: Ballantine Books.

Berkowitz, S. (2003). Children exposed to community violence: The rationale for early intervention. *Clinical Child & Family Psychology Review, 6*(4), 293–302.

Bokszczanin, A. (2008). Parental support, family conflict, and overprotectiveness: Predicting PTSD symptom levels of adolescents 28 months after a natural disaster. *Anxiety, Stress & Coping, 21*(4), 325–335.

Bowman, R. P. (1987). Approaches for counseling children through music. *Elementary School Guidance & Counseling, 21,* 284–291.

Brand, A. G. (1987). Writing as counseling. *Elementary School Guidance & Counseling, 21,* 266–275.

Burton, A. (2006, August). Health disparities: Crisis not over for hurricane victims. *Environmental Health Perspectives, 114*(8), A462.

Carter, S. R. (1987). Use of puppets to treat traumatic grief: A case study. *Elementary School Guidance & Counseling, 21*(3), 210–215.

Children and War Foundation. (n.d.). *The children's impact of event scale.* Retrieved December 18, 2007, from http://childrenandwar.org/files/Billeder/instruments%20articles/CRIES-13.doc

Cohen, J. A., Berliner, L., & March, J. S. (2000). Treatment of children and adolescents. In E. B. Foa, T. M. Keane, & M. J. Friedman (Eds.), *Effective treatments for PTSD: Practical guidelines from the International Society for Traumatic Stress Studies* (pp. 213–216). New York: Guilford.

Cohen, J., Goodman, R. F., Brown, E. J., & Mannarino, A. (2004). Treatment of childhood traumatic grief: Contributing to a newly emerging condition in the wake of community trauma. *Harvard Review of Psychiatry, 12,* 213–216.

Dripchak, V. (2007). Posttraumatic play: Towards acceptance and resolution. *Clinical Social Work Journal, 35*(2), 125–134.

Drucker, K. (2001). Why can't she control herself? A case study. In J. Murphy (Ed.), *Art therapy with young survivors of sexual abuse: Lost for words* (pp. 101–125). New York: Brunner-Routledge.

Dyregrov, A., & Yule, W. (2005). A review of PTSD in children. *Child and Adolescent Mental Health, 11*(4), 176–184.

Elsass, P. (2001). Individual and collective traumatic memories: A qualitative study of post-traumatic stress disorder symptoms in two Latin American localities. *Transcultural Psychiatry, 38*(5), 306.

Eth, S., & Pynoos, R. S. (1985). Developmental perspective on psychic trauma in childhood. In C. R. Figley (Ed.), *Trauma and its wake: The study of post-trauma stress disorder* (pp. 36–52). New York: Brunner/Mazel.

Figley, C. (2007, May). *Clinical applications of a model of combat stress injury management.* Paper presented at Argosy University's third annual Traumatology Symposium, Sarasota, FL.

Foa, E. B., Johnson, K. M., Feeny, N. C., & Treadwell, K. R. H. (2001). The child PTSD scale: A preliminary examination of its psychometric properties. *Journal of Community Psychology, 30,* 376–384.

Fogarty, J. A. (2000). *The magical thoughts of grieving children.* Amityville, NY: Baywood.

Gaffney, D. A. (2006). The aftermath of disaster: Children in crisis. *Journal of Clinical Psychology, 62*(8), 1001–1016.

Gladding, S. T. (1987). Poetic expressions: A counseling art in elementary schools. *Elementary School Guidance & Counseling, 21,* 307–311.

Gunn, F. X. (2007). Spiritual issues in the aftermath of disaster. *Southern Medical Journal, 100*(9), 936–937.

Hamblen, J. (1998). *PTSD in children and adolescents: A National Center for PTSD fact sheet.* Retrieved January 9, 2008, from http://www.ncptsd.va.gov/ncmain/ncdocs/fact_shts/fs_children.html

Holtz, T. H. (1998). Refugee trauma versus torture trauma: A retrospective controlled cohort study of Tibetan refugees. *Journal of Nervous and Mental Disease, 186*(1), 240–34.

Hovey, J. D. (2000). Acculturative stress, depression, and suicidal ideation in Mexican immigrants. *Cultural Diversity and Ethnic Minority Psychology, 6*(2), 134–151.

Husain, S., & Nair, J. (1998). Stress reactions of children and adolescents in war and siege conditions. *American Journal of Psychiatry, 155*(12), 1718.

Irwin, E. C. (1987). Drama: The play's the thing. *Elementary School Guidance & Counseling, 21,* 276–283.

James, R. K. (2003, April). *Drawing out the trauma.* Paper presented at the Twenty-Seventh Annual Convention of Crisis Intervention Personnel, Chicago.

James, R. K. & Gilliland, B. E. (2005). *Crisis intervention strategies.* Belmont, CA: Thomson Publishing.

James, R. K., & Myer, R. (1987). Puppets: The elementary counselor's right or left arm. *Elementary School Guidance & Counseling, 21,* 292–299.

Johnson, D. R. (2000). Creative therapies. In E. Foa & T. Keane (Eds.), *Effective treatments for PTSD: Practice guidelines from the International Society for Traumatic Stress Studies* (pp. 356–358). New York: Guilford.

Johnson, K. (1989*). Trauma in the lives of children: Crisis and stress management techniques for counselors and other professionals.* Alameda, CA: Hunter House.

Johnson, R. G. (1987). Using computer art in counseling children. *Elementary School Guidance & Counseling, 21,* 262–265.

Jones, L. (2008). Responding to the needs of children in crisis. *International Review of Psychiatry, 20*(3), 291–303.

Kraybill-Greggo, J. W., Kraybill-Greggo, M. J., & Collins, T. M. (2005). The crisis of death. In B. G. Collins & T. M. Collins (Eds.), *Crisis and trauma* (pp. 319–361). New York: LaHaska.

Kruczek, T., & Salsman, J. (2006). Prevention and treatment of posttraumatic stress disorder in the school setting. *Psychology in the Schools, 43*(4), 461–470.

Lamberg, L. (2008). Psychiatrists strive to help children heal mental wounds from war and disasters. *JAMA: Journal of the American Medical Association, 300*(6), 642–643.

Landreth, G. L. (1987). Play therapy: Facilitative use of child's play in elementary school counseling. *Elementary School Guidance and Counseling, 21,* 253–261.

Landreth, G. L. (2002). *Play therapy: The art of the relationship.* New York: Brunner-Routledge.

Lee, T. (2006). New Freedom Schools in New Orleans help Katrina youth. *Crisis, 113*(4), 5–6.

Math, S. B., Girimaji, S. C., Benegal, V., Kumar, G. S., Uday, H. A., & Nagaraja, D. (2006). Tsunami: Psychosocial aspects of Andaman and Nicobar islands. Assessments and intervention in the early phase. *International Review of Psychiatry, 18*(3), 233–239.

Miller, L. (1999). Treating posttraumatic stress disorder in children and families: Basic principles and clinical applications. *The American Journal of Family Therapy, 27,* 21–34.

Minkowski, A., Morisseau, L., Marciano, P., Hurau-Rendu, C., Cukier-Hemeury, F., & Guillaumet, C. (1993). Mental stress on children exposed to war and natural catastrophes. *Infant Mental Health Journal, 14*(4), 273–282.

National Association of School Psychologists. (2002). *Memorials/activities/rituals following traumatic events.* Retrieved May 22, 2007, from http://www.naspweb.org/resources/crisis_safety/memorials_ general.aspx

National School Safety Center. (n.d.). *School associated violent deaths.* Retrieved December 28, 2007, from http://www.schoolsafety.us/School-Associated-Violent-Deaths-p-6.html

Patten, S., Gatz, Y., Jones, B., & Thomas, D. (1989). Posttraumatic stress disorder and the treatment of sexual abuse. *Social Work, 34*(3), 197–203.

Psalms. *Holy bible: The NIV study bible.* (1995). Grand Rapids, MI: Zondervan.

Purtscher, K. (2005). Preparing and responding to major accidents and disasters. *International Journal of Injury Control and Safety, 12*(2), 119–121.

Pynoos, R. S., Frederick, C., & Nader, K. L. (1987). Life threat and post-traumatic stress in school-age children. *Archives of General Psychiatry, 44*, 1057–1063.

Pynoos, R. S., Steinberg, A. M., & Goenjian, A. (1996). Traumatic stress in childhood and adolescence: Recent developments and current controversies. In B. A. van der Kolk, A. McFarlane, & L. Weisaeth (Eds.), *Traumatic stress: The effects of overwhelming experience on mind, body, and society* (pp. 331–358). New York: Guilford.

Ruzek, J. L., Brymer, M. J., Jacobs, A. K., Layne, C. M., Vernberg, E. M., & Watson, P. J. (2007). Psychological first aid. *Journal of Mental Health Counseling, 29*(1), 17–49.

Silverman, W. K., & Albano, A. M. (1996). *ADIS: Anxiety disorders interview schedule for DSM-IV.* San Antonio, TX: Psychological Corporation.

Sluckin, A., Weller, A., & Highton, J. (1989). Recovering from trauma: Gestalt therapy with an abused child. *Maladjustment and Therapeutic Education, 7*, 147–157.

Steinhausen, H., Mas, S., Ledermann, C., & Metzke, C. (2006). Risk factors for the development of emotional and behavioral problems in children born to drug-dependent mothers. *European Child & Adolescent Psychiatry, 15*(8), 460–466.

Tolan, P. H., & Dodge, K. A. (2005). Children's mental health as a primary care and concern. *American Psychologist, 60*(6), 601–614.

University of the State of New York. (n.d.). *Crisis counseling guide: Age-related reactions of children to disasters.* Retrieved May 22, 2008, from http://www.emsc.nysed.gov/crisis/counsel.htm

U.S. Department of Health and Human Services, Substance Abuse and Mental Health Services Administration. (2005). *Tips for talking to children in trauma: Interventions at home for preschoolers to adolescents* (Paper No. NMH02–0138). Washington, DC: Author.

Vijayakumar, L., Kannan, G., & Daniel, S. (2006). Mental health status in children exposed to tsunami. *International Review of Psychiatry, 18*(6), 507–513.

Vinturella, L., & James, R. K. (1987). Sandplay: A therapeutic medium with children. *Elementary School Guidance & Counseling, 21*, 229–238.

Webb, N. B. (Ed.). (1999). *Play therapy with children in crisis: Individual, group, and family treatment.* New York: Guilford.

Worden, J. W. (1996). *Children and grief: When a parent dies.* New York: Guilford.

Provider Perspectives on Serving the Needs of Displaced Disaster Survivors Following Hurricane Katrina

J. Brian Houston

Gilbert Reyes

Betty Pfefferbaum

Karen Fraser Wyche

Major disasters that affect wide geographic areas, such as the Indian Ocean tsunami of 2004, are likely to displace large numbers of people. The same is true with eruptions of widespread violence, such as wars and other forms of armed conflict. Whatever the source of massive death and destruction, the consequences will bear similarities, as people flee their homes and communities in search of relatively secure locations. Secure locations are typically inhabited by populations that are willing to provide temporary security, shelter, and support, until conditions become more favorable for the displaced people to either return to their homes or relocate more permanently to hospitable places of their choosing. A variety of terms are used to describe displaced groups, including *evacuees*, *refugees*, and *internally displaced persons*. For the purposes of the present chapter, the term *displaced disaster survivors* is used to describe people who have evacuated their communities for a sustained time in response to severe environmental disturbances that threatened their lives, their health, or their livelihoods.

In August and September 2005, Hurricane Katrina ravaged the coastal region of the United States that borders on the Gulf of Mexico. When the storm was gathering force and making landfall, hundreds of thousands of people began to evacuate the Gulf Coast. In the immediate wake of the hurricane, levee failure caused flooding that nearly destroyed New Orleans and necessitated the long-term relocation of thousands or more residents. It is estimated that 600,000 to 1.2 million people were ultimately evacuated as a result of these events (Abramson, Redlener, Stehling-Ariza, & Fuller, 2007), with well over 400,000 of those experiencing lengthy displacement. Hurricane Katrina, with its massive impact and extended period of displacement, created significant strains and challenges for the survivors, the host communities where they relocated, and the disaster relief establishment. In addition, Hurricane Katrina had profound repercussions for the economics and politics of the region and the nation. Most important, the impact of the storm was unique in terms of the extent of displacement and was aptly compared to disasters in other parts of the world that Americans had previously observed from a safe distance and from which they felt insulated.

Hurricane Katrina evacuees were disbursed to host communities throughout the United States, where they received support for their basic needs from disaster relief organizations, community and governmental agencies, faith-based organizations, social service agencies of various kinds, and health care professionals. Among the displaced were approximately 200,000 children, a majority of whom required educational placement at schools in their host communities (Abramson et al., 2007). All displaced survivors required food, clothing, housing, furnishings, transportation, and other items necessary to establish new domiciles and sustainable livelihoods (Leadership 18, 2006). The need for less tangible forms of sustenance, such as a sense of community membership, social support, familiarity, comfort, and security, also emerged (Chamlee-Wright, 2006; Mills, Edmondson, & Park, 2007; Reich & Wadsworth, 2008).

The complexity of meeting these needs was compounded by the diverse characteristics of both the displaced populations and the host communities to which they were relocated. Based partly on her observations as a disaster mental health provider shortly after Hurricane Katrina, Dass-Brailsford (2008) classified and summarized some of the barriers to care and other issues that influenced the quality of care for the displaced populations. Among the barriers she identified were an insufficient availability of multiculturally competent providers, difficulties with language and communication, poverty and other socioeconomic factors, mistrust of institutions, historically informed distrust between culturally distinct groups, differences in worldviews regarding the interests of individuals and the collective interest, differing perceptions of help and healing, the roles of religion and spirituality in adapting to adversity, the positive and negative influences of the news media, and the exposure of service providers to secondary traumatic stress (i.e., secondary traumatization). This extensive list of barriers and complicating factors illustrates the challenges faced by Hurricane Katrina survivors, the host communities where they relocated to, and the multitude of disaster relief service providers that were mobilized in response to this unique crisis.

In the years since Hurricane Katrina precipitated such a massive displacement, researchers have conducted numerous studies to assess the acute and enduring effects experienced by survivors. An early tracking survey by the Hurricane Katrina Community Advisory Group (Brewin et al., 2006), designed to establish baseline data on the needs and reactions of the disaster, found that a vast majority of those surveyed experienced multiple major stressors, with roughly 23% experiencing "extreme psychological adversity" (p. iii). Survey respondents also reported facing a number of practical challenges, including problems with finances, services, housing, employment, and insurance claims. Signs and symptoms of psychological problems were reported at prevalence levels substantially higher than those observed in the general population, as were signs of optimism and resilient adaptation in the face of profound adversity. The need for mental health support was also suggested in an early surveillance report by the Centers for Disease Control and Prevention (2006), and subsequent research found that residents of the disaster-affected areas experienced substantial hardship and exposure to many potentially traumatic events (Weems et al., 2007).

CHAPTER HIGHLIGHTS

+ Describes a study that focused on identifying the challenges to adaptational resilience among displaced survivors of Hurricane Katrina from the vantage point of service providers in the greater Houston metropolitan area;

+ Discusses provider perspectives informed both by their backgrounds in working with people affected by profoundly stressful events and by their experiences with displaced survivors of Hurricane Katrina;

+ Compares observations across the cases encountered after Hurricane Katrina and cases previously encountered in other disaster settings; and

+ Identifies the most common problems and needs encountered by service providers and identifies the types of services and solutions that were found to be effective.

METHOD

In August 2007, approximately 2 years after Hurricane Katrina made landfall, the Terrorism and Disaster Center at the University of Oklahoma Health Sciences Center, a member of the National Child Traumatic Stress Network, conducted training focused on working with displaced families at a community mental health center in Houston, Texas. Participants at the training were providers from the Houston area who had worked or were working with Katrina survivors. As part of this training, participants were invited to complete a survey assessing their experiences with Katrina survivors and their perceptions of the psychosocial needs and difficulties faced by survivors, the adequacy of community services, survivor integration in the host community, and the role of the media in supporting or delaying recovery. Development of the survey was informed by our earlier work with Katrina survivors (see Houston et al., 2009; Pfefferbaum et al., 2008). Participants who chose to complete the survey signed informed consent forms approved by the University of Oklahoma Health Sciences Center Institutional Review Board.

Participants

The participants were 28 providers from the Houston metropolitan area and included case managers, social workers, clinicians (including school counselors; child, marriage, and family therapists; psychotherapists; and psychiatrists), disaster specialists, career counselors, and a juvenile probation officer. Participants worked for organizations such as the DePelchin Children's Center, Houston Independent School District, the United Way, and the American Red Cross, as well as with other local social service providers. Participant involvement with Katrina survivors included providing counseling or therapy ($n = 20$), referring survivors to other services and resources in the community ($n = 16$), providing education and skills-based training ($n = 5$), offering case management ($n = 4$), offering direct assistance in the form of money or goods ($n = 4$), and advocating for survivors ($n = 1$). Some providers had worked intimately with a handful of Katrina survivors, while others had spoken with hundreds of survivors by phone or through office visits. Most of the participants ($n = 23$) were still working with Katrina survivors 2 years after the hurricane (the time of this survey).

RESULTS

Psychosocial Needs and Difficulties

Respondents were asked to indicate how many of the Katrina survivors they worked with had difficulties with a variety of psychosocial issues during two time periods: since arriving in the new community and currently (see Table 7.1 for all issues queried and results). A majority of respondents indicated that most of the survivors they worked with had difficulty obtaining a car for personal use (74%) and finding employment (56%) since arriving in the host community. In addition, many providers reported that since arriving in the new community, most survivors had difficulty keeping employment (48%), becoming part of the new community (48%), learning the laws of the new community (46%), paying for health care (46%), making decisions about whether to return home or stay in the new community (44%), succeeding in school (42%), keeping housing (41%), using public transportation (41%), getting and paying for mental health care (41%), and trusting people in the new community (41%). Each of these difficulties was reported to be less common at the time the survey was conducted (2 years after Katrina), with the exception of trusting people in the new community, which was reported by 44% of providers to be a difficulty among most Katrina survivors. Other current difficulties experienced by Katrina survivors included obtaining a car for personal use (39%), finding employment (39%), becoming a part of the new community (39%), learning the laws of the new community (36%), finding food they like in the new community (35%), and paying for health care (35%).

Respondents were also asked to compare psychosocial difficulties experienced by Katrina survivors with the difficulties experienced by clients the providers normally work with (see Table 7.2). A majority of the respondents reported that Katrina survivors experienced more difficulties with all issues queried than did clients that providers normally work with. The most frequent endorsement of greater difficulty among Katrina survivors occurred for issues related to school (75%), employment (71%), and transportation (67%).

TABLE 7.1 Provider perceptions of frequency of difficulties among Hurricane Katrina survivors								
	Since arriving				Currently			
	n	Few	Some	Most	n	Few	Some	Most
Housing difficulties								
Finding housing	25	20%	48%	32%	23	44%	39%	17%
Keeping housing	27	26%	33%	41%	23	39%	52%	9%
Transportation difficulties								
Using public transportation	27	22%	37%	41%	23	22%	57%	22%
Obtaining a car (personal use)	27	11%	15%	74%	23	22%	39%	39%
Employment difficulties								
Finding employment	27	7%	37%	56%	23	22%	39%	39%
Keeping employment	25	16%	36%	48%	21	29%	43%	29%
School difficulties								
Succeeding in school	26	15%	42%	42%	22	23%	46%	32%
Getting help with any school issues or problems	27	22%	44%	33%	22	27%	41%	32%
Health, mental health, and social service difficulties								
Getting health care	27	15%	56%	30%	23	17%	57%	26%
Paying for health care	27	14%	36%	46%	23	30%	35%	35%
Getting mental health care	27	22%	37%	41%	23	17%	57%	26%
Paying for mental health care	27	41%	19%	41%	23	26%	44%	30%
Getting social services	27	19%	44%	37%	22	14%	68%	18%
Social support difficulties								
Making new friends	27	11%	63%	26%	23	17%	65%	17%
Staying in touch with friends and/or family from home	27	19%	48%	33%	23	35%	39%	26%
Integration in host community difficulties								
Becoming part of the new community	27	4%	48%	48%	23	17%	44%	39%
Learning the laws of the new community	26	15%	39%	46%	22	27%	36%	36%
Finding food they like in the new community	26	19%	42%	39%	23	35%	30%	35%

TABLE 7.1 (Continued)								
		Since arriving				*Currently*		
	n	*Few*	*Some*	*Most*	*n*	*Few*	*Some*	*Most*
Understanding the way people talk in the new community	27	30%	48%	22%	23	26%	57%	17%
Enjoying the popular music or musical styles in the new community	26	42%	46%	12%	22	36%	59%	5%
Adjusting to the weather or climate of the new community	26	50%	42%	8%	22	46%	36%	18%
Trusting people in the new community	27	7%	52%	41%	23	22%	35%	44%
Decision-making difficulties								
Accessing information about the home or city they left	27	15%	52%	33%	23	26%	48%	26%
Making normal, routine decisions	27	15%	52%	33%	23	22%	61%	17%
Making decision about whether to return home or stay in the new community	27	7%	48%	44%	23	26%	48%	26%

Note: Respondents were asked: "*Since arriving in the new community,* how many Hurricane Katrina survivors that you worked with had difficulty . . ." and "How many of the Hurricane Katrina survivors that you are *currently* working with are having difficulty . . ." for each of the difficulties listed in the first column. Possible responses ranged from 1 = *None* to 7 = *Most*; analyses were grouped into the following categories: 1, 2, = *Few*; 3, 4, 5 = *Some*; and 6, 7 = *Most*. Rows may not equal 100% due to rounding.

TABLE 7.2 Provider perceptions of difficulties among Hurricane Katrina survivors compared to clients not affected by the disaster				
		Amount of difficulty compared to other clients		
	n	*Less*	*Same*	*More*
Finding housing	26	12%	39%	50%
Paying for housing	27	19%	26%	56%
Transportation	27	7%	26%	67%
Finding and keeping employment	24	0%	29%	71%
Schools	24	4%	21%	75%

Note: Possible responses ranged from 1 = *Much less difficulty* to 5 = *Much more difficulty*. For analyses, responses were grouped into the following categories: 1, 2 = *Less*; 3 = *Same*; and 4, 5 = *More*. Rows may not equal 100% due to rounding.

In an attempt to further clarify the specific issues underlying overall difficulties among Katrina survivors in the areas of transportation and employment, providers were asked to report on the specific problems experienced by Katrina survivors in these areas (see Table 7.3). With regard to transportation, a majority of respondents indicated that survivors were unable to afford a car or personal transportation (81 %) or the maintenance on personal transportation (77 %) and that there were logistical issues with public transportation (e.g., 54 % of respondents reported that the buses did not serve the areas where the survivors lived and that survivors did not have information about bus schedules; and 50 % reported that buses did not run frequently enough).

TABLE 7.3 Provider perceptions of frequencies of specific problems experienced by Hurricane Katrina survivors	Problem experienced by Katrina survivors	
	Yes	No
Transportation (n = 26)		
Do not have information about bus schedule or route	54%	46%
Buses do not run often enough	50%	50%
Buses do not serve the area where survivors live	54%	46%
Buses do not serve the area where survivors work	35%	65%
Survivors are unwilling to use public transportation	46%	54%
Survivors are unable to afford a car or other personal transportation	81%	19%
Survivors are unable to afford maintenance for a car or other personal transportation	77%	23%
Survivors are not aware of driving laws or rules in the new community	12%	89%
Employment (n = 26)		
Survivors lack educational requirements for available employment	69%	31%
Survivors lack appropriate skills for available employment	69%	31%
Survivors are overqualified for available employment	19%	81%
Employment for survivors is not available in the new community	31%	69%
Survivors are unable to find transportation to available employment	73%	27%
Survivors are unwilling to accept available employment	39%	61%

Note: Rows may not equal 100 % due to rounding.

Transportation was also related to employment difficulties, as 73% of respondents reported that survivors were unable to find transportation to travel to places of employment. Employment difficulties were also linked to the qualifications of survivors, as 69% of respondents indicated that Katrina survivors lacked the education or skills required for available employment. Only 31% of the respondents indicated that there was no employment available for survivors in the community, leading to the conclusion that the transportation and employment qualification issues described previously were the main impediments to Katrina survivors attaining employment as opposed to an overall unavailability of jobs.

Responding to Psychosocial Needs and Difficulties

In addition to describing the frequency of psychosocial difficulties faced by Katrina survivors, respondents were also asked to describe the ways in which they or the organizations for which they worked were able to assist survivors with these issues.[1] With regard to addressing the housing difficulties experienced by Katrina survivors, many respondents reported referring survivors to community programs specializing in housing, some reported directly placing survivors in housing, and one reported serving as an advocate for survivors with the Federal Emergency Management Agency (FEMA) and the U.S. Department of Housing and Urban Development (HUD).

Providers helped address transportation problems by making referrals to organizations in the community that provided transportation assistance in the form of bus passes, taxi vouchers, or financial assistance for purchasing cars or making repairs. Some providers worked for organizations that helped survivors with transportation by driving them to counseling appointments or providing vans for travel to job interviews or work. One respondent reported providing tours of the city that focused on the location of essential and important destinations such as hospitals, social service agencies, and schools, to help survivors acclimate to the new community and prepare to get around on their own.

Employment difficulties among survivors were addressed by providers, mainly through making referrals to employment counseling, training, and education programs in the community. Some of the employment programs were focused specifically on helping Katrina survivors, while others were pre-existing social service programs focused on helping increase people's skills and knowledge so that they could attain employment. One provider reported referring survivors directly to a local temporary employment agency in the community that had work available, while another provider referred some survivors directly to a local construction company that needed workers.

Providers and their organizations helped address school difficulties by delivering counseling in schools and in community health centers; offering after-school programs, tutoring, and career services for students; holding community meetings with students, parents, and teachers; helping establish a school exclusively for students displaced due to Katrina; and directly providing uniforms and school supplies to displaced students. Respondents also provided suggestions about what additional activities they thought could be offered to help survivors with school difficulties. These suggestions included providing more mental health counseling for children affected by the disaster, offering group sessions that allowed students to process their experiences together, facilitating ongoing community meetings to discuss the needs of new students in the community, training school staff to understand the effects of disaster and displacement on students and the impact of culture on these experiences, and providing social services in the school and/or having schools directly link with social service providers in the community to make sure students received necessary services.

Community Services and Survivor Integration in the Host Community

Respondents were asked several questions about the level of services available for Katrina survivors in the host community (see Table 7.4). Overall, a majority of respondents agreed that the local community had responded to the needs of Katrina (71%), while disagreeing that the local (61%) and federal (79%) governments had done enough to address the needs of survivors. A slight majority of respondents (54%) perceived host community residents to be angry about the level of services available for Katrina survivors. Respondents were split on whether the overall level of services available in the community was sufficient to meet the needs of survivors and whether the services made available to Katrina survivors took away from the services available to other community residents.

As part of community integration, respondents were asked about the extent to which they agreed that conflict existed in schools between new students and students already living in the community, since the new students arrived, and currently.[2] Providers overwhelmingly agreed that conflict existed between new and old students since the new students arrived ($n = 26$; *Agree* = 85%; *Neutral* = 4%; *Disagree* = 12%), and a majority of providers reported that such conflict continued 2 years after the disaster ($n = 24$; *Agree* = 54%; *Neutral* = 17%; *Disagree* = 29%).

TABLE 7.4 Provider perceptions of community service availability				
	n	*Disagree*	*Neutral*	*Agree*
The local community has responded to the needs of Katrina survivors.	28	21%	7%	71%
There are sufficient services in the local community for Katrina survivors.	27	37%	26%	37%
Services that were provided to Katrina survivors have decreased the services available to other community residents.	28	39%	18%	43%
Community residents are angry about the amount of services that have been offered to Katrina survivors.	28	21%	25%	54%
Local government has done enough to help Katrina survivors.	28	61%	11%	29%
The federal government has done enough to help Katrina survivors in my community.	28	79%	4%	18%

Note: Responses ranged from 1 = *Disagree* to 7 = *Agree*. For analyses, responses were grouped into the following categories: 1, 2, 3 = *Disagree*; 4 = *Neutral*; and 5, 6, 7 = *Agree*. Rows may not equal 100% due to rounding.

Providers were also asked to list any barriers they perceived as making it difficult for Katrina survivors to integrate into the new community. Participants listed a variety of barriers, including stigma and negative labels associated with being Katrina survivors; differences between Katrina survivors and the host community in terms of values, culture, language, and education; perceptions in the host community that survivors would only be in Houston temporarily; transportation, employment, and financial difficulties; and the overall difficulty in trying to meet the needs of survivors and to integrate such a large number of new residents into the community.

The Role of the Media

Providers were asked how often they perceived Katrina survivors to be depicted negatively and positively in the local media currently and since arriving in the new community.[3] A majority of providers perceived that Katrina survivors were often depicted negatively in the local media since arriving in the new community ($n = 28$; *Often* = 75%; *Sometimes* = 21%; *Rarely* = 4%), though these depictions were perceived to occur less often currently ($n = 28$; *Often* = 46%; *Sometimes* = 39%; *Rarely* = 14%). Conversely, a majority of respondents perceived Katrina survivors to rarely be depicted positively both since arriving and currently ($n = 28$; *Often* = 4%; *Sometimes* = 36%; *Rarely* = 61%).

Providers were also asked several questions about the perceived accuracy and influence of local Hurricane Katrina media coverage (see Table 7.5). Overall, a majority of providers disagreed that local media coverage helped the community understand the problems faced by Katrina survivors (59%) or that the local media coverage of survivors was accurate (71%); and

TABLE 7.5 Provider perceptions of the role of media in displacement situation				
	n	*Disagree*	*Neutral*	*Agree*
Local media coverage of Katrina survivors has helped the community understand the problems that Katrina survivors face.	27	59%	15%	26%
Local media coverage of Katrina survivors is largely accurate.	28	71%	18%	11%
The local media has been helpful in getting information to Katrina survivors.	28	46%	21%	32%
Local media coverage of Katrina survivors has influenced the way the local community thinks about Katrina survivors.	28	11%	7%	82%
Local media coverage is biased against Katrina survivors.	28	21%	25%	54%
Local media coverage of Katrina survivors has influenced how much aid is available for Katrina survivors in the local community.	27	22%	33%	44%

Note: Responses ranged from 1 = *Disagree* to 7 = *Agree*. For analyses, responses were grouped into the following categories: 1, 2, 3 = *Disagree*; 4 = *Neutral*; and 5, 6, 7 = *Agree*. Rows may not equal 100% due to rounding.

a majority thought that media coverage of Katrina survivors was biased against the survivors (54%). Most of the providers surveyed (82%) believed that the media depictions of Katrina survivors influenced the way that the local community thought about those survivors, and a fewer number (44%) believed that these media depictions influenced the amount of aid available for Katrina survivors in the local community. Last, 46% of the providers surveyed did not think that the local media did a good job of communicating information to Katrina survivors.

DISCUSSION

To better understand the psychosocial needs and difficulties of Katrina survivors, the types and availability of community services for disaster survivors, the integration of survivors in the host community, and the influence of media reports on the perception of Katrina survivors, social service providers working in the Houston, Texas, area were surveyed about their experience working with Katrina survivors. The survey conducted as part of this study was informed by earlier work with Katrina survivors (Houston et al., 2009; Pfefferbaum et al., 2008) and addressed a variety of psychosocial issues.

Overall, the results of the provider survey indicate that numerous issues posed difficulties for people who were displaced from their homes and communities due to a major disaster. Among the most commonly identified problems were finding and keeping housing; using public transportation or obtaining a car; finding and keeping employment; succeeding in school and getting help with school problems; getting and paying for health, mental health, and social services; making new friends and staying in touch with friends and family from the old community; becoming part of and trusting people in the new community; and making both routine and major decisions. As might be expected, the prevalence of these difficulties decreased by the time of this survey (2 years after Hurricane Katrina), but they had not decreased to the point where one could consider them insignificant.

Moreover, most of the providers surveyed reported that the difficulties that Katrina survivors experienced in terms of finding and paying for housing, finding transportation, finding and keeping employment, and dealing with school issues were greater than the difficulties experienced by the clients these providers normally served. The increased difficulties faced by displaced disaster survivors may be related to their unfamiliarity with the new community and/or the overall traumatic experience of having one's home, neighborhood, and/or community destroyed by a disaster. The increased difficulty of displaced disaster survivors addressing their needs compared to other social service clients justifies expanding efforts to provide services or assistance to people who are displaced due to a disaster.

The providers surveyed in this project often helped Katrina survivors meet their most pressing psychosocial needs by linking survivors to available services in the area. Referrals to available services are helpful when working with people who have been displaced due to a disaster, because in addition to providing a source of direct help for a specific need, the provider is also helping the individual find assistance in an environment in which that person is unfamiliar or addressing a need for which that person does not have a great deal of experience. For instance, survivors who may not have needed help arranging transportation in the past may require such assistance after suffering major losses and when faced with unfamiliar environments.

In addition to making appropriate referrals, many of the providers surveyed in this project were proactive in their assistance by driving Katrina survivors around Houston so that they could become familiar with the area, advocating for survivors as they interacted with federal agencies such as FEMA or HUD, and directly connecting survivors to places in the new community with available employment. These examples of active assistance may not be necessary when working with clients who are familiar with the area, but this type of assistance may be instrumental in orienting the displaced to the new community.

Although the results of this survey indicate that addressing basic psychosocial needs is a priority when working with displaced survivors, assisting them with integration into their new community was also strongly emphasized. Becoming part of the new community and adjusting to the culture in the new community was a problem for some or many of the Katrina survivors, according to a majority of the providers surveyed. In fact, a large number of providers believed that most Katrina survivors had more difficulty trusting people in the new community 2 years after Katrina than they had on their initial arrival into the community. This was the only difficulty in our survey that increased over time for Katrina survivors.

Some of the challenges with community integration may be related to how Katrina survivors were depicted in the local media. A majority of the providers surveyed as part of this project perceived local media coverage of Katrina survivors to be negative, inaccurate, and biased against the survivors. Although this research did not assess whether Katrina survivors shared these opinions of local media coverage, we can assume that if survivors perceived themselves depicted negatively in the media, then this might contribute to a conscious or unconscious decision to avoid engaging the local community and perceptions of the community as untrustworthy. Therefore, providers who have experience working with displaced populations and who are aware of the importance of community integration in helping displaced survivors recover from a disaster may wish to intervene in a situation where local media coverage is perceived to be negative or biased. Such an intervention might involve contacting local television stations or newspapers to offer viewpoints and expertise on the challenges faced by displaced people, to describe the positive influences of disaster survivors on the local community, and to provide stories that demonstrate resiliency. This will give both journalists and consumers of local media opportunities to gain a broader perspective about the overall displacement situation and about displaced survivors who are striving to recover and rebuild their lives.

PRACTICAL IMPLICATIONS

- People who have been displaced experience numerous needs and difficulties.
- The difficulties experienced by people who have been displaced due to disaster are often greater than those experienced by social service clients who have not been displaced.
- A host community will need to provide additional services to help people who have been displaced, because the normal level of social services will not be sufficient.
- Providers and organizations working to help people who have been displaced should communicate and collaborate with each other to prevent duplication of efforts, improve the overall assistance provided to disaster survivors, and identify

survivor needs that are not being met by existing services or organizations in the community.

- Providers can help people who have been displaced, by orienting them to the new community.
- Community integration and the establishment of social support in the new community may be difficult for people who have been displaced. Providers should be aware of these issues and intervene to help survivors increase social connections in the new community, because establishing social support contributes positively to coping, mental health, and physical health.
- Media depictions of displaced disaster survivors may influence how disaster survivors are perceived in the host community. If media depictions of survivors are negative, then providers should be prepared to advocate on behalf of survivors through the local media.

CONCLUSION

The research described here used the perspectives of providers working with children and adults who were displaced from their homes due to Hurricane Katrina to identify the survivors' psychosocial needs and difficulties, the types and availability of community services, the integration of survivors in the host community, and the influence of media reports on the perception of Katrina survivors. The results provide several important lessons that can be used by providers and organizations to prepare for the next major disaster as well as to inform disaster interventions.

The first lesson learned from the providers surveyed is that the needs of people who have been displaced due to a disaster are numerous (and include things such as employment; housing; transportation; access to health care, mental health care, and social services; school issues; integration into the new community; and decision making). The difficulties that displaced disaster survivors experience generally exceed those experienced by the clients that providers normally serve. Therefore, simply adding displaced individuals to the caseload of existing social service providers and organizations is not likely to be sufficient in addressing displacement-related needs. Not only can a major disaster result in a significant number of displaced people suddenly appearing in a host community and needing assistance, but also given their psychosocial issues, the host community will likely have to expand services to meet the additional needs.

It is unlikely that any single social service, volunteer, or faith-based organization will have the resources or expertise to address all of these needs. Therefore, it is recommended that providers and organizations in the host community collaborate with each other to coordinate response efforts (see Houston et al., 2009). This collaboration will allow providers to appropriately refer people who have been displaced to the organizations in the community that are in the best position to address their various and multiple needs. The collaboration may also decrease duplication of effort among providers and organizations. For example, it will be of little support to those who have been displaced if there are 10 organizations in the host community ready to assist with transportation issues but no organizations available to help them locate and attain housing.

Communication among response organizations and providers will help prevent such duplication of efforts. In addition, it will identify gaps in a community's network of disaster service providers.

Another lesson learned in this study is that providers can assist people who have been displaced by orienting them to the new community or environment. Where one should go to get services or information is a major issue for many people who have been displaced by a disaster. Displaced disaster survivors may not be familiar with how to access social services and will also likely not know the location of such services in a new community. Therefore, providers can play an important role in orienting displaced survivors to available resources and the location of such resources.

The next lesson learned from this research is that community integration is a major and ongoing issue for people who have been displaced. The providers surveyed in this project perceived distrust of the new community to be an issue that increased over time among people who were displaced due to Hurricane Katrina. If survivors do not feel welcome in their new community, then it is likely that they will not make the necessary interpersonal connections that can result in positive social support. This is important, because social support has been found to help adults and adolescents cope with traumatic events (Cook & Bickman, 1990; Henrich & Shahar, 2008) and has been found to be generally associated with good health and mental health (Cohen, 2004; Kawachi & Berkman, 2001). It is possible that those who have been displaced may be resistant to investing their time or emotions in becoming part of the new community, especially if they are uncertain about the length of time they will spend in the new community. Unfortunately, if what happened in New Orleans after Hurricane Katrina is the exemplar, displacement following a major disaster could last far longer than we can predict. Therefore, it behooves providers to encourage those who have been displaced to seek opportunities to make new relationships and participate socially in the new community. Even if someone who has been displaced does not stay in the new community permanently, making social connections will be of value to that person while he or she is displaced from his or her original home.

The final lesson emerging from this research is that providers must be aware of the role that the media has in the recovery of displaced survivors. The providers surveyed here clearly perceived the local media as playing a negative role in survivors' adjustment in the host community. Therefore, providers and the organizations they work for must be prepared to advocate on behalf of displaced survivors in the local media. This advocacy includes providing the local media with accurate information about the experience of displaced survivors, details about survivors' resiliency, and examples of how survivors may be contributing positively to the local community. Although advocating for those who are in need is a common function of social service providers, advocating through the local media may be a new approach for some. However, if the local media's depiction of disaster survivors is as powerful as perceived by the providers who participated in this survey, then providers working with other displaced populations should be prepared to work with the local media in the hope that this interaction will positively influence how displaced disaster survivors are depicted in the media. Ultimately, successful media advocacy can influence host community perceptions of displaced survivors, improve relationships between new and old community members, and support the adjustment of those displaced by disasters.

REFERENCES

Abramson, D., Redlener, I., Stehling-Ariza, T., & Fuller, E. (2007). *The legacy of Katrina's children: Estimating the number of at-risk children in the Gulf Coast states of Louisiana and Mississippi* (National Center for Disaster Preparedness research brief). New York: Columbia University Mailman School of Public Health.

Brewin, C., Galea, S., Jones, R. T., Kendrick, D., Kessler, R., King, D., et al. (2006). *Overview of baseline survey result: The Harvard Medical School Hurricane Katrina Community Advisory Group Report.* Retrieved December 14, 2008, from http://www.hurricanekatrina.med.harvard.edu/pdf/baseline_report%208-25-06.pdf

Centers for Disease Control and Prevention. (2006). Assessment of health-related needs after Hurricanes Katrina and Rita—Orleans and Jefferson Parishes, New Orleans area, Louisiana, October 17-22, 2005. *MMWR Morbidity & Mortality Weekly Report, 55*(2), 38–41.

Chamlee-Wright, E. (2006). *After the storm: Social capital regrouping in the wake of Hurricane Katrina* (Global Prosperity Initiative Working Paper No. 70). Washington, DC: George Washington University, Mercatus Center.

Cohen, S. (2004). Social relationships and health. *American Psychologist, 59,* 676–684.

Cook, J. D., & Bickman, L. (1990). Social support and psychological symptomatology following a natural disaster. *Journal of Traumatic Stress, 3,* 541–556.

Dass-Brailsford, P. (2008). After the storm: Recognition, recovery, and reconstruction. *Professional Psychology: Research & Practice, 39,* 24–30.

Henrich, C., & Shahar, G. (2008). Social support buffers the effects of terrorism on adolescent depression: Findings from Sderot, Israel. *Journal of the American Academy of Child and Adolescent Psychiatry, 47,* 1073–1076.

Houston, J. B., Pfefferbaum, B., Reyes, G., Wyche, K. F., Jones, R. T., & Yoder, M. (2009). *The domestic disaster displacement (3D) manual: Working with people who have been displaced due to disaster.* Oklahoma City: University of Oklahoma Health Sciences Center, Terrorism and Disaster Center.

Kawachi, I., & Berkman, L. F. (2001). Social ties and mental health. *Journal of Urban Health, 78,* 458–467.

Leadership 18. (2006). *Voices from the Gulf Coast.* Retrieved June 14, 2007, from http://dir.unitedway.org/files/pdf/Voices_from_the_Gulf_Coast_Report_ii.pdf

Mills, M. A., Edmondson, D., & Park, C. L. (2007). Trauma and stress response among Hurricane Katrina evacuees. *American Journal of Public Health, 97,* S116–S123.

Pfefferbaum, B., Houston, J. B., Wyche, K. F., Van Horn, R. L., Reyes, G., Jeon-Slaughter, H., et al. (2008). Children displaced by Hurricane Katrina: A focus group study. *Journal of Loss and Trauma, 13,* 303–313.

Reich, J. A., & Wadsworth, M. (2008). Out of the floodwaters, but not yet on dry ground: Experiences of displacement and adjustment in adolescents and their parents following Hurricane Katrina. *Children, Youth and Environments, 18*(1), 354–370.

Weems, C. F., Watts, S. E., Marsee, M. A., Taylor, L. K., Costa, N. M., Cannon, M. F., et al. (2007). The psychosocial impact of Hurricane Katrina: Contextual differences in psychological symptoms, social support, and discrimination. *Behavior Research and Therapy, 45,* 2295–2306.

NOTES

1. These were open-ended questions.

2. Responses to these questions ranged from 1 = *Disagree* to 7 = *Agree*; and analyses were grouped into the following categories: 1, 2, 3 = *Disagree*; 4 = *Neutral*; and 5, 6, 7 = *Agree*.

3. Possible responses to these questions ranged from 1 = Never to 5 = Always; and analyses were grouped into the following categories: 1, 2 = *Rarely*; 3 = *Sometimes*; and 4, 5 = *Often*.

Older Adults and Natural Disasters

Lessons Learned From Hurricanes Katrina and Rita

Katie E. Cherry

Priscilla D. Allen

Sandro Galea

People are living longer today than ever before. By the year 2030, one fifth of the U.S. population is expected to be 65 years of age and older. Persons 85 years of age and older, often called the "oldest-old," are of particular concern, because they comprise the fastest growing segment of the population with the greatest health care needs (U.S. Department of Health and Human Services, Administration on Aging, 2007). The growing proportion of older adults in today's society brings many issues and challenges for individuals, families, and society as a whole, which may become magnified in times of crisis. When a natural disaster strikes, concerns about the safety and practical needs of older people may become particularly acute among family members and senior service providers.

In this chapter, we explore the impact of Hurricanes Katrina and Rita on older adults, defined here as people age 65 years and older. Our guiding assumption is that these disasters revealed both strengths and weaknesses at an individual level (i.e., human responses to a significant environmental stressor) as well as at a societal level (i.e., community preparedness and disaster recovery).

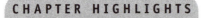

CHAPTER HIGHLIGHTS

✦ Provides insight into psychological reactions to disaster and suggests directions for planning and preparedness related to serving an older population;

✦ Examines commendable responses to the storms, including the notable efforts made by schools and universities, faith-based organizations, and the goodwill of the people of South Louisiana and the nation;

✦ Examines problematic storm responses that led to evacuation dilemmas in which older people were adversely affected (e.g., the St. Rita's Nursing Home tragedy);

✦ Addresses four points of practical consideration for crisis counselors and social planners related to older adults in a disaster context, which include (a) the heterogeneity of older adults, (b) the role of pre-existing mental conditions on postdisaster reactions, (c) the role of prior hurricane experience and resilience in a natural disaster, and (d) the long-range effects of Hurricanes Katrina and Rita on an aging population; and

✦ Discusses implications for advocacy, disaster planning, and preparedness for seniors, including consideration of policy initiatives to protect those whose destiny is often dependent on others.

OLDER ADULTS AND DISASTER: THE KATRINA AND RITA IMPACT

On the morning of August 29, 2005, Hurricane Katrina made landfall in the Gulf Coast region, which includes Mississippi and the lower Plaquemines and Orleans parishes in South Louisiana. Community destruction was widespread and loss of life was considerable, with an estimated death toll of 1,577 people in Louisiana (Sharkey, 2006). Death reports still remain controversial as to when the count ended and what was directly and indirectly caused by the storm. For example, people who died after relocating to a nursing home may not have had their death attributed to the hurricanes. On September 24, 2005, less than a month after Katrina, Hurricane Rita made landfall, primarily affecting Calcasieu, Cameron, and Vermilion parishes on the western side of Louisiana. Rita, also a destructive Category 3 hurricane at landfall, directly caused seven fatalities with property damage estimated at $11.3 billion (National Hurricane Center, 2007), and indirect consequences of the disaster are still undetermined. With toxic waters remaining, newly homeless people dispersed all over the country, and officials still collecting and counting the dead, Hurricane Katrina all but eclipsed Hurricane Rita. The disproportionate coverage of Hurricane Katrina left Hurricane Rita an afterthought and led to the coining of the term *Rita Amnesia* (Hancock, 2006).

In retrospect, we know there were both notable and detrimental responses to Hurricanes Katrina and Rita, and sometimes the two are not mutually exclusive. For example, the weather advisory was successful in providing longer and more accurate warnings of specific wind mileage and the prospective devastating consequences of a Category 5 storm more than 56 hours in advance, yet officials took longer than usual to call a mandatory evacuation. Still, many households, hospitals, and nursing facilities made plans well in advance of the epic storm to shelter the most vulnerable people. In the following paragraphs, we consider the extraordinary efforts of many individuals and organizations in the aftermath of the hurricanes. We also cast a spotlight on those dark events in which errors in judgment and unfortunate responses took a disproportionate and, in some cases, devastating toll on elderly persons.

Commendable Responses and Successful Outcomes

As Margaret Mead stated, it is more often the efforts of a small group of dedicated individuals that changes the world for the better (Aycinena, 2003) than attempted large-scale efforts caught in bureaucratic tape. Several responses after Hurricane Katrina follow this adage. In the next section, we describe select examples of those who gave of their own heart and time, assisting with the recovery and aftermath response of Hurricanes Katrina and Rita.

University and faith-based organizations. Extraordinary response efforts occurred on university campuses, schools, and churches statewide. Private and public partnerships were established with Louisiana State University (LSU) in Baton Rouge, where the largest disaster field hospital in U.S. history was housed to treat and triage more than 20,000 people (Bacher, Devlin, Calongne, Duplechain, & Pertuit, 2005). In spite of a massive influx of people who lost everything, volunteers remained optimistic and dedicated. In fact, the mantra in the Pete Maravich Center, an acute field hospital on the grounds of LSU that triaged some 15,000 evacuees and treated 6,000 others, was simply "get it done" (Bacher et al., 2005, p. xiii). Next door to the acute facility, LSU housed a Special Needs Shelter, an 800-bed field nursing home that was open for 5 weeks. In the LSU field hospitals, 3,000 students, staff, and community members provided services for days and weeks after the wake of the storm. Medical and human service professionals, along with community volunteers, picked up the pieces often barricaded by the federal government. Physicians, nurses, and mental health professionals flew in from all over the country into storm-ravaged areas as well to provide direct hands-on care, many on their own dime. Angel Flight, a volunteer organization comprised of pilots who help in times of need, provided its own fuel and airplanes for emergency travel of special needs residents from the Maddox Fieldhouse on the LSU campus. This was especially helpful, as the large airlines were not providing free travel in days and weeks following Hurricane Katrina (Allen, 2007). Volunteers, including social workers and psychologists, were some of the unsung heroes of the devastation as they stepped in to respond to the unprecedented mental health, physical, and case management needs in the aftermath of the disaster.

Southern University, a largely African American university in north Baton Rouge, also took a primary role in providing shelter and medical services for the evacuees in the F. G. Clark Activity Center (Southern University, 2005). Administrators, faculty, and staff associated with Southern University's Agricultural Research Extension Center developed a disaster response plan with immediate and long-term responses to those directly affected by Hurricane Katrina. Their disaster response plan included family assistance with immediate food, shelter, and clothing needs; community renewal and restoration through assistance to local officials; and community resource and economic development through job training opportunities. Agriculture extension agents provided disaster relief and immediate assistance in the shelters, working to aid displaced families to relocate, find loved ones, and navigate the system (Williams, 2007).

The immediate and widespread responses of area churches and faith-based organizations also made a positive contribution. Baton Rouge has a vital and active church community with more than 600 churches in the Greater Baton Rouge area. In a recent study, Cain and Barthelemy (2008) found that 75% of the religious community supported relief efforts, primarily through establishment of shelters—some that operated for as long as 2 months after the hurricanes—as well as financial support, case management, linkage to benefits and services, and help finding loved ones and securing housing. Faith-based responses were cited as superior to federal and coordinated agency response such as the Federal Emergency Management Agency (FEMA), the Red Cross, and the Salvation Army (Cain & Barthelemy, 2008).

Many churches provided shelters to the more able-bodied evacuees and aided in coordination and referrals for those needing more extensive help. People used their own time, power, resources, and care to counter one of the worst catastrophes in U.S. history. There are countless stories about how regular citizens commandeered buses and boats to save hundreds of people in the floodwaters. Also, the National Guard provided heroic support in times of horror, lifting 1,200 distraught and disoriented residents—many of them older persons—out of their homes.

National and international attention focused on the plight of the thousands of Katrina evacuees. A lesser known fact is that many of them faced the separation or loss of beloved pets, an integral part of their lives for numerous individuals and families. In this context, another success story is how LSU provided an animal shelter providing care to more than 2,300 pets of evacuees. A record 2,000 animals were reunited with their owners (Bacher et al., 2005). The shelter was a massive effort of the LSU School of Veterinary Medicine and the Agricultural Center, the Louisiana Veterinary Medical Association, the Louisiana Department of Agriculture and Forestry, the Louisiana Society for the Prevention of Cruelty to Animals, and the Louisiana Animal Control Association.

Those who stayed and cared. First responders, along with countless other well-meaning citizens, did whatever they could, despite much hardship, to save others. In some cases, caregivers had to make a choice between caring for their own family or providing care for those they were responsible for at work. Many caregivers devoted tremendous energy, dedication, and love to those whom they helped relocate before the storm and the devastating flooding. Ironically, those medical personnel, law enforcement officers, and local officials who were required to stay in flooded New Orleans to maintain stability even in the throes of disaster often faced the harshest judgment from the public. Health care professionals who continued to provide care in the sweltering heat with little support were later interrogated, arrested, and faced with criminal charges. For example, Dr. Anna Pou and two nurses who provided palliative care and treatment to patients in Memorial Medical Center in New Orleans were accused of killing four critically ill patients by giving them lethal doses of pain-killing drugs to ease their suffering (known as "mercy killing"), but a grand jury failed to indict them on criminal charges related to the patients' deaths (Foster, 2007).

Nursing home administrators and staff who cared for the growing number of admissions to nursing facilities in times of crisis are to be commended for working marathon-length days and handling burgeoning caseloads. The following describes a typical scenario:

Thirty persons all at once entered the facility. Caregivers, mostly women, were lifting residents and getting them situated. We also had a couple of Jane Does; one woman (who had previously suffered a stroke) could not verbalize well. One day, the survivor uttered her family member's first name. We finally found this survivor's family, weeks after Katrina. . . . It was amazing to see people who were essentially bed-bound make a 10-hour trip on a school bus. (a social worker at the Louisiana Nursing Home Association Annual Meeting, May 3, 2006)

Nursing home residents arrived at shelters exhausted, dehydrated and hungry, and at times disoriented.

Although it is often easier to recount stories of horror, it is comforting to remember that many individuals were responsible for saving others and helping despite a fragmented system and a slow institutional response by organizations and agencies mandated to supporting the well-being of those affected by disasters. A month after Hurricane Rita, local asset building and social action were called into play, and it is safe to say that the local can-do attitude of volunteers and regular citizens made substantial contributions in the disaster response.

Problematic Responses and Negative Outcomes

Extreme weather changes may adversely affect seniors who have limited income and other limitations such as restricted driving, sight, hearing, and mobility (Hutchins & Norris, 1989). Disaster response to the elderly must take into account these and other age-related limitations and needs, such as an older person's chronic and acute physical conditions, medications, and changes in health stability brought on by unexpected emergencies. Even those who were functioning independently prior to the hurricanes of 2005 may have experienced a decline brought on by the extent of the disasters and forced relocation (Sanders, Bowie, & Bowie, 2003). In this section, we focus on problematic storm responses that led to negative outcomes for older persons. With the hope that catastrophic personal loss and suffering can be avoided or minimized through careful planning and resource management in future storms, we examine how older adults responded to storm warnings and evacuations as well as the effects of storm-related relocation on them.

Evacuation dilemmas and tragic happenings. The conditions of devastation for those who remained in the affected areas during the post-impact period were horrific. Within a day after Hurricane Katrina, the Superdome, a huge sports and entertainment arena, took in 9,000 homeless evacuees. Conditions in the disorganized and neglected Superdome were substandard, without working toilets and other supplies, including water for drinking or bathing, yet for some people, it was all there was. On the second day following the disaster, a reported 20,000 residents were in the Superdome and were required to evacuate under an order by Louisiana Governor Kathleen Blanco. Reports of crime and bedlam across the city were widespread—some realities worse than the rumors—but others, such as people with substance addictions forced out of their homes without proper support, were in impossible and grave situations for themselves and those around them (Horne, 2006). Looting and theft became widespread throughout a city that seemed all but forgotten. Perhaps chaos arose as a response to the lack of support and feeling of desperation. Reports of looting not only included regular citizens but also those charged with recovery efforts.

Some of the hardest stories relate to the most vulnerable older persons who were under the care of people who lacked or did not follow protocol, or perhaps found themselves in impossible situations in the eleventh hour. Many elderly adults were left in hospitals and nursing facilities with limited staff and relief efforts. The Associated Press (2005) reported that more than 215 bodies were recovered from hospitals and nursing homes in Hurricane Katrina's aftermath. Some died during or before the August 29th storm, or drowned in the rushing floodwaters that ensued, or perished in 100-degree heat following the disasters. Others died in transit or while waiting. The St. Rita's Nursing Home tragedy is another story of insurmountable horror and loss in which 35 residents drowned in the rising floodwaters because the facility did not evacuate prior to the storm. Among the survivors included Salvador and Mabel Mangano, the two operator-administrators who opted to stay in the facility and who were found after the flooding, paddling offsite in a boat, leaving the dead at the nursing home (Kern, 2007b). The Manganos faced criminal charges of negligent homicide related to the deaths of 35 residents and 24 counts of cruelty to the infirm for those who survived. Their ill-fated decision to shelter in place was thought at the time to be less risky than to move frail residents in a lengthy evacuation. Defense lawyers argued that there was no state or local mandatory evacuation order and the facility would have been fine had the levee protection system surrounding St. Bernard Parish not failed. Two years later, the Manganos were acquitted of these charges by a six-member jury in West Feliciana Parish (Kern, 2007a).

In retrospect, transportation planning may have been the single-most important factor in terms of getting people to safety. Pre-flood plans were secured through facility-arranged services by van, bus, and ambulance companies. Nursing homes are not unfamiliar with disaster planning, as it is a required part of their ongoing secured policies regulated by the licensing agency. One of the less familiar stories was the manner in which a facility transported the residents. Because there were few caregivers, despite the policy that certified nursing assistants and other medical personnel were required to be on buses providing transport to frail and medically compromised residents, the staff instead followed a school bus in their car. The bus, of course, was not equipped with toileting facilities for the residents, who were reportedly tied to the seats to make them stay in place (L. Sadden, personal communication, November 6, 2005). Another tragedy occurred after Hurricane Rita, when residents from Brighton Garden Home for the Aged in Texas were on a bus that caught fire. Their oxygen tanks exploded and killed 23 of the residents (Gross, Griffin, Wilder, & Lyles, 2005; Horne, 2006).

Older adults and storm warnings. Older persons may heed warnings differently than their younger counterparts. For instance, they may struggle with determining a best course of action in a crisis, compounded by confusion, added challenges of not being able to stand in line for prolonged periods, or muscular and mobility limitations in regard to taking the stairs or walking (Hutchins & Norris, 1989). Age alone is not a predictor of warning compliance

(Perry & Lindell, 1997). Compliance and ability, however, may be among two challenges for older persons because of possible physical and cognitive limitations that may interfere with successful evacuation. In Hutchins and Norris's (1989) study, more than half of community-dwelling older adults had some kind of physical limitation that required assistance if a disaster were to occur. Many seniors rely on transportation from others. Due to the late call for a mandatory evacuation in New Orleans, many did not have enough time to plan and were left to fend for themselves. In addition, many were not practical and compared the coming storm to other storms they had managed to survive (e.g., Hurricane Camille in 1965). Also, those older adults in the institutional settings that were not relocated before the storm had little in the way of options unless their families picked them up. However, mounting physical challenges limited even this option. When under the care of 24-hour skilled nursing services, one expects housing and nursing needs to be met, even when crises occur. Unfortunately, because of poor planning among a few nursing homes, many older adults had to stay in the Superdome in New Orleans or relocate to makeshift shelters across state lines.

Those most at risk had health care needs compounded by transportation barriers. Bob Johannessen, Lousiana Department of Health and Hospitals spokesman, expressed, "The elderly were much more likely to be in hospitals and nursing homes as well as possibly homebound and not able to access transportation in order to evacuate from the storm" (Associated Press, 2005, n.p.). But nothing came close to the horror of the ill-planned "Dome" following Katrina, where bathroom facilities were lacking, water and food scarce, and safety was a constant concern.

How do we know that older persons were at a disproportionate level of risk? One way is to examine reports of those who perished. Sixty-six percent of all citizens who died were over the age of 65 (Sharkey, 2006). In addition, many older survivors in need of housing and physical or mental health care were faced with their worst nightmare. They were separated from loved ones for an extended time, and one of the most pressing issues aside from essential care needs was locating loved ones of evacuated citizens. Many people who were living independently for years were virtually forced to relocate to nursing homes overnight.

Older adults, post-disaster relocation, and temporary housing. Transitions and relocation can be stressful for almost anyone under normal circumstances but especially for frail elderly adults who may have diminished control over their relocation (Oswald & Rowles, 2006). When elders are plucked from known support systems and familiar surroundings, a host of adverse psychological hardships hit, such as increased depression, pain, further impaired functioning, and a decline in perception of health, as well as increased isolation (Gallagher & Walker, 1990; Grant, Skinkle, & Lipps, 1992, as cited in Sanders et al., 2003). The urgency of relocating, or forced relocation as it is referred in the literature, requires multiple levels of readjustment for older persons. Maintaining a sense of routine and control over life choices was impossible; survival was the routine.

Relocation for those who had lost their housing meant living in the outskirts of Baton Rouge in the largest FEMA village in the state, Renaissance Village. However, placing people in temporary housing structures such as FEMA trailers has been problematic, especially for older adults. FEMA trailers, in comparison to permanent structures, are precarious and pose a risk during storms. Safety issues are an added hazard. After about 1 year of occupancy, several trailers were discovered to have the same locks (MSNBC,

2006). The materials used in the building materials are biohazardous for humans and the formaldehyde levels are unsafe (Burdeau, 2007). In addition, when power is knocked out in the summer months, which is not uncommon in Louisiana, trailers can easily reach temperatures well over 95 degrees, proving deadly to those most vulnerable, such as older residents. The blur of white, nondescript, and boxlike structures sheltering hundreds of people in crisis with minimal access to transportation and support services left elderly residents in a dangerous situation.

Older adults and nursing home relocation. Whether the devastation of Hurricanes Katrina and Rita led to premature placements in nursing homes is unanswerable. Nursing homes are rarely the desired setting for older people, yet in many cases there were few options other than a nursing home for dislocated older persons with medical needs. Whether the nursing home industry helped or exploited older survivors of the 2005 hurricanes is debatable; options were minimal and nursing home care was a dire necessity for some individuals.

There was little question about the sudden increased occupancy in areas unaffected by the storm where survivors were ultimately relocated. It has been difficult to acquire solid data on relocation statistics for older survivors. A typical facility may have had a pre-storm occupancy rate of 65%. Months following Hurricanes Katrina and Rita, this jumped to a 96% occupancy rate.

Sadly, there were few alternatives to caring for others, and even Governor Blanco noted embarrassment and shame in how slowly state authorities evacuated elderly residents from nursing homes and hospitals. The disasters essentially caused one of the largest influxes of residents into nursing homes virtually overnight; they included individuals who were relocated from other inoperable facilities and those who were living independently in their own homes at the time of the storm. Louisiana thus has the highest nursing home use rate in the nation (GOVERNING, 2004). A contributing factor is that Louisiana directs the majority of its Medicaid budget into institutional settings rather than home-based and community-based services. In fact, $4 out of every $5 goes toward nursing home care, and only $1 out of $5 goes toward community-based services (Stanford University, Center for Deliberative Democracy, 2005). Whether physically and/or mentally compromised elders will ever return to their home is yet to be seen. The massive devastation and the flimsy policy responses, together with diminished organizational support in the most storm-affected areas, make a best-case scenario outcome unlikely.

OLDER ADULTS AND NATURAL DISASTERS: IMPLICATIONS FOR CRISIS COUNSELORS

Historically, older people have been considered an at-risk group in times of intense stress or uncertainty. The elderly may be more vulnerable to the consequences of natural disasters than other age groups because they may be less likely to receive warnings, less willing to evacuate, and thus more likely to experience disruption and disturbance in their lives after a disaster and less likely to survive (see Cherry, Galea, & Silva, 2008). Other researchers doubt whether older adults are more vulnerable to disasters than other age groups (e.g., Phifer, Kaniasty, & Norris, 1988). Understanding the emergent needs and issues associated with an aging population in times of disaster is vitally important for crisis counselors as well as federal, state, and local officials who are responsible for ensuring the safety and well-being of all citizens in the aftermath of hurricanes and other catastrophic natural disasters.

Although natural disasters differ by type and impact, there are several fundamental aspects in disaster science related to older persons. Considering all that we have learned and continue to process related to these epic storms, there are lessons and practical considerations pertaining to older persons that must be borne in mind. The next section describes four points that counselors and others who may interact with older adults in a disaster context should recognize and appreciate to provide optimal assistance during a crisis.

(1) Heterogeneity of the Older Adult Population

National demographic trends have drawn increased attention to the challenges associated with meeting the complex needs of an aging population. What may be less well known is the striking heterogeneity of the senior population. The majority of those age 65 years and older are relatively healthy and live independently in the community. The probability of an illness or chronic condition that leads to disability, immobility, or chronic pain increases with age, possibly reducing one's ability to exert control over everyday activities and future events. When disaster strikes, community-dwelling older persons are less likely to access formal care and financial support compared to other age groups. They may also be slower to respond to disaster than their younger counterparts (Perry & Lindell, 1997).

In the wake of Hurricanes Katrina and Rita, we know that older people faced disproportionate hardship and challenges due to multiple factors of vulnerability. For instance, reluctance in leaving, lack of transportation, limitations in mobility, and limited resources were a problem for some. For others, physical health needs, such as respiratory and heart conditions, or mental health issues created undue hardship. For reasons such as these, older adults are often considered a special risk group for post-disaster distress (Massey, 1997), although research yields a complicated picture of disaster impact on elderly persons. Some researchers have found a significant impact of natural disasters on older adults' physical health (Phifer et al., 1988) and psychological symptoms (Phifer, 1990; Phifer & Norris, 1989). Others have argued that older adults may be less vulnerable and better able to cope with stressful situations compared to their younger counterparts (Tracy & Galea, 2006). These contrasting viewpoints underscore the heterogeneity of older people, a factor that should not be overlooked by crisis counselors and in future hurricane planning and preparation.

(2) Role of Pre-Existing Mental Conditions

Physical and psychological distress may occur in the post-disaster period for victims and non-victims alike, although few who experience a disaster develop a psychological disorder. For those who have experienced disaster-related losses, psychological symptoms are likely, but such reactions typically do not mark the beginning of clinical disorder (Phifer, 1990; Phifer & Norris, 1989). Rather, those who suffer from existing mental health symptoms, such as trait anxiety, generalized anxiety disorder, and depression, may be more vulnerable to adverse psychological sequelae in the post-disaster period than those without pre-existing conditions. For example, Weems, Piña, et al. (2007) found that negative affect states present before Hurricane Katrina predicted symptoms of posttraumatic stress and general anxiety among children and youth in the greater New Orleans area. For older adults, the presence of depressive symptoms prior to a stressful event may also contribute to subsequent depression symptoms (Kraaij, Pruymboom, & Garnefski, 2002). In addition, persons with a history of posttraumatic stress disorder, depression, anxiety disorders, and substance abuse disorders are more vulnerable to new trauma due to their latent emotionality and inability to handle the considerable demand that follows a natural disaster (Franklin, Young, & Zimmerman, 2002).

Substantial differences are seen in personal responses to stressful events such as natural disasters. Psychological vulnerability after stressful life events varies widely, although greater risk is noted for certain sociodemographic groups (e.g., women; unmarried people; those with lower education, lower income, or lower occupational status; Thoits, 1982). Thompson, Norris, and Hanacek (1993) remind us that people who live through natural disasters bring along their personal histories, including social support resources and coping skills and abilities. These individual characteristics, coupled with disaster-related burdens unique to the person and his or her situation, may ultimately determine who will be the most or least vulnerable to adverse disaster effects. The effects of a natural disaster, then, should be evaluated in the context of the life course of the individual (Norris & Murrell, 1988).

Approximately 15% to 25% of older adults in the general population are thought to have symptoms of mental health problems. Available data underestimate the mental health of older people because they tend to avoid using mental health services (Oriol, 1999). Under stressful situations such as natural disasters, there are many factors to consider that may affect mental health outcomes for older persons. For example, older persons often experience greater declines in physical health, decreased functional capacity, declines in sensory abilities, and fewer social and economic resources compared to younger people (Massey, 1997; Oriol, 1999; Phifer, 1990). The occurrence of a natural disaster such as Hurricane Katrina has an unquestionably detrimental effect on social ties and support systems, disrupting access to friends, family, and community (Weems, Watts, et al., 2007). For people of all ages, pre-existing major depressive disorder is generally thought to double the risk for developing posttraumatic stress disorder after exposure to a traumatic event (Breslau, Davis, Andreski, Peterson, & Schultz, 1997).

For older persons suffering from poor mental health, a natural disaster may worsen their condition, while physical health problems are exacerbated by changes in social functioning and disruption in care-seeking behaviors (Tracy & Galea, 2006). Careful consideration of a person's psychological state prior to a disaster is necessary for an accurate assessment of mental health in the post-disaster period. One of the poignant lessons learned from Hurricanes Katrina and Rita concerns special needs evacuees suffering from mental illness. Many did not have medical records or access to prescriptions after evacuating their homes, which further complicated assessment and treatment. In addition, those who were confused and disoriented after the storm were not able to remember the medications they were taking. Discussions on electronically registering special needs citizens' medications have occurred in the elderly service network. However, challenges in the cost, portability, updates, and organization have handicapped progress in this area of disaster preparation.

(3) Role of Prior Storm Experience and Psychological Resilience

Cherry et al. (2008) have made the point that natural disasters provide a context for examining adaptation and resilience after a significant environmental stressor and may provide new insights into successful aging. It stands to reason that older adults who live in the Gulf Coast region may have considerable prior experience with hurricanes, floods, and storms. Other potentially relevant lifetime experiences, such as military combat or other personal hardships, may also provide a backdrop for older people when dealing with current challenges in the wake of disaster. Previous hurricanes and storms, coupled with other unique life experiences, may serve a protective function for older adults, insulating them from psychological distress and strong emotional reactions to subsequent natural disasters. This positive view of prior storm experience finds its conceptual roots in Eysenck's (1983) inoculation hypothesis, which purports that stress exposure actually increases people's ability to tolerate future stresses. Thus, older people are thought to fare better than one might expect and be more resilient in the event of a future disaster as a result of their earlier flood and hurricane experiences. Some studies have found that past experiences are protective factors among older people by reducing stress following a similar disaster later in life (Ferraro, 2003; Knight, Gatz, Heller, & Bengtson, 2000).

Findings showing adaptation and resilience among older adults in the post-disaster period lend support to the inoculation perspective (Norris & Murrell, 1988). Moreover, such findings imply that those who may meet the criteria for successful aging continue to thrive despite the obstacles, hurdles, and adversity they may have to overcome in the post-disaster recovery period. According to Phifer (1990), several factors may account for the relative resilience of older adults. Older people may have a higher incidence of past resolved stressful experiences, so in a general sense, they are "experienced" victims (Norris & Murrell, 1988). Older people may have rich histories of coping with prior crises that lessen the impact of an immediate disaster. They may also experience fewer life changes within a given time interval compared to younger adults, resulting in a lower incidence of unresolved stressful experiences in their daily lives. For younger adults, the simultaneous occurrence of other life stressors and/or crises may exacerbate the impact of a given crisis, leaving them overwhelmed and vulnerable to the adverse effects of a natural disaster.

From a practical vantage point, those resilient older persons who adapt and cope successfully in the wake of a natural disaster may be in a unique position to offer assistance. For instance, they could be a valuable resource for post-disaster victim advocacy and other less physically strenuous disaster relief efforts in communities that have suffered natural disasters (Norris & Murrell, 1988; Thompson et al., 1993). Moving from a vision of older people as victims to those with remarkable resilience and lessons to teach younger generations may be the way to learn productive aging and unlearn ageism. Remembering those older persons in the community who have the capacity and interest to be part of the solution is a critical piece of the puzzle for local and state officials who are responsible for disaster planning and preparedness efforts. Morrow (1999) has made the point that just because persons may have been viewed as vulnerable or disenfranchised in the past does not suggest that they are unwilling to be part of the process. She illuminates women as those who often provide ongoing care but are excluded in formal disaster planning, management, response, and leadership. Much could be said about older people, as they may serve essential roles in responding to disasters in terms of experience and support. In the shelters, it was common to see older people, neighbors, and families supporting each other in the aftermath of disaster. An older man disclosed to a first responder that his 90-year-old tenant urged him to get to the second floor of the apartment and to be airlifted with her out of the window. He said without her help, he would not be alive (Allen, 2007).

(4) Uncertain Long-Range Effects on the Aging Population

We are still witnessing the effects of the hurricanes of 2005 and will continue to do so for some time. Kilijanek and Drabek (1979) note that loss can be particularly hard for older persons, particularly those who are frail and impoverished as they face compounded losses; loss of sentimental items is found to result in "heightened sense of deprivation for older as compared to younger victims" (p. 556). These researchers paint a particularly bleak picture that one of the "detrimental consequence[s] of disaster is impaired physical functioning" (p. 555). Older persons may also experience what the authors refer to as a "pattern of neglect," whereby older victims are less likely than younger victims to receive formal and informal support. Nearly 20% of sampled participants received no support from nine potential resources (family, friends, religious organizations, American Red Cross, Salvation Army, other voluntary organizations, governmental agencies, strangers, and employers).

Disaster literature cites the impact and definition of recovery in the way in which the system returns to normalcy or a state of equilibrium after disasters (Friesema, Caporaso, Goldstein, Lineberry, & McCleary, 1979). Such equilibrium usually depends on geographic regions, status of unemployment, economic growth or decline, health, and hospitalization rates. Normalcy is compromised when many are not able to return to their original homes. The aftermath effect may make a temporary situation permanent (Friesema et al., 1979). Such a state is evident at this juncture in New Orleans, by the reality of more than 40,000 citizens continuing to reside in FEMA trailers 3 years after the storm.

One of the long-standing arguments that remains is whether Hurricane Katrina was a natural or man-made disaster. Science and experience tells us that it was both. Due to the poor maintenance of levee systems as well as delays and barriers in responding, the response to a massive catastrophic event was weakened. Zakour and Harrell (2003) raise dimensions of environmental disadvantages of lower income people in urban settings. Those who live in older, urban areas with declining physical infrastructures such as cheaper rents are stratified by income and class (Zakour & Harrell, 2003). Vulnerability is constructed not only by chance but also by social construction and economic circumstances of life (Morrow, 1999). Certain groups of people will always be disproportionately at higher risk. These include but are not limited to the poor, elderly, disabled, ethnic minorities, single parents—people living in high-risk areas with mounting environmental threats. As Poulshock and Cohen (1975) suggested, "the study of a population group and the community it lives in under stress of a natural disaster yields significant insights into the behavior of that population group under more normal circumstances" (p. 360).

PRACTICAL IMPLICATIONS

- Older adults comprise a vulnerable population, and efforts should be made to ensure their safety in disasters.
- Sustainable disaster planning involves a collaboration between both local and federal government agencies.
- Community agencies and local individuals should be an integral part of disaster planning.
- It is necessary to develop a registry of special needs patients to plan evacuations and transfers to special needs shelters.

CONCLUSION AND FUTURE DIRECTIONS

Although disasters may be caused by natural events, the preparation and responses to disasters are based on human efforts. With older people soon to account for one fifth of the total population in the United States, planning for the care and support of older persons is an absolute necessity. From a global perspective, convergent evidence arises from other natural disasters to underscore the vulnerability of the elderly in large-scale emergency situations. For example, older adults were more likely to die in the 2003 heat waves in Europe, and older persons in Indonesia were also less likely to survive the Indian Ocean tsunami of 2004 (World Health Organization, 2007). These death statistics, together with other public health indicators, highlight the need for policies to ensure the safety and well-being of elderly persons and other vulnerable groups following a disaster.

Sustainable disaster plans require involvement at the local as well as federal level (Morrow, 1999), yet planning for disasters in high-risk areas of Louisiana remains very formative. Khanna (2006) further indicates that nursing home evacuation plans, although required and executed as part of standing policy, are often loosely followed, based on a handshake or a verbal agreement than on formalized, implemented, and practiced policy. One of the lessons learned and reviewed in this chapter has been the essential role that local citizens and organizations played in rescue efforts and meeting the immediate needs of first responders and evacuees. Hurricanes Katrina and Rita have shown us that local individuals and communities rose to meet an unprecedented challenge and emerged as clear heroes. Thus, an integral part of disaster planning is the involvement of local individuals and community organizations. In short, advocacy is called for through educational campaigns about risks related to older persons whereby citizens take on an active role for mutual support. In addition, as discussed in this chapter's section on problematic responses and negative outcomes, it is necessary for hurricane- and disaster-prone areas to develop a registry of special needs patients to better plan safe and supportive evacuations and transfers to special needs shelters. Some regions in Florida have required efforts coordinated by the state's Agencies on Aging. In Louisiana, no such coordination exists to date (Poiley, 2007).

Because older people may either delay action to evacuate based on existing patterns of neglect and reluctance to use formal services, extra vigilance is needed to assess the location of older persons in the communities. Securing consensual organizational responses and networking between what has often been referenced to as "separate silos of human service delivery" will better serve those in need after a disaster. However, we must also consider predisposing medical, physical, and cognitive conditions that may shape recovery from disaster. It is clearly a priority to formulate better plans for people residing in institutions, such as hospitals, nursing homes, and structured living arrangements (e.g., assisted living communities and homes for the aged). Working to maximize independence and get support well in advance of a storm is essential.

Following Hurricane Andrew, Silverman and Weston (1995) urged that any comprehensive disaster plan must include attention to the special care of older and frailer members in the community. Also, for the elderly who may be hard to reach, special outreach activities should continue well after the disaster has ended. Disasters are likely to occur in the future, but they do not have to be deadly for older members of society if we plan appropriately. It is time for society to reconsider the ways of treating the elderly and the support provided for their care. It is important to develop strict policies on their standard of care in disaster situations by clear planning and relocation strategies.

In closing, the 2005 hurricanes opened the eyes of Americans to the consequences of poor disaster planning in relation to the needs of older persons affected by a natural disaster. From the reality and risk of relocating citizens in buses that were not safe enough to transport them over long, poorly planned routes, to the unparalleled tragedy of St. Rita's Nursing Home, the concerns about poor planning and disaster management far outweigh any useful efforts that were made. Still, it is important to remember the countless stories of survival and humanitarian efforts in which people put the needs of others before their own.

REFERENCES

Allen, P. D. (2007). Social work in the aftermath of disaster: Reflections from a special needs shelter on the LSU campus. *Reflections, 13,* 127–137.

Associated Press. (2005, October 23). *Rich or poor, most Katrina victims were seniors.* Retrieved October 26, 2007, from http://www.msnbc.msn.com/id/9797302/

Aycinena, P. (2003). *From Margaret Mead to Caesar's wife. EDA Café.* Retrieved February 9, 2009, from http://www10.edacafe.com/nbc/articles/view_weekly.php?articleid=209270

Bacher, R., Devlin, T., Calongne, K., Duplechain, J., & Pertuit, S. (2005). *LSU in the eye of the storm: A university model for disaster response.* Retrieved August 30, 2007, from http://www.lsu.edu/pa/book/EYEofTheSTORMtxt.pdf

Breslau, N., Davis, G. C., Andreski, P., Peterson, E. L., & Schultz, L. R. (1997). Sex differences in posttraumatic stress disorder. *Archives of General Psychiatry, 54,* 1044–1048.

Burdeau, C. (2007). *FEMA moves to get people out of trailers.* Retrieved August 22, 2007, from http://www.boston.com/news/nation/articles/2007/08/10/

Cain, D. S., & Barthelemy, J. (2008). Tangible and spiritual relief after the storm: The religious community responds to Katrina. *Journal of Social Service Research, 34,* 9–42.

Cherry, K. E., Galea, S., & Silva, J. L. (2008). Successful aging and natural disasters: Role of adaptation and resiliency in late life. In M. Hersen & A. M. Gross (Eds.), *Handbook of clinical psychology. Vol. 1: Adults* (pp. 810–833). New York: John Wiley.

Eysenck, H. J. (1983). Stress, disease, and personality: "The inoculation effect." In C. L. Cooper (Ed.), *Stress research* (pp. 121–146). New York: John Wiley.

Ferraro, F. R. (2003). Psychological resilience in older adults following the 1997 flood. *Clinical Gerontologist, 26*, 139–143.

Foster, M. (2007, July 25). No indictment for Pou. *The Advocate*, pp. A1, A6.

Franklin, C. L., Young, D., & Zimmerman, M. (2002). Psychiatric patients' vulnerability in the wake of the September 11th terrorist attacks. *Journal of Nervous and Mental Disease, 190*, 833–838.

Friesema, H. P., Caporaso, J., Goldstein, G., Lineberry, R., & McCleary, R. (1979). *Aftermath.* Beverly Hills, CA: Sage.

Gallagher, E., & Walker, G. (1990). Vulnerability of nursing home residents during relocations and renovations. *Journal of Aging Studies, 4*, 31–46.

GOVERNING. (2004). *Government Performance Project: A case of neglect.* Retrieved September 13, 2007, from http://www.governing.com/GPP/2004/long.htm

Grant, P., Skinkle, R., & Lipps, G. (1992). The impact of an institutional relocation of nursing home residents requiring a high level of care. *The Gerontologist, 32*, 834–842.

Gross, J., Griffin, L., Wilder, C., & Lyles, T. (2005). Storm and crisis: The evacuation; luck and fate seated victims on a doomed bus. *New York Times.* Retrieved August 23, 2007, from http://select.nytimes.com/gst/abstract.html?res=F30E13F63B540C708CDDA90994DD404482&n=Top%2fReference%2fTimes%20Topics%2fSubjects%2fB%2fBuse

Hancock, M. (2006). Many in Louisiana, Texas lament Rita "amnesia." *USA Today.* Retrieved December 21, 2007, from http://www.usatoday.com/news/nation/2006-01-25-rita_x.htm

Horne, J. (2006). *Breach of faith: Hurricane Katrina and the near death of a great American city.* New York: Random House.

Hutchins, G. L., & Norris, F. H. (1989). Life changes in the disaster recovery period. *Environment and Behavior, 21*(1), 33–56.

Kern, E. (2007a, September 8). Manganos not guilty. *The Advocate*, pp. A1, A4.

Kern, E. (2007b, August 30). St. Rita's relived. *The Advocate*, pp. B1–B2.

Khanna, R. (2006). *Nursing homes remain ill prepared for disaster.* Retrieved August 2, 2007, from http://www.chron.com/disp/story.mpl/front/4191315.html

Kilijanek, T. S., & Drabek, T. E. (1979). Assessing long-term impacts of a natural disaster: A focus on the elderly. *The Gerontologist, 19*, 555–566.

Knight, B. G., Gatz, M., Heller, K., & Bengtson, V. L. (2000). Age and emotional response to the Northridge earthquake: A longitudinal analysis. *Psychology and Aging, 15*, 627–634.

Kraaij, V., Pruymboom, E., & Garnefski, N. (2002). Cognitive coping and depressive symptoms in the elderly: A longitudinal study. *Aging and Mental Health, 6*, 275–281.

Massey, B. A. (1997). Victims or survivors? A three-part approach to working with older adults in disaster. *Journal of Geriatric Psychiatry, 3*, 193–202.

Morrow, B. H. (1999). Identifying and mapping community vulnerability. *Disasters, 23*(1), 1–18.

MSNBC. (2006). *FEMA says same key opens many trailers: Agency to replace locks on up to 118,000 homes of Katrina evacuees.* Retrieved September 13, 2007, from http://www.msnbc.msn.com/id/14349568

National Hurricane Center (2007-01-23). November 2005 Atlantic Tropical Weather Summary. NOAA. Retrieved January 20, 2009, from http://www.nhc.noaa.gov/archive/2005/tws/MIATWSAT_nov_final.shtml

Norris, F. H., & Murrell, S. A. (1988). Prior experience as a moderator of disaster impact on anxiety symptoms in older adults. *American Journal of Community Psychology, 16*, 665–683.

Oriol, W. (1999). *Psychosocial issues for older adults in disasters.* Retrieved February 9, 2009, from http://www.ce-credit.com/articles/100113/psychosocialOlderAdultsDisasters.pdf

Oswald, F., & Rowles, G. D. (2006). Beyond the relocation trauma in old age: New trends in today's elders' residential decisions. In H.-W. Wahl, C. Tesch-Römer, & A. Hoff (Eds.), *New dynamics in old age: Environmental and societal perspectives* (pp. 127–152). Amityville, NY: Baywood.

Perry, R. W., & Lindell, M. K. (1997). Aged citizens in the warning phase of disasters: Re-examining the evidence. *International Journal of Aging and Human Development, 44,* 257–267.

Phifer, J. F. (1990). Psychological distress and somatic symptoms after natural disaster: Differential vulnerability among older adults. *Psychology and Aging, 5,* 412–420.

Phifer, J. F., Kaniasty, K. Z., & Norris, F. H. (1988). The impact of natural disaster on the health of older adults: A multiwave prospective study. *Journal of Health and Social Behavior, 29,* 65–78.

Phifer, J. F., & Norris, F. N. (1989). Psychological symptoms in older adults following a natural disaster: Nature, timing, duration, and course. *Journal of Gerontology: Social Sciences, 44,* S207–S217.

Poiley, J. (2007). *Evacuating elderly a major concern for EOC managers.* Retrieved August 23, 2007, from http://www.baynews9.com/content/36/2007/7/24/270344.html#

Poulshock, S. W., & Cohen, E. S. (1975). The elderly in the aftermath of a disaster. *The Gerontologist, 15*(4), 357–361.

Sanders, S., Bowie, S. L., & Bowie, Y. D. (2003). Lessons learned on forced relocation of older adults: The impact of Hurricane Andrew on health, mental health, and social support of public housing residents. *Journal of Gerontological Social Work, 40*(4), 23–35.

Sharkey, P. (2006). Survival and death in New Orleans: An empirical look at the human impact of Katrina. *Journal of Black Studies, 37*(4), 482–501.

Silverman, M., & Weston, M. (1995). Lessons learned from Hurricane Andrew: Recommendations for care of the elderly in long-term care. *Southern Medical Journal, 88*(6), 603–609.

Southern University. (2005, September 3). *Southern University aids evacuees.* Retrieved August 19, 2007, from http://www.subr.edu/hurricanerelief/releasesept3.htm

Stanford University, Center for Deliberative Democracy. (2005). *Louisiana healthcare issues.* Retrieved September 13, 2007, from http://cdd.stanford.edu/docs/2005/btp-cities/batonrouge.pdf

Thoits, P. A. (1982). Life stress, social support, and psychological vulnerability: Epidemiological considerations. *Journal of Community Psychology, 10,* 341–362.

Thompson, M. P., Norris, F. H., & Hanacek, B. (1993). Age differences in the psychological consequences of Hurricane Hugo. *Psychology and Aging, 8,* 606–616.

Tracy, M., & Galea, S. (2006). Post-traumatic stress disorder and depression among older adults after a disaster: The role of ongoing trauma and stressors. *Public Policy & Aging Report, 16*(2), 16–19.

Uekert, B. K. (2005). *Future trends in state courts: Elder abuse and neglect.* Retrieved January 8, 2008, from http://www.ncsconline.org/WC/Publications/Trends/2005/EldAbuNeglectTrends2005.pdf

U.S. Department of Health and Human Services, Administration on Aging. (2007). *Profiles of older Americans.* Retrieved January 8, 2008, from http://www.agingcarefl.org/aging/AOA-2007profile.pdf

Weems, C. F., Piña, A. A., Costa, N. M., Watts, S. E., Taylor, L. K., & Cannon, M. F. (2007). Predisaster trait anxiety and negative affect predict posttraumatic stress in youths after Hurricane Katrina. *Journal of Counseling and Clinical Psychology, 75,* 154–159.

Weems, C. F., Watts, S. E., Marsee, M. A., Taylor, L. K., Costa, N. M., Cannon, M. F., et al. (2007). The psychosocial impact of Hurricane Katrina: Contextual differences in psychological symptoms, social support, and discrimination. *Behaviour Research and Therapy, 45,* 2295–2306.

Williams, K. (2007). *Southern University Ag Center responds to Hurricane Katrina.* Retrieved August 23, 2007, from http://www.suagcenter.com/News%20Archives/Sept-Dec2005/SUAREC_Responds.html

World Health Organization. (2007). *10 facts on ageing and the life course.* Retrieved December 21, 2007, from http://www.who.int/features/factfiles/ageing/en/index.html

Zakour, M. J., & Harrell, E. B. (2003). Access to disaster services: Social work interventions for vulnerable populations. *Journal of Social Service Research, 30*(2), 27–54.

The Spiritual Dimensions of Caring for People Affected by Disasters

Harriet G. McCombs

The spiritual responses to trauma closely resemble psychological responses and may be effectively addressed in a counseling relationship. Spirituality has traditionally been a source of support for people who seek to make meaning of their lives and as a coping mechanism for those who feel estranged from the core aspects of their lives. The spiritual dimensions of coping have been a long-standing interest of psychiatry, social work, psychology, pastoral care, and counseling. In *Care of Mind, Care of Spirit*, Gerald May (1982), a psychiatrist and spiritual director, advanced the imperative to respond to both the mental health and spiritual needs of clients while honoring the distinction between the disciplines. It is not surprising that spirituality has also been a source of support for coping with the distress caused by disasters and tragedies. People who seek counseling as a result of experiencing disasters have a variety of needs, including making sense of the tragic event and alleviating psychological and spiritual distress.

Counseling that incorporates spirituality offers clients an environment and framework for finding meaning, relief from grief and emptiness associated with loss of possessions, and establishing new connections. It addresses suffering in a real way, confirming that suffering can have significance and meaning. The ability of counselors to incorporate spiritual recovery and connection is critical. It is in the movement toward recovery that people are able to draw on spiritual resources and act on their deeply held beliefs to resolve soul-searching issues. Assessing the impact of the event through clients' stories provides an opening to explore and affirm the spiritual interpretations of the event. The disaster is not a static event. The telling of the story and the commitment to successfully resolve the coping tasks are shaped and reshaped by new interpretations of the meaning of the incident in their lives. Counselors can affirm client spiritual values, accept their venting, assist in the discovery of the personal meaning of loss and suffering, and redefine hopes and goals in a context of client spiritual beliefs and practices. Counseling environments for spiritual affirmation and support in which clients tell their stories and articulate their core beliefs, especially those around suffering, and the value placed on material possessions and estrangement from God and others are much needed. The task of the counselor is to discover resources to explore spiritual beliefs within effective counseling models.

CHAPTER HIGHLIGHTS

+ Enhances a counselor's abilities to assess and support adaptive spiritual attitudes and behaviors that facilitate coping after disasters;

+ Provides an understanding of the different dimensions of spirituality, how they are affected by a disaster, and tools for addressing them in counseling;

+ Illustrates the importance of incorporating clients' spirituality as part of an overall counseling strategy to address trauma. Brief excerpts from client statements and design methodology from large-scale counseling programs are included as examples of how spirituality emerges in counseling; and

+ Discusses the adoption of a spiritual strategy that complements and enhances existing therapeutic techniques to support client recovery.

TRAUMA AND SPIRITUALITY

Mental health practitioners agree that trauma refers to "a wide range of intensely stressful experiences that involve exposure to levels of danger and fear that exceeds normal capacity to cope" (Schlenger, 2006, slide 3). Disasters are by nature intensely stressful and exceed the normal range of daily experiences. They destroy the anchoring points of reality in a swift, devastating, and numbing fashion. Whether disasters are natural or human-made, large-scale hurricanes or local school shootings, the felt experience is pervasive, invasive, and brutal, because they dislodge established concepts about life and how it is arranged. Tragic local events can produce felt experiences with an effect similar to that created by large-scale disasters. Events like school shootings may create distress and suffering in such a way that the entire community is redefined by the event. The impact of events, like those of September 11, 2001, the 2005 hurricanes Katrina and Rita, and the 2008 Midwest tornadoes and floods, can overwhelm the minds and spirits of individuals, communities, and the entire nation. For many people, disasters erase beliefs in an orderly and predictable world and the existence of a benevolent deity who was involved in protecting innocent people from danger and maintaining order over natural phenomena.

The client's usual skills for comprehending and managing are stretched beyond limits and sometimes fall apart. People are often unable to make sense of the event in a cognitive or emotional way, resulting in enormous tension in managing the internal or external world (Antonovsky, 1987). In addition, people may experience frustration with those who do not understand or empathize with the depth of their experience and how they interpret the event. The spiritual malaise engendered by disasters brings many clients to counseling.

An important challenge is to distinguish between spiritual and psychological aspects of coping with trauma. Spirituality is an extensive system of core values and beliefs about an individual's relationship with what is transcendent, divine, and sacred (i.e., God). Within the spiritual system are interconnected constructs about human nature, the purpose of life, morality, and life after death. Knowledge of spiritual beliefs (e.g., the existence and nature of a deity or multiple deities, a personal or universal force for good, the origin and end of life, and issues of morality) facilitates listening and understanding in the counseling process. Other helpful constructs are human nature, relationships with others, meaning of life, the spiritual aspects of human personalities, intervention by spiritual powers on behalf of human beings, and the sacredness of times and spaces. Spirituality includes the possibility that life may have a central purpose such as helping to make the world a better place, having a relationship with God, obtaining liberation from the cycle of rebirth, developing inner virtues, or learning to choose good over evil. It is expressed as an enduring way of living that is in alignment with one's view of God, human nature, purpose, and morality and attempts to fulfill one's belief about life's purpose. Spirituality organizes life around those values, people, and things that provide meaning, direct the purpose of life, and help the individual connect to a larger reality.

Awareness of the distinguishing features of disasters can increase counseling effectiveness. It is important to assess the impact on clients in the context of the disaster's cause, intensity, duration of exposure, and availability of medical and psychological support (Benedek, Fullerton, & Ursano, 2007). The interaction of the specific features of the event and client resiliency produces a variety of coping strategies. The majority of the U.S. population is exposed to at least one potentially traumatic event in a lifetime, and many are exposed to more than one. What is perhaps most intriguing is that across a broad range of large-scale, potentially traumatic events, most of those who are exposed experience some distress (e.g., intense fear, anger, sorrow, uncertainty) but do not have any clinically significant mental health sequelae (Schlenger, 2006). However, in the absence of clinically significant mental health sequelae, other significant effects may be overlooked, one of which is spiritual distress: "Because human beings are spiritual beings, trauma affects our relationship with God, and our relationship with God contributes to our healing from trauma" (Day et al., 2006, p. 2).

SPIRITUALITY AND PSYCHOLOGICAL RESPONSES

Counseling requires assessing spirituality, the consequences of the event, and the coping skills and resources of clients. Not all individuals are traumatized by disasters. Most people will experience mild, transient distress; some will experience more persistent symptoms; and a smaller group will develop psychiatric illnesses such as posttraumatic stress disorder or major depression. Those who experience persistent symptoms may not seek counseling. Of those who seek counseling, there are those who will not want to address their spiritual distress. They may feel they that are unable to articulate the distress, do not feel comfortable with a counselor who may not share or understand their spirituality, or feel that they do not have a right to feel as distressed as they do. The importance of integrating spirituality with the experience of trauma thus becomes important (Day et al., 2006), particularly when a trauma is disaster related (Kajeski, 1998; McGee, 2005). The recent and growing focus on the integration of spirituality with counseling has made this once marginalized approach to counseling more mainstream and acceptable. The spiritual dimensions of health, especially mental health and trauma, have posed a challenge for theorists, researchers, and practitioners alike. Yet the conclusions are the same: Care of the mind and the spirit are necessary aspects in counseling people who have experienced disaster-associated trauma. Clients need to be encouraged to articulate their experiences and interpretations of the cause, intensity, duration of exposure, and available sources of support. Studies have shown that people who have a strong spiritual foundation are better able to cope and respond to a vast array of devastating change (Pargament, 1997).

When people are faced with devastating events, they often turn to strongly held spiritual beliefs or faith. After the tragic events of September 11, 2001, a survey was taken that asked people how they were coping. Ninety percent of the respondents indicated they coped by turning to their faith (Schuster et al., 2001). It is in the spiritual realm that people find meaning and direction when assumptions about an orderly and reliable world need reconstructing.

Disasters are disruptive to long-held beliefs, and they create spiritual tension and distress that raise questions such as, Where was God in all this? How do we pray or feel ourselves in God's presence when one of the fundamental elements of trauma is that trust has been ruptured? (McGee, 2005). Clients may often struggle with beliefs about their mortality, the spiritual power that influences human behavior, natural phenomena, and most importantly their futures. These beliefs and their associated values and practices are highly personal. The illusive and highly personal nature of spirituality is a major reason why it often goes unaddressed in counseling sessions. Clients' psychological and spiritual distress related to questions about mortality and meaning of life (e.g., Is there life after death?) can be effectively resolved in a safe environment where spiritual interpretations and spiritual resources for recovery are openly addressed.

When spirituality is affirmed in counseling, clients are empowered to draw on their spiritual resources to regain hope and to reconnect. More important, it links the traumatizing experience to a larger, more stable reality. This larger reality is often described as the Sacred, the Divine, the Source, the Supreme Being, and/or God.

To open the door to sacred, spiritual dimensions within counseling requires an appreciation and respect for the clients' belief about the ability of spiritual resources to transform brokenness in human nature and the world into a new wholeness. This appreciation forms the basis of a spiritual strategy that allows counselors to identify and integrate spiritual perspectives into their existing therapeutic approaches to grief, loss, and trauma. It also provides tools for managing and talking about loss, abandonment, death, and dying in the context of hope, everyday kindnesses, good and evil, and miracles.

FAITH COMMUNITIES AND TRAUMA

Spiritual responses are closely related to psychological responses. However, the themes of disassociation, grief, and anger take on a broader, deeper, more urgent meaning. They are likely to be expressed in terms of sense of direction, meaning, and purpose in life; feelings of connectedness with oneself, with others, and with God; and clarification on what is trivial and what is truly vital in life (Miller & Thorsen, 1999). Clients with a mature connection to faith communities often have a strong support network in these communities that can facilitate their recovery. Tragic local events can produce felt experiences with a similar effect to that of large-scale disasters. Events such as school shootings may create distress and suffering in such a way that the entire community may be redefined by the event.

In the aftermath of a disaster, client beliefs may be changed through exposure to new and often conflicting spiritual interpretations of the critical incident. Conflicting spiritual attributions of the cause of massive loss and devastation are often the source of the clients' distress and anger. This is especially true when responsibility for the event is shifted or financial restitution is denied because events are interpreted as "acts of God." The following excerpts are illustrative of this conflict.

> Buffalo Creek was the scene of a major flood in 1972. Coal waste dumped in a mountain stream—on a hillside in West Virginia by the Pittston Coal Company. After several days of rain and four days after having been declared "satisfactory" by a federal mine inspector, the dam burst. The resulting flood unleashed approximately 132 million gallons of black waste water, over 30 ft high, upon the residents of 16 coal mining hamlets in Buffalo Creek Hollow. Out of a population of 5,000 people, 125 people were killed, 1,121 were injured, and over 4,000 were left homeless. (*Buffalo Creek Flood*, 2008)

> Three separate commissions studying the disaster—federal, state, and citizen— found that Buffalo Mining had blatantly disregarded standard safety practices. The Pittston Coal Company officials called the flood an "Act of God" and said the dam was simply "incapable of holding the water God poured into it." Rev. Charles Crumm, a disabled miner from the Buffalo Creek area who testified before the Citizens' Commission to Investigate the Buffalo Creek Disaster, disagreed that it was an act of God. (West Virginia Division of Culture and History, 2008)

Suffering, trauma, stress, grief, and loss are all part of the human condition, yet reducing them to a form of physical or psychological pain denies that they can have any spiritual significance. Moreover, it overlooks important spiritual resources such as stories, rituals, and communities to alleviate suffering. For centuries, spiritual symbols, beliefs, and spiritual practices have been used to make sense of and to restore wellness after traumatic events. Long before Abraham Maslow (1954) developed his theory of personality describing a hierarchy of needs, Jennie Wilson wrote a hymn, "Hold to God's Unchanging Hand," as a roadmap to recovery for millions during the difficult post–Civil War years. Addressing the need for hope, her assessment and counsel were presented through a commonly held spiritual framework. She encouraged people to draw on an unchanging spiritual resource to find meaning associated with the swift loss of possessions and connections.

> *Time is filled with swift transition,*
> *Naught of earth unmoved can stand,*
> *Build your hopes on things eternal,*
> *Hold to God's unchanging hand.*

CONTINUITY AND NEWLY FOUND SPIRITUALITY

When critical incidents stir up a deeper spiritual awareness and stimulate spiritual growth or a newly found spirituality, people attempt to integrate these new aspects of spirituality by seeking counseling within their faith communities. Spiritual caregivers within faith communities are ideal first responders in disasters. For example, the purpose of the Johns Hopkins Center for Public Health Preparedness is to provide disaster mental health training and psychological first aid for spiritual caregivers (McCabe et al., 2008). The training is an important effort to engage and prepare the faith community to participate in the early stages of disaster relief. Faith-based organizations may provide emergency relief for emotional trauma but may not be able to address the psychological distress in a sustained manner. Although faith communities available to share empowering beliefs and supportive networks, not all clients will be connected with a faith community.

Counselors, not associated with a particular faith community, are capable of providing support. A sense of alienation often emerges once the initial shock has passed and volunteers have moved on and forgotten about the clients' continuing needs. Clients may discover that their faith communities have shifted their focus to other aspects of community service and are unable to provide trauma counseling. Moreover, long-term post-disaster pastoral counseling related to trauma is rare. The depth of clients' needs, the level of pastoral demands, and support for seeking help outside the congregations may often combine to create barriers to long-term counseling. In the absence of a supportive faith-based network to assist them in integrating new aspects of spirituality into their recovery process, clients may turn to mental health counselors for continuing support.

Day et al. (2006) have developed a curriculum for faith communities interested in supporting trauma survivors. Although their work is about interpersonal traumatic events, it does lend itself to natural disasters. Natural disasters may not always have the elements of betrayal, victimization, and exploitation, as do interpersonal traumas: "However, at the spiritual level where the trauma survivor feels betrayed by God for the violation of his or her safety, the distinction between natural disasters and interpersonal trauma fades" (Day et al., 2006, p. viii). Day et al. present a trauma model based on seven principles. Most relevant here is the fifth principle: Respect, Information, Connection, and Hope (RICH), which they describe as the four most important things a helper can offer survivors. They provide a model illustrating how trauma disrupts relationships and how it can lead to spiritual distress because of a sense of disconnection from God, loss of meaning, disrupted feeling and faith, disrupted judgment, disrupted spiritual beliefs and needs, and disconnection between the self and the body. They also illustrate ways in which spirituality can promote healing and how recovery from trauma can lead to spiritual growth.

THE TRAUMA STORY

The recovery process centers on the telling of the trauma story. The focus on recovery, wholeness, and connection is critical and begins with assessing the relative impact of the event on those who experienced it. A counselor may readily identify overt physical and psychological symptoms such as sleep disturbance, anger, and increased use of tobacco or alcohol, but fail to hear the trauma story and assess the client's spiritual resiliency. It is important to listen to the story for both the conflicts and resources that allow clients to explore the soul-searching questions (e.g., Why me? How could God let this happen?). Trauma affects spiritual thought, motivation, and feeling. Clients with a strong spiritual orientation may experience a level of spiritual distress in which they must reconcile holding onto a belief in a benevolent God who has presumably abandoned them but is the source of hope for recovery, wholeness, and reconnection with life. The excerpt below from a disaster survivor is illustrative of an unwavering spiritual faith.

> A story of divine support: James, a 76-year-old man displaced from New Orleans to one of the distant suburbs of Atlanta without any family, possessions, or transportation to get to the disaster services in the downtown area of the city, states with tentative confidence: "I've lost everything. I still have my life. And my health. I don't know how. But, I'm going to make it. With the help of the Lord, I will. I will."

In James's brief expression of aspects of his spirituality, he reveals his resource for overcoming loss and isolation, as well as the source of his hope and confidence.

The cause, exposure, intensity, duration, and resources available in disasters have differing repercussions on groups affected by the event. For example, there are differences in exposure among groups of people who experienced the attack on the World Trade Center. Some people were evacuated, others narrowly escaped, some lost loved ones, and others by divine providence were able to avoid the event altogether.

As clients begin to tell their stories, counselors can assist by exploring and affirming the spiritual interpretations of the characteristic. The following extract presents a portion of a client's story in which the protection of his son-in-law was attributed to divine providence.

> A story of divine grace: J.W. is a 56-year-old New Jersey man who views spirituality as central to his life. His son-in-law worked for a prestigious firm in the World Trade Center. J.W. experiences great difficulty in telling his story because of the strong sense of undeserved divine protection and gratitude. "Every time I had asked my son-in-law to go fishing, he always said he had to go to work—always— he always had to go into work. I was just about tired of asking. Then I asked again. I asked him the week before (the event). He surprised me and said yes. We went fishing that day. If my son-in-law had gone into work that day . . ." (J.W., personal communication, September 28, 2001)

He was overwhelmed by the timing of the incident and his depth, humility, and gratitude to a divine power for averting the loss and suffering.

Among those who experienced Hurricanes Katrina and Rita, there were groups that evacuated and experienced the event at a distance but lost their homes, rode out the storm and experienced the event directly, narrowly escaped, left their homes for a month, and/or never went back. Although there are differences, there are also similarities in their stories such as symptoms of hypervigilance when the sky darkens and profound expressions of deep gratitude when they describe the devastation and what could have happened.

Subsequent coping tasks are shaped by spiritual beliefs and through recalling the horror or grace of the trauma story while reinterpreting its meaning for their lives. Clients may resolve the immediate distress by viewing disasters as "acts of God" or accepting that there was nothing anyone could do to avert it and "giving thanks because it could have been worse." The client may interpret the critical incident as divine retribution, divine punishment, a divine gift, or "a second chance at life." Adopting spiritual interpretations requires adopting a plan of recovery that is consistent with those interpretations: There is a need to resolve spiritual issues with God and align future actions with those interpretations. For some, the critical incidents are viewed as powerful transforming lessons in accepting suffering as a part of life, fighting injustice, accepting the changes with grace, building safer communities, or offering forgiveness.

The trauma story and need of each client is unique because of the intensity and duration of exposure. For example, effects of the bombing of Oklahoma City in 1995 included injuries, death, damage, and loss, which were experienced differently by the people who lived and worked there (Smith, Christiansen, Vincent, & Hann, 1999). The Oklahoma hospital staff's experience was different from the experience of dental students who identified bodies of victims. As a result of their experiences, many of the dental students who identified bodies of victims did not return to complete their course of study at the dental school. Spiritual issues emerged differently among those who could not bring themselves to return to work or attend coworkers' funerals and those whose official duty required them to attend funerals and memorials on a daily basis.

Integrating this awareness of group differences in existing therapies can enhance the counseling relationship. It is helpful to understand the differences in groups' experiences, especially those of first responders and people who care for first responders. After emergencies and disasters, first responders report significant increases in measures of posttraumatic stress disorder symptoms, depression, anxiety, general psychological morality and global symptom severity, helplessness, panic disassociation, horror response, and aggression toward coworkers (Benedek et al., 2007). Although the general public experiences the event at a distance by way of radio, television, and the Internet to send "thoughts and prayers" to affected victims, first responders experience the site directly through touch, sight, sounds, and odors that wedge the event into their changing sense of reality. It is especially helpful to have knowledge of the event's exposure and duration as well as the availability of resources to clients who are nontraditional responders (e.g., teachers, clergy, medical examiners, funeral directors, news reporters, sanitation department employees, and others who handle the emotions and physical or spiritual debris of the event). Their stories may reveal fragile coping mechanisms. Other clients may have escaped the direct effects of a disaster, yet experience high social disruption, resulting in a negative impact on psychological and emotional well-being. The aftermath of Hurricanes Katrina and Rita resulted in a wide range of effects, including injuries and death; damage and loss of job, home, and social support; massive relocation; missing persons; widespread uncertainty about the future; and loss of confidence in officials to provide order and protection, health care, and education (Schlenger, 2006).

The trauma story reveals a spiritual meaning when clients evaluate their losses against the investment of time, money, and energy into building homes, relationships, or businesses that no longer exist. Clients report that they have nothing to show by way of accomplishment or relationships for their lives and thus a spiritual search for meaning begins.

There are often signs of uprooted hope when listening carefully to clients' stories about feeling vulnerable, exposed, and disconnected. Without a spiritual underpinning, the person loses a vital element in healing: hope. Hope gives a person the will, the desire to seek new horizons, and the ability to move from a place of desolation to solace and comfort (Yahne & Miller, 1999).

During disasters, hope related to beliefs about the goodness of human nature is usually affected. Questions emerge about the nature of suffering and compassion for hurting people. Social disruption causes disaster survivors to rethink their views on the meaning of human relationships. The following two excerpts provide examples of client beliefs about human nature that were questioned and reshaped.

> A story of indifference and neglect of others: A 41-year-old New Orleans woman who experienced the aftermath of Katrina raised angry and puzzling questions about why an elderly woman survived the initial disaster but did not receive follow-up care. The elderly woman died shortly after because of neglect. "What's the world coming to? I don't understand it. I don't. Didn't they see that old woman? Didn't they see she needed help? Why didn't they help? They could have done something. Something. They did not have to let her die like that. God don't like ugly!" [The reference to God disliking ugliness addresses the ugliness of neglecting someone in obvious need.]

> A story of kindness from a stranger: A 38-year-old woman in her haste to avoid the impending disaster left her medications behind. As a result, she experienced visible distress related to the symptoms of her disease: "People started asking me what was wrong. I could barely talk but I told them I didn't have my medicine. They asked me what kind of medicine? I could hear them talking, 'She forgot her medicine. . . . She forgot her medicine.' There was another woman there and she had the same medicine. She took hers out and gave me some of hers. She didn't know me. She didn't know me! Never seen me in her life. She just gave me some of hers. Just gave it to me, I tell you!"

EFFECTIVELY INTEGRATING SPIRITUALITY

Counseling effectively integrates spirituality and encourages hope for people to move through the irrepressible "why" questions. Understanding clients' spirituality assists in the framing of the event so that meaning can emerge. When individual, social, and spiritual supports are not readily accessible (internal or externally), there is even more struggle to create meaning.

It is difficult, especially for a spiritually oriented client, to make meaning of what does not make sense, face an urgent uncertainty about the future, and/or feel cut off from everything and everyone (including God). At some point, the questions emerge, "Why did this happen to me?" and "How could God have let this happen?" It is in response to these existential questions that the power of faith, hope, and connection is urgently needed. Partnering with spiritual communities to provide spiritual counseling is helpful in that they can provide a framework about the events' causes, the ultimate outcome, and connection and support until recovery or resolution is experienced. Traumatic events may overwhelm individuals, but spiritual communities are likely to possess some resources to find additional meaning within the trauma story. Communities may support the process by providing additional understanding of client stories, interpretations, spiritual struggles, and the role of deity in the event and recovery.

Client views of morality need understanding. Clients may experience guilt as a result of surviving and weigh the merits of their lives against those who lost theirs. In a culture that encourages people to "just get over it," slow recovery from traumatic events can also raise issues of guilt. Furthermore, engaging in counseling or other mental health services, especially when spiritual issues are involved, can be stigmatizing within some faith communities. Clients may have to overcome the stigma of seeking counseling if their faith community discourages seeking counseling outside of the faith community or from secular counselors. In other faith communities, clients may be offered a diverse set of helpful frameworks and tasks for coping with trauma. For example, the 2006 Pennsylvania school shooting in the Amish community raised universal concern for the families of the slain children. It also raised questions about the senselessness of the act and the mental health of the perpetrator. The Amish community focused on the brokenness of human nature and the opportunity for their community to demonstrate love toward one another—even the one who committed the heinous act. It was an event that caused them not to question God but rather to question their own morality and how they should respond. They chose to respond by working out the tensions among the event, God, human nature, and self by offering forgiveness to the man who had committed the act.

Observations of clients' attempts to articulate a spiritual task (e.g., forgiveness) will guide their recovery or circumvent the process, often with a simple acknowledgment that there is a higher purpose that is unfolding and will be revealed later (e.g., "Everything happens for a reason"). This is at the heart of recovery work. It is precisely the unknown reasons that create the spiritual tensions and open the door for exploring ways to resolve the issues.

IMPLICATIONS FOR POLICY AND LARGE-SCALE COUNSELING PROGRAMS

Spirituality as part of an overall disaster counseling strategy has implications for public policy and community rebuilding. As noted in the Amish example, individual recovery is linked to community recovery. Spirituality shapes both individual and community perceptions of coping, evaluations of how well people cope, and the choice of care providers. Provided are two policy examples that show how spirituality became a key issue in the design for counseling specific segments of a community and the willingness of individual clients to engage in therapy. The first example involved a group in Nairobi, Kenya, and the second a clergy group in the United States.

In the 1998 bombing of the U.S. Embassy in Kenya, approximately 212 people were killed, and an estimated 4,000 were injured. The U.S. Agency of International Development supported the development of community mental services to victims and families of the U.S. Embassy bombing. As mental health services were being designed for the affected populations, distinctive professional and spiritual pathways to the services emerged. The effects of the bomb blast were framed culturally along a mental well-being continuum, ranging from psychiatrically or psychologically "injured" to quasi-psychologically "hurt." Use of counseling services was influenced by the counselor and client religious communities. Clients who were psychiatrically or psychologically injured or traumatized sought nonmedical, outpatient mental health services. Those who described themselves as "hurt" welcomed treatment by a professional, lay, or spiritual counselor. The question of the counselor's religion (e.g., Christian, Muslim, Hindu, or no expressed affiliation) emerged as an important issue for both providers and clients.

Some clients clearly stated that they would not see a counselor of another faith. Others expressed preferences for same-faith counselors who would affirm their spiritual values, accept their venting, assist in the discovery of the personal meaning of loss and suffering, and help to redefine hopes and goals in a context of their spiritual beliefs. They wanted counselors to pay attention to spiritual themes within their faith tradition (Miller & Thorsen, 1999). Counseling opportunities were created for clients to address trauma and use spiritual and emotional support from counselors who affirmed their spiritual perspectives.

The second example is a series of incidents in communities throughout the United States. In response to the large number of communities affected by church arson, Congress passed in 1996 the Church Arson Prevention Act, a bill that gave additional tools to federal prosecutors and provided federal loan guarantees to assist in the rebuilding effort. By October 1998, the U.S. Department of the Treasury's National Church Arson Task Force opened investigations into 670 arsons, bombings, or attempted bombings that occurred at houses of worship between January 1, 1995, and September 8, 1998. As the rebuilding effort continued, the National Coalition of Burned Churches focused attention on the trauma experienced by the clergy.

Clergy, their families, and mental health professionals interpreted the events as "traumatic." The clergy were desirous of care from any appropriate mental health professionals and lay counselors. The spiritual dimension was salient and complex. The complexity centered not only on their individual losses but also on the spiritual meaning of the destruction of their icon of worship—the church. The destruction of a spiritual meeting place, the repository of memorials of significant spiritual life events, and the symbol of the communities' relationship with God left those who led spiritual communities without the external tools to assist in recovery and resolution. Furthermore, the event affected their spiritual identities as leaders of a traumatized spiritual community. The nature of their questions was almost exclusively framed along spiritual dimensions. Affected clergy wanted counseling that not only addressed the spiritual dimension but also held spirituality as the starting point and core of their recovery. They expressed a preference for counselors who could authentically affirm the spiritual dimensions of their trauma and recovery through dual training in counseling and pastoral ministry.

In the process of counseling pastoral communities and other clients with complex spiritual and emotional needs the counselor should be clear about offering a safe and supportive place that is affirming of the clients' spirituality. Clients must be able to trust opportunities to explore the critical event, the responses of others who do not share their spiritual interpretations, and the event's impact on a wide range of spiritual beliefs including seeking mental health counseling as opposed to spiritual counseling. Clients must be able to trust that their stories and interpretations of unseen spiritual forces will be heard and support will be offered to integrate these interpretations into their ongoing recovery. Affected clergy in the church burning incidents were offered the opportunity to explore their spiritual leadership by way of rebuilding their houses of worship and assisting parishioners to cope; at the same time, they explored their own understanding of the spiritual rationale for the "attacks" on the "houses of worship or houses of God." Their recovery process included re-evaluating their roles and relationships with their immediate families, parishioners, fellow clergy, local mental health providers, and other sources of support. It also required the clergy to reconcile the acts of the arsonists with their own spiritual path toward recovery and forgiveness.

A HEALING SPACE

Clients who have experienced disasters enter counseling for support through the process of discerning and articulating core beliefs. Initially, client statements may lack a spiritual dimension; however, while exploring their belief systems many factors connected to spirituality may emerge. The task of the counselor in such situations is to discover and explore ways to approach clients' spiritual beliefs and religious practices within effective counseling models.

Spiritual issues are deeply personal and require authentic expression and exploration for effective resolution. Authentic language and relationships, based on a mutual understanding of the expectations for counseling, open doors to recovery. Some individuals believe that spiritual forces are available to assist in recovery (e.g., an angel's rescue, a saint's protection or guidance of self or missing family members). The underlying premise in attending to spiritual issues is the clients' hope and belief that in the middle of their disrupted lives and suffering, God still takes an interest in the plight of people. In the absence of a miraculous intervention, there is always the promise of presence, encouragement, and strength to face the future (Greek, 2004).

In counseling clients with strong spiritual needs, the use of spiritual terminology is just the beginning. Without an authentic and effective spiritual strategy for addressing these needs, the counselor's efforts may be perceived as hollow and lacking in substance. With authentic attention to spiritual needs, however, clients gain a sense of healing as a result of being seen, heard, and assisted in a way that provides meaning. Meaningfulness is experienced in a way that is consistent with the values and commitments of faith and the path that one's faith has taken. Issues related to humanness, life, death, loss, suffering, justice, and goodness can be introduced in the counseling process. The recovery process will come to an abrupt halt if counselors focus only on the facts of the event and not on the narrative of the client's story and his or her underlying philosophy about life.

Counselors will find a myriad of spiritual beliefs among different individuals and cultures. The interplay of spirituality and exposure as well as clients' beliefs about recovery and specific attributes of God (i.e., God intervenes directly in human affairs) influence therapy, whether or not beliefs are discussed explicitly. It can be a challenge to address spiritual matters, because they are often connected to very personal experiences and are difficult to articulate. Appreciating these different views of trauma will help the counselor to contextualize the impact in terms of a community's spiritual interpretation, prescribed tasks for resolutions, and clients' expectations for recovery. Not all individuals will desire to address spiritual issues; many may not view them as important in their recovery. Religious or not, survivors of disaster are spiritually wounded and sometimes disconnected from the realities of life, their feelings about other people, and their sense of purpose.

Central to recovery from trauma is reconnection. Establishing or regaining a sense of purpose and reconnection to important people, places, and values is an important link in the recovery process. Counselor unawareness of client feelings of animosity toward religion and God will allow underlying spiritual tension to go unresolved and minimize progress toward recovery. There is a paradox with reconnecting: Clients seek interpersonal connection and safety in and from connection (Day et al., 2006). In the counseling relationship, the client may experience being connected with the self, others, and God, while anticipating the kindness of strangers, the return to home, the rebuilding of community spaces, and reconnection with those people thought to be lost or missing.

At some point, the counselor will be required to connect with the suffering of the client. If counselors are unable to build relationships that include spiritual issues, the recovery process may become short-circuited. Whether or not spiritual concerns are presented in explicit terms, there is always a spiritual element in healing relationships. Offering continuity within the spiritual framework of the client is an important aspect in the art of healing. This continuity is a key to integrating and transforming the traumatic event into one that acquires meaning and reconnections rather than estrangement.

Creating a safe healing space to improve grief management and coping, restoring hope and meaning, and building connections requires listening to the deeper meaning of the client's story. Spiritual issues are a significant feature of the story, but not the whole story of a person's life (Patton, 1983). Acquiring skill-based training or involving the advanced training of pastoral counselors can be important in addressing the more complex spiritual issues that may have been exacerbated by the disaster. Referring clients who need further help to work through complicated spiritual issues widens opportunities for recovery.

Disasters disconnect people from communities. Clients may find themselves abandoned and exiled from their local spiritual communities. Counseling with sensitivity to spiritual issues can be provided by offering a spiritual presence to people in need, in pain, or in transition. Acknowledging the fragility of the human condition and the power of spirituality to transform suffering are powerful tools for the counselor that open a space in the session to address the response to pain resulting in the emotional and spiritual meaning that the pain has in one's life (Emerson, 1986; Kestenbaum, 2001).

Somewhere in the efforts to rebuild lives and communities, places must be created for legitimate suffering, which allow all persons affected to grieve the loss of life as they knew it. Legitimate suffering allows individuals to express all their issues as they undertake the process of seeking a satisfactory level of physical, psychological, and spiritual resolutions. Along with the material aid, social support, grief work, and positive resolution of psychological issues, there is a need to recognize the signs and opportunities for spiritual counseling to restore meaning, faith, hope, and love for the self and the community.

Spiritual healing happens in many contexts beyond that of religious settings. It happens when counselors show up with caring attitudes. Healing and recovery happens when individuals are allowed to express their spiritual doubts and fears, encouraged to find or continue their spiritual journeys, and relate their stories of despair and faith. Ultimately, it is up to each counselor to decide how to respond to the suffering of those who experience a traumatic event. Suffering can be endured, and there is an ultimate meaning and victory as a result of going through and emerging from the distress of loss, hopelessness, and abandonment.

OPENING THE DOOR

Opening the door to spiritual concerns and issues informs clients that their spiritual life is valuable and affirms the interconnectedness and boundaries of physical, mental, and spiritual health. Care and vigilance is needed so as not to relegate important spiritual care to an afterthought or to treat spiritual issues as psychological ones. Opening the door to the trauma story requires the counselor to be spiritually attuned to the meaning and interpretations of the event and to be aware of a client's pre-existing "sustained threshold" for trauma as well as their religious beliefs about mental health care. It also requires a willingness to address spirituality at each counseling session. Through a collaborative relationship with trained, spiritual caregivers—ideally one with mental health skills—counselors can increase their effectiveness with clients.

Tools for brief assessment can clarify gaps between the counselor's spiritual understanding of the event's impact and the client's willingness to explore his or her spirituality. Puchalski's (2002) and Puchalski and Romer's (2000) assessment and algorithm called FICA can be used to introduce spirituality into the counseling session. FICA questions can be used as a tool to determine the client's *faith* and belief (F), its *importance* and influence (I), its connection with a faith *community* (C), and how it is to be *addressed* in care (A):

- Some of my clients have found it helpful to talk about their faith and their spirituality after the event. Is that something you want to talk about?
- Do you consider yourself spiritual?
- Do you have a spiritual belief that helps you with stress?
- How would you like for me to address that?

Because of the deeply personal nature of these questions, clients are likely to ask counselors where they stand with regard to their spirituality. It is important for counselors to be prepared to answer questions about their own spirituality, clearly and honestly state their beliefs, and recommend spiritual counseling for issues that are best addressed in pastoral counseling.

When counselors have a high degree of awareness about the self and others, are comfortable to explore and connect with the spiritual dimensions of their clients, and have an attitude and posture of humility, clients can experience recovery along spiritual dimensions. The challenge for counselors is to reflect on their own qualities, competencies, and spiritual resources in relation to the spiritual aspects of the traumatic experience for their clients. Care must be taken when addressing spiritual issues so that the boundaries between professional and religious roles is not neglected; honoring religious authority; affirming religious values of clients or being sensitive to their values; and practicing within the boundaries of professional competence (Richards & Bergin, 1997).

Finally, the physical meeting place (i.e., the office) is as important as the psychological and spiritual space. Counselors can assess the meeting space by asking the question, What is it about this space that contributes to or hinders a healing experience along spiritual dimensions? Also, are there objects in the counselor's office that are indicative of his or her spiritual attitude, and if so, how will this shape a client's willingness to talk about his or her own spirituality? These are valid concerns that counselors should consider ahead of time.

PRACTICAL IMPLICATIONS

- Augment existing counseling approaches that provide opportunities for exploring spirituality. Be creative in adapting approaches if necessary. A fuller understanding of a client's spirituality can be achieved by sharing with the client that it is appropriate to address issues of spirituality in therapy.
- Clearly identify the needs that are perceived by the client as important. Clients must also be able to recognize their spiritual needs and invite counselors to hear their spiritual beliefs and interpretations.
- Assess the challenges and barriers to utilizing spiritual resources, the resources already in place, and resources that the clients have been using or wish to use.
- Identify available personal and community resources, including spiritual support. Explore the potential for support outside the counseling relationship.
- Acknowledge and be knowledgeable of local resources. How can the practice benefit or complement other counseling practices? How can both practices work together to serve affected clients?
- Incorporate clients' sense of resolution. How is the resolution experienced by the client?
- Develop realistic expectations for client recovery based on the willingness of the client to explore the spiritual aspects of the disaster and the human, moral, social, and spiritual consequences and resources.
- Be specific about counseling expectations: what and how needs can and will be addressed.
- Start small, think long term, and plan for ways to expand the focus on spirituality, even if progress may appear to be distant.

CONCLUSION

People have psychological and spiritual ways of framing traumatic events and seeking care for recovery. Counselors can create a healing space that allows spiritual dimensions to emerge by being aware of their own attitudes and environment, searching for the trauma and recovery story, possessing a willingness to hear and assist with reflection and reframing, and enlisting the support of colleagues in pastoral counseling or spiritual direction.

Clients need to know that it is permissible to talk about spiritual resources within counseling sessions. A successful counseling session includes using the client's own spiritual outlook and practices as an added resource in the process of healing and recovery while respecting and honoring the principles of spiritual counseling, spiritual direction, and pastoral counseling. Occasionally, the disaster may trigger a turbulent period of spiritual challenges or transformation or conflicting spiritual interpretations where the process of spiritual emergence or integration becomes unmanageable for the client. In such cases, referrals to spiritual counselors may be warranted.

It is important to implement practical, spiritually appropriate, and authentic spirituality in post-disaster counseling. There are several serious challenges to the introduction of spirituality to meet clients' needs, including ways to approach and interpret spiritual viewpoints. However, there are steps that can be integrated into existing counseling approaches to support client recovery.

Evaluating one's own counseling experience with the treatment of post-disaster trauma survivors is important. It is critical to know whether the skills one already possesses is effective in counseling people who have witnessed disasters and clients who remain affected by its aftermath. Word of effective counseling gets around fairly quickly to communities of people experiencing trauma. Preparation to initiate a long-term, sustainable program of trauma counseling that addresses spirituality is vital to the recovery of clients.

Integrating spirituality into counseling services may appear daunting. Early efforts will set the stage for necessary adaptation of past approaches to better serve the needs of individual clients and communities. These efforts have the potential to support individual and community recovery.

Addressing the spiritual dimension creates the opportunity to hear words that speak to the core of what it means to be alive, to stir life within us, and to instill hope into empty spaces filled with despair, fear, fury, and frustration (Crabb, 2003). Recovery will come to an abrupt halt if we listen to the facts of the event and not the story of a spiritual reality that is supporting the recovery process. Learning to listen to the voice telling the hidden story of the event is a process. The hidden story should include life-changing events that taught the client the meaning of life. When clients face a core loss (their sense of well-being, protection from God, connection with God), they experience a desperate hopelessness. Providing the healing space for clients to simultaneously experience profound disappointment and persevering hope leads to recovery and wholeness.

REFERENCES

Antonovsky, A. (1979). *Health, stress, and coping.* San Francisco: Jossey-Bass.

Antonovsky, A. (1987). *Unraveling the mystery of health—How people manage stress and stay well.* San Francisco: Jossey-Bass.

Benedek, D. M., Fullerton, V., & Ursano, R. J. (2007). First responders: Mental health consequences of natural and human-made disasters for public health and public safety workers. *Annual Review of Public Health, 28,* 55–68.

Buffalo Creek Flood. (2008, June 26). Retrieved July 24, 2008, from http://en.wikipedia.org/wiki/Buffalo_Creek_Flood

Crabb, L. (2003). *Soul talk: The language God longs for us to speak.* Nashville, TN: Thomas Nelson.

Day, J. H., Verilyea, E., Wilkerson, J., & Giller, E. (2006). *Risking connection in faith communities: A training curriculum for faith leaders supporting trauma survivors.* Baltimore: Sidran Institute.

Emerson, J. C. (1986). *Suffering: Its meaning and ministry.* Nashville, TN: Abingdon.

Greek, J. (2004). Spiritual care: Basic principles. In S. Sorajjakool & H. Lamberton (Eds.), *Spirituality, health and wholeness: An introductory guide for health professionals* (pp. 95–112). New York: Haworth Press.

Kestenbaum, I. (2001). The gift of a healing relationship: A theology of Jewish pastoral care. In D. A. Friedman (Ed.), *Jewish pastoral care: A practical handbook from traditional and contemporary sources* (pp. 3–15). Woodstock, VT: Jewish Lights.

Krajeski, R. L. (1998, 2005). *Comfort ye, my people: Disasters and emotional, cognitive and spiritual vulnerability reduction (mitigation) and emotional, cognitive, and spiritual capacity building (preparedness): An alternative view of disaster mental and spiritual health.* Mannington, WV: Community Response Management.

Maslow, A. (1954). *Motivation and personality.* New York: Harper & Row.

May, G. (1982). *Care of mind, care of spirit: A psychiatrist explores spiritual direction.* San Francisco: Harper & Row.

McCabe, O. L., Mosley, A. M., Gwon, H. S., Everly, G. S., Lating, J. M., Links, J. M., et al. (2008). The tower of ivory meets the house of worship: Psychological first aid training for the faith community. *International Journal of Emergency Mental Health, 9*(3), 171–180.

McGee, T. R. (2005). *Transforming trauma: A path toward wholeness.* Maryknoll, NY: Orbis.

Miller, W. R., & Thorsen, C. E. (1999). Health and spirituality. In W. R. Miller (Ed.), *Integrating spirituality into treatment: Resources for practitioners* (pp. 3–18). Washington, DC: American Psychological Association.

Pargament, K. I. (1997). *The psychology of religion and coping: Theory, research, practice.* New York: Guilford.

Patton, J. (1983). *Pastoral counseling: A ministry of the church.* Nashville, TN: Abingdon.

Puchalski, C. M. (2002). Spirituality and end-of-life care: A time for listening and caring. *Journal of Palliative Medicine, 5,* 289–294.

Puchalski, C. M., & Romer, A. L. (2000). Taking a spiritual history allows clinicians to understand patients more fully. *Journal of Palliative Medicine, 3,* 129–137.

Richards, P. S., & Bergin, A. E. (1997). *A spiritual strategy for counseling and psychotherapy.* Washington, DC: American Psychological Association.

Schlenger, W. (2006, June). *Disasters and trauma: What we have learned from 9/11 and Hurricane Katrina.* PowerPoint slides presented at the meeting of the Academy Health's Behavioral Health Services Research Interest Group, Seattle, WA.

Schuster, M. A., Stein, B. D., Jaycox, L. H., Collins, R. L., Marshall, G. N., Elliott, M. N., et al. (2001). A national survey of stress reactions after the September 11, 2001, terrorist attacks. *New England Journal of Medicine, 345,* 1507–1512.

Smith, D. W., Christiansen, E. H., Vincent, R., & Hann, N. E. (1999). Population effects of the bombing of Oklahoma City. *Journal of the Oklahoma State Medical Association, 92*(4), 193–197.

West Virginia Division of Culture and History. (2008). *Buffalo Creek: The aftermath.* Retrieved July 24, 2008, from http://www.wvculture.org/history/buffcreek/buff3.html

Yahne, C. E., & Miller, W. R. (1999). Evoking hope. In W. R. Miller (Ed.), *Integrating spirituality into treatment: Resources for practitioners* (pp. 3–18). Washington, DC: American Psychological Association.

Working With Rural and Diverse Communities After Disasters

Beth Boyd

Randal P. Quevillon

Ryan M. Engdahl

The disaster mental health field in the United States has grown rapidly in recent years. With this growth has come the recognition that good intentions are not enough when it comes to providing help to those who are hurting. Large-scale disaster responses such as the terrorist attacks of September 11, 2001, and the hurricanes of 2005 have led to new awareness about the need for community-based culturally responsive services.

CHAPTER HIGHLIGHTS

+ Addresses important issues in responding to disasters at the community level, with specific attention to rural and ethnic minority communities;

+ Discusses issues that affect disaster response services in diverse communities;

+ Explores issues of diversity highlighted in the aftermath of Hurricane Katrina;

+ Discusses the lessons learned in serving diverse communities in past disasters;

+ Reviews the importance of supporting resilience through use of local cultural resources; and

+ Addresses questions that must be attended to in order to further our knowledge of providing services that are truly culturally responsive.

Responses to disaster at the individual level are now well known. Persons exposed to a traumatic event may experience the effects in all of the domains of their lives—emotionally, psychologically, behaviorally, physiologically, and spiritually. It is also important to note that, just as an individual has strengths and weaknesses and coping resources and liabilities, so each community has ways of handling crises and "patterns of difficulty." Looking at communities from an ecological perspective (Kelly, 1966, 2002) helps to promote understanding of how community resources can be mobilized in times of catastrophe and recognition of areas in need of external support.

DISASTER MENTAL HEALTH AT THE COMMUNITY LEVEL

Just as the effects of trauma may be experienced at the individual level, they may also be experienced at the community level (Hobfall & deVries, 1995; Williams, Zinner, & Ellis, 1999). Communities may experience communal grieving, disorientation, unconstructive behaviors, and the inability to make sense of what has happened. Just as an individual who experiences trauma must go through a period of grieving and find meaning in the loss, a community must also come to see itself as a stronger, more cohesive, resilient version of itself in order to heal. A community's ability to recover after a disaster depends, to a large extent, on the degree to which it has made sense of what has happened, the degree to which interventions have contributed to making the event manageable, whether resources for recovery are sufficient to the need, and how the community reframes the event into a challenge (Zinner & Williams, 1999). Connecting with one's community is an important source of identity, meaning, and resilience for those who have experienced a traumatic event. For example, mere hours after Oklahoma City was hit by an F5 tornado in May 1999, community leaders helped residents to reframe the disaster by reminding them of the community mobilization and communal strength following the Alfred P. Murrah Federal Building bombing in 1995. Conversely, a community might be harmed by the context of a disaster and a lack of support from their community, as was the case in the Buffalo Creek community in West Virginia. Following the catastrophic flood of 1972, which was brought about by the collapse of a dam, there was much blame focused on the local mining company and a lack of cohesive, constructive messages to community members. Displaced residents were moved to camps with disregard of their prior neighborhoods. The dislocation fragmented communities and harmed their traditional patterns of social support that had existed before the flood. The resultant feelings of powerlessness, anomie, and alienation on the part of community members and their loss of a sense of community led to a very negative outcome: The pre-existing communities were never effectively re-established (Erickson, 1976; Murray & Kupinsky, 1982). Although the Buffalo Creek disaster happened more than three decades ago, actions following Hurricane Katrina illustrate how prior lessons on effective disaster responses were unheeded. We cannot afford to repeat errors in disaster management.

The Buffalo Creek disaster highlights the special vulnerabilities of rural communities in the United States to the effects of disaster and community trauma. Although some of our most recent examples of community-wide trauma include the Midwest floods of 2008, rural communities also experience disasters in the form of rapid economic decline and environmental change (e.g., drought and forest fires). Any of these events can have devastating effects on the lifestyle and well-being of rural communities.

Rural disasters can be viewed as "rocking in a small boat," in that the lower population and resource levels, among other factors, make the impact of the disaster even more acutely felt. Rural social support networks tend to be smaller and more dense (Quevillon & Trenerry, 1983). That is, an individual's pattern of friends, neighbors, and acquaintances usually consists of fewer members, but these members often fill multiple roles (e.g., fishing buddy, coworker, fellow church member, and neighbor). Large disasters often affect the social fabric of a rural community in especially pernicious ways. Individuals affected by disasters in rural communities need increased support and are often less able to help others. Thus, dense networks are quickly diminished in capacity. Community support structures are likewise hard hit. For example, emergency and medical services in rural communities—already modest in resources—might quickly be overtaxed, and the situation might be made more acute by the likelihood that service providers will be attempting to deal with their own family members and friends while trying to fulfill job-related duties.

The effects of disaster and trauma in rural communities include all of the same effects that any individual or community might experience. In addition, disasters have several unique effects on the rural community:

- The primary economic base is often dependent on natural resources that may have been destroyed or compromised as part of the disaster;
- The sparse population base often makes it difficult to attract the economic or political attention to needed resources;
- The final agricultural and agribusiness impact of the disaster may not be realized until weeks or months after the event; and
- Rural citizens often do not apply for assistance, or underestimate their needs when they do apply for assistance.

Additional stress in rural communities may be generated by issues such as uncertainty about level of crop damage or price fluctuations, time limits on applying for assistance, distrust of outsiders or government intervention, and a cultural value of self-reliance.

Residents of rural areas are less likely than urban residents to seek outside help, particularly for mental health issues (New Freedom Commission on Mental Health, 2004). Some of the issues that may affect rural help seeking in the aftermath of a disaster include the following:

- Accessibility issues such as distance, transportation, and insurance coverage of mental health services;
- Availability of mental health services and providers in rural areas; and
- Acceptability due to the stigma attached to seeking mental health services.

Rural areas can be as culturally or economically diverse as any urban community. Even when a rural community appears homogeneous, there may be significant differences in ethnic background, religious beliefs, education, socioeconomic status, country versus town dwelling backgrounds, farmers versus ranchers, and so forth. Disaster relief efforts must be able to respond to these contextual issues. In rural areas where there are often fewer structured resources, the community-based disaster recovery effort must work especially hard to use the existing local resources to help the community find meaning in the traumatic event and empower its natural healing mechanisms. Building broad participation and mobilizing residents to advance the psychosocial well-being of the community will help to ensure that healing efforts are context appropriate. A community-focused approach to disaster recovery lends itself well to working with the heterogeneity of the rural community.

A community-based approach to disaster recovery recognizes that individual healing is dependent on the community's ability to heal. This must be achieved from the inside out, which means that healing efforts must be initiated within the community and with full community collaboration. Every community and every disaster is unique, and for disaster recovery services to be effective, the special needs, cultural values, and characteristics of each community must be understood by those who seek to help. A successful community-based disaster recovery effort builds local capacity, works within the culture of the community, fits psychosocial support into the broader recovery context (e.g., economic development, primary health care, etc.), and empowers the community to activate its natural healing process (Wessells, 1996). This model includes the following:

- Providing psychosocial support (e.g., social support, networking, psychological first aid and public education on the normal effects of traumatic stress, self-care, and ways to support others and when to seek help);
- Outreach and coordination between local and outside resources;
- Collaborative care that interfaces with the primary health care system;
- Ongoing vigilance to guard against abuses of human rights; and
- Attention to issues of social justice and constructive societal transformation.

Disaster relief workers from outside a community should also avoid the pitfall of viewing a community as a monolithic structure. To understand the full impact of the disaster, it is critical to recognize that various groups coexist within the community and that each may recover to differing degrees and at their own pace (Williams et al., 1999). A community may be cohesive or split into fragments prior to and/or after a disaster. For example, in New Orleans, following Hurricane Katrina, there was a clear delineation and tension between the experiences of low-income African Americans and middle-class White residents. Although it is sometimes tempting to view the disaster as causing the tension, it is more likely that these tensions were pre-existing and exacerbated by the disaster.

Previous experiences with disaster or trauma may also have an impact on how the current event is viewed within the community (Williams et al., 1999). For example, if the community has had a history of similar losses, it will be important to understand what those losses were; how they were perceived; what secondary losses occurred (e.g., hopes, dreams); the overall impact of the event; what community actions were helpful or not helpful; what legacy of loss has remained in the community; and how the community has grown or found meaning in that event.

DISASTER MENTAL HEALTH IN ETHNIC MINORITY COMMUNITIES

While responding to disasters requires extreme flexibility, disaster mental health interventions in ethnic minority communities require specific attention to the cultural norms and traditions of the particular group (Dubrow & Nader, 1999). Although the field of disaster mental health begins with the belief that people in crisis simply need help, events such as Hurricane Katrina have provided an awareness that what is perceived as helpful to survivors is always grounded in the context of their culture, race, ethnicity, and sociopolitical history.

Culture is a lens through which people view their experiences (deVries, 1996). It affects every aspect of one's being and relationship with others. It also affects what is experienced as wellness, illness, hurt, and healing. To provide help in the recovery from a traumatic event, crisis, or disaster, one must first understand how that community defines these concepts. For example, in Native American culture, wellness is not just a reflection of physical health—it is, rather, a balance between the physical, mental, emotional, and spiritual aspects of the self. If any one of these areas is neglected, "dis-ease" may result. Healing requires restoring a balance between these critical areas (Boyd & Thin Elk, 2008).

Culture also influences how individuals and communities express traumatic reactions (deVries, 1996; McFarlane & Van Der Kolk, 1996). It affects one's interpretation of what is a traumatic event as well as how the traumatic event should be interpreted. Although the basic physiological reactions to trauma may be similar across cultures, the specific manifestations of trauma may differ significantly. The individual's culture defines healthy pathways to healing as well as what is acceptable in the context of that culture. Although it is impossible to intimately know every single culture, perspective, and community, one can learn to ask the right questions to access diverse communities and provide help that is truly useful to the community.

Service Delivery System Issues Affecting Diverse Communities

There are a number of issues in the service delivery system that have contributed to the difficulties that ethnic minority communities face in accessing appropriate and helpful services.

Long-standing problems with access to services. The lack of coordination between multiple service delivery systems often creates delays of service, and people in need of help can "fall through cracks" in the system. For example, most states assume that Native Americans will get needed services from the Indian Health Service and as a result do not often include Native American reservations in statewide disaster and mental health planning.

Media attention. Media attention is critical in improving public awareness and influencing the priorities of helping agents and organizations. Because ethnic minority and rural communities seldom receive the kind of media attention that is seen in affluent and urban areas, these communities do not receive the outpouring of support from the general public that they may in fact need. Conversely, there are other cases where substantial media attention is present, but it is attention that can damage a community by casting it in a negative light. For example, the media characterizations of African Americans "looting" in the aftermath of Hurricane Katrina juxtaposed with White people "finding food and supplies" had a devastating impact on public perceptions of the African American community.

Definition of disaster. To meet the requirements necessary to receive resources, a crisis needs to fit the criteria of a disaster—both for the community and for relief organizations. The definition of *disaster* is subjective and can vary widely across groups. Community members may view a situation to be a "disaster," whereas the service agencies or providers do not. On the other hand, those outside of a community may perceive a situation to be disastrous when the community members view it differently. Following the Midwest floods of 1993, contact with Native American (Lakota and Dakota) communities that had been affected by the floods revealed that, although the people were experiencing flood-related crises, concepts of disaster were clearly inappropriate. Lakota and Dakota cultures view natural events as part of the natural world or "Acts of the Creator;" there is no word in the Lakota language for *disaster*. In some communities, applications for disaster assistance were not made. In a particular community, the 1993 flooding resulted in basements that were flooded for more than 4 years, overloaded domestic sewer systems, and contaminated wells. Tribal officials filed for disaster assistance 2 years after the initial flooding when the ground remained saturated and water in basements had nowhere to drain. However, this type of long-term underground flooding did not fit the Federal Emergency Management Agency's definition of flooding at that time: only overflowing rivers and streams were considered in need of disaster services. It is clear that issues related to what is perceived as a disaster are critical. These issues can exacerbate existing tensions between groups and/or a community may not welcome the influx of professionals to help deal with the disaster that the community is handling on its own.

Levels of acculturation. Different levels of acculturation of individuals in a community also influence the service delivery system in the time of a disaster. Helping professionals who respond to a community need to recognize and understand that multiple levels of acculturation to the mainstream culture may exist in a community. The acknowledgment of a traditional part of the community is necessary but not sufficient if there is also a part of the community that is bicultural or completely acculturated to the dominant culture. For example, some people in Native American communities rely on traditional Native spirituality for support and healing, whereas others in the same community have a strong Christian-based spiritual and support network. Still, others may draw on both traditions for support. This may have a big impact on how affected individuals respond to the help that is offered following a disaster.

Social contexts. In some communities where poverty, oppression, violence, and discrimination are prevalent, trauma is chronic and the cumulative effect of multiple traumas is viewed as primary to the identified crisis. Disasters are often conceptualized as temporally linear, involving a specific event, a post-impact phase, and a recovery/restoration phase. But life in some communities involves so many traumatic incidents and occurrences that residents' experiences more closely resemble an ongoing disaster. Peter Ventevogel's (2008) model of a cyclical disaster may better capture the experiences of these communities. This cycle of trauma may have a significant impact on the experiences of the individual and community and the way the current disaster is perceived. Knowledge of the social context of the current crisis and a community's history of trauma is critical when providing assistance to communities that have experienced prolonged and repeated trauma (Herman, 1992).

Hurricane Katrina

Hurricane Katrina, which occurred in August 2005, provided us with discouraging evidence of many of the issues discussed earlier. The disaster that Hurricane Katrina left in its wake affected over a million people, mostly African Americans. It also affected some 34,000 naturalized citizens, an estimated 5,000 to 6,000 Native Americans, 72,000 documented immigrants, and an unknown number of undocumented immigrants (Bourne, 2006).

For the hundreds of thousands of African Americans who were affected by Hurricane Katrina, their inability to evacuate and later their experiences of serious inequities in rescue and recovery efforts heaped insult on injury. Following the hurricane, the media labeled African Americans negatively with terminology such as "looters," "refugees," and "renegades." There was lack of awareness from relief agencies and workers about the importance of kinship bonds and spirituality, which resulted in the separation of many families throughout the rescue and recovery process. The additional stress that resulted from the displacement of families, communities, and spiritual support systems was overwhelming. For many survivors, being loaded onto buses and airplanes, without knowing where they were going, how long they would be away, or how they would come back home, triggered the historically traumatic image of slave ships.

Approximately 4,500 Vietnamese American people living on the Gulf Coast were also affected by Hurricane Katrina (Mississippi Center for Justice, 2007, January 4). Some 800,000 Vietnamese people came to the United States during the 1970s and 1980s as refugees from war and political oppression following the Vietnam War. Many of them settled around the Gulf Coast and worked as shrimpers or in the seafood industry, mostly in the Biloxi, Mississippi, area. Over 70% of the Biloxi Vietnamese American community lived inside the 100-year flood zone and did not have flood insurance (Le, 2006). Language barriers were evident as evacuation orders were not properly translated into Vietnamese, and this confusion continued well into the recovery period, causing much distress, fear, and confusion among Vietnamese Americans. The manner in which they were treated by rescue operations triggered memories of their earlier dislocation from Vietnam. Seventy percent of Vietnamese American shrimpers lost their boats in the storm, and most of them lost their homes. Vietnamese Americans were most likely to turn to religious and community institutions such as temples, churches, homes, or make-shift shelters for help and relief rather than official disaster recovery centers where workers did not understand their language or culture (Lum, 2005).

The effect of Hurricane Katrina on the Mexican American community is more difficult to trace (Bourne, 2006). Many people from the Mexican American community turned to their families in Mexico for help, while undocumented immigrants sought aid underground, because of misleading public information and official policies. The fear of deportation loomed heavily for some members of this community. Applications at the Federal

Emergency Management Agency Disaster Relief Centers included a notice that information would be shared with Immigrations and Customs Enforcement. Stories circulated in the community of American Red Cross shelters requiring proof of citizenship and police raids on shelters in Mississippi. It is likely that many victims of the storm avoided these relief centers due to fears of reprisal and deportation. Furthermore, the presence of U.S. customs officers at Federal Emergency Management Agency Disaster Relief Centers provides another reason why some individuals did not seek safety at these shelters.

Native American communities affected by Hurricane Katrina included six federally recognized tribes and several smaller unrecognized tribes along the Gulf Coast (Indianz.com, 2005, September 2). The Mississippi band of Choctaw suffered the most damage. An estimated 4,500 United Houma Nation people lost everything they owned in Katrina, and another 5,000 to 6,000 Native people along the Louisiana coast were left homeless after Hurricane Rita, which occurred 4 weeks after Hurricane Katrina. The Native American communities were largely ignored by governmental and major relief organizations, and what help was received came primarily from other tribes and Native organizations across the country. There was almost no coverage on Native Americans affected by the hurricanes in the mainstream media.

WHAT HAVE WE LEARNED?

Hurricane Katrina, a disaster that disrupted and displaced over a million people, has afforded the relief community the opportunity to learn about the process of responding to a disaster and the importance of understanding communities. The following are some of the lessons learned from this disaster:

Not all Americans have the means to evacuate. Even when given early warnings, not all people are able to leave a dangerous situation. Trauma, poverty, and ethnic minority status is a high-risk combination in the United States, and this results in individuals and families not having the means, the transportation, or access to the information needed to evacuate. It is important for the relief community to understand that people do not choose to stay in a hazardous situation, and effective disaster planning must recognize the critical role of economic status.

Labeling and the language used following a disaster affects survivors. Disaster survivors are not "refugees," "renegades," "rapists," or "looters"—all terms that were applied to African American survivors of Hurricane Katrina. In his presidential message to the Association of Black Psychologists regarding the response to Hurricane Katrina, Dr. Robert Atwell (2005) emphasized that not only are these psychologically damaging terms insensitive and inaccurate, but they also delay much-needed assistance when survivors are viewed as dangerous.

The beliefs that survivors have about governmental and mainstream relief organizations play a role in how emergency directives are followed or believed. Fear and mistrust of these organizations can lead to situations in which people do not follow critical warnings about evacuations or impending disaster. Effective messaging in times of crisis depends on the transmission of accurate information and feasible options for maintaining safety. The benefits of the recommended behavior must outweigh the risk of the impending threat. If people do not find the message or the messenger credible and trustworthy, the message becomes ineffective. The previous experiences that individuals and communities have had with authority figures and relief organizations may prevent them from following directives or accessing available resources.

Ethnocultural realities play a role in response to a traumatic event. Poverty and racism heavily influence the effect that a crisis event has on individuals and communities. Trauma responses are often increased due to the ongoing stress of living with limited resources. Existing racial tensions between groups can also become magnified in times of disaster. When national insecurity becomes prevalent, people of visible difference or those belonging to a minority group may be scapegoated. For example, following the terrorist attacks of September 11, 2001, racial profiling increased, and the Us and Them mentality became more prevalent; the targeting of Latinos and East Indians increased because they looked Middle Eastern and similar to the perpetrators of the 9/11 attacks (Dudley-Grant, Comas-Diaz, Todd-Bazemore, & Hueston, 2003).

Historical trauma affects communities. Historical trauma is the cumulative emotional and psychological wounding over the life span and across generations (Brave Heart & De Bruyn, 1998). The American Indian Holocaust in which generations of traumatic losses occurred is an example of historical trauma. Traditional spiritual and ceremonial ways of healing were outlawed until 1978, leaving generations of Native Americans with no cultural mechanism for healing. The resulting Historical Trauma Response has included high levels of substance abuse, suicide, depression, anxiety, low self-esteem, anger, difficulty recognizing and expressing emotions, and difficulty recognizing unresolved historical grief. These experiences affect whole communities across many generations. When a disaster occurs on top of this cumulative and intergenerational trauma, the effects are magnified. Help in the form of disaster relief hardly scratches the surface of the wounds that need to be healed.

People with a strong spiritual foundation are better able to cope with stress and trauma. The spiritually centered lives of many ethnic minority communities are different from the mainstream. In many cultures, the physical and spiritual worlds are one and the same. The visible community is merely an extension of the ancestral community. Connection with ancestors is valued, and relationships with ancestors guide community actions in the present. The spiritual meaning of life experiences is considered most important and has the greatest psychological impact. If those responding to such spiritually centered communities miss these important nuances, they lose valuable resources for healing within the community.

Psychological stress occurs in the context of poverty, chronic oppression, discrimination, extreme physical need, and ecological and social disruption. Communities cannot be expected to heal and grow in the midst of stressors that are chronic and rooted in the sociopolitical history of the community (Wessells, 1996). When new losses occur, they heighten the issues that already exist. There can be no real healing in the face of these stressors. Relief, assistance, and healing mean that, as helping professionals, we must step outside of our usual disciplines and roles to advocate for social justice and constructive societal transformation.

Help must be holistic. The Western psychological emphasis on trauma and posttraumatic stress disorder leads us to a fragmented view of psychosocial problems (Wessells, 1996). Emphasis on individual diagnosis and intervention leads us to see signs and symptoms independent of their societal contexts and to pathologize situations that may be driven by political or economic needs. On the other hand, if we understand that healing requires hope and empowerment and if we see psychosocial well-being as the goal, we understand that healing cannot occur without access to jobs, education, physical reconstruction, and resumption of culturally appropriate patterns of living. Healing comes best at the community level. This requires that mental health workers take a long-term perspective and go beyond the usual boundaries of the discipline to understand the situation within the social context in which it occurs. People may be most in need of tangible services such as housing, clothing, transportation, and medical assistance after a disaster; helpers must be willing to work with other community agencies to make sure that these services are provided.

Help must be culturally responsive. Effective strategies for helping should always be focused around culturally specific needs. Effective mental health service delivery includes awareness of the cultural issues as well as the unique trauma responses that ethnic minority populations may experience. Planning an intervention without any knowledge of the affected group or the care they may need is grossly inappropriate. To be grounded in the local culture, relief efforts must include the perspectives of the community, the assistance of traditional and natural helpers from the community, and the local cultural resources that have sustained the community for generations (Wessells, 1996).

The community is central in the healing process. A connection to the community provides a source of identity, meaning, and resilience for residents, so it is critical to encourage local participation, community mobilization, and empowerment (Wessells, 1996). Responders should use local, culturally appropriate resources that are led by people who understand the culture, language, and situation. The focus should be on building broad participation and mobilizing everyone to advance the psychosocial well-being of the community. In this way, the community is involved in its own healing. Outsiders (relief agencies and workers) facilitate change best through partnering with the community, empowering the people, and building local capacity while staying in the background and avoiding the development of dependency. Mental health and other disaster relief workers should be aware that it is the community—and not the relief structure—that will truly heal the community.

SUPPORTING LOCAL CULTURAL RESOURCES

The Inter-Agency Standing Committee's (IASC; formed in 1992 by the United Nations General Assembly Resolution 46/182) *Guidelines on Mental Health and Psychosocial Support in Emergency Settings* identifies several important areas of working with local cultural resources to mobilize communities following a disaster. This document was finalized in the spring of 2007 and provides an extremely useful framework, highlighting the essential nature of community participation, capacity building, and attention to human rights issues in disaster responding. Designed to guide complex humanitarian emergencies worldwide, the guidelines emphasize the cultural appropriateness of psychosocial interventions and provide action sheets with suggested activities and process indicators of success. The guidelines also provide practical resources to aid program planning and coordination and are intended as a lever for advocating better practices in disaster response (Wessells, 2008). In the United States, the IASC guidelines might prove especially valuable for those responding to disasters that involve rural communities with less developed resources, culturally diverse urban communities, and communities that live on reservations.

In keeping with the IASC guidelines, relief workers need to be aware of locally available cultural resources. These resources may include traditional and spiritual healers, spiritual leaders, elders, and the natural helpers who understand the heart of their communities. These people are often also the gatekeepers to the community and allow others access and authority to be in the community. Relief workers may not have their presence validated without the approval of these key community leaders. To appropriately enter the community, these people must be sought out and the appropriate access rituals must be engaged to build trust. This might include sharing a meal, presenting a traditional gift, explaining where one comes from, providing details about one's family, or simply listening to the gatekeeper's perspective of the situation. It is important to remember that this may not be the official authority of the community—it may be the grandmother who meets people at her kitchen table, the local bartender, or the priest. To even find this important person or persons in the community, one needs to understand the traditional power structure, norms for dialogue and consultation, the rules for entering the community, methods to communicate respect, the different constituencies that need to be heard, and the key people who know how to get things done. Body language, eye contact, pace of conversation, and other culturally specific communications styles must be understood and practiced. Local communities have specific methods and tools for healing that are grounded in the beliefs, values, and traditions of the local culture, and these methods of healing are more appropriate and sustainable than outside methods. They should be embedded in every step of the needs assessment, program planning and design, training, implementation, monitoring, and evaluation processes. It is important to recognize that these traditional local tools may be weakened or disrupted by oppression but that the community is resilient because it is still there and these are the tools that will help regenerate it. Responders must also recognize that their mere presence in the community may be a political act and thus must continually ask themselves whose interests are being served and whose interests may be overlooked through their work (Wessells, 1996).

RESILIENCE

A discussion of community, culture, and disaster cannot be complete without addressing the issue of resilience. The connections between culture and resilience are intertwined. The culturally learned values and practices of communities are what promote positive coping and adaptive reactions to trauma and disaster (Chemtob, 1996). Embracing community identity and valuing community welfare strengthens one's cultural identity, which in turn increases one's resiliency. The connection between culture and resiliency transcends even death as the relationships that many communities share with their ancestors help guide current activities. The very fact that a community has survived hardship in the past helps to provide an expanded definition of resilience. Spirituality helps in coping with trauma by addressing questions regarding the meaning of life, loss of hope, victimization, and demoralization. Meeting and overcoming adversity promotes personal and communal growth and development. Generativity, the desire to promote the well-being of future generations, helps in the healing process of individuals and communities. An emphasis on community well-being, both past and future, promotes resilience. Creativity is also related to resilience, as it provides ways to cope with oppression through humor, music, art, and poetry.

Supporting resilience is an important disaster response goal, because it allows the community to access its own resources as well as avoid becoming dependent on the response effort. Disaster responders from outside of the community can support resilience by supporting strong ethnic identity through conscious participation in cultural activities, encouraging individuals to increase their community ties through actions with and for others, promoting positive meaning-making constructs, working within the spiritual framework of the community, and using story-telling and drawing on past experiences of overcoming trauma for present-day application. The use of traditional knowledge and the ancient ways of knowing and healing that have sustained communities for generations should also be encouraged in the healing process and survivors should be encouraged to use traditional ceremonial ways of healing and feel supported in their reaching out for help from extended family. The community should be empowered to engage its natural healing mechanisms.

Resilience and healing are difficult to achieve in the face of invalidation. For those communities that have experienced oppression, discrimination, racism, prejudice, and disproportionate losses, it is important that the people's experiences be heard, acknowledged, and validated. It is not enough to have a sympathetic response—to be truly culturally responsive, one must acquire cultural knowledge, skills, and the ability to see the disaster through the eyes of the community.

QUESTIONS THAT CAN WAIT NO LONGER

Cultural responsiveness requires more than good intentions. We need to be willing to openly see, understand, and discuss the painful reality of institutionalized racism and the role of power and oppression. To provide help and healing, we must allow ourselves to see the economic, political, and social contexts in which communities exist. As helping professionals, we must be willing to ask ourselves some important questions. The following questions can wait no longer for substantive answers:

- How do rural and ethnic minority communities fit into existing systems of disaster relief services?
- How do existing systems of disaster relief services meet the needs of rural and ethnic minority communities?

- How do the existing systems need to change to meet the needs of rural and ethnic minority communities?
- What do service providers, disaster relief workers, governmental organizations, and nongovernmental organizations need to know about rural and ethnic minority communities?
- How should organizations be trained for work in rural and ethnic minority communities?
- What standard of competency or responsiveness can rural and ethnic minority communities expect?
- How will we define care?
- How will we measure care?
- Whose perceptions are valid?
- Who defines what is traumatic?
- Who defines what is effective?
- When does a disaster response end?

Practical Implications

When offering disaster response services in rural and ethnic minority community settings, it is critical to remember the following:

- Communities must be involved in every aspect of their own healing from disaster.
- Disaster responders should understand the culture, worldview, spirituality, and sociopolitical history of the community—or find those who do.
- Disaster response efforts must be grounded in the community's concepts of wellness, trauma, healing, and help.
- Healing cannot fully occur in the face of social injustice, poverty, discrimination, oppression—disaster response may mean advocating for positive societal transformation.
- Outsiders (relief agencies and workers) facilitate change best through partnering with the community, empowering the people, and building local capacity while staying in the background and avoiding building dependency.
- Supporting a community's natural resilience and capacity to heal itself may be the most important disaster response goal.

Conclusion

The recent history of disasters in the United States has painfully shown us that there are many things we must learn to provide culturally responsive disaster mental health services in the community setting. We need to know the specific needs of the population being served, the sociopolitical history of the group, appropriate cultural protocols for gaining entry into a specific community, and the community's tradition and infrastructure for managing crisis and long-term trauma. We need to know about the true accessibility of basic health and mental health services within a community. As outsiders to the communities that we seek to help, we need to gain some knowledge about how the community understands health, illness, wellness, and healing, as well as the role of the spiritual healing systems, culture, and the practices of the community in response to crisis.

REFERENCES

Atwell, R. (2005, September 6). *National president's statement on Hurricane Katrina: Black psychologists response to Hurricane Katrina.* Retrieved September 10, 2008, from http://www.abpsi.org/hurricane.htm

Bourne, D. R. (2006, March). Evacuation patterns of ethnic minority populations affected by Hurricane Katrina. *Communique: Hurricane Katrina: A multicultural disaster* [Special section], xiv–xvi.

Boyd, B., & Thin Elk, G. (2008, August). Indigenous perspectives on healing. *Communique: Psychology and Racism* [Special section], 44–46.

Brave Heart, M. Y. H., & De Bruyn, L. M. (1998). The American Indian Holocaust: Healing historical unresolved grief. *American Indian & Alaska Native Mental Health Research, 8,* 56–78.

Chemtob, C. M. (1996). Posttraumatic stress disorder, trauma, and culture. In F. L. Mak & C. C. Nadelson (Eds.), *International review of psychiatry* (pp. 257–289). Arlington, VA: American Psychiatric Publishing.

deVries, M. W. (1996). Trauma in cultural perspective. In B. A. van der Kolk, A. C. McFarlane, & L. Weisaeth (Eds.), *Traumatic stress: The effects of overwhelming experience on mind, body and society.* New York: Guilford.

Dubrow, N., & Nader, K. (1999). Consultations amidst trauma and loss: Recognizing and honoring differences among cultures. In K. Nader, N. Dubrow, & B. Hudnall Stamm (Eds.), *Honoring differences: Cultural issues in the treatment of trauma and loss.* Philadelphia: Brunner/Mazel.

Dudley-Grant, R. G., Comas-Diaz, L., Todd-Bazemore, B., & Hueston, J. D. (2003). *Fostering resilience in response to terrorism: For psychologists working with people of color.* Washington, DC: American Psychological Association.

Erickson, K. T. (1976). *Everything in its path.* New York: Simon & Schuster.

Herman, J. (1992). Complex PTSD: A syndrome in survivors of prolonged and repeated trauma. *Journal of Traumatic Stress, 5*(3), 377–391.

Hobfall, S. E., & deVries, M. W. (Eds.). (1995). *Extreme stress and communities: Impact and intervention.* Dordrecht, Netherlands: Kluwer.

Indianz.com. (2005, September 2). *Indian Country responds to victims of Katrina.* Retrieved September 8, 2008, from http://www.indianz.com/News/2005/010151.asp

Inter-Agency Standing Committee. (2007). *IASC guidelines on mental health and psychosocial support in emergency settings.* Geneva, Switzerland: Author.

Kelly, J. G. (1966). Ecological constraints on mental health services. *American Psychologist, 21,* 535–539.

Kelly, J. G. (2002). The spirit of community psychology. *American Journal of Community Psychology, 30,* 43–63.

Le, U. (2006, August 26). *The invisible tide: Vietnamese Americans in Biloxi, MS. An update one year after Hurricane Katrina.* National Alliance of Vietnamese American Service Agencies. Retrieved September 11, 2008, from http://www.navasa.org/pdf/BiloxiReport.pdf

"Legal clinic to meet needs of Coast's Vietnamese residents" (2007, January 4). Mississippi Center for Justice. Retrieved September 9, 2008, from http://www.mscenterforjustice.org/vietnameseclinic.swf

Lum, L. (2005). Swept into the background. *Diverse Issues in Higher Education, 22,* 22–27.

McFarlane, A. C., & Van Der Kolk, B. A. (1996). Trauma and its challenge to society. In B. A. van der Kolk, A. C. McFarlane, & L. Weisaeth (Eds.), *Traumatic stress: The effects of overwhelming experience on mind, body and society.* New York: Guilford.

Murray, J. D., & Kupinsky, S. (1982). The influence of powerlessness and natural support systems on mental health in the rural community. In P. A. Keller & J. D. Murray (Eds.), *Handbook of rural mental health* (pp. 62–73). New York: Human Sciences Press.

New Freedom Commission on Mental Health. (2004). *Subcommittee on rural issues: Background paper* (SMA-04-3890). Rockville, MD: Author.

Quevillon, R. P., & Trenerry, M. R. (1983). Rural depression research: Implications of social networks for theory and treatment. *International Journal of Mental Health, 12,* 45–61.

Wessells, M. (1996). Culture, power, and community: Intercultural approaches to psychosocial assistance and healing. In K. Nader, N. Nubrow, & B. Hudnall Stamm (Eds.), *Honoring differences: Cultural issues in the treatment of trauma and loss* (pp. 267–282). Philadelphia: Brunner/Mazel.

Wessells, M. (2008, September). *Inter-Agency Standing Committee (IASC) guidelines on mental health and psychosocial support in emergency settings—Getting beyond the "anything goes" approach.* Paper presented at the 11th annual conference on Innovations in Disaster Psychology, Vermillion, SD.

Williams, M. B., Zinner, E. S., & Ellis, R. R. (1999). The connection between grief and trauma: An overview. In E. S. Zinner & M. B. Williams (Eds.), *When a community weeps: Case studies in group survivorship* (pp. 3–22). Philadelphia: Brunner/Mazel.

Ventevogel, P. (2008, September). *The IASC guidelines: Opinions and experiences.* Paper presented at the 11th annual conference on Innovations in Disaster Psychology, Vermillion, SD.

Zinner, E. S., & Williams, M. B. (1999). Summary and incorporation: A reference frame for community recovery and restoration. In E. S. Zinner & M. B. Williams (Eds.), *When a community weeps: Case studies in group survivorship* (pp. 237–254). Philadelphia: Brunner/Mazel.

Voices of Hope

A Commentary on Dislocation and Relocation

Sylvia A. Marotta

Many voices can be heard when a natural disaster occurs. Some of those voices describe the event as news (Lipton, Drew, Shane, & Rohde, 2005); others recite statistics of loss (Berggren & Curiel, 2006); still-others describe the losses in terms of disease burden (Norris, Friedman, & Watson, 2002). When the disaster is of the magnitude of Hurricane Katrina, which destroyed the Gulf Coast in the New Orleans area in 2005, followed closely in the same year by Hurricane Rita, these familiar voices of incalculable loss and suffering can overwhelm and drown out the very real voices of those whose lives were incontrovertibly changed. Some of these voices are those of survivors and other voices are those of caregivers and professional helpers. The purpose of this chapter is to provide a commentary, using composite voices of those people who were displaced by the two hurricanes, to illustrate how mental health professionals and governmental policy makers might incorporate lessons learned from survivors and helpers into the design and delivery of mental health services in future hurricane disasters. The chapter is an attempt to "manage knowledge" gained from the experience of taking care of hurricane survivors who had relocated to a shelter. It is an unfortunate reality that over the course of the 20th century, many lessons have been learned and stored about ways to manage natural disasters, but those lessons have not been disseminated or reused as often as they should have been (Gheytanchi et al., 2007). Although it is helpful to learn from experiences, learning must be applied for its benefit to be evaluated and shared.

My fundamental premise is that mental health needs can and should be woven into and through the entire ecology of disaster preparedness planning, at individual, community, governmental infrastructure, and policy levels. When an ecological system is damaged, there is a role for everyone—survivors and policy makers and helpers—in managing knowledge in preparation for the next occurrence. Only then will comprehensive infrastructures be available to provide for the mental and physical needs of individuals and communities affected (Schonfeld, 2005). All case examples are drawn from experiences of working with a national disaster relief organization as part of a Disaster Mental Health

Team, and with the Society for Counseling Psychology, Division 17 of the American Psychological Association's project with mental health professionals, a year after Hurricanes Katrina and Rita in New Orleans. Cases are composites to protect the anonymity of survivors and their caregivers. Ten case vignettes and the resulting lessons learned from their stories are described.

CHAPTER HIGHLIGHTS

✦ Identifies the major components of the ecology of disaster preparedness planning and describes a role for each component;

✦ Discusses how to provide safety and stabilization to those who seek treatment and those who do not seek treatment after natural disasters;

✦ Outlines the differences among existing models of early intervention and evaluates their outcomes; and

✦ Formulates strategies for professional associations and academics to incorporate disaster lessons into training and education programs.

LESSON 1: Safety matters. Imagine that you're a single mother with two children ages 5 and 10. You struggle to pay the mortgage on your small house, but it is your home and you have lived in the city all your life. For several days, television news reports say that the hurricane is approaching, and between going to work and caring for your children, you find time to stock up on water, canned food, and batteries. You do this without a car because you've never needed one here and you couldn't afford one anyway. All your life you've prepared in this way for a storm and you'll do it again for this one. Your plan is to hunker down with the kids and ride the storm out, even though you know that the mayor recommended an evacuation. Your oldest child is anxious but your youngest one only knows that Mommy won't have to go to work and that will be fun. The storm hits early in the morning and through the afternoon and while the waters are high, you think you've made it. In the afternoon, though, the National Guard comes to your door with guns drawn and orders you to leave. You and your children leave your home at gunpoint, eventually making your way to the airport and a shelter in Texas.

When a storm ultimately causes more than 1,800 deaths, physical safety is a primary concern. When levees break, whole communities disappear and the need to move great numbers of people quickly has to be the first order of business. The psychological safety of adults and children facing drawn weapons in addition to the hurricane catastrophe must not be a distant second concern, however, as the consequences of inattention to this form of safety can be long lasting. Most trauma treatment models include a prolonged period of safety and stabilization. It is difficult to process traumatic exposures or to make meaning without having stability in at least one domain. This fact stands out in stark relief through the repetitive descriptions by the mother and children of what it was like to leave their home at gunpoint, often superseding their descriptions of the storm itself. From a preparedness perspective, one wonders whether first responders like the National Guard are given training scenarios that discuss when weapons should and should not be used. What tabletop exercises exist to train police officers in moving groups of people when there is a likelihood of resistance to being moved and especially when the bulk of the population does not own private means of transport? Are there discussions among first responders about the advantages and disadvantages of using weapons to get women and children to safe havens? The answers to these questions could be informative to those charged with preparing for the next disaster.

Because not everyone who is exposed to an extreme stressor develops a diagnosable mental disorder, it is likely that this woman and her children might never be seen in any treatment setting. It is also possible that acute stress reactions in the aftermath of a disaster will resolve themselves without treatment. Indeed, a whole range of responses is likely, including no reaction, psychological adaptation, and posttraumatic growth (Sheikh & Marotta, 2008). Following Hurricane Katrina, approximately 25% of survivors reported symptoms of posttraumatic stress disorder 6 months later (Weisler, Barbee, & Townsend, 2006). This compares to 8% lifetime prevalence rates reported for adults exposed to extreme stressors in general (American Psychiatric Association, 2000). Those rates increase markedly when there is comorbidity with another Axis I condition such as depression (North, Kawasaki, Spitznagel, & Hong, 2004). Moreover, in one study, children of individuals with comorbid mental conditions were 2.5 times more likely to have psychological problems following exposure than those whose parents had little or low levels of symptomatology (Weisler et al., 2006). For mental health professionals, assessing for comorbidities while providing psychological first aid, and not therapy, might prove to be an effective first-line intervention. Assessment of children in the aftermath of a disaster for pre-existing conditions among parents would also help in triage decision making.

> **LESSON 2. Voices *will* be heard.** Imagine that you're in a shelter and happy to be alive. You keep playing the events of the last couple of days over and over in your mind. You compare stories with your neighbors in the sleeping area and over meals in the eating area. You are amazed at being alive and safe. You're grateful that all these volunteers are here and you want to be helpful, too. There is a spirit of community here in the shelter, and the horrors that brought you here begin to diminish.

For mental health professionals, it is important to remember that the vast majority of people exposed to extreme stressors will recover from their adversity exposure without any treatment. In fact, the first line of intervention is to encourage conversations among family members and neighbors. There is an inverted pyramid of helpful resources, and the broadest portion of that pyramid is the help that survivors provide for each other (see Figure 11.1).

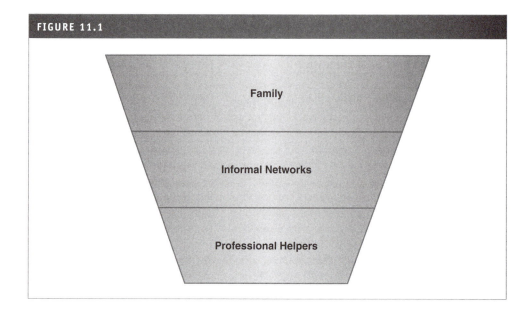

FIGURE 11.1

Professional helpers are in the cone at the bottom of the inverted pyramid, accessible to those whose personal resources are not sufficient enough to help them cope, usually a far smaller group that will need psychotherapy or counseling. By encouraging families and neighbors to voice their experiences, people can provide support and comfort to each other, triggering the curative factor of altruism and promoting natural resilience and eventually healing.

> **LESSON 3. Water is powerful.** You went to bed that night hoping you'd made the right decision to stay in your house during the approaching hurricane. As is your routine, you awake to go to the bathroom in the early hours of the morning. As you stumble to the bathroom, you notice that the floor in your bedroom feels damp on your bare feet. When you reach the bathroom, you are stepping in a pool of water. In the time it takes you to use the facility, the water reaches your ankles. By now you're shouting to everyone in the house to wake up because the water is getting to knee level. Thirty minutes after you first woke up, you and your family have climbed through the attic and onto the roof of your house, waiting for rescue.

It is paradoxical that water destroys and water nourishes. Flood waters drive people out of their homes and into shelters. Flood waters contain toxins that can cause infectious diseases. For some survivors, images of bodies floating in water or loved ones disappearing in water contribute to acute stress reactions. On the life-giving side of the equation, one very visible marker of safety in the shelter is the ubiquitous bottled water. Water is essential to physical survival. Drinking water that is clean and safe is especially vital after a flood. Cases of bottled water arrive on flatbed trucks every day during a shelter's existence. Water is heavy, and shelter workers and survivors spend time moving cases from one place to another. The task of moving cases of water can be curative as survivors and caregivers bond over the moving and distributing of bottled water. Not all curative factors have to come from counseling or therapeutic modalities.

Social support is a protective factor against developing mental illness, and the lack of it is a risk factor. For children, the experience of having survived rising water can have lasting psychological effects. A year after Hurricanes Katrina and Rita, some children still could not take baths because being immersed in water was too vivid a reminder of their ordeal.

The lesson for caregivers to apply lies in "languaging" about water as a life-giving as well as a life-threatening force. *Languaging* is a term used by social constructivists (Neimeyer, 1995) to describe one of the changes that happens in therapy through meaning making. Conversations with adults and children about their experiences with water will be affected by the cognitive and affective developmental level of the individual, the previous history of an individual's access to resources in the community before the storm, and the severity of someone's exposure to the destructive power of water. In the immediate aftermath of a hurricane, helpers should be aware that water is a loaded term and that realities are being co-constructed around the words that we use. Adults and children will have differential abilities to process both negative and positive experiences with water during the acute phase of exposure. The ability to make meaning after a loss as big as that which resulted from Hurricane Katrina may require longer time frames for children than for adults (Andrews & Marotta, 2005). Indeed, every developmental stage might bring reconsideration of the consequences of exposure and an accommodation to existing cognitive frameworks.

In treatment settings, the best practice literature suggests that psychoeducation is not a first-line intervention for treatment of posttraumatic stress disorder (Foa, Davidson, & Frances, 1999). First-line interventions are defined as those that are appropriate for initial treatment and include therapies such as exposure, anxiety management, and cognitive therapy. Psychoeducation is only recommended as a first-line intervention during the acute phase of a stressful exposure to normalize symptoms. It is also used when individuals cannot tolerate first-line treatments or to promote compliance with treatment among adults. Helpers can use information to empower people to explore their experiences verbally, being careful to avoid framing the information in ways that could become self-fulfilling prophecies. When people hear helpers talk more about "traumatic symptoms" than they do about "natural resiliencies," meaning making may be skewed toward the expectation that a disorder will naturally follow. Like water, words are double-edged.

Survivors who do go on to develop diagnosable disorders will benefit from helpers who facilitate meaning making around the role of water in daily life following a hurricane exposure. Talk therapies acknowledge the centrality of language in adaptive processing as well as in meaning making (Anderson, 1995). For adults, the treatment efficacy literature supports the use of therapies such as cognitive-behavioral therapy, eye movement desensitization and reprocessing, and exposure in the treatment of posttraumatic stress disorder (Foa, Keane, & Friedman, 2000). Although randomized clinical trials on treatments for children are fewer in number, there is some support for these same forms of treatment for children and adolescents (Feeny, Foa, Treadwell, & March, 2004).

LESSON 4. A little information can be a lot. You're a licensed mental health counselor with more than 15 years' experience in your own private practice. You've developed a specialty in trauma treatment, and when you hear about the devastation of Hurricane Katrina, you want to offer your services to those in need. Over several days, you are on the phone and on various government Web sites. You register on some of these sites but don't hear back from anyone. You complain to your colleagues that no one seems to be in charge of volunteers and you worry that people are not getting the care they need. Later you learn that those professionals in the helping industry who were working in the shelters felt overwhelmed by the magnitude of the services needed.

There are lessons here for professional associations and for individual helpers, as well as for government policy makers. The proliferation of helping models and help providers, both governmental and private, makes it difficult for would-be volunteers to know what to do when a disaster strikes. In our post-9/11 society, the complexities of service delivery have grown even more complicated. Titles and definitions of roles are used interchangeably in the literature, making it difficult for prospective helpers to know how and where to volunteer services. The title "emergency worker," for example, encompasses helpers such as police and firefighters, but is also used for those who provide medical and health care (Weiss, Marmar, Metzler, & Ronfeldt, 1995). Although police, firefighters, and physicians may be referred to as "first responders" (Hyman, 2004), they are to be distinguished from those who perform psychological first aid or crisis intervention (Ursano, Fullerton, Benedek, & Hamaoka, 2007). Some disaster relief roles are organized toward survivor care and others are focused on first responder care.

For professionals providing mental health services, the primary criterion for becoming a disaster relief worker is to hold a license in a particular state. This is not the only entry point, however. What is required of all licensed professionals is a training course in a model of disaster relief such as that provided by the American Red Cross. These models teach safety and relaxation strategies but do not provide psychotherapy or counseling. The licensed professional who would like to be a disaster helper has to be willing to suspend his or her therapeutic style and follow the model of the disaster relief service.

The time to consider being a disaster helper is before a disaster occurs. Professional associations often offer training and education in disaster response to prepare members appropriately. Although some training does happen following a disaster, it is best to acquire the appropriate credentialing and to register with an organization that provides disaster services before the need presents itself. In addition, once a mental health professional is registered with a relief organization, he or she will have opportunities to participate in simulation exercises to prepare for later work in disaster situations. For example, mental health professionals might be asked to provide support to volunteers who are engaged in a mock terrorist attack, where the primary purpose of the simulation is to test the coordination of community agencies in the event of a real attack. These simulations can be very real to volunteer victims who play roles of victims with grotesque physical injuries, and the presence of a mental health professional can diffuse any potential emotional consequences arising from the simulation itself.

For professional associations, offering continuing education programs in disaster preparedness on a regular basis helps ensure that there are enough registered volunteers within the organization. Most state psychological associations now have disaster response groups. Perhaps professional associations could use Web-based networks to share information on training and continuing education programs in disaster relief. There is at least one federation of disaster relief organizations at the national level; The National Voluntary Organizations Active in Disasters has 49 members, and its goal is to improve communication between its member agencies and the federal government during a disaster (Government Accountability Office, 2008). This goal is critical, but to date, the member organizations are seriously under-resourced and do not have the technology resources that would facilitate electronic communication. Are there analogous federations or coalitions of various professional groups that provide disaster relief, and are databases mined for information on dilemmas to be expected when one is in the field? In addition to initial training provided by professional associations, it would be helpful to have a continuing education function within the involved professions focused on using the problems and solutions derived from work in disaster situations to manage the knowledge gained from those experiences. Both inter-agency and intra-agency sharing of collective experiences would be a way to ensure transfer of knowledge.

Graduate education programs in universities and colleges could become part of the ecology of disaster preparedness by incorporating disaster relief models into their curriculum, thus ensuring that the next generation of professionals will be aware and ready to serve. Training and education would then be woven throughout helpers' professional lives, decreasing the confusion that can happen when one tries to be helpful in the acute phase of a natural disaster. Crisis intervention competencies are being added to some degree programs as the need for these penetrates the national consciousness. For example, the Council for Accreditation of Counseling and Related Education Programs added a curriculum change called the "Emergency Preparedness Initiative" to its standards revision process. The Council received a federal contract to consider establishing guidelines and standards that will prepare counselors to work as health care providers in national emergency situations. The standards revision process was extended for an additional year, pending this potential set of competencies being developed and feedback received from the field.

> **LESSON 5. Need is timeless.** You are one of the working poor. You've always worked full-time at a variety of service jobs but never at only one job. You've been able to scratch a living together working two or more jobs, depending on the season. Because you are working part-time with each employer, your employer doesn't have to provide you with health insurance. You limit your health care to emergency room visits when you know you have no other choice. For everything else, you do without. As long as you can remember, you've had trouble sleeping, have little appetite or energy, and find yourself feeling hopeless on a regular basis. When Hurricane Katrina threatens your city, you comply with the evacuation and go to the Superdome where you join the 26,000 or so other people riding out the storm. You spend most of your time at the shelter in your cot behind the curtains. This storm seems like just another catastrophe with which you will find it difficult to cope.

Mental wellness and mental illness exist on a continuum. Although there are many definitions of what constitutes good mental health, it is generally accepted that some level of functionality in relationships and work is fundamental. Another characteristic of good health is adaptation to adversity. Mental illness or mental disorders are those states that can be assessed and diagnosed using existing classification systems such as the *Diagnostic and Statistical Manual of Mental Disorders* (4th ed., Text rev.; American Psychiatric Association, 2000). In between wellness and illness are conditions or features that are not severe enough to meet the criteria for any one disorder but which nonetheless are associated with distress. The U.S. Surgeon General Satcher in a U.S. Department of Health and Human Services (1999) report noted that approximately 20% of adults in the United States can expect to have a mental illness in any given year. Hurricanes are an example of a trigger that can change manageable distress or subclinical symptoms into a diagnosable condition.

Workers at shelters for disaster survivors know that when a disaster occurs in a community, there will be some mentally ill people among the survivors. Some undiagnosed conditions are always present. In addition, homeless people are often placed in shelters, and the correlation between homelessness and mental illness is well known (cf., Pickett-Schenk, Cook, Grey, & Butler, 2007). Thus, first responders and helpers may have to assist people to manage the acute symptoms of mental illness that may predate the effects of the disaster itself and that have been untreated. The more remote the shelter is from the direct impact of a storm, the more likely it will be that that particular shelter will have people needing services that may not be directly related to the disaster. It is to meet the needs of this group of shelter inhabitants that mental health training can be invaluable.

One lesson from Katrina at the systemic level is that most survivors had inadequate health care delivery and insurance coverage before the storm. New Orleans was ranked the lowest in the United States in terms of citizen access to health care (Rodriguez & Aguirre, 2006). Today, the health care system in New Orleans remains decimated and is being rebuilt very slowly (Conrad, Townsend, & Buccola, 2008). Less than 50% of a shelter population in one study was covered by health insurance after the hurricane (Rosenbaum, 2006). Rosenbaum advocates for using a preparedness approach to obtaining national health insurance reform. This approach builds reform by considering natural disasters as a public health emergency that will require service delivery systems accessible to low-income populations.

There is considerable cultural resistance to changing the current system of employer-provided health insurance, but for people such as our imaginary survivor, insurance was never accessible for part-time employees or those without jobs at all. Access to services that would help alleviate mental distress and prevent mental illness is denied to those with part-time or no employment. In the months after the two disasters, there was a spirit of collaboration among the dominant political parties that resulted in funding that partially covered Medicaid services for survivors (Lambrew & Shalala, 2006). Although this funding was insufficient to manage the sheer numbers of low-income individuals affected by the storms, it did provide some short-term relief to the states of Louisiana, Mississippi, and Alabama. In the long term, however, even several years after the 2005 hurricanes, people continue to be unable to find appropriate health care practitioners for either their mental or their physical health needs (Cerise, 2007). However, this situation offers an opportunity to construct service delivery systems in places that went below the radar previously. Opponents of change in the health care system cannot make the argument that the status quo is preferable when the system nearly disappeared overnight in New Orleans. As Voelker (2006) notes, the entire health care system, from the workforce to the facilities that housed the system to its medical records, has to be reconstructed simultaneously.

LESSON 6. There is no "they" in disaster. Imagine that you've been in the shelter now for 5 days and you don't know whether or not your home is still standing. You stay away from the sleeping and eating areas because several people there have taunted you about your disability. You walk around town, trying to kill time while you wait for the services you need. You hear news stories about the part of town where you live. These stories report that that part of town had relatively little damage. You want to go see for yourself, but there are problems with getting money for short-term needs once you return and even for immediate needs while you're at the shelter. You go to the Red Cross housing table, you get sent to FEMA on the other side of the shelter, you wait in lines at both places. Finally you're told to go stand in yet another line and after several days of this, you've had enough and you begin shouting at the worker. The worker shouts back, having worked those tables as many days as the survivor has visited them. The worker hasn't been taking the rest periods because there was just too much to do. The worker also doesn't know if her house is still there or not.

When a disaster of the magnitude of Hurricane Katrina strikes, it does not discriminate in its level of destruction. Caregivers and survivors struggle with similar issues of loss, grief, and uncertainty. Those who provided support after Hurricane Katrina were sometimes caught in the dilemma of being required to help others when they weren't sure whether their own families were safe. Like many mental health professionals, those who worked in New Orleans before the storm had developed resource and referral networks for managing their caseloads. After the storm, many of these resources were no longer available and they had to adapt to working with little resources and poor networks after the storm. A year later, many were still struggling to cope with a decimated in-patient treatment system. It is not surprising that less than half of outpatient providers have returned.

Although crisis intervention for survivors has a long history, crisis intervention for caregivers, and especially first responders, dates only to the 1990s, when it was recognized that there were inherent psychological and physical risks that first responders might encounter in the course of fulfilling their responsibilities (Castellano & Plionis, 2006). The inverted pyramid of support mentioned earlier might be the preferred strategy for increasing resilience among helpers. Sharing experiences with other professionals of what it means to be both a helper and a victim can counter the effects of working without adequate support. Agencies in affected areas can promote the well-being of their employees by providing opportunities for self-care during the workday. Reading groups made up of coworkers and staff meetings with open forums on the agenda might help to promote social support and decrease the potential for burnout. In addition to these structural and organizational supports, individual healthy practices such as exercise, yoga, and massage can be helpful.

LESSON 7. Science has a voice, too. Imagine that you are a volunteer for a national organization. You've been trained in the Disaster Mental Health Model, and though you're a licensed professional, you know that this is not a place where you will be doing therapy. You notice that there is one hurricane survivor who spends each day alone, walking around aimlessly or smoking a cigarette outside. As each day passes, the survivor seems more anxious and depressed. You make it your routine to be in those places where the survivor is, and you talk about inconsequential things with the person, sharing a joke here and there, asking the survivor to help you move cases of water or help you put up signs for the town hall meeting that will be held the next day. When the survivor finally is ready to leave the shelter, he comes to you and thanks you for being there at this difficult time. He seems less anxious and depressed.

There are many forms of early intervention that have evolved in response to the needs of people in natural disasters. These theoretical and technical approaches are referred to as crisis intervention, psychoeducation, psychological debriefing, and defusing (Reyes & Elhai, 2004). The essential feature of crisis intervention models is safety and stabilization of people who are in crisis. Strategies are not designed to be psychotherapeutic and referral is often the outcome of assessment. Psychoeducation in early intervention models is based on the principle that knowledge is power and people who feel powerless will benefit from having accurate information about the consequences—positive and negative—of having survived a disaster. The essential feature of the various debriefing models that have evolved in the disaster relief field is that people will benefit from discussing their experiences in a structured way. Debriefing models can be applied either individually or in a group format, by peers or by professionals. The essential feature of defusing models is verbal processing of stressful events with a focus on the present. This latter category of models can focus on survivors or on first responders and helping professionals. It is beyond the scope of this chapter to comment on the efficacy and effectiveness of these models. Considerable controversy exists in the literature about the current state of the evidence base of each practice model (Devilly, Gist, & Cotton, 2006). Suffice it to say that there is no form of early intervention that can be considered empirically supported as of yet. There are, however, some points of consensus that can be gleaned from the literature base. One of these is that people who experience early interventions appear to be grateful for the support. Another consensus is that those organizations that provide interventions in the acute phase of disasters do so because survivors appreciate it and because society has come to expect disaster relief organizations to provide some response in the aftermath. Appreciation and social expectations, however, are not to be confused with a positive psychological or mental health outcome. The scientific method requires a preponderance of evidence about a model or approach before it can be said that posttraumatic stress disorders or any mental disorder might be prevented following any particular form of early intervention.

Currently, it can only be said that effective outcomes from helping models are less about any intervention and more about managing the crisis effectively. It appears that effective communication between and among the various levels of affected organizations is associated with recovery. A final consensus point appears to be in favor of interventions with flexible components that can be adapted to the situation rather than a one-size-fits-all model.

> **LESSON 8. Location, location, location.** Imagine yourself having survived Katrina, temporarily living in a shelter in a part of the country you've never even visited. Your partner of 20 years is not with you. You don't know where your partner is because in the confusion at the airport, you were told to get in one line and your partner was told to get in another. No one was told where the flights were going, only that you needed to get on the plane quickly. You don't have any means of contacting your partner because your cell phones were left in your house in New Orleans. You know no one in the area and the only thing you hear from the Red Cross is that no one is being allowed to go back yet. You worry that your house will be gone when you return. You worry that your partner who is diabetic won't have access to medications. You worry alone.

In any disaster, there will be a period when people will be displaced from their natural environments. The bigger the disaster, the more likely it will be that displacement periods will be long. This resulting isolation from partners or relatives can be mitigated, however, by actions on the part of everyone in the ecology, from the displaced person, to the community, and to the national disaster relief agency. Individuals and families can develop their own plans for how and where they will meet should they ever become separated. In a post-9/11 world, these family plans and logistics should be a preparatory staple for everyone. One key aspect of these plans is to select a point of communication and rendezvous far enough away from an individual or family residence that it would not be similarly affected by a disaster. Such a location, agreed upon in advance, can provide a safety net to ensure that communication continues in the event of a separation. Sharing these plans with extended family members or with friendship or kinship networks can help diminish the effect of emergency displacements with their potential isolating and retraumatizing consequences.

People with chronic illnesses usually know that they must provide themselves several days' worth of medication in the event of an emergency. Disasters of the magnitude of Hurricane Katrina, however, will require more than a few days of medications. What is the role of prescription providers and pharmacies in facilitating access to medications? Is there such a thing as a disaster prescription that people can carry with them, such as an emergency medical bracelet? Malone (2007) mentions e-prescriptions as a possible way to address prescription access for people displaced by disasters. In the aftermath of Hurricane Katrina, it became apparent that paper-based prescriptions could not meet the needs of people who left homes without time to collect existing prescriptions or request new ones from their health care providers. Malone suggests that networks of providers and pharmacies can create databases where patient health information and current prescriptions can be accessed remotely. Like other forms of health information that require the use of technology, there are some concerns about privacy and the need to conform to Health Insurance Portability and Accountability Act protections on the use of private health information, but the benefits in the event of disaster could be greater than the negative consequences. One unintended but positive consequence would be that medication errors that arise from pharmacist readings of physician handwriting would be eliminated in an electronic system.

At the state level, and especially among people who are enrolled in state Medicaid programs, there should be ongoing discussions about allowing short-term access to out-of-state

Medicaid systems when people receiving Medicaid in disaster states are temporarily displaced. In the immediate aftermath of the two storms, there were temporary measures passed by neighboring states that suspended eligibility requirements about residency for displaced hurricane survivors who had been on Louisiana Medicaid (see, e.g., North Carolina Department of Health and Human Services, 2005). A year after Hurricane Katrina, Lambrew and Shalala (2006) were advocating a more permanent long-term response that would require federal legislation, but this has not materialized. A more permanent national Medicaid authorization would go a long way toward facilitating recovery for displaced people with chronic illnesses.

Borrowing from public health models of disease management, it might be feasible to use call-in radio programs to educate people about how to manage chronic diseases should they be displaced by a natural disaster or other extreme crisis. This type of programming could be developed in collaboration with professional associations of the various health care providers. Again, these efforts are best done before the occurrence of a regional or national emergency.

LESSON 9. The whole ecology may suffer and the whole ecology may also be satisfied. Imagine that you are a FEMA staff person managing a team of disaster workers in a shelter 1,000 miles away from the primary hurricane site. This is the third time that you've been away from home in 18 months. Each time you leave for several months, you return home, only long enough to do paperwork before being sent to the next site. You've heard all the jokes about FEMA incompetence and long ago stopped reading the media's criticisms of your agency. Next to the FEMA area at the shelter is the Family Services Red Cross table. The Family Services manager comes from the local area, and this is the first time she's had full responsibility for a team. Having served as a volunteer herself, she knows what to expect in her team members' reactions to hearing survivors' stories. Next to that area is the local Health and Human Services office staff. They all live in the area and are assigned to the shelter to interface with the others by providing a resource-and-referral network to those workers who are not familiar with area capabilities. There have been no natural disasters of this magnitude in the area. All the teams, both volunteers and staff, have struggled with setting up the computer networks and organizing the paperwork that will help manage the flow of people and data as the shelter provides service.

The experience level of people working in disaster relief in any one shelter will range from first-time volunteers to veterans with decades of disaster service experience. Because stress is based on subjective appraisals, and because repeated exposures can increase stress, mental health professionals must be prepared to apply varying approaches to stress management. The potential for vicarious trauma will be as variable as the people themselves.

Workers in temporary workplaces can be expected to experience stressors that come from conflicts in the way they see their roles as well as ambiguities that exist in how those roles are executed. Sometimes the roles themselves may be evaluated externally and found to be deficient, as was the case with FEMA in the aftermath of Hurricane Katrina. Just as psychological recovery is the hoped-for outcome for survivors, so, too, mental health professionals may experience a positive outcome in the form of compassion satisfaction

(Stamm, 2002); burnout or secondary trauma is not the only potential consequence. The literature on predictors of positive and negative outcomes of secondary exposure is in the very early stages of definition. In a review of vicarious trauma and secondary traumatic stress, Baird and Kracen (2006) reported persuasive evidence that supports a positive correlation between repeated exposures and the occurrence of secondary traumatic stress. Only three of the studies they reviewed were specific to disaster mental health workers, however. They also reported that how one perceived and evaluated one's ability to cope with stress was a protective factor against negative outcomes. The disaster responder's access to supervision can also be a protective factor. Increasing the repertoire of self-care strategies when mental health workers are repeatedly deployed can ameliorate the consequences of long-term exposure to traumas experienced in disasters.

> **LESSON 10. Hope springs eternal.** Imagine that you are in a shelter in a part of the country that you never thought you would be in, largely because you'd never left the city in which you were born. You wait patiently for permission to leave the shelter, and being a bit extroverted, you soon develop a group of buddies to sit with during the day. Your conversation tends to be about the present, and though you don't lose sight of why you're at the shelter, you are also very aware of the goodness of people who provide food and housing to you and your buddies. You tell them that you'd never had a piece of meat like the one you ate for dinner the previous night, and all agree that the food here is pretty spectacular. Not like the food at home, of course, which is excellent. For now, you thank God that you are alive and enjoy your first taste of prime rib.

There is a vast amount of literature on resiliency and what it takes to build it. Personality characteristics such as extroversion and agreeableness, for example, predict resiliency, as do social conditions such as belonging to an extended family and identifying with a specific cultural group. Spirituality has also been associated with resiliency among people with a history of trauma (Connor, Davidson, & Lee, 2003). Both spirituality and resilience are correlated with positive outcomes such as physical and mental health and diminished symptom severity among those people diagnosed with posttraumatic stress disorder. The African American community, which was disproportionately affected by Hurricanes Katrina and Rita, relied on religion to support their well-being and enhance the quality of their lives. Perhaps the message of hope that these survivors highlighted is that it is possible to cope adequately with adversity when one has a group of friends and a spiritual belief system on which one can depend.

PRACTICAL IMPLICATIONS

- Everyone has a role in preparing and managing the knowledge gained from Hurricanes Katrina and Rita—each level of analysis, whether individual, group, organization, community, or policy, can be explored, and its lessons consolidated to provide effective disaster relief in the future.

- At the individual level of analysis, it is helpful to remember that human beings are among the most adaptive of all organisms. The natural tendency toward healing will propel survivors toward resolution of the exposure and a return to adaptive functioning.
- For those individuals with pre-existing mental health issues, it may be necessary to provide services that acknowledge the destabilization and again presume that a return to the previous level of functioning will be the outcome.
- From the perspective of individual human development, mental health professionals can remind themselves that meaning-making is a lifelong process and that each subsequent stage of development following disaster exposure may require further metabolizing of the experience.
- At the group level, mental health professionals and other first responders must keep abreast of the literature on efficacy and effectiveness of early intervention models.
- The science of disaster relief is developing rapidly, and what is learned in the academy and applied in practice is constantly being reformulated, if not being replaced by new research findings.
- Professional groups can provide professional development on ways for their members to manage self-care, especially for those helpers who will go to many disaster sites, thereby increasing long-term exposures to extremely stressful conditions.
- Professional organizations are key in developing a continuing cadre of helpers trained in evidence-based models of disaster response. Graduate programs in the various disciplines can re-examine the competencies expected of those who will intervene in crisis situations and infuse the concepts throughout the curriculum.
- At the community level, collaborative partnerships between professional associations and community service organizations could develop public information campaigns about the best way to prepare for a disaster. Efforts such as the "Clean hands save lives!" campaign (Centers for Disease Control and Prevention, 2008), for example, have been found to be remarkably effective in a hospital's ability to reduce nosocomial infections.
- For those community organizations charged with training first responders such as police and firefighters, adding mental health professionals to the planning teams might help prevent retraumatizing participants in the process of ensuring their safety.

CONCLUSION

Lakoff and Halpin (2005) note that a central role of government is to promote the common good by relying on basic human values such as empathy, responsibility, and fairness. In the immediate aftermath of Hurricane Katrina, survivors and caregivers exemplified empathy and responsibility in their interactions during displacements and relocations, and they asked and continue to ask for fairness from government. Perhaps the crisis of the 2005 hurricanes provides an opportunity for creating an infrastructure that uses the knowledge base that was acquired at such great cost, to prepare for the devastating aftermath of disasters still to come.

REFERENCES

American Psychiatric Association. (2000). *Diagnostic and statistical manual of mental disorders* (4th ed., Text rev.). Washington, DC: Author.

Anderson, H. D. (1995). Collaborative language systems: Toward a postmodern therapy. In R. H. Mikesell, D. Lusterman, & S. H. McDaniel (Eds.), *Integrating family therapy: Handbook of family psychology and systems theory* (pp. 27–44). Washington, DC: American Psychological Association.

Andrews, C. R., & Marotta, S. A. (2005). Spirituality and coping among grieving children: A preliminary study. *Counseling and Values, 50,* 38–50.

Baird, K., & Kracen, A. C. (2006). Vicarious traumatization and secondary traumatic stress: A research synthesis. *Counselling Psychology Quarterly, 19,* 181–188.

Berggren, R. E., & Curiel, T. J. (2006). After the storm: Health care infrastructure in post-Katrina New Orleans. *New England Journal of Medicine, 354,* 1549–1552.

Castellano, C., & Plionis, E. (2006). Comparative analysis of three crisis intervention models applied to law enforcement first responders during 9/11 and Hurricane Katrina. *Brief Treatment and Crisis Intervention, 6,* 326–336.

Centers for Disease Control and Prevention. (2008). *Clean hands save lives!* Retrieved May 12, 2008, from http://www.cdc.gov/cleanhands/

Cerise, F. P. (2007). *Testimony for "Post Katrina Health Care: Continuing Concerns and Immediate Needs in the New Orleans Region."* Retrieved May 14, 2008, from http://www.dhh.louisiana.gov/offices/publications/pubs-81/Cerise_Testimony_31307.pdf

Connor, K. M., Davidson, J. R. T., & Lee, L. C. (2003). Spirituality, resilience, and anger in survivors of violent trauma: A community survey. *Journal of Traumatic Stress, 16,* 487–494.

Conrad, E. J., Townsend, M. H., & Buccola, N. (2008). Restoration of mental health services in New Orleans. *American Journal of Psychiatry, 165,* 33.

Devilly, G. J., Gist, R., & Cotton, P. (2006). Ready! Fire! Aim! The status of psychological debriefing and therapeutic interventions: In the workplace and after disasters. *Review of General Psychology, 10,* 318–345.

Feeny, N. C., Foa, E. B., Treadwell, K. R. H., & March, J. (2004). Posttraumatic stress disorder in youth: A critical review of the cognitive and behavioral treatment outcome literature. *Professional Psychology: Research and Practice, 35,* 466–476.

Foa, E. B., Davidson, J. R. T., & Frances, A. (Eds.). (1999). Treatment of posttraumatic stress disorder. *The Journal of Clinical Psychiatry, 60*(Suppl. 16), 1–76.

Foa, E. B., Keane, T. M., & Friedman, M. J. (Eds.). (2000). *Effective treatments for PTSD: Practice guidelines from the International Society for Traumatic Stress Studies.* New York: Guilford.

Gheytanchi, A., Joseph, L., Gierlach, E., Kimpara, S., Housley, J., Franco, Z. E., et al. (2007). The dirty dozen: Twelve failures of the Hurricane Katrina response and how psychology can help. *American Psychologist, 62,* 18–130.

Government Accountability Office. (2008). *National disaster response: FEMA should take action to improve capacity and coordination between government and voluntary sectors* (Report No. GAO-08-369). Retrieved May 6, 2008, from http://www.gao.gov/new.items/d08369.pdf

Hyman, O. (2004). Perceived social support and secondary traumatic stress symptoms in emergency responders. *Journal of Traumatic Stress, 17,* 149–156.

Lakoff, G., & Halpin, J. (2005, October 7). *Framing Katrina: The American prospect online.* Retrieved January 11, 2008, from http://www.rockbridgeinstitute.org/research/lakoff/framingkatrina/view

Lambrew, J. M., & Shalala, D. E. (2006). Federal health policy response to Hurricane Katrina: What it was and what it could have been. *The Journal of the American Medical Association, 296*(11), 1394–1397.

Lipton, E., Drew, C., Shane, S., & Rohde, D. (2005, September 11). Breakdowns marked path from hurricane to anarchy. *New York Times*. Retrieved February 9, 2009, from http://www.nytimes.com/2005/09/11/national/nationalspecial/11response.html

Malone, R. B. (2007). *Health information technology, e-prescribing and Hurricane Katrina: Could electronic health records have made a difference?* Retrieved May 19, 2008, from http://www.okjolt.org/articles/20070kjoltrev38.cfm

Neimeyer, G. J. (1995). The challenge of change. In R. A. Neimeyer & M. J. Mahoney (Eds.), *Constructivism in psychotherapy* (pp. 111–126). Washington, DC: American Psychological Association.

Norris, F. H., Friedman, M. J., & Watson, P. J. (2002). 60,000 disaster victims speak: Part II. Summary and implications of the disaster mental health research. *Psychiatry: Interpersonal and Biological Processes, 65*, 240–260.

North, C. S., Kawasaki, A., Spitznagel, E. L., & Hong, B. A. (2004). The course of PTSD, major depression, substance abuse and somatization after a natural disaster. *Journal of Nervous and Mental Disorders, 192*(12), 823–829.

North Carolina Department of Health and Human Services. (2005). *Revised policy concerning evacuees from areas devastated by Hurricane Katrina* (Food and Nutrition Services Letter No. 9-2005). Retrieved February 12, 2009, from http://info.dhhs.state.nc.us/olm/manuals/dss/ei-30/adm/ES_AL-9-2005.htm

Pickett-Schenk, S. A., Cook, J. A., Grey, D. D., & Butler, S. B. (2007). Family contact and housing stability in a national multi-site cohort of homeless adults with severe mental illness. *Journal of Primary Prevention, 28*, 327–339.

Reyes, G., & Elhai, J. D. (2004). Psychosocial interventions in the early phases of disasters. *Psychotherapy: Theory, Research, Practice, Training, 41*, 399–411.

Rodriguez, H., & Aguirre, B. E. (2006). Hurricane Katrina and the healthcare infrastructure: A focus on disaster preparedness, response and resiliency. *Frontiers of Health Services Management, 23*, 13.

Rosenbaum, S. (2006). U.S. health policy in the aftermath of Hurricane Katrina. *Journal of the American Medical Association, 295*, 437–440.

Schonfeld, D. J. (2005). Rebuilding a region: 200 billion dollars restoring communities: Priceless. *Journal of Developmental and Behavioral Pediatrics, 26*(6), 419–420.

Sheikh, A. I., & Marotta, S. A. (2008). Best practices following the trauma of cardiac disease. *Journal of Counseling & Development, 86*, 111–119.

Stamm, B. H. (2002). Measuring compassion satisfaction as well as fatigue: Developmental history of the compassion satisfaction and fatigue test. In C. R. Figley (Ed.), *Treating compassion fatigue* (pp. 107–112). New York: Brunner-Routledge.

Ursano, R. J., Fullerton, C. S., Benedek, D. M., & Hamaoka, D. A. (2007). Hurricane Katrina: Disasters teach us and we must learn. *Academic Psychiatry, 31*(3), 180–182.

U.S. Department of Health and Human Services. (1999). *Mental health: A report of the Surgeon General.* Rockville, MD: Author.

Voelker, R. (2006). In post-Katrina New Orleans, efforts under way to build better healthcare. *The Journal of the American Medical Association, 296*(11), 1333–1334.

Weisler, R. H., Barbee, J. G., & Townsend, M. H. (2006). Mental health and recovery in the Gulf Coast after Hurricanes Katrina and Rita. *Journal of the American Medical Association, 296*(5), 585-588.

Weiss, D. S., Marmar, C. R., Metzler, T. J., & Ronfeldt, H. M. (1995). Predicting symptomatic distress in emergency service personnel. *Journal of Consulting and Clinical Psychology, 63*, 361–368.

The Federal Government in Disaster Mental Health Response

An Ever-Evolving Role

Daniel Dodgen

Jessica Meed

T he unprecedented scale of destruction from the 2005 hurricane season inspired many federal agencies to find new ways to use existing authorities and resources to serve the people affected by the devastation. This assistance came in the form of direct action and indirect assistance through federal support to state and local entities. The government response, though not faultless, produced many positive outcomes and served as a catalyst for improving future responses.

The immediate federal mental health response to Hurricane Katrina was dramatic. Between September 2005 and June 2006, the Substance Abuse and Mental Health Services Administration (SAMHSA), part of the U.S. Department of Health and Human Services (HHS), supported numerous vital activities. One example of a program is the Louisiana Spirit program, which made more than 775,000 person contacts, 144,000 individual crisis counseling sessions, and 125,000 phone or e-mail contacts, and distributed more than 7 million educational materials (Louisiana Department of Health and Hospitals, 2006). SAMHSA also sent behavioral health experts to be part of the HHS secretary's Emergency Response Team in the field and the secretary's Operation Center in Washington, DC.

Both the Indian Health Service (2005) and the Health Resources and Services Administration (HRSA; Duke, 2005) deployed U.S. Public Health Service–commissioned corp officers to assist with the provision of counseling services and provide logistical support for the medical response. In keeping with pre-existing response plans, other federal behavioral health specialists temporarily left their normal assignments to be deployed to the Gulf Coast. Additional human resources were pulled from other federal agencies.

The hurricanes destroyed much of the Gulf Coast area's infrastructure, including clinical and laboratory facilities needed for public health surveillance and medical research. With these resources temporarily out of commission, local health officials were hindered in monitoring emerging public health threats. The Centers for Disease Control and Prevention (CDC) stepped in to fill the void. This permitted an expedited process of carrying out necessary health surveillance and rapid needs assessments. In addition, CDC collected data on the behavioral health needs in affected areas (U.S. Government Accountability Office, 2008). These data allowed the state of Louisiana to better document needs in applying for a Crisis Counseling Program grant from the Federal Emergency Management Agency (FEMA).

Similarly, the National Institutes of Health (NIH, 2005) used Rapid Assessment Post Impact of Disaster (RAPID) grants to quickly fund mental health research. RAPID grants had been designed in response to NIH's recognition that traumatic stress research must include the study of the immediate aftermath of a disaster, which would be impossible if researchers had to wait the minimum 9 months typically required between the time that a grant is submitted and the time that funds are transferred to the researcher (NIH, 2002).

Furthermore, several agencies took immediate steps to help with the dissemination of best practices in behavioral health prevention and treatment. The National Institute of Mental Health (NIMH), part of NIH, has a long history of supporting research and education on traumatic stress (Insel, 2005). NIMH used this experience to provide technical assistance to researchers, trainees, and community public health providers. It also provided disaster-related material that targeted the needs of children (NIH, 2009). Similarly, the U.S. Department of Veterans Affairs (VA) immediately began to disseminate resources for practitioners and for the general public through the National Center for Posttraumatic Stress Disorder (NCPTSD). The NCPTSD also published a paper summarizing the research on the impact of hurricane and other large-scale emergencies (Norris, 2005). This information was used extensively by applicants for various grant programs.

Finally, several federal agencies waived certain documentation requirements that were difficult to fulfill due to the destruction of records or the displacement of an organization's employees or service recipients. Certain agencies also provided additional grant money to help recipient organizations rebuild their services. In some cases, this additional grant money was also used to reach out to new individuals who were affected by the storm. A considerable amount of grant money was specifically used to support behavioral health efforts.

As this chapter illustrates, there are many federal agencies and programs that support response to psychological trauma. These programs are diverse in focus, scope, and budget, but they have all provided significant assistance in times of need.

CHAPTER HIGHLIGHTS

✦ Describes how mental health fits into the National Response Framework;

✦ Provides an overview of the Crisis Counseling Training and Assistance Program and other response grants focused on mental health and substance abuse;

+ Describes the role of deployable clinical assets such as the National Disaster Medical System;

+ Discusses federal research activities related to disaster mental health; and

+ Reviews other federal activities in the aftermath of Hurricanes Katrina and Rita.

HOW THE FEDERAL GOVERNMENT SUPPORTS EMERGENCY RESPONSE

According to the National Response Framework (U.S. Department of Homeland Security, 2007), which governs the federal response to emergencies, "Public Health and Medical Services includes behavioral health needs consisting of both mental health and substance abuse considerations for incident victims and response workers." The term *behavioral health services* may include treatment for chronic mental health conditions, counseling and treatment for acute traumatic stress, psychosocial interventions designed to improve the resiliency of the general population, and services to help individuals with substance abuse issues. In this chapter, unless otherwise specified, the term *behavioral health services* is assumed to include everything covered under the broadest definition of the term.

The federal role in addressing psychological aspects of disaster preparedness and response is quite complex. To help the reader understand the federal role, this chapter addresses the underlying principles behind the design of federal disaster policy in behavioral health and the legislation that gives federal agencies the authority to respond to behavioral health needs following a disaster. It also discusses the federal assets that currently exist, including how those assets were deployed during the 2005 hurricanes. Finally, the chapter discusses the future direction of federal behavioral health response.

Because the authors work primarily on federal efforts, this chapter focuses on issues at the federal and national levels. The authors acknowledge that the focus on federal-level efforts provides only one piece of the picture. State and local governments, community and nongovernment organizations, and individual providers all make a significant contribution that cannot be underestimated (see Hamilton & Dodgen, 2008). Although all of these partners are important to the process, this chapter focuses on describing the process from the perspective of the federal government. Given the old adage that "all disasters are local," many readers may wonder about the relevance of the federal government to the behavioral response to a disaster. The authors believe that the federal role is significant because of its impact on services, research, and planning efforts by states. Furthermore, awareness of the federal policy process should foster a more seamless cooperation between various agencies, different layers of government, and the public and private sectors.

The Federal Role: An Overview

Federal disaster assistance programs are designed to balance two principles. The first principle is recognition that the federal government has an obligation to provide assistance when the surge of need, created by a sudden catastrophe, temporarily overwhelms the capacity of state and local resources. This need must be balanced with the principle that the provision of federal assistance should not undermine the long-term integrity of the local system (Dodgen & Meed, 2008).

Fundamentally, federal disaster policy must address the need to balance the constitutional rights of states, with recognition that the federal government has resources that state and local governments lack. The U.S. Constitution leaves all authority not explicitly given to the federal government to the states. State and local authorities have primary control of most of the nation's public health systems. The state regulates medical professionals, hospitals, medical insurance, and the Medicaid program. As such, state and local governments are in the position to know which policies will best support the public health response to an event. The primary role of the federal government is to support state and local programs through funds, guidelines, and technical assistance.

The federal response is designed to reinforce local capabilities without undermining the long-term stability of the local system. An example of how temporary help could hinder long-term recovery efforts in the area of behavioral health service follows: After a disaster, there may be a surge of demand for crisis counseling. At the same time, the capabilities of the local health system may have been affected by the disaster. The combination may overwhelm the resources of the local health system, requiring additional support from outside the community. The federal government can assist with the provision of additional services through FEMA contractors or, in limited instances, through direct services provided by HHS assets. However, there is concern that extended existence of subsidized services provided by federal resources may replace the demand for local providers, possibly causing those providers to leave the community and undermining the long-term recovery of the community. To minimize the risk of federal services displacing local services, most disaster aid has been in the form of grants to states that promote spending money on locally provided services before importing additional services from outside the community (Dodgen & Meed, 2008).

Key Factors in Federal Responding to Psychosocial Needs

From a federal perspective, behavioral health concerns resulting from disasters can be broken into two broad types of mental health needs. The first need is one generated by the disaster itself. After a disaster, it is common for survivors and responders to exhibit some level of psychological distress. This distress may manifest itself as traumatic stress or as symptoms that mimic physical illness (White House, 2007). Although a distress reaction can range from mild to debilitating, its population prevalence generally decreases over time (Galea, 2007; Morren, 2007). For this reason, trauma-linked behavioral health problems are thought of as a temporary surge—a problem that can be appropriately addressed by time-limited federal resources. At the same time, the disaster does not erase the pre-existing mental and behavioral health needs of the community. For example, one of the most comprehensive surveys of Hurricane Katrina survivors found that 21.3% of respondents reported having a mental disorder in the 12 months prior to Katrina (Wang et al., 2007). Individuals being treated for behavioral health conditions before the event require ongoing care throughout the response and recovery process. In addition, having pre-existing psychosocial problems could put these individuals at higher risk than the general population for having a severe traumatic stress reaction to the disaster. Although the federal government can help the local public health system in building its capacity to provide continuity of care to this population, federal response assets are generally ill equipped to directly provide that care, because they are, by definition, temporary and crisis focused.

Although specific federal disaster support of the local public health system has time limits, federal support of local entities is ongoing. Normally the federal government has a role in supporting research, infrastructure, and patient care, including work intended to increase the resiliency of local communities. For example, CDC, HRSA, and the Department of Homeland Security have a role in funding the ongoing development of state and local preparedness for the psychological consequences of disasters (U.S. Government Accountability Office, 2008). Furthermore, HRSA—through its funding of community health centers—and the Center for Medicare and Medicaid Services (CMS)—through reimbursement and support to local hospitals and other behavioral health services—have a significant role in addressing the ongoing needs of communities. For all of these agencies, disaster response support grows out of pre-existing relationships between the agency and stakeholders within the local public health system. These ongoing programs are critical because, ultimately, they must absorb (or reabsorb) the affected populations when temporary, crisis-focused programs end.

The programs described in this chapter all follow a series of steps that must be completed before a federal program can begin to fulfill its function. First, Congress must authorize the existence of the program and assign its mission to one or more government agencies. This bill must pass both houses of Congress before being signed into law by the president. Next, Congress must specifically authorize funds for the program. These funds are allocated through separate appropriations bills that must also pass both houses of Congress and be signed by the president. Once funds have been appropriated, it is up to the agency receiving the funds to determine a policy that will execute the services mandated by the new law. At this stage, the agency may gather input from other stakeholders, such as state and local government, representatives of the private sector, expert opinion, nonprofit organizations, and other agencies. Once the conceptual framework of the program has been developed, it is time to determine the implementation strategy for the program. This is the step where equipment is purchased, grant proposals are requested, and staff are hired and trained. Only then is the ultimate goal of having a usable disaster response program realized.

In this chapter, we distinguish between the different steps. Legislation is the legal basis for a federal agency's ability to respond to a disaster. A response program is the formal policy that the agency has created to operationalize the intention of the legislation. A deployable asset is a specific asset (personnel, equipment, or published material) that has been fully developed by the agency and is ready for deployment during a disaster. A deployable asset can be anything from a mobile hospital, to team of medical providers, to an emergency stockpile of medication.

PROGRAMS THAT SUPPORT DISASTER BEHAVIORAL HEALTH

The following section describes major legislation authorizing federal support of services either directly or by grant support to local programs.

Stafford Act/Crisis Counseling Program

The 1974 Stafford Act, also known as the Disaster Relief Act Amendments of 1974 (PL 93–288, S 3062), provides the basis for all disaster legislation. In fact, because the Stafford Act authorizes the president to use federal assets during a declared national disaster, many federal disaster relief funds are known as Stafford Act programs. The Act authorizes the performance of essential community services, public information, assistance in health and safety measures, technical assistance, and distribution of medicine, as well as other types of aid (42 USC 5145). Included in the statute's language is authorization for the provision of services to responders and victims who have mental disorders that are caused or aggravated by the disaster.

In the original legislation, crisis counseling was to be performed by the NIH. This specification was removed in 1988, allowing any professional provider to provide crisis counseling. This change increased the role of private providers and employees of state and local government in response activities.

The Stafford Act authorizes FEMA to run the Crisis Counseling Training and Assistance Program (CCP; U.S. Government Accountability Office, 2008). The CCP helps local entities provide short-term interventions to populations experiencing psychological sequelae after disasters. This program is primarily directed at populations that are not considered to be suffering from a chronic mental illness. CCP grants fund programs that provide victims with coaching and supportive listeners as they process and respond to the disaster. FEMA provides technical assistance, consultation, training, grant administration, and program oversight through interagency agreements with SAMHSA (U.S. Government Accountability Office, 2008). Although CCP grants may assist with the crisis needs of individuals with chronic mental conditions, they may not be used to fund long-term care, because that is the domain of the local public health system (Dodgen & Meed, 2008; FEMA, 2006, 2007).

SAMHSA Emergency Response Grants (SERG) Program

The Children's Health Act of 2000 gave SAMHSA the authority to use up to 2.5% of appropriated funds to provide noncompetitive aid to local communities experiencing substance abuse or mental health emergencies. Known as SAMHSA SERG, these funds support services in cases that are rapid in onset and have a definite conclusion, and are considered funds "of last resort" (U.S. Department of Health and Human Services [HHS], 2008). Authority to declare a mental health emergency belongs to the Secretary of Health (42 USC Sec. 290aa). Although this program allows SAMHSA the flexibility to respond in an emergency, it must be noted that all SERG grants come at the expense of regular SAMHSA mental health programming (Dodgen & Meed, 2008).

Assistant Secretary for Preparedness and Response and the Pandemic and All-Hazards Preparedness Act

Although historic in scale, the scope of the federal government response to behavioral health needs after the 2005 hurricanes still built on prior emergency response activities. The federal government has long played an important role in the response to disaster-related behavioral health problems. FEMA's primary mission is disaster response, but most other federal behavioral health response activities have come from individual agencies applying their regular nondisaster mandates to the task of emergency response. As such, the nature of an agency's response has historically been determined by the individual agency rather then by an overarching federal plan. As our society's understanding of the interplay between predisaster preparedness, disaster response, and psychosocial health has evolved, the federal government has moved to coordinate the many assets that individual agencies have created. In the future, as these efforts continue, there will also be an emphasis on creating a system that will provide better national-level support without undermining the self-determination of state and local agencies (White House, 2007).

The Pandemic and All-Hazards Preparedness Act (PAHPA) of 2006 formally legislated this process by creating an Assistant Secretary for Preparedness and Response (ASPR) position within the Office of the Secretary of HHS (PL n. 109-417). The ASPR was mandated to coordinate the nation's disaster response policy and assets, with the goal of creating a nation prepared. PAHPA gave the secretary of HHS the responsibility to lead the federal response to public health emergencies through the ASPR. This leadership includes coordination between the divisions of HHS (such as NIH, CDC, and SAMHSA) and other federal departments, particularly the Departments of Defense (DOD), VA, and U.S. Department of Homeland Security (which includes FEMA), in all matters related to public health preparedness and response (Dodgen & Meed, 2008). The implementation of PAHPA obviously had not yet begun when Hurricanes Katrina and Rita hit the Gulf Coast states in the fall of 2005. Although the subsequent federal support of behavioral health services demonstrated the strength of the agencies' individual programs, it also illustrated the need for the ASPR's mission of coordinating preparedness and response efforts as they relate to public health and mental health.

One of the ASPR's jobs is to develop the federal government's proactive role in promoting resilience as part of disaster preparedness. ASPR policies integrate federal disaster response into social support programs that already exist locally, including programs that provide behavioral health services. ASPR may also coordinate the sending of mental health experts from an HHS agency to support local entities developing their own response to a disaster.

Unlike the CCP, which targets a mentally healthy population, ASPR has a mandate to create specific response plans that protect at-risk individuals in the event of a disaster. At-risk individuals include those people who might be especially vulnerable to the turmoil of a catastrophe and may include people with mental health problems (Dodgen & Meed, 2008).

1984 Victims of Crime Act and the Crime Victims Fund

One last statute that deserves mention is the 1984 Victims of Crime Act, which gave the federal government a means to help individuals who develop traumatic stress as a result of crime. The law created a fund that is used to compensate victims of crime. Initially, the fund helped individual crime victims; in recent years, however, the fund has been used to compensate victims of crimes for health and mental health treatments and provide support services for victims of multiple-victim crimes, such as those directly affected by September 11, 2001. The fund did not play a large role in the response to Hurricane Katrina but could be important in responding to future man-made events such as terrorist attacks (U.S. Department of Justice, Office for Victims of Crime, 2007).

Deployable Assets

In addition to the programs described, HHS controls three types of personnel assets that can be mobilized in a disaster. The first and the only one to serve HHS throughout the year is the U.S. Public Health Service, one of the seven uniformed services of the United States. Throughout the year, officers serve as providers at federal facilities, as well as planners and administrators within federal agencies. In domestic or international disasters, multidisciplinary teams are deployed by the Office of the Surgeon General to provide humanitarian relief. Recent deployments include the 2004 Indonesian tsunami, the 2005 hurricanes, and the 2006 earthquake in Hawaii (U.S. Public Health Service, 2008).

The next two groups of personnel assets are the civilian responders who provide direct care to the general population and provide force protection to the disaster responders. The National Disaster Medical System (NDMS) is a component of ASPR's civilian response and is composed of intermittent federal employees assigned to 90 general disaster and specialty teams. A mental health provider may be deployed with each NDMS team. In addition to NDMS, providers contracted through the HHS Employee Assistance Program and through Federal Occupational Health provide psychosocial support to federal employees who are responders to or victims of the disaster (U.S. Department of Homeland Security, 2007).

The final category of human resources is made up of volunteer professionals. The Medical Reserve Corp (MRC) was founded in 2002 as part of the push to create a national network of volunteers dedicated to local community security following the terrorist attacks of September 11, 2001. MRC was conceived as a means of organizing citizen volunteers with health services skills to respond to disasters and promote healthy living throughout the year. Although the MRC is controlled at the local level, the volunteer members of the MRC units are trained and prepared to respond to national and local emergencies. Local MRC volunteers can include mental health providers such as psychiatrists, psychologists, pharmacists, and social workers. MRC units supplement existing emergency and public health resources and agencies such as FEMA, the American Red Cross, and local public health, fire, police, and ambulance services. Because MRC roles are determined at the local level, they are in a position to tailor their roles to the needs of the local community. Although the primary mission of the MRC is local, they can be deployed to other areas in the event of a large-scale disaster such as Hurricane Katrina. The Office of the Surgeon General, which sponsors the MRC program, plays a role in coordinating nonlocal deployments (Office of the U.S. Surgeon General, 2008).

The Emergency System for the Advance Registration of Volunteer Health Professionals (ESAR-VHP) program is a state-based, standardized, volunteer registration system. The establishment of these standardized systems enhances each state's ability to quickly identify and better assign health professional volunteers in emergencies and disasters. The mental health provider category includes volunteer professionals such as psychiatrists, psychologists, clinical social workers, and mental health counselors. In addition, these state systems enable the sharing of these preregistered and credentialed health care professionals across state lines and even nationally. Each state's ESAR-VHP system maximizes the size of the population. ESAR-VHP was formerly funded and coordinated through the HRSA but is now part of ASPR (HHS, 2008).

Individual providers may want to know these things about the federal role in disaster response:

- The HHS ASPR coordinates the nation's public health (including mental health) disaster response policy and assets. These efforts support rather than supplant local efforts. ASPR may also coordinate sending mental health providers and experts to support local entities. ASPR connects to local, state, and regional efforts through the Incident Command Structure.
- CCP grants are frequently available from FEMA to states after a disaster. CCP grants can be used for the provision of services to responders and victims, particularly short-term interventions to populations experiencing distress. Although CCP grants may assist with the crisis needs of individuals with chronic mental conditions, they may not be used to fund long-term care.
- The Crime Victims Fund has been used to compensate and provide support services for victims of multiple-victim crimes, such as those directly affected by the terrorist attacks on September 11, 2001.
- HHS controls several types of personnel who can be deployed to assist in a disaster. U.S. Public Health Service mental health providers can provide direct support to victims or consultation to community leaders. The NDMS uses its mental health teams to support responders. The Medical Reserve Corp is a national network of volunteers dedicated to local communities and includes mental health providers such as psychiatrists, psychologists, pharmacists, and social workers. The Emergency System for the Advance Registration of Volunteer Health Professionals program is a state-based, standardized, volunteer registration system that includes volunteer professionals such as psychiatrists, psychologists, clinical social workers, and mental health counselors. Mental health providers interested in disaster work can volunteer with the latter three programs.

FEDERAL RESEARCH IN TRAUMA AND DISASTER MENTAL HEALTH

Over the past few decades, the federal government has invested in another mechanism for reinforcing local and state public health agencies in their disaster response efforts. A number of federal agencies, including CDC, SAMHSA, NIMH, and the VA, fund research to develop best practices in treatment and prevention of traumatic stress. These agencies offer literature, training, and technical assistance that can be used by local authorities to develop preparedness and response plans. The lead HHS agency for research on traumatic stress in civilian populations is NIMH, which provides extramural funding for research ranging from neuroscience to health services delivery. The NIMH Web site also provides a link for individuals wishing to participate in clinical trials to treat traumatic stress. NIMH also began funding a disaster mental health research center in 2008.

The CDC has a smaller grant-making ability than NIMH, with the majority of its studies focused on epidemiological questions. In particular, the CDC's National Institute for Occupational Safety and Health (NIOSH) looks at work-based traumatic stress. Under this focus, NIOSH supports research into causes and prevention strategies and interventions for workplace stress, including traumatic stress (CDC, 2008). The CDC and NIMH, along with SAMHSA, play a large role in ensuring that lessons learned from the research are disseminated to providers, policy makers, and the larger population (HHS, 2008).

Traumatic Stress Services for the Military

In addition to the HHS activities described, the Departments of Defense and Veterans Affairs also play a large role in developing our understanding of behavioral health problems that are linked to traumatic stress. The VA coordinates its research through the previously mentioned NCPTSD. The VA researchers use the Veterans Health Administration's network of hospitals to conduct research into traumatic stress and its treatment. VA researchers have found that common causes of traumatic stress among veterans include combat exposure and sexual violence. Extensive research has been conducted on managing both causes (U.S. Department of Veterans Affairs [VA], 2007). In addition to providing information on ongoing VA studies, the NCPTSD also provides validated tools that can be used by non-VA providers to study PTSD in civilian populations (VA, 2008).

HOW FEDERAL CAPABILITIES WERE USED DURING HURRICANES KATRINA AND RITA

This chapter has provided a brief overview of many federal response capabilities. The beginning of the chapter highlighted some activities undertaken during Katrina and its aftermath. It may be helpful now to discuss how the programs just described made possible those response activities. One of the ironies of the federal response to Hurricanes Katrina and Rita was that many of the most effective federal actions were invisible. With the exception of the Uniformed Services and a portion of FEMA's operations, the goal of most federal interventions was to buttress state or local operations. This was done through emergency grants, supplemental staff, waivers on documentation requirements, and technical support. When this was done successfully, the program maintained the character and structure that the state had intended; the programs that the federal government supported did not look like federal programs. However, federal agencies were often in the background, making sure that state leaders were provided with the support they needed to keep their programs running.

For example, when Hurricane Katrina first made landfall in late August 2005, senior personnel from HHS agencies convened at headquarters to determine how the mandates of each division of the department could be called out to maximize the response capabilities of federal behavioral health assets. Beginning August 29, 2005, as the storms were hitting the Gulf Coast, the agencies launched a series of initiatives that would provide support for local projects for years to come.

By the time the storm made landfall, the following steps had already occurred. Thirty-eight U.S. Public Health Service officers had arrived in Jackson, Mississippi, to assist with direct patient care (HHS, 2005d). As members of one of the uniformed services, these officers provided a recognizable face for federal disaster assistance. Meanwhile, additional experts from CDC and FDA were already being identified to assist the states with public health concerns once the storm had passed. As part of an ongoing project to create a Strategic National Stockpile, 27 pallets of medical supplies assembled by the CDC had been delivered to Louisiana. Before the storm hit, HHS had identified alternative hospital beds in the area and had begun to make plans with the VA and DOD to move patients to those beds once the storm had passed.

By the time the storm cleared on August 30, it was evident that damage from Hurricane Katrina exceeded everyone's worst expectations. On September 2, HHS, with support from the DOD, took steps to open 10 federal medical shelters. On that day, an additional 500 U.S. Public Health Service officers were deployed to assist with patient care. NDMS, the VA, and the DOD also sent hundreds of extra medical providers (HHS, September 2, 2005c). In addition to the medical shelters, HHS, through SAMHSA, created a crisis hotline to serve the immediate mental health needs of hurricane victims (HHS, September 7, 2005a).

Although many federal agencies contributed to the mental health response, SAMHSA's normal mission as a key supporter of mental health programs gave it responsibility for taking the lead on HHS mental health efforts. By September 13, SAMHSA had awarded $600,000 in SERG grants to the four states most affected by Hurricane Katrina. These grants were used by the state official to fund mental health and substance abuse treatments for evacuees. The state of Louisiana used some of the funds to provide counseling to disaster workers and first responders (HHS, September 13, 2005b). Many more resources from SAMHSA followed in the ensuing months.

At the same time, several federal agencies made moves to streamline the process of accessing benefits for the hurricane survivors. The states worked with CMS to enroll evacuees who lacked personal identification documentation in the Medicaid program. In many cases, CMS granted waivers to allow enrollment or the delivery of services to individuals with little or no documentation regarding income, age, or residence. Similar waivers were applied to recipients of programs administered by the Administration for Children and Families and mental health and substance abuse programs (Substance Abuse and Mental Health Services Administration [SAMHSA], 2005a).

The SERG grants and waivers were just a first step. Over the next few weeks, as states got a better sense of their programmatic needs, the federal government increased its efforts to provide assistance. In October, the Mississippi Department of Health launched Project Recovery, a statewide in-person and helpline-based crisis counseling program, overseen by FEMA and SAMHSA. Although the program was run by the state, SAMHSA facilitated obtaining providers for the services. FEMA funded the program using the CCP grants (FEMA, 2005). In all, FEMA and SAMHSA worked together to administer a total of $25.8 million in crisis counseling grants to 29 states during the first few weeks of the recovery period (SAMHSA, 2006).

Outreach continued and grew to include programs throughout the county. In December 2005, HHS Secretary Mike Leavitt unveiled a series of public service announcements designed by SAMHSA and the ad council to encourage responders and evacuees to seek appropriate mental health care (SAMHSA, 2005b). SAMHSA continued to deliver grant money to fund state programs in states that were directly affected as well as those that were affected through their reception of evacuees.

As FEMA, SAMHSA, CMS, and HRSA (Duke, 2005; U.S. Government Accountability Office, 2008) worked with other federal agencies to ensure that hurricane survivors and responders had access to services, other federal agencies were taking action to ensure that the opportunity to learn more about disaster mental health was not wasted. SAMHSA convened a National Summit to Address the Nation's Disaster Behavioral Health Preparedness and Response (SAMHSA, 2006b). As discussed in the introduction, the CDC and NIH further assisted communities by conducting their own needs assessments while also supporting research by educational institutions. One of the largest of these research projects was the Hurricane Katrina Community Advisory Group study, which was assigned with monitoring the behavioral health aspects of the response recovery phase. This ongoing project is currently being conducted by faculty at a number of academic institutions with funding from multiple federal grants. NIH, the HHS Office of the Assistant Secretary for Planning and Evaluation, and FEMA have all contributed funds to the project (Hurricane Katrina Advisory Group, 2005).

THE AFTERMATH OF HURRICANES KATRINA AND RITA

About 6 months after Hurricane Katrina made landfall, the White House (2006) published *The Federal Response to Hurricane Katrina: Lessons Learned*. The report notes that despite numerous individual successes of federal, state, and local personnel, a lack of coordination across federal agencies hindered the efficiency of the public health response. While the report was being finalized, ASPR was already meeting with key personnel across HHS and other departments with the goal of creating a clear organizational structure for the nation's response efforts. Employees of HHS, in conjunction with DHS (including FEMA), and the Departments of Transportation, Housing and Urban Development, Defense, Agriculture, and Veterans Affairs, regularly met to take stock of the resources that already existed and talk through, step by step, what would be required to use those resources to respond to man-made events or natural disasters.

As part of this assessment process, ASPR undertook a survey of HHS behavioral health assets. The survey looked at the assets and capabilities in each of the agencies and offices of the department. It considered organizational problems that might hinder the effective deployment of each asset and recommended possible avenues for mitigating those programs. The survey also reviewed what gaps existed in the federal behavioral health response program and solicited potential solutions.

There are growing realizations that rather than invest solely on developing better responses to disaster behavioral health needs, the federal government should play a role in helping state and local authorities proactively build the ability of their community to be resilient in the face of a disaster. Consistent with this growing recognition, the White House (2007) issued the *Homeland Security Presidential Directive-21*, which notes that "the impact of the 'worried well' in past disasters is well documented, and it is evident that mitigating the mental health consequences of disasters can facilitate effective response." The directive instructed the secretary of HHS to work with the DOD, VA, and DHS to address this concern. Toward that end, the presidential directive mandated the establishment of an expert panel to develop a set of recommendations for "protecting, preserving and restoring individual and community mental health in catastrophic health events settings" (White House, 2007). The White House–level expert panel will make recommendations to the secretary of HHS regarding these issues. Following the issuance of *Homeland Security Presidential Directive-21*, HHS moved quickly to establish the Disaster Mental Health Subcommittee of the National Biodefense Science Board.

PRACTICAL IMPLICATIONS

Although Hurricane Katrina provided an opportunity for federal agencies to offer significant assistance, it also uncovered gaps in the current system. The knowledge resulting from this event has served as a catalyst for change and an impetus to address the many challenges regarding federal policy on traumatic stress. For example HHS undertook a comprehensive survey of all existing assets and capabilities related to behavioral health (HHS, 2008).

One challenge is the limitation of the current literature regarding interventions that mitigate traumatic stress. Without knowledge about which interventions work, it is difficult to know which interventions the government should support or encourage. These evidence-based guidelines will have to come from research and providers as the field develops. However, the federal government can assist with this process by supporting research.

Traumatic stress services, particularly in the area of disaster response, are reactive by nature. Because we do not know who will be a victim of a disaster or traumatic event before it happens, it is difficult to take steps to minimize the emotional impact of that event. Researchers and policy makers are increasingly looking at what factors put an individual at risk for pathological traumatic stress in hopes of creating successful early interventions.

Finally, in creating national policies to address traumatic stress, there is a tension between the need to disseminate best practices in an organized fashion and the need to allow local authorities to tailor responses to local needs. All of this must be done without hindering individual researchers and practitioners from developing innovative intervention strategies.

CONCLUSION

Disaster response remains a local responsibility and thus "all disasters are local." However, the federal government plays a significant role in supporting local people when responding to an emergency event. That support can come through grants and waivers that empower states to create their own response systems. The support can also be through the provision of direct services or allocation of other resources. Regardless of the form that support takes, there are many mechanisms by which federal support can be delivered. During the response to Hurricanes Katrina and Rita, the mental health response was not perfect. Nevertheless, significant assistance was provided that made an impact in the lives on thousands of survivors. Since Katrina made landfall with such devastating results, much work has been done to evaluate lessons learned and use those lessons to improve future responses. The impact of this process is still being felt, but the authors are hopeful that it will yield an even better result in the next major national emergency.

REFERENCES

Centers for Disease Control and Prevention. (2008). *NIOSH safety and health topic: Occupational health psychology (OHP)*. Retrieved February 13, 2009, from http://www.cdc.gov/niosh/topics/stress/ohp/ohp.html

Dodgen, D., & Meed, J. (2008). Laws, legislation, and policy: The role of government in addressing traumatic stress. In G. Reyes, J. Elhai, & J. Ford (Eds.), *Encyclopedia of psychological trauma* (pp. 377–380). Hoboken, NJ: Wiley.

Duke, E. (2005, October 18). *Remarks to the Maternal and Child Health Federal/State Partnership meeting*. Retrieved August 3, 2008, from http://newsroom.hrsa.gov/espeeches/2005/Duke-MCH.htm

Federal Emergency Management Agency. (2005, October 5). *Mississippi project recovery available to all affected by Hurricane Katrina*. Retrieved July 20, 2008, from http://www.fema.gov/news/newsrelease.fema?id=19438

Federal Emergency Management Agency. (2006). *Crisis counseling and mental health treatment–similarities and differences*. Retrieved August 3, 2008, from http://www.fema.gov/txt/media/2006/ccp_mh.txt

Federal Emergency Management Agency. (2007). *An overview of the Crisis Counseling Assistance and Training Program*. Retrieved July 28, 2007, from http://www.fema.gov/txt/media/2006/ccp_over.txt

Galea, S. (2007). The long-term health consequences of disasters and mass traumas. *Canadian Medical Association Journal, 176*(9), 1293–1294.

Hamilton, S., & Dodgen, D. (2008). Nongovernmental organizations. In G. Reyes, J. Elhai, & J. Ford. (Eds.), *Encyclopedia of psychological trauma* (pp. 448–451). Hoboken, NJ: Wiley.

Hurricane Katrina Advisory Group. (2005). *Project overview*. Retrieved February 13, 2009, from http://www.hurricanekatrina.med.harvard.edu/

Indian Health Service. (2005). *Phoenix area HIS deployments to aid Hurricane Katrina survivors*. Retrieved February 13, 2008, from http://www.ihs.gov/facilitiesServices/AreaOffices/Phoenix/phx_feature200509.cfm

Insel, T. (2005). *Coping with Hurricane Katrina*. Retrieved May 11, 2009, from http://www.nimh.nih.gov/about/director/updates/2005/coping-with-hurricane-katrina.shtml

Louisiana Department of Health and Hospitals. (2006). Data evaluation of the CCP. *Inside Louisiana Spirit, 1*(2), 1–4.

Morren, M. (2007). The influence of a disaster on the health of rescue workers: A longitudinal study. *Canadian Medical Association Journal, 176*(9), 1279–1283.

National Institutes of Health. (2002). *Rapid assessment post-impact of disaster*. Retrieved July 20, 2008, from http://grants.nih.gov/grants/guide/pa-files/PAR-02-133.html

National Institutes of Health. (2005). Notice of mechanism for time-sensitive research opportunities: PAR-05-150, expansion to include alcohol and drug research pertaining to Hurricane Katrina. Retrieved August 3, 2008, from http://grants.nih.gov/grants/guide/notice-files/NOT-DA-05-013.html

National Institutes of Health. (2009). *Coping with traumatic events*. Retrieved May 11, 2009, from http://grants.nih.gov/grants/guide/pa-files/PAR-02-133.html

Norris, F. (2005). *Range, magnitude, and duration of the effects of disasters on mental health: Review update 2005*. Retrieved February 13, 2009, from http://www.redmh.org/research/general/REDMH_effects.pdf

Office of the U.S. Surgeon General. (2008). *About the Medical Reserve Corps*. Retrieved July 10, 2008, from http://www.medicalreservecorps.gov/About

Pond, M. (2006). Hurricane recovery guides preparedness planning. *SAMHSA News, 14*(4).Retrieved May 11, 2009, from http://www.samhsa.gov/SAMHSA_NEWS/VolumeXIV_4/index.htm

Substance Abuse and Mental Health Services Administration. (2005a, September 13). *Secretary Leavitt tours Gulf Region; Announces streamlined access to benefits for Hurricane Katrina victims*. Retrieved July 20, 2008, from http://www.samhsa.gov/news/newsreleases/050913_hhs_leavitt.htm

Substance Abuse and Mental Health Services Administration. (2005b, December 7). *HHS secretary Leavitt unveils national PSA campaign to provide mental health services to hurricane survivors.* Retrieved July 20, 2008, from http://www.samhsa.gov/news/newsreleases/051207_hurricane.htm

Substance Abuse and Mental Health Services Administration. (2006, February 15). Mississippi, Arkansas, Indiana, Maryland, New Jersey, Utah receive over $22 million for Hurricane Katrina crisis counseling assistance. Retrieved July 10, 2008, from http://www.samhsa.gov/news/newsreleases/060215_katrina.htm

U.S. Department of Health and Human Services. (2005a, September 7). *Crisis hotline available for victims of Hurricane Katrina.* Retrieved July 19, 2008, from http://www.hhs.gov/news/press/2005pres/20050907.html

U.S. Department of Health and Human Services. (2005b, September 13). *HHS awards $600,000 in emergency mental health grants to four states devastated by Hurricane Katrina.* Retrieved July 19, 2008, from http://www.samhsa.gov/news/newsreleases/050913_hhs_leavitt.htm

U.S. Department of Health and Human Services. (2005c, September 2). *HHS designates first medical shelters and provides vital medical supplies and medical assistance.* Retrieved July 20, 2008, from http://www.hhs.gov/news/press/2005pres/20050902.html

U.S. Department of Health and Human Services. (2005d, August 29). *HHS supports medical response to Hurricane Katrina.* Retrieved July 10, 2008, from http://www.hhs.gov/news/press/2005pres/20050829a.html

U.S. Department of Health and Human Services (2008). Summary of HHS Disaster Behavioral Health Assets and Capabilities. Washington, DC: Office of the Assistant Secretary for Preparedness and Response.

U.S. Department of Homeland Security. (2007). *National Response Framework: Worker safety and health support annex.* Retrieved August 4, 2008, from http://www.fema.gov/emergency/nrf/

U.S. Department of Justice, Office for Victims of Crime. (2007). *Grants and funding.* Retrieved August 5, 2007, from http://www.ojp.usdoj.gov/ovc/fund/welcome.html

U.S. Department of Veterans Affairs. (2007). *HSR&D studies sorted by keywords.* Retrieved February 99 http://www.hsrd.research.va.gov/research/keywords.cfm

U.S. Department of Veterans Affairs. (2008). *National Center for PTSD.* Retrieved August 3, 2008, from http://www.ncptsd.va.gov/ncmain/index.jsp

U.S. Government Accountability Office. (2008). *Federal efforts help state prepare for and respond to psychological consequences, but FEMA's* crises counseling program needs improvements. Washington, DC: Author.

U.S. Public Health Service. (2008). *About the Commissioned Corps: Emergency response.* Retrieved July 8, 2008, from http://www.usphs.gov/aboutus/emergencyresponse.aspx

Wang, P., Gruber, M., Powers, R., Schoenbaum, M., Speier, A., Wells, K. M., & Kessler, R. (2007). Disruption of existing mental health treatments and failure to initiate new treatments after Hurricane Katrina. *American Journal of Psychiatry, 165*(1), 34–41.

White House. (2006). *The federal response to Hurricane Katrina: Lessons learned.* Retrieved June 10, 2008, from http://www.whitehouse.gov/reports/katrina-lessons-learned/

White House. (2007). *Homeland security presidential directive-21 (HSPD-21): Subject public health and medical preparedness.* Retrieved July 21, 2008, from http://www.whitehouse.gov/news/releases/2007/10/20071018–10.html

A Community-Based Approach to Coping With Crises in Africa

Karen F. Carr

The focus of this chapter is to describe the crises and traumas faced by cross-cultural workers in an international setting, to identify the resilience factors that help them to cope, and to review a community-based approach that proactively addresses the skills and strengths needed to adapt and cope. Challenges and benefits of doing this kind of work are discussed. The writer specifically focuses on Africa, because she has lived and worked there as a clinical psychologist on a multidisciplinary team, providing training and crisis response for cross-cultural workers since 2000.

CHAPTER HIGHLIGHTS

+ Explains the unique aspects of trauma and grief responses in African cultures;

+ Identifies ways that cross-cultural workers can effectively provide crisis care in an African context;

+ Lists the factors that promote resiliency in cross-cultural workers;

+ Explores a preventative community-based approach as a way of addressing traumatic reaction and increasing resilience;

+ Examines the Mobile Member Care Team model as a way of using peer responders to promote healthy coping and longevity; and

+ Identifies the challenges and benefits of working cross-culturally.

CRISIS AND TRAUMA FOR AFRICANS

"I talked to a boy who had been kidnapped and turned into a child soldier. The children were ordered to club men and women to death. One boy was forced to be the first one to beat his mother as she was clubbed to death."

—Ugandan humanitarian aid worker

"During the war, terrible things happened—the belief was that if you raped a woman, you wouldn't be killed by your enemies. So, many women were raped, sometimes with the use of inanimate objects. People were buried alive."

—Conglese translator

"It was a senseless war. Ideologies changed from day to day. Anyone who was disgruntled had a way to vent their hostilities. The atrocities rose to new levels. Two rebel soldiers wagered with each other over the gender of an unborn fetus. To find out who had won the bet, they disemboweled the woman, killing her and her unborn baby. People were told to clap when their houses were set on fire. Women were told to laugh when their children were killed. Rebel soldiers amputated people's hands and arms—they had been told to bring bags of hands back to their leaders. One time I had to hide in my residence for 17 days as bullets and bombs went off around me."

—Sierra Leonian educator

"My family fled from the war in Liberia into Sierra Leone. Then we had to flee Sierra Leone because of the war there. The rebels shot my brother because he was a doctor and had treated government soldiers. We had to step over his body as we fled the rebels and my 4-year-old son could not understand why his uncle wasn't coming with us."

—Liberian pastor

Most Westerners have never experienced these kinds of horrific trauma. Meanwhile, those living in many countries in Africa have experienced many years of war—battles between government troops and rebel soldiers that can drag on for years and include atrocities that we cannot fathom. The rules of rebel fighting in Africa are different. Methods that are designed to annihilate certain ethnic groups, destabilize governments, and ensure complete intimidation and submission are used. Some of these methods include systematically raping women, cutting the fetuses out of wombs, abducting children and forcing them to become soldiers, amputating arms and legs with machetes, forcing children to murder their parents, and forcing people to eat the body parts of someone they have just murdered.

Africans have suffered tremendously. And yet, there is an inner core of strength and resilience that leads many to persevere in the face of tremendous suffering. There are aspects of certain African cultures that seem to enhance one's ability to endure hardship. Some African values that seem to promote resilience and community are a strong sense of loyalty to family and community, a lack of entitlement, a tendency to apply grace when mistakes are made, and a high value placed on generosity and hospitality. There is also an expectation that life will be difficult, such that most people are not taken by surprise when bad things happen. In cases of death, it is common for the bereaved to be surrounded by friends and family who patiently and quietly sit with them, providing companionship and comfort. There seems to be a familiarity with pain and loss that allows one to be near suffering without being afraid or having a need to escape.

How can an outsider, who has never been through this level of suffering, bring understanding, empathy, and trauma care? Having a humble, learner attitude goes a very long way in international settings. Rather than assuming that academic education prepares one to provide competent care, one can consciously and respectfully observe, ask questions, listen, and learn before offering alternative or new means of coping. It also helps to understand that although many human reactions are universal and transcend culture, the way these emotions are expressed may vary greatly across country, tribal affiliation, family, and individual personality.

Some grieving ritual norms in certain African cultures seem to prevent healthy coping. Cross-cultural sensitivity for those working in this context involves learning the values and embracing differences but can also include occasionally challenging cultural norms that hinder adaptive responses to trauma.

In Rwanda, there is a proverb that says a man should swallow his tears. Many African men say that it is very unusual for an African man to cry (although it really does depend on the ethnic group he comes from). Of course, we often hear this from North American men as well. In a recent training seminar in Ghana that included both Westerners and Africans, a Nigerian facilitator became tearful as he shared a personal story. Rather than being ashamed of this behavior or rejecting it, several of the Africans stood up at the end of the workshop and thanked this man for being a role model and for communicating that it was acceptable to cry. This was a shift from the traditional norm that requires men to remain stoic and unexpressive when grieving. The power of this intervention came from the model of an African man in a position of leadership and authority.

In some African cultures, women who are raped are unable to talk about their trauma because their community will not accept or care for them. The woman is blamed and rejected, and her feelings of shame are perpetuated by community attitudes. Some trauma trainings designed for Africans are providing community leaders with education about how to respond to women who have been raped in ways that foster healing and recovery.

In 1997, I traveled to Rwanda and worked with a number of families who had personally experienced the trauma of the genocide. Men and women who were raising orphans—who had witnessed their parents being killed—came with questions about why their adopted children were having nightmares, crying, acting out, refusing to go to school, and demonstrating many other typical posttrauma symptoms. They reported that their traditional methods of telling the children not to cry and refusing to talk about what had happened did not seem to be working. They were open to the concept of asking the children to describe what they had experienced and providing an environment of safety and nurture. Some of these guardians later reported seeing improvements in the children's functioning after the children had the opportunity to express their pain in a context of acceptance and love.

Some of the ways that cross-cultural workers can effectively provide crisis care include building credibility by respecting cultural values (e.g., proper greetings, appropriate nonverbal language), providing a safe context for listening to traumatic stories, shaping attitudes related to healthy expressions of pain, and assisting in culturally appropriate coping responses.

CRISIS AND TRAUMA FOR CROSS-CULTURAL WORKERS IN AFRICA

Many Western humanitarian aid workers and missionaries (hereafter referred to as cross-cultural workers) coming from North America and Europe live and work in Africa. More recently, there has been a rising trend for cross-cultural workers to come to Africa from Asia, Latin America, and other African nations. They come for various reasons, including refugee resettlement, food programs, micro or small business enterprise, medical care, translation, church planting, AIDS education, literacy, and community development programs. Workers have a wide range of motivations, which might include a desire to give, a need to be needed, hope for adventure, peer or family pressure, vocational advancement, a call to serve God, and compassion. The possibilities for personal rewards are often the internal, intangible ones that last forever. Those include an expanded worldview, increased feelings of gratitude, a sense of fulfillment, greater cross-cultural competence, feeling closer to God, and meaningful relationships.

Regardless of motivation or type of service, the cross-cultural learning curve is steep and the practical day-to-day experience often does not match one's expectations. Some of the most common chronic stressors are heat, language difficulties, challenges resulting from witnessing poverty, lack of understanding or acceptance of cultural norms or cues, difficult traveling conditions, corruption in government officials, and infrastructure breakdown (e.g., intermittent or lack of electricity, water, trash removal, phones, and Internet). There is the threat of malaria, typhoid, dysentery, parasites, meningitis, AIDS, and injury or death from traffic accidents. There are constant demands and pressures, coupled with a lack of time and personnel. A person may not be in a job that suits his or her skills. Leaders may feel that they did not receive adequate training for the positions they have. They may also feel isolated and have the sense that there is no one they can talk to about their stressors. Interpersonal crises may stem from the unresolved conflicts and tensions that come from being on a multicultural team. Many team members are living and working with each other under very high-pressure situations. Finally, there are many losses for cross-cultural workers, including separation from family (parents, adult children, or younger children placed in boarding schools); premature death of friends and colleagues; loss of security, safety, familiarity, possessions, hopes, and dreams; and a constant change of friends and living situations.

Cross-cultural workers of all nationalities may personally experience the crises and traumas that are common to Africa, such as war, evacuation, armed robberies, carjackings, burglaries, and assault. Schaefer et al. (2007), in a study on 206 missionaries working in West Africa, found that 91.6% of male and 84.5% of female missionaries reported one or more severe traumas in their lives. In comparison, in the U.S. general population, 60.7% of men and 51.2% of women reported the same. Furthermore, 71.1% of male and 64.2% of female West African missionaries had experienced three or more severe traumas, compared to 9.5% of men and 5.0% of women in the U.S. population. The most common traumas experienced by West African missionaries were serious medical illness (61%); car, train, or plane accidents (56%); unexpected death of family member or close friend (51%); immediate exposure to fighting, civil unrest, or war (48%); burglary in the home without serious confrontation (41%); serious threat or harm to family member or close friend (38%); experience of seeing another person seriously injured or dying as a result of accident or violence (34%); burglary outside the home without confrontation (33%); evacuation (31%); experience of being in the midst of a mob or riot (29%); and robbery with confrontation (25%).

A Personal Account of Trauma in Bouaké, Côte d'Ivoire, September 19, 2002

"In the early hours of the morning, I woke up to the sound of automatic gunfire in the distance. The radio informed us that there had been an attempted coup and that the city was in the control of rebel forces. We were running a workshop and had 18 cross-cultural workers who had come from all over Africa. We could not leave the conference center. African employees were still there at the center and they started to bring in a supply of food for us, realizing that we might have to stay there for a while. Then they went home to their families and we began to manage things on our own.

For the next few days, we continued on with the workshop despite the constant distraction of gunfire and the general tension in the air. We decided to form a crisis management committee and started the preparations for a possible long-term siege and a possible evacuation. We divided up tasks and ran parallel tracks of workshop facilitation and crisis management, which included plans for how to conserve our water and food supplies.

On some days there was shooting and explosions all around us so we would stay in the hallway as a group, lying flat on the floor with mattresses against the windows, praying, comforting each other, and answering the phone which was ringing about every ten minutes.

One day we opened the gate to receive 40 Liberian men, women and children who were fleeing those who had decided that foreigners were to blame for the war and were retaliating with machete attacks. One of the worst moments was when we heard the sound of a mob in the distance and we feared they were coming to massacre the men, women and children we were hiding. After staying for one night, the Liberian families started to leave in small groups, fearing that they were in more danger as one large group.

Finally, on the eighth day of the siege, we were able to leave in our own vehicles as the French troops had temporarily secured the town and had negotiated a 48-hour cease-fire between the rebel troops and loyalist troops so that we could safely evacuate. When we arrived in Abidjan, we had a time together as a group processing our experience and affirming the role that each person had played in getting us safely through the experience. Later in the week, some counselors arrived from the U.S. and gave us opportunity to talk further about how this experience had impacted us."

SOURCE: Carr, K. (2002, November). Bouaké diary: In the midst of the battle in Côte d'Ivoire. *World Pulse, 37* (21), 5.

WHAT IS THE IMPACT OF TRAUMA AND STRESS ON CROSS-CULTURAL WORKERS?

The psychological consequences of living with these types of stressors on a daily basis without adequate resources to respond to them most typically include depression, anxiety, acute stress disorder, posttraumatic stress disorder, and the exacerbation of pre-existing psychological conditions (e.g., personality disorders). When people or their organizations request counseling, the most typical presenting problems are burnout (fatigue, apathy, irritability, etc.), depression, anxiety, interpersonal conflicts, marital difficulties, or behavioral problems with children. Many of these symptoms are related to unresolved grief or an accumulated response to ongoing stress or trauma.

Schaefer et al. (2007) found the types of traumas for West African missionaries that were the most closely associated with posttraumatic or depressive symptoms were "immediate exposure to fighting, civil unrest, and war"; "serious threat or harm to family member or close friend"; and "unexpected death of family member or close friend." In a sample of the U.S. population, approximately 2% were suffering from posttraumatic stress disorder (PTSD) and 4% qualified for posttraumatic stress syndrome (PTSS). In the sample of West African missionaries, 5% had PTSD and 15% had PTSS. Among those missionaries who evacuated from Ivory Coast and live in higher risk areas such as Ivory Coast, Guinea, and Nigeria, the combined rate of PTSD and PTSS was higher at 28%.

It is striking that an increased resilience and strong sense of purpose was noted among missionaries in West Africa who had experienced higher rates of traumatic events. The resilience factors associated with less posttraumatic distress were "a sense of control in one's life" and "a tendency to bounce back after adversity."

FACTORS THAT PROMOTE RESILIENCY

What factors have helped those cross-cultural workers who continue to work internationally be so resilient and cope so well? Some interpretations can be made based on these data and previous research, but more research will need to be done to further identify the reasons for this hardiness.

Brown (2007) discovered several core pretrauma and posttrauma themes among those missionaries who had experienced trauma (and particularly evacuation) but continued to stay in high-risk areas. The four pretrauma factors were a strong personal call to be where they were, a sense of having been prepared to do this work from birth, a sense of God's presence and input, and sturdy relationships. The four self-identified posttrauma factors that most contributed to their resilience were experiencing the closeness and protection of God, a sense of supportive and authoritative leadership, quickly finding a new ministry focus, and being part of a supportive network. Brown also identified seven things that leaders in mission agencies can do to enhance resiliency and longevity among their missionaries. These included creating networks of relationships across organizations and cultures, acknowledging the trauma and its impact, sending evacuees initially to another country in the region (as opposed to returning them immediately to their home country where they would have a hard time finding anyone who can relate to what they had experienced), providing well-timed words of support, helping members to develop a theology of risk and suffering, fostering a sense of duty, and affirming the call to continue their cross-cultural ministry.

The concept of a "call" appears in both pretrauma and posttrauma resilience. Those who feel that they are fulfilling their life's purpose are more able to endure loss, hardship, and disappointments than those who live and work cross-culturally for other motivations such as attraction to the job, a sense of adventure, or pressure from a spouse or family.

Strong social and emotional support also plays a significant role in both pretrauma and posttrauma resilience. The literature has identified two key areas of support contributing to resilience, which are team cohesion and consultative leadership style (J. Fawcett, 2002, 2003). Team cohesion is a means of promoting resilience and lowering overall stress level. It can be logically concluded, therefore, that programming aimed at increasing resilience should be designed to promote better communication and to develop skills related to conflict management. Second, many cross-cultural workers reference the presence and attitude of their leaders as being a critical factor in how they coped with various traumas and stressors. In fact, there seems to be a distinct negative correlation between expressions of bitterness toward or disappointment in leadership during times of crisis and ability to adapt successfully to the losses of the trauma. This may be related to the actual support given by the leadership as well as the person's perception of and trust in leadership in general (G. Fawcett, 2003). Although a more directive leadership style may be needed in times of crisis, a consultative style may have the most benefits in non-crisis times. Hay et al. (2007) found that missionaries who were given freedom to shape and develop their post-trauma ministry were more likely to stay in their place of service.

WHAT ARE THE BENEFITS OF A PREVENTATIVE, COMMUNITY-BASED APPROACH?

Solomon, Shklar, and Mikulincer (2005) found that 20 years after the 1982 Lebanon War, traumatized soldiers who received frontline treatment had lower rates of posttraumatic and psychiatric symptoms, experienced less loneliness, and reported better social functioning than similarly traumatized soldiers who did not receive treatment on the front lines of combat. The treatment provided was based on the three principles of proximity (treatment was administered close to the front line), immediacy (treatment was administered close to the time of symptom onset), and expectancy (the expectation was communicated that soldiers would recover rapidly and resume functioning). The intervention offered practical support; relief from stress; interpersonal contact; normalizing of reactions; and the opportunity to express emotions such as grief, guilt, and shame, thereby curtailing avoidant coping mechanisms.

It has been demonstrated that the level of social support as well as the perception of organizational support during and after a crisis affects one's ability to cope with it and one's overall resilience (Forbes & Roger, 1999; Keane, Scott, Cavoya, Lamparski, & Fairbank, 1985). A specific goal of any crisis intervention or prevention program then should be to improve or affirm one's support system. Trained peer responders can be in the unique role of coaching organizational leaders to provide ongoing support to trauma victims.

Trained peer responders and leaders can provide practical support to those in crisis, which is also part of evidence-based psychological first aid (The National Child Traumatic Stress Network and National Center for PTSD, 2006). This might include provision of money, making meals, providing temporary housing, replacement of personal items, care of children, options for future employment, or the opportunity to continue their work, even if from a distance (J. Fawcett, 2002).

Crisis training for cross-cultural workers should contribute to participants' sense of mastery and control, which is directly related to their ability to cope with crisis situations. Peer responders and leaders can give trauma victims educational handouts such as "Common Post-Trauma Reactions and Symptoms" (accessible at http://www.mmct.org/common_post.php). This gives people an opportunity to identify, anticipate, and talk about normal reactions to trauma.

Providing linkage to resources is another key aspect of psychological first aid. This might include facilitating people to find peers who have experienced similar traumatic events, helping them to have meaningful contact with family and friends who are able to be supportive, reminding them of spiritual resources, or arranging follow-up appointments with a mental health professional. Training events that include cross-cultural workers from a variety of organizations allow for networking connections that facilitate increased technical, practical, logistical, and emotional support in times of crisis.

An early intervention model of peer response provides an opportunity to observe and assess those who may need further care and link them to those who are qualified to provide specialized care. Crisis training ideally includes skill building in crisis assessment as well as debriefing. Assessing a person's risk for complications following trauma is a key element of crisis intervention and an essential skill for potential debriefers.

In a community-based approach, peer responders, leaders, and mental health professionals are available to those who go through stress and crisis, giving them the opportunity to talk about what they have been through and the impact it has had on them. This is not forced or required but rather is made available. As cross-cultural workers have the opportunity to express their concerns and receive support, they are encouraged to cope with trauma in a way that protects them from using avoidance as a defense mechanism. Avoidance has been identified as a key risk factor in the development of PTSD.

Leaders play a key role in preventative care. J. Fawcett (2002) asserts that team cohesion and trust in competent leadership—factors that must exist before the crisis—are key elements in promoting healthy adaptation to the crisis event. In recommending pre-crisis training for leaders, Fawcett mentions things such as team cohesion, morale, and consultative leadership style as ways of increasing social support and reducing stress. A workshop that focuses on helping participants to build trust, manage stress, listen well, and address conflicts in relationships will contribute significantly to the quality of relationships between leaders and their staff. A crisis workshop designed for leaders can specifically build skills in understanding normal crisis response, providing crisis care, proactively building and enhancing trust, and reducing stress among members.

World Vision has found that the level of organizational support is more important than the debriefings (J. Fawcett, 2002). Specifically, the staff reported that the presence of a senior manager during and following a critical event was perceived as a demonstration of organizational support and care and was a significant factor in how they coped with the trauma. Leaders can make a crucial impact through phone calls, e-mails, and personal visits when they are communicating support, concern, and care, as well as a commitment to help and stay involved. Given the key role of leaders and the amount of pressure and responsibility they face, any preventative program should also take into account the emotional needs of the leaders before, during, and after crisis events.

The research suggests that a key way of reducing posttraumatic stress is to engage in behaviors even before the trauma, which enhance stress management and increase the quality of social supports. Providing resources that focus on the development of interpersonal skills, management of conflicts, team building, crisis preparation, and stress management through training, consultation, pastoral care, and appropriate counseling interventions are an essential part of an effective strategy for reducing posttraumatic stress and enhancing cross-cultural workers' ability to cope with the inevitable traumatic stressors in international settings.

CRISIS RESPONSE PROGRAMS IN AFRICA

Programs that focus on psychological recovery from trauma in Africa are few, and many more are needed. One program called "Healing the Wounds of Trauma: How the Church Can Help" (Hill, Hill, Bagge, & Miersma, 2001) was developed by cross-cultural workers and brings together African church and community leaders to train them in crisis response skills. Content areas include beliefs about suffering, grief, AIDS, rape, children's issues, and contingency planning. The workshop includes time to translate the materials from French and English into local African dialects. Participants are trained to be trainers so that they can offer the workshop in their communities.

Crisis programs, which are specifically for cross-cultural workers, can potentially provide training, crisis response, counseling, and consultation. One such program is the Mobile Member Care Team (MMCT; Jerome, 2001; Jerome & Carr, 2002). MMCT-West Africa (MMCT-WA) serves more than 10,000 cross-cultural workers living in the 14 countries of West Africa—from Senegal to Nigeria (a geographic area about two thirds the size of the continental United States). These workers come from many areas of the world (including the United States, Canada, Europe, Brazil, South Korea, Nigeria, Ghana, and other African countries) and are members of a variety of organizations that focus on different services, including medical care, community development, relief work, education, literacy, Bible translation, and church planting.

MMCT's goal is to help cross-cultural workers cope and function effectively and with perseverance in the midst of crises and constant exposure to stress. They achieve this using a community psychology model, aimed at improving community life by promoting psychological well-being and mitigating stress and trauma reactions. Using a primary prevention approach, they provide psychoeducation that teaches practical skills such as how to manage conflicts, how to grieve, how to handle stress, and how to help others during crisis and trauma. These workshops serve the purpose of building awareness of needed skills, increasing existing skills, building and strengthening relationships within the communities, increasing knowledge, and creating networks. The training is interactive, using various methods of adult learning, including small-group tasks, whole-group interaction, case studies, skill demonstrations, skill practicum, and personal reflection. Believing that there are already strengths and skills within the community that can be enhanced and accessed, they provide specialized crisis response training as a way of expanding helping resources within the community (Carr, 2006; Reissman, 1990).

Sharpening Your Interpersonal Skills (SYIS)

The SYIS is a 4½-day workshop that has been offered and refined for nearly 30 years by Dr. Ken Williams (2002) of International Training Partners. This workshop provides training in key knowledge, attitudes, and skills needed for developing and maintaining healthy relationships. Some of the topics are listening, building trust, living in community, helping others manage grief, confrontation, conflict resolution, and managing stress.

Aside from the personal growth that many experience through this workshop, there are other benefits. The facilitators of the workshop are able to identify the natural "people helpers" who are potential peer responders for the future. In addition, MMCT staff is able to form working relationships with organizational leaders who take the workshop, which later makes a difference when they are called in as consultants during crisis situations. Also, cross-cultural workers from several organizations who have worked in the same area for years may find themselves, for the first time, in a setting where they can build community and informal support networks across organizational lines. This is crucial on the front lines of cross-cultural work but is far too often not the case.

In addition, for many of these cross-cultural workers attending one of these workshops, it may be the first time they have interacted with a psychologist. This gives them an opportunity in a nonthreatening environment to develop a relationship with mental health professionals and break down negative stereotypical views about them.

Recently, for example, a cross-cultural couple, who had lived overseas for many years, attended the SYIS workshop and said this to the MMCT facilitator:

A few years earlier, an older couple in our mission took this workshop. We had never gotten along with them. It seemed like whenever we were with them, they were just one-upping everyone else with how much they had or were suffering. They were not caring at all. But they changed drastically after doing the SYIS. They were caring and reaching out to others.

Peer-Response Training (PRT)

Building on the basic interpersonal skills covered in the SYIS, the PRT is a 6-day workshop designed for those already coming alongside their peers as helpers. Admission to the PRT workshop requires an application process that includes recommendations from SYIS facilitators affirming applicants' basic interpersonal skills; from their organizational leader confirming their confidence in them, their availability to serve, and the organization's intention to use them once trained; and from a colleague who expresses confidence in their interpersonal skills in crisis situations.

MMCT has offered this workshop multiple times and over 100 cross-cultural workers have trained to become peer responders. Participants learn about the typical impact and effects of a crisis and its potentially pathological effects, how to make initial contact with a person in need, and how to provide psychological first aid. The workshop also includes personal assessment of attitudes toward suffering. Other topics include when and how to make referrals and ethical issues such as confidentiality and boundaries. The last session of each day provides coaching when a group of four participants meet with the same staff person to share with each other what they have learned and experienced. These coaching relationships lend themselves to ongoing mentoring after the workshop through e-mail, phone, and occasional visits as MMCT staff travel through the region.

Events have demonstrated the efficacy of PRT training. In Guinea, political tensions and civil unrest began to escalate, and a number of expatriates evacuated to the surrounding countries. Trained peer responders in Senegal and Mali helped to provide these evacuees with practical support such as housing and meals. They spent one-on-one time with them, listened to their stories of what they had witnessed, and helped them to think through their options as they waited for things to calm down. Within months, most of these individuals had returned to their work in Guinea. In Nigeria, hundreds of widows were given the opportunity to talk about the trauma they experienced when their husbands were killed during fighting between Muslims and Christians in central Nigeria. A Nigerian peer responder translated the common posttrauma reactions handout into the Hausa language and worked alongside American peer responders who also spoke Hausa and were very familiar with the culture.

One missionary couple that attended an MMCT workshop had suffered two armed robberies and two evacuations. When asked what had helped them to cope, they immediately referred to two fellow missionaries in Nigeria who had played a key role in supporting them by listening and caring for them. These two missionaries had been through the PRT workshop and were peer responders available to help those in crisis.

The ongoing mentoring relationship between MMCT staff and trained peer responders is a crucial aspect of the community development approach. This training provides opportunity for practice and feedback in the midst of the workshop and support before, during, and after crisis events that occur after the training is complete.

Member Care While Managing Crises (MCMC)

Given that pre-crisis preparation has been cited as an important variable in coping with crises (Danieli, 2002), it seems a wise investment of time and resources for leaders to make sure that they and others who will give care during a crisis will receive crisis response training. By participating in the 5-day MCMC workshop, a leader will learn about normal responses to crisis and how to support others through the necessary stages of grief after loss or trauma. MCMC addresses the strategic role that an administrator plays in crisis situations. Given the evidence that team cohesion and trust in leadership are two key factors in the mitigation of acute stress reactions in traumatic situations, this training is a key strategy in enhancing the strength and skills of organizational leaders and increasing their leadership competence in crisis situations (J. Fawcett, 2002). Specific topics include the impact of crisis; development of policies, procedures, and protocols; the dynamic of trust for leaders in crisis situations; confidentiality and communication; information management; assessment of vulnerable members; unique needs in cases of depression, sexual assault, or evacuation; leadership styles in crisis; and the when, why, and how of debriefings and crisis management committees.

After the evacuation of about 200 missionaries from Côte d'Ivoire, a regional administrator who had been through this training and has also been involved on the MMCT governing board wrote the following, related to the efficacy of the MMCT crisis training:

> An evacuation of a large country is taking place with no members of MMCT-WA
> on the continent and yet every mission group seems to be well cared for through

the joint efforts of an army of trained peer debriefers. So, the hours registering people, writing materials, hauling suitcases from airport to airport, workshop training, coaching and sleeping in less than adequate conditions has paid off. Six years ago that wouldn't have happened, or at best it would have been a fumbling attempt. Now because of MMCT, there is a sort of missions without borders happening where the various mission communities are no longer in their own little boxes, but they know and are friends with others through common workshops and training and now they are helping each other and working for each other's well-being.

In addition to the training and mentoring, MMCT provides direct care to cross-cultural workers with psychological assessments, brief therapy, crisis intervention, and the mentoring of individuals (called peer responders) who can provide psychological first aid to their peers (Carr, 1997; Jerome & Carr, 2002). West Africa is a setting where there is a high incidence of crises and trauma (e.g., war, evacuation, civil unrest, serious medical illness, and armed robberies) and very few resources for psychological care. In the past when there was no on-site counseling care available, many cross-cultural workers left their field of service and returned to their home countries prematurely, often with a sense of failure and shame.

SELF-CARE FOR INTERNATIONAL WORKERS

International caregivers live in a very intense, highly stressful environment and are vulnerable to posttrauma reactions, stress-related reactions, and interpersonal difficulties. An aggressively proactive approach to building and maintaining quality personal and team life with built-in accountability and support structures is essential to long-term resilience. Some supports might include a regional advisory councils that uniquely provides protection, support, and guidance; an intentional community approach to team life; and a group of supporters in home countries that provides financial, emotional, and spiritual care.

Finding the balance of work, rest, and play is not easy in this setting but is crucial to professional longevity. There is a tendency among cross-cultural workers to work to the point of exhaustion or illness. The work can be intense and often involves long hours and a rigorous travel schedule. Taking vacations can present logistical and financial challenges. Making a commitment to take a few weeks away on a regular basis for a retreat is beneficial. Reading and other pleasurable activities can provide professional and personal renewal.

Maintaining healthy relationships, particularly on the work team, is a very important aspect of self-care. This means confronting when necessary, giving grace often, forgiving daily, serving sacrificially, and listening well. It takes hard work, surrender of rights, and intentionality to be a part of a team community that fosters mental health and perseverance; but if successful, this kind of other care (which is a form of self-care) will sometimes be the one thing that helps a cross-cultural worker deal with challenging times.

CHALLENGES OF CRISIS WORK IN AN INTERNATIONAL SETTING

Often in international crisis work, the workers are a part of the community they serve. Like being in a rural setting or serving on a naval ship, caregivers in Africa often do not have the luxury of separating personal life from their professional life. Because there are so few licensed mental health professionals available to serve cross-cultural workers, multiple relationships are hard to avoid. This means that the family you had dinner with is the same family that you see for a crisis debriefing the next day. Although this is a challenge, these multiple relationships can enhance the quality of service as long as awareness of limitations, a certain degree of objectivity, and healthy boundaries are maintained.

However, this boundary crossing, which is inevitable, can take an emotional toll. In one situation, one of our staff and her husband were the victims of a carjacking by three gunmen. Their care and debriefing was provided by their coworkers on the team who all experienced a certain degree of posttraumatic symptoms because of their proximity to the victims.

The above example is reflective of another challenge, which is that there are very few options for referrals to other caregivers. In this setting, the number of caregivers is extremely limited, and sending someone back to their home country for care is only used in severe cases.

The chronic exposure to genuine need and suffering brings the challenges of feelings of hopelessness, weariness, and being overwhelmed. Cross-cultural workers are vulnerable to burnout unless they are able to maintain priorities and vision and are able to accept their own limitations in meeting the needs of those they serve.

Another challenge in international work is being separated from loved ones who remain in the worker's home country. It is a major loss to miss a birth or a death or a wedding or a graduation. Family members in the home country may have struggles or needs that bring internal conflicts for the worker who wants to be available in both places.

BENEFITS OF DOING CRISIS WORK IN AN INTERNATIONAL SETTING

Given all that has been described in terms of the effects of trauma, stress, and challenges of doing this kind of work, why would someone choose it? It is hard to give an intellectual response to this question. The answer lies in the indescribable experience of being with someone when he or she goes from bitterness, helplessness, and despair to hope, encouragement, and strength. One who has crisis response skills, cross-cultural experience, and lives in an international setting earns that opportunity over and over again. The need is there; the workers are few; the joy and fulfillment of meeting that need and bringing life and hope to those who have suffered surpasses any challenges experienced.

PRACTICAL IMPLICATIONS

- Cross-cultural workers can provide effective crisis care by respecting cultural values, providing a safe context for expression, maintaining a learner attitude, shaping attitudes related to healthy expressions of pain, and assisting in developing culturally appropriate coping responses.

- The most common traumas experienced by cross-cultural workers in Africa are serious medical illness, accidents, unexpected deaths, and war.
- An increased resilience and strong sense of purpose was noted among missionaries in West Africa, who had higher rates of experience with traumatic events than missionaries in Europe.
- Factors that promote resiliency include sense of a call, sense of God's presence, sturdy relationships, consultative leadership, and team cohesion.
- A preventative community-based approach such as MMCT can increase resilience by enhancing social support networks and mobilizing practical supports through training programs and the ongoing mentoring of peer responders and leaders.

CONCLUSION AND FUTURE DIRECTIONS

One aspect of crisis care in international settings that is likely to change in the coming years is the formation of multicultural teams. As organizations grow and become more culturally aware and diverse, more teams will need to address their internal cultural differences as it affects decision-making styles, lifestyle choices, child-rearing practices, humor, and communication. Proactively engaging in team-building exercises will help to increase the understanding, acceptance, and appreciation of these value differences.

Another possible future development is that humanitarian aid organizations will acknowledge and support the need for proactive care of their members. This will result in increased budget lines, not just for crisis response but also for proactive training, mentoring, and debriefing, which will contribute to the overall mental health and coping capacity of cross-cultural workers.

Finally, as those from developing countries have an opportunity to access resource materials and training opportunities in crisis care, the focus of Western caregivers may shift from provider roles to training roles. The future will likely see more of an emphasis on adult learning models, which incorporate active participation through discussion, reflection, and the opportunity to practice skills.

Web Sites For Further Information

www.mmct.org (The MMCT Web site)
www.itpartners.org (The International Training Partners Web site)

REFERENCES

Brown, R. (2007). Resilience in ministry despite trauma. In R. Hay, V. Lim, D. Blocher, D. Ketelaar, & S. Hay (Eds.), *Worth keeping: Global perspectives on best practice in missionary retention* (pp. 315–318). Pasadena, CA: William Carey Library.

Carr, K. F. (1997, October). Crisis intervention for missionaries. *Evangelical Missions Quarterly, 33*(4), 451–458.

Carr, K. F. (2006). The Mobile Member Care Team as a means of responding to crises: West Africa. In L. Barbanel & R. J. Sternberg (Eds.), *Psychological interventions in times of crisis* (pp. 75–97). New York: Springer.

Danieli, Y. (Ed.). (2002). *Sharing the front line and the back hills.* Amityville, NY: Baywood.

Fawcett, G. (2003). Preventing trauma in traumatic environments. In J. Fawcett (Ed.), *Stress and trauma handbook* (pp. 40–67). Monrovia, CA: World Vision International.

Fawcett, J. (2002). Preventing broken hearts, healing broken minds. In Y. Danieli (Ed.), *Sharing the front line and the back hills* (pp. 223–232). Amityville, NY: Baywood.

Fawcett, J. (Ed.). (2003). *Stress and trauma handbook.* Monrovia, CA: World Vision International.

Forbes, A., & Roger, D. (1999). Stress, social support and fear of disclosure. *British Journal of Health Psychology, 4,* 165–179.

Hay, R., Lim, V., Blocher, D., Ketelaar, J., & Hay, S. (Eds.). (2007). *Worth keeping: Global perspectives on best practice in missionary retention.* Pasadena, CA: William Carey Library.

Hill, M., Hill, H., Bagge, R., & Miersma, P. (2001). *Healing the wounds of trauma: How the church can help.* Nairobi, Kenya: Paulines.

Jerome, D. (2001). Mobile Member Care Team—West Africa: Our journey and direction. In K. O'Donnell (Ed.), *Doing member care well: Perspectives and practices from around the world* (pp. 117–126). Pasadena, CA: William Carey Library.

Jerome, D., & Carr, K. (2002). Mobile Member Care Teams. In J. Powell & J. Bowers (Eds.), *Enhancing missionary vitality* (pp. 399–407). Palmer Lake, CO: Mission Training International.

Keane, T. M., Scott, W. O., Cavoya, G. A., Lamparski, D. M., & Fairbank, J. A. (1985). Social support in Vietnam veterans with posttraumatic stress disorder: A comparative analysis. *Journal of Consulting and Clinical Psychology, 53,* 95–102.

The National Child Traumatic Stress Network and National Center for PTSD. (2006). *Psychological first aid field operator's guide* (2nd ed.). Retrieved February 2, 2009, from http://www.ncptsd.va.gov/ ncmain/ncdocs/manuals/nc_manual_psyfirstaid.html

Reissman, F. (1990). Restructuring help: A human services paradigm for the 1990's. *American Journal of Community Psychology, 18*(2), 221–230.

Schaefer, F. C., Blazer, D. G., Carr, K. F., Connor, K. M., Burchett, B., Schaefer, C. A., et al. (2007). Traumatic events and posttraumatic stress in cross–cultural mission assignments. *Journal of Traumatic Stress Studies, 20,* 529–539.

Solomon, Z., Shklar, R., & Mikulincer, M. (2005). Frontline treatment of combat stress reaction: A 20-year longitudinal evaluation study. *American Journal of Psychiatry, 162,* 2309–2314.

Williams, K. (2002). *Sharpening your interpersonal skills.* Colorado Springs, CO: International Training Partners.

Secondary Trauma Among Disaster Responders

The Need for Self-Care

Priscilla Dass-Brailsford

Responding to the needs of traumatized individuals can take its toll on the psyche of mental health professionals. People who are involved in disaster-related assistance are more likely to need support (Boscarino, Figley, & Adams, 2004; Pearlman, 2005; Stamm, 1999) because as first responders they generally work long hours without breaks and have intense interactions over a protracted period with severely traumatized individuals; these activities produce many negative consequences. Listening to unrelenting stories of suffering and survivorship can be emotionally and physically depleting. In addition, observing social injustices and the institutional challenges faced by survivors can be demoralizing and disillusioning; it may sometimes trigger a responder's own personal history of loss and hardship.

Figley (1995) defines the normative occupational hazard of working with traumatized clients as compassion fatigue, derived from empathic contact with traumatized clients and listening to their traumatic experiences. Although providing mental health support during times of disaster is a noble and humanitarian act that can be spiritually enriching, organizations that send volunteers into the disaster field should be aware that such work makes them susceptible to secondary traumatization. Thus, efforts should be made to provide volunteers with enough support, which can serve as an antidote to the stress they experience at the disaster site. This support should not end with the volunteer assignment but continue to be provided during the transition period when first responders return home and resume their regular activities, because it is in this period of normalcy, in the safety and comfort of their homes, that secondary stress reactions may first emerge.

> **CHAPTER HIGHLIGHTS**
>
> ✦ Reviews the definitions of secondary trauma and vicarious trauma, compassion fatigue, and burnout;
>
> ✦ Discusses the warning signs of burnout (cognitive, emotional, physical, spiritual, and behavioral);
>
> ✦ Outlines the challenges of working in disaster settings, which include a lack of structure, resources and rewards, and adaptation to changing leadership; and
>
> ✦ Discusses self-care and coping strategies that can curtail the negative consequences of secondary trauma.

BACKGROUND

An inevitable consequence of responding to a disaster is exposure to many physical and emotional stressors. Such exposure is likely to increase the mental health responder's risk for posttraumatic stress disorder (PTSD). Compared to the national PTSD prevalence rate of 4% for the general population (Kessler, Chin, Demler, Merikangas, & Walters, 2005), the prevalence rate for those involved in rescue and recovery occupations ranges from 5% to 32% (Fullerton, Ursano, & Wang, 2004), with the highest prevalence rates documented among search and rescue personnel (25%; Ozen & Aytekin, 2004), firefighters (21%; Chang et al., 2003), and workers with no prior disaster training (33%; Guo et al., 2004).

The mental health status of rescue and recovery workers who were involved in the World Trade Center disaster in 2001 provides some useful data on secondary stress. An assessment conducted 2 weeks after September 11th found that 22% of World Trade Center workers had acute posttraumatic stress symptoms (Fullerton, Ursano, Reeves, Shigemura, & Grieger, 2006), while a later study conducted a year after the disaster found PTSD symptoms among 13% of the rescue workers (Smith et al., 2004). The reduced number of affected workers in the second study indicates that PTSD is more prevalent in the acute phase of a disaster but as time passes, individuals appear to be less symptomatic. Perhaps they are able to adapt to changed circumstances and to some extent integrate the traumatic experiences so that PTSD reactions become less prevalent.

The adverse consequences of working with traumatized clients have been described under a variety of terms: *vicarious trauma* or *secondary trauma*, and *compassion fatigue*. The concepts of vicarious trauma and secondary trauma are often used interchangeably. Vicarious trauma is the "negative transformation of a helping professional's inner experience as a result of empathic engagement with traumatized clients" (Saakvitne, 2003, p. 143) and describes the mental health professional's reactions to exposure to a client's traumatic experience (Tripanny, White Kress, & Wicoxon, 2004). Changes in self-image and disruptions in identity, memory, and belief systems are likely to occur as a result of this transformation (Pearlman & Saakvitne, 1995). Listening to repeated stories of pain and suffering can deleteriously affect the professional's core beliefs and perceptions about others and the world. Mental health professionals who see a large number of traumatized clients belong to this high-risk group. Additional factors that may influence a helping professional's vulnerability to vicarious trauma include a personal trauma history, the meaning attached to traumatic life events, psychological and interpersonal style, current stressors, and poor support systems (Pearlman & MacIan, 1995).

Some individuals are at a higher risk than others for developing vicarious trauma. For example, research on stress indicates that individuals from lower socioeconomic and disadvantaged groups, including women, the elderly, and ethnic minorities, are most vulnerable and prone to becoming debilitated by stress (Pearlin, 1989; Thoits, 1995). Similarly, Schauben and Frazier (1995) found that female counselors who saw a large number of victims of sexual violence reported experiencing an increase in vicarious trauma. A personal history of trauma increases helping professionals' susceptibility to vicarious trauma and compromises their ability to ward off its deleterious effects (Kassam-Adams, 1999; Nelson-Gardell & Harris, 2003). Other research has found that counselors who work with sexually abused clients experience profound and disruptive psychological effects that persist months and years after working with such clients (Cunningham, 2004).

Pearlman and Saakvitne (1995) propose that secondary trauma reflects neither pathology on the part of the helper nor intentionality on the part of the victim or survivor; it should therefore be perceived not as pathology (Cunningham, 2004) but as a consequence of sensitive therapeutic engagement when helping professionals attempt to empathically understand a survivor's traumatic experience. Although issues of countertransference and other unresolved personal factors may complicate the therapeutic process, vicarious reactions are predictable, just as posttraumatic stress reactions are predictable reactions to violent and abusive environments. Mental health professionals who compassionately engage with trauma survivors and feel a strong sense of responsibility in helping others carry the dual risks of experiencing vicarious or secondary trauma, which can develop into burnout (Figley, 1995).

Compassion fatigue, a term coined by Figley (1995), is described as a normative occupational hazard of working with traumatized clients. It affects most professionals who respond to disasters (police officers, firefighters)—not just mental health workers—and the primary symptom is a decreased ability to maintain empathy as a result of repeatedly listening to traumatic stories. In addition, mental health professionals who suffer from compassion fatigue are unable to establish healthy psychological boundaries from their clients' traumatic material; they may begin to feel as if the client's trauma were directly happening to them and, as a result, display reactions similar to those of their clients.

Because the symptoms of compassion fatigue parallel the symptoms of posttraumatic stress syndrome, with the mental health professional affected by "hearing about" rather than "directly experiencing" a traumatic event, it has been referred to as secondary traumatic stress disorder (Figley, 1995) and meets the diagnostic Criterion A, or "the event" criterion of PTSD (American Psychiatric Association, 1994):

> The person has been exposed to a traumatic event in which both of the following were present: (1) the person experienced, witnessed, or was confronted with an event/s that involved actual or threatened death or serious injury, or a threat to the physical integrity of self or others. (2) the person's response involved intense fear, helplessness or horror. (p. 467)

Similar to PTSD the symptoms of compassion fatigue occur in the areas of arousal, intrusion, avoidance depression, and dissociative symptoms. First responders who experience such symptoms are likely to be assailed by feelings of ineffectiveness and lowered functioning. Both vicarious trauma and compassion fatigue can develop into burnout. In comparison to burnout, compassion fatigue presents itself with very little warning, although affected individuals can recover more rapidly from compassion fatigue than burnout (Figley, 1995).

Burnout is described as general malaise, psychological stress, and a "chronic tedium in the workplace" (Jenkins & Baird, 2002, p. 425). Burnout usually results from psychological depletion and may be accompanied by feelings of physical exhaustion; helplessness; hopelessness; disillusionment; negative self-concept; and negative attitudes toward work, people, and life itself (James & Gilliland, 2005).

In the early stages of a disaster, first responders may have abounding energy, motivation, and a strong sense of altruism. Their training, neutrality (many may come from outside the affected area), and expertise make an important contribution to communities affected by a disaster. However, if a crisis or disaster takes a long time to resolve, first responders may begin to find the time they spend in a disaster location exceeding their initial expectations, motivation, and enthusiasm. In the beginning, they may not realize the toll of the work, but eventually physical and psychological burnout are likely to set in, especially if the responder does not practice self-care on a regular basis. As disaster responders witness continuous images of despair, loss, and hardship, feelings of hopelessness and helplessness can quickly emerge, and even the most seasoned responders will eventually feel worn out.

Finally, the concepts of secondary or vicarious trauma, compassion fatigue, and burnout share similarities and differences. The onset of secondary or vicarious trauma and compassion fatigue is sudden and identifiable, whereas the development of burnout is gradual; it is the cumulative effect of working under unrelenting stress and insufficient support. Unfortunately, the slow progression of burnout eludes early detection.

WARNING SIGNS OF BURNOUT

Burnout affects several areas of disaster responders' functioning. Cognitively, they may find that they cannot stop thinking about the crisis, the victims, and the disaster itself. They may lose their sense of objectivity the longer they remain in the disaster-affected area. Personal identification with disaster victims and their families can develop. Moreover, as their ability to get adequate sleep and a nutritional diet decreases, frequent clock watching and an inability to concentrate or focus on tasks may increase. Most important, they may lose focus, find their attention wavering, and experience difficulty in listening attentively.

In the physical area, first responders may experience major sleep disturbances, nightmares, and dreams about the disaster. Chronic fatigue, gastrointestinal problems, headaches, and other body pains are likely physical reactions. Experiencing a loss of appetite in an environment where many people are hungry is expected. A yearning for comfort foods that are high in sugars, fats, and carbohydrates may also become prominent.

Burnout is marked by emotional exhaustion, depersonalization, and reduced personal accomplishment. First responders who are overworked and who are excessively concerned about their clients become psychologically and emotionally burdened and may entertain suicidal thoughts, suffer from depression, and become irritable and impatient, especially when they are unable to meet the needs of their clients. Under these circumstances, cynicism and pessimism are likely to become pervasive. In contrast, some responders may become overinvolved in every crisis intervention activity, even though they may not have the physical stamina to do so. They may be unable to let go of their involvement in the disaster. The intensity of the work acts as an adrenaline rush, and returning to their normal responsibilities is perceived as dull and boring. A desire to remain in the disaster-affected area for an indefinite amount of time strengthens, and the disaster dominates the first responder's daily thoughts and actions. Even when they cannot physically remain at the disaster, they do so vicariously by thinking and talking about it all the time. Some responders may exceed the limits of the helping profession by maintaining contact with crisis victims beyond the disaster.

Other clear danger signs of burnout are when first responders feel overextended and overloaded by the work; face organizational challenges of large client caseloads, a lack of adequate supervision, and isolation from their professional community; and experience other institutional and bureaucratic factors. Finally, in an attempt to alleviate stress, some first responders may resort to unhealthy and impulsive behaviors such as the consumption of alcohol and other addictive substances. Supervisors and other peers have a responsibility to intervene should they notice such behaviors, because over time, this can develop into a major problem that handicaps the mental health professional's ability to conduct his or her daily activities.

THE CHALLENGES OF WORKING IN A DISASTER SETTING

Responding to a disaster is an intense and emotionally challenging experience that affects the disaster mental health responder in several ways. Applying self-care strategies on a regular basis is invaluable in preventing secondary traumatic stress and compassion fatigue and maintaining a healthy attitude to work. Mental health professionals teach their clients how to better care for themselves but fail to do the same for themselves. It is not unusual for such professionals to behave as if they are protected by a shield of invulnerability that makes them impervious to the negative effects of stress.

Eustress Versus Distress

In disasters, mental health responders are exposed to two different kinds of stress. Eustress is stress that is motivating and performance enhancing; it is the kind of stress that motivates first responders to volunteer to work in challenging situations in the first place. The adrenaline rush produced by eustress overshadows the hardship and other challenges prevalent at disaster sites and allows helping professionals to sometimes go without regular meals and sleep for extended periods of time. However, disaster sites inherently are places of immense pain and suffering and eustress can soon turn into distress with its accompanying negative consequences such as compassion fatigue and burnout. It begins when the disaster is perceived as burdensome and wears the first responder down; feelings of impatience and irritability increase rapidly under such circumstances.

Lack of Structure

Disaster sites are often confusing and chaotic places that can be overstimulating and overwhelming. In the midst of such an environment, the mental health disaster responder is expected to remain calm and collected while making difficult decisions. This can quickly develop into a highly stressful task. Working long hours under adverse conditions adds to the challenges that the first responder faces. Under normal circumstances, most mental health professionals work within a structured, organized, and professional environment; similar conditions are unlikely to exist in disaster settings (e.g., simply securing a private space to talk with a client in a disaster setting can be a major challenge). In addition, mental health responders often reside in the same building as their clients; thus, separating work time from personal time becomes virtually impossible.

Disaster mental health providers are expected to see a large number of clients on a daily basis. This is a serious risk factor that can contribute to burnout. Disaster organizations can better support their volunteers by diversifying the tasks of the first responder and reducing the number of clients they are required to see on a daily basis. In addition, keeping changes to work schedules at a minimum increases the first responders' feelings of stability and creates a positive work environment.

Lack of Resources

Being away from home isolates first responders from a familiar and supportive professional community; they may go for weeks without supervision and professional guidance. Thus, opportunities to process the intense and overwhelming reactions that emerge in disaster settings are reduced.

In addition, resources for both mental health professionals and survivors are generally scarce at disaster sites, and when available, they are severely rationed. Since meal and sleep times are strictly scheduled, first responders who miss a meal time may have to go without sustenance or seek other alternatives. A lack of sleep and inadequate nourishment is likely to wear down even the healthiest individual and usual coping abilities become severely tested.

Changing Leadership

The schedules of supervisors and team leaders often change, requiring the mental health professional to constantly adapt to a new schedule and leadership style. This can increase feelings of instability in the disaster environment; even the most patient volunteers can become overwhelmed by constant adaptation. Speaking from a personal experience, in a 2-week deployment as a mental health responder, I had four different supervisors, each of whom had different work styles and different expectations of volunteers. Other basic administrative tasks (paperwork, notes, etc.) also require acclimatization. Learning new ways of doing things is always challenging, but this worsens under stressful conditions.

Direct Victims

Unlike other mental health settings, the first responder at the disaster site runs the additional risk of becoming a primary victim of trauma. For example, first responders who were deployed to the tsunami in Southeast Asia saw decaying corpses and human limbs strewn around the disaster-affected areas before it was cleaned up. Thus, these first responders were not only required to support survivors in the aftermath of the disaster but, at the same time, had to deal with their own traumatic reactions that emerged as a result of what they had seen.

Lack of Rewards

Survivors expect mental health professionals to remain calm and to take away their emotional pain. When this does not occur, they may become disappointed and express frustration. This in turn may contribute to mental health professionals questioning their efficacy and efforts; they may worry unreasonably about their suitability for the profession; their level of motivation may begin to dwindle and low morale may become prominent as feelings of invalidation increase. A vicious cycle sets in as increased feelings of hopelessness result in a simultaneous increase in errors and poor decisions.

Personal Challenges

Mental health providers who are residents of disaster-affected areas are more prone to experiencing adverse consequences; they may have to deal with their own direct losses of family members and personal property in addition to supporting other survivors of a disaster. Including such individuals in disaster relief efforts may not be wise.

For example, in a study done among students enrolled in a social work program in New York when the September 11th attacks occurred, Tosone et al. (2003) found that the students' physical proximity to the disaster site caused them to experience reactions similar to those of their clients. This shared sense of trauma resulted in a blurring of therapeutic boundaries, and the students struggled to keep a neutral perspective. It was clear that they had to first deal with their own feelings before helping others.

Similarly, first responders who have current personal stressors will find that these stressors are exacerbated in the disaster setting. Furthermore, first responders who have histories of personal trauma and those who lack adequate social and family resources are most susceptible to burnout.

What Can Be Done?

As first responders immerse themselves in the disaster culture, it becomes easy to feel more fortunate, to count one's blessings, and to set aside one's personal needs. Some responders, however, may feel that it is selfish to even entertain thoughts about their own self-care in the midst of a crisis. Motivated by professional invulnerability, they may become passionate about helping others while postponing and/or neglecting to take care of themselves.

However, because untreated vicarious trauma is detrimental to the psychological well-being and healthy functioning of a mental health professional, the sooner it is detected and attended to the better. Mental health providers who practice self-care techniques they usually teach their clients will experience less stress. Such self-care can act as a protective shield for the disaster responder. Unfortunately, although mental health professionals are able to detect stressors in clients and intervene with adequate therapeutic strategies, they are seldom able to do the same for themselves.

Despite the hazards of providing support during disasters, many first mental health professionals are inspired to continue doing the rewarding work of crisis and disaster intervention. There are many things that can be done to circumvent secondary trauma and compassion fatigue.

It is important to remember that self-care strategies are culture specific and are often determined by the availability of resources and other limitations that may be present at a disaster site. Three important principles should be borne in mind in the practice of self-care strategies:

- Self-care strategies should include attainable, concrete, and easily available tasks. For example, taking a walk outside may be more feasible than planning to go to a movie. The completion and control of activities are important, and adequate time should be set aside for these activities; they should not become an additional task for an already stressed individual.
- Self-care strategies should be related to the reactions that a mental health professional is already experiencing. For example, those who feel isolated as a reaction to stress should plan an activity with a colleague, call family members, or engage in other social activities.
- Self-care strategies can have both negative and positive consequences; mental health professionals should always choose the latter. For example, consuming a glass of wine may be perceived as a way to relax and destress after a hard day's work. However, alcohol is an addictive substance, and the first responder should be careful that this self-care strategy does not lead to an excessive consumption of alcohol; self-care strategies that lead to additional problems defeat their purpose.

Planning for Self-Care

Two things are indispensable in a disaster responder's survival kit: a self-care plan and a symbolic red flag that alerts the mental health professional that things are going awry. The red flag is an identifiable indicator of stress. It signals a challenge to affected counselors to stop, take stock of their psychological functioning, review the situation that may be unfolding, and strategize on how to ameliorate the situation by resorting to a self-care plan.

A self-care plan involves knowing what strategies one should use before, during, and after a disaster response. This is a plan that cannot be constructed in the moment but must be carefully planned, rehearsed, and practiced before embarking on a disaster response. It involves intentionality and attentiveness to one's emotional health. Everly (1995) describes constructing a plan according to a self-care pyramid. At the base of the pyramid lie internally focused self-care practices that support changes in attitude and perception. As the pyramid narrows upwards, external aspects of connection and support and problem solving become the focus of the self-care plan.

Self-Awareness

Self-awareness is a critical ingredient in counselor self-care. Knowing one's limitations and what one is comfortable handling or not handling is an important first step. This requires mental health first responders to have insight into their own feelings, their capacity for empathy, and the ability to differentiate between their own needs and the needs of the client (Miller, 1998).

As first responders find themselves immersed in environments in which individuals possess overwhelming and unending needs, they may exceed the limits of what they can logically offer. For example, workdays on disaster sites are often quite busy and lengthy, making it easy for the first responder to overwork. Indeed, some responders may choose to continue working rather than taking a break. Taking walks, visiting a store, and attending education and supervision groups that may be available on site for first responders are helpful self-care exercises that can provide a necessary diversion.

First responders working under disaster conditions should not be surprised to find themselves experiencing symptoms of secondary trauma such as unwanted recollections of the traumatic event, sudden re-experiencing of the event, detachment, difficulty concentrating, and sleep disturbances (Hafeez, Hertz, Kefer, & Motta, 1999). However, recognizing that these reactions are normal and expectable consequences of listening to traumatized clients will help put things in perspective. This awareness and mindfulness supports the first responder's self-care. The question is not whether the responder will be exposed to traumatizing experiences (this can always be anticipated in a disaster setting) but rather how the effects of these experiences are managed.

Maintaining a Routine

Although not always possible, once a first responder is out in the field, attempts should be made to maintain a normal and predictable daily routine; regular sleep and eating patterns are seriously compromised by the stressful environment at disaster sites. Eating healthy meals and maintaining a regular sleep regimen helps create structure in a chaotic environment and supports adjustment. The body anticipates getting rest and food at a particular time; honoring this schedule helps in reducing unnecessary stress. Physical exercise is also invaluable in releasing stress. Although it is not always possible to visit a gym on a disaster site, other simple physical activities such as taking a walk outside or doing some stretch and yoga exercises in one's designated sleeping area are quite possible and highly recommended.

Setting Boundaries

Establishing strict guidelines on the amount of time the responder spends on a disaster site is supportive of the first responder's self-care. Even the most resilient first responder becomes overwhelmed upon arriving on the scene of a disaster; feelings of powerlessness and futility, including questions about whether one can make a difference, quickly emerge. In contrast, some responders may have abounding energy and become completely immersed in the rescue effort. These responders often remain at the disaster site for an extended period of time that exceeds their initial deployment. However, they face the risks of increasing vulnerability and a predisposition to posttraumatic reactions. For example, among first responders to the Oklahoma City bombing, the length of time spent at the disaster site was strongly associated with the development of PTSD (Bernard & Driscoll, 2006).

Similarly, an investigation conducted among first responders to the World Trade Center disaster found that PTSD was elevated for those who worked for more than 3 months at the disaster site Stratified analyses also revealed that the relationship between time worked at the site and the probability of PTSD was strongest for those who started on September 11th, when exposure to trauma and risk of injury was the greatest (Perrin et al., 2007).

Although a mental health responder may be committed to working longer hours and remaining at a disaster site for several weeks, it is important to focus on what can be accomplished in a short period of time. This can be achieved by thinking small, thinking constructively, and thinking creatively in terms of the operation of a shelter and the limits presented by the context of the disaster. Such thinking can prevent the first responder from getting overwhelmed by the enormity of a problem.

Importance of Collaboration

Collaboration is a valuable and productive mechanism for reducing stress among mental health professionals in disaster locations. It makes helpers feel like they are members of a team and diminishes unnecessary duplication of efforts. Some disaster organizations set up a buddy system in which responders are partnered with others so that all activities are conducted in a dyad format. The buddy system can be quite beneficial in supporting the self-care of a disaster responder. An astute buddy helps slow down an overzealous colleague and is able to detect the early signs of secondary stress and compassion fatigue. At the same time, the buddy system offers opportunities for peer consultation and becomes an invaluable resource when the first responder feels overwhelmed.

Support

Generating social and emotional support from significant others outside the disaster setting can alleviate the stress of disaster work. This support can come from family, friends, coworkers, and supervisors in the responder's home environment. Those with few social supports are a vulnerable group who are likely to suffer greater psychological and physical consequences. The simple act of carrying photos of close friends and family and other personal mementoes can be stress reducing. It is a good strategy to arrange a personal space with these personal items after one settles into the disaster site and is assigned sleeping quarters.

In this technological age, maintaining contact with loved ones by telephone or e-mail is possible even from a disaster location. Taking a few minutes each day to connect with trusted friends and family members is a good reminder that the disaster activities are temporary; it is also a reminder of what one can look forward to upon returning home.

Mindful Activities

It is preferable to practice self-care strategies that are mindful and are derived from a health-oriented perspective. Such strategies should be comforting, healing, and restorative. They should balance work and personal life and allow the individual to become fully present and focused in the moment (Kabat-Zinn, 1994). Mindful activities are reminders of the importance of living each moment to the fullest (Cunningham, 2004). Self-care strategies should be experienced as recharging and refueling activities; if it is experienced as restorative, then it probably works and should be repeated on a regular basis.

Organizational Support

There are many ways in which organizations that send volunteers to disaster sites can adequately support them. For example, in a study conducted among rescue and recovery workers who responded to the September 11th disaster and who continued to experience substantial psychological distress years later, Perrin et al. (2007) concluded that to reduce the psychological burden associated with participation and to decrease PTSD among future workers and volunteers, disaster preparedness training, shift rotations, and a shorter duration of service at the site should be mandated.

A supportive organizational environment mitigates the secondary stress experienced by trauma workers. For example, those who received empathic support from coworkers following the Oklahoma City bombing had lowered levels of secondary traumatization and psychological distress (Batten & Orsillo, 2002). In contrast, first responders who had high-intensity work assignments over an extended period of time were constrained and not fully available to their clients, they felt unappreciated by coworkers or supervisors, and showed higher burnout rates (Savicki & Cooley, 1987). Organizations that do not clearly delineate the tasks of their volunteers create role conflict and ambiguity (Barber & Iwai, 1996). Thus, disaster organizations have a responsibility to recognize and take appropriate steps to ameliorate the stress of the work environment (Everly, 1989).

A tangible organizational strategy to reduce secondary traumatization and work-related stress is a smaller and manageable caseload. This allows mental health professionals time to process their clinical experience and complete administrative tasks between seeing clients. In contrast, a larger caseload is strongly associated with disruptions in cognitive schemas, increased PTSD symptoms, and secondary trauma (Schauben & Frazier, 1995). Ethical and practice guidelines from professional organizations such as the American Counseling Association and the American Psychological Association provide standards on the appropriate size of client caseloads for mental health professionals (Pearlman, 2005).

Benefits of Debriefing

Disaster organizations should make every attempt to debrief disaster responders after their deployment; debriefings have been demonstrated to lower compassion fatigue and increase the coping behaviors of first responders when they return home (Adams, Figley, & Boscarino, 2008). For example, Jenkins (1996) found that emergency medical workers reported better psychological health after participating in debriefing sessions. The debriefing also serves as an acknowledgment of the challenging work of the mental health disaster responder. When conducted as a group, it provides dual opportunities to hear from others who have had similar experiences and gain recognition for involvement in challenging disaster work. Lack of recognition was seen as partially responsible for an increase in psychological distress among construction and sanitation workers at the World Trade Center. Unlike other workers who responded to the World Trade Center, they did not receive recognition for their efforts, and this apparently prevented them from obtaining closure after engaging in the traumatic search and rescue work after 9/11 (Perrin et al., 2007).

Adequate Preparation and Training

It is incumbent on training and other academic programs to impress upon their trainees the value of practicing regular self-care, especially if they plan to work as first responders. Such training programs can help reduce secondary trauma by communicating the message to first responders that self-care should be ongoing and intentional. It should be viewed not as an option that can be fulfilled when the responder has extra time but as a responsibility that has to be met on an ongoing and consistent basis. Disaster responders who take good care of themselves take good care of their clients as well. Depth of training and experience are additional protective factors that support the well-being of first responders.

Baum (2004) suggests that it is critical that supervisors convey to their supervisees the importance of balancing personal and professional life; supervisees must be encouraged to communicate concerns and other pertinent issues to supervisors on a regular basis. Supervisors who ensure that first responders are held accountable and practice adequate self-care strategies prevent the build-up of secondary trauma.

It may be helpful to provide mental health professionals who may not have acquired adequate training with curricula ahead of their deployment to help them deal with some of the challenges of providing direct services to disaster survivors (Dane, 2000). An awareness of the impact of secondary trauma would be a key feature of such a curriculum. In this way, mental health responders can anticipate what may occur cognitively, emotionally, physically, and behaviorally when working with traumatized clients.

The Role of Transition

Finally, before mental health responders get ready to resume their normal schedules, it is critical that they set aside a transition time, which acts as a buffer period between deployment and regular work activities; it is an invaluable destressing mechanism. Mental health responders can expect to experience unremitting guilt when they return home; they may find themselves preoccupied by memories of those they have left behind, some of whom continue to experience hardship. This transition period offers a time to work through and integrate the experiences of the deployment so that they can focus on the commitments and responsibilities of their current life. Professional colleagues in the local environment can play an important role in supporting the mental health responder's adjustment.

Research has shown that altruism is life enhancing and can add to a person's self-esteem and mental health (Post, 2005; Schwartz, Meisenhelder, Ma, & Reed, 2003). Similarly, volunteering and engaging in other helping behaviors has been shown to have many physical health benefits (Moen, Dempster-McCain, & Williams, 1993) as well as contributing to increased longevity (Oman, Thoresen, & McMahon, 1999). Providing instrumental and emotional support to others has also been associated with decreased mortality (Brown, Nesse, Vonokur, & Smith, 2003).

PRACTICAL IMPLICATIONS

- Secondary trauma is an inevitable consequence of engaging in disaster work. To prevent burnout, self-care strategies should be practiced on an ongoing basis.
- There are several warning signs to burnout that affect mental health professionals cognitively, emotionally, physically, and behaviorally.
- A lack of structure, rewards, and resources are some of the challenges of working in disaster settings. Adapting to changing leadership and dealing with personal issues can intensify the situation.
- Organizations can better support first responders. Providing adequate training, ongoing support and supervision, and mandating the amount of time volunteers spend on site and the number of clients they serve are some supportive mechanisms.
- Mental health professionals have a responsibility to take care of themselves; they can do so by setting good boundaries and limits on the amount of time spent at the disaster site, having better self-awareness, maintaining a regular routine, and seeking support and collaboration.

CONCLUSION

As mental health professionals, the ethical principle of not harming others is integral; yet so often we fail to apply the same principle to ourselves. In this way, we neglect to practice what we teach; inattention to self-care can be considered self-harming behavior. Perhaps for those of us who put our clients before ourselves, remembering that engaging in self-care activities improves clinical competence can be a motivating strategy; ultimately our clients stand to gain from working with a mental health professional who is relaxed, empathic, and fully present. We tend to focus on restoring resiliency and empowerment among our clients; similarly, it behooves us to strive toward achieving the same for ourselves. Tosone et al. (2003) wrote, "Only by taking care of themselves can clinicians truly be in a position to help others" (p. 73).

In this chapter, the various shortfalls of failing to practice self-care strategies have been reviewed by examining vicarious trauma, compassion fatigue, and burnout, all of which result from the interaction between a helping professional's worldview and the traumatic material of a client. Vicarious trauma reactions develop from simply hearing about a client's traumatic experience; it is the cumulative effect of counseling traumatized clients (McCann & Pearlman, 1990; Pearlman, 2005; Pearlman & Saakvitne, 1995).

A mental health professional's reactions to disaster work often mirror the reactions of their clients and should be viewed as a normal response to an abnormal occupational hazard. This is an inevitable and expectable consequence of engaging in the work of disaster responding. However, the way in which mental health professionals manage their reactions to stress determines whether these reactions become debilitating and dysfunctional. Disaster responders have a tendency to believe that they are immune to stress; such attitudes can have long-term harmful consequences. Acknowledging the stressful nature of disaster work on an ongoing basis benefits the well-being of mental health professionals.

This chapter has included concrete ideas on how to manage and avert the negative consequences of secondary trauma. These strategies are to be applied before, during, and after a disaster deployment. Although disaster work is challenging, many people continue to do it because it is spiritually meaningful and a humanitarian way of supporting fellow citizens.

REFERENCES

Adams, R. E., Figley, C. R., & Boscarino, J. A. (2008). The compassion fatigue scale: Its use with social workers following urban disaster. *Research on Social Work Practice*, *18*(3), 238–250.

American Psychiatric Association. (2000). *Diagnostic and statistical manual of mental disorders* (4th ed., Text rev.). Washington, DC: Author.

Barber, C., & Iwai, M. (1996). Role conflict and role ambiguity as predictors of burnout among staff caring for elderly dementia patients. *Journal of Gerontological Social Work*, *26*(1–2), 101–116.

Batten, S. V., & Orsillo, S. M. (2002). Therapist reactions in the context of collective trauma. *Behavior Therapist*, *25*, 36–40.

Baum, N. (2004). Social work students' treatment termination. *Clinical Supervisory*, *23*(1), 165–178.

Bernard, B. P., & Driscoll, R. J. (2006). Health hazard evaluation of police officers and firefighters after Hurricane Katrina. *MMWR Weekly*, *55*, 456–458.

Boscarino, J. A., Figley, C. R., & Adams, R. E. (2004). Compassion fatigue following the September 11 terrorist attacks: A study of secondary trauma among New York City social workers. *International Journal of Emergency Mental Health*, *6*, 57–66.

Brown, S., Nesse, R. M., Vonokur, A. D., & Smith, D. M. (2003). Providing social support may be more beneficial than receiving it: Results from a prospective study of mortality. *Psychological Science*, *14*, 320–327.

Chang, C., Lee, L., Connor, K. M., Davidson, J. R. T., Jeffries, K., & Lai, T. (2003). Posttraumatic distress and coping strategies among rescue workers after an earthquake. *Journal of Nervous Mental Disorders*, *191*, 391–398.

Cunningham, M. (2004). Avoiding vicarious traumatization: Support, spirituality, and self-care. In N. B. Webb (Ed.), *Mass trauma and violence* (pp. 327–346). New York: Guilford.

Dane, B. (2000). Child welfare workers: An innovative approach for interacting with secondary trauma. *Journal of Social Work Education*, *36*, 27–38.

Everly, G. S. (1989). *A clinical guide to the treatment of the human stress response*. New York: Plenum.

Everly, G. S. (Ed.). (1995). *Innovations in disaster and trauma psychology, Volume 1: Applications in emergency services and disaster response*. Ellicott City, MD: Chevron.

Figley, C. R. (1995). Compassion fatigue: Toward a new understanding of the costs of caring. In B. H. Stamm (Ed.), *Secondary traumatic stress: Self care issues for clinicians, researchers, and educators* (2nd ed., pp. 3–28). Lutherville, MD: Sidran.

Fullerton, C. S., Ursano, R. J., Reeves, J., Shigemura, J., & Grieger, T. (2006). Perceived safety in disaster workers following 9/11. *Journal of Nervous Mental Disorders*, *194*, 61–63.

Fullerton, C. S., Ursano, R. J., & Wang, L. (2004). Acute stress disorder, posttraumatic stress disorder, and depression in disaster or rescue workers. *American Journal of Psychiatry*, *161*, 1370–1376.

Guo, U., Chen, C., Lu, M., Tan, H. K., Lee, H., & Wang, T. (2004). Posttraumatic stress disorder among professional and non-professional rescuers involved in an earthquake in Taiwan. *Psychiatry Residency*, *127*, 35–41.

Hafeez, S., Hertz, M. D., Kefer, J. M., & Motta, R. W. (1999). Initial evaluation of the secondary trauma questionnaire. *Psychological Reports, 85,* 997–1002.

James, R. K., & Gilliland, B. E. (2005). *Crisis intervention strategies* (5th ed.). Pacific Grove, CA: Brooks/Cole.

Jenkins, S. R. (1996). Social support and debriefing efficacy among emergency medical workers after a mass shooting incident. *Journal of Social Behavior and Personality, 11,* 477–492.

Jenkins, S. R., & Baird, S. (2002). Secondary traumatic stress and vicarious trauma: A validational study. *Journal of Traumatic Stress, 15*(5), 423–432.

Kabat-Zinn, J. (1994). *Wherever you go, there you are: Mindfulness meditation in everyday life.* New York: Hyperion.

Kassam-Adams, N. (1999). The risks of treating sexual trauma: Stress and secondary trauma in psychotherapists. In B. H. Stamm (Ed.), *Secondary traumatic stress: Self-care issues for clinicians, researchers, and educators* (pp. 37–48). Towson, MD: Sidran.

Kessler, R. C., Chin, W. T., Demler, O., Merikangas, K. R., & Walters, E. E. (2005). Prevalence, severity, and comorbidity of 12-month DSM-IV disorders in the National Comorbidity Survey Replication. *Archives of General Psychiatry, 62,* 617–627.

McCann, I. L., & Pearlman, L. A. (1990). Vicarious traumatization: A framework for understanding the psychological effects of working with victims. *Journal of Traumatic Stress, 3,* 131–149.

Miller, L. (1998). Our own medicine: Traumatized psychotherapists and the stresses of doing therapy. *Psychotherapy, 35*(2), 137–142.

Moen, P., Dempster-McCain, D., & Williams, R. M. (1993). Successful aging. *American Journal of Sociology, 97,* 1612–1632.

Munroe, J. (1995). Ethical issues associated with secondary trauma in therapists. In B. H. Stamm (Ed.), *Secondary traumatic stress* (2nd ed., pp. 211–229). Baltimore: Sidran.

Nelson-Gardell, D., & Harris, D. (2003). Childhood abuse history, secondary traumatic stress, and child welfare workers. *Child Welfare, 82,* 5–26.

Oman, D., Thoresen, C. E., & McMahon, K. (1999). Volunteerism and mortality among the community-dwelling elderly. *American Journal of Public Health, 4,* 301–316.

Ozen, S., & Aytekin, S. (2004). Frequency of PTSD in a group of search and rescue workers two months after 2003 Bingol (Turkey) earthquake. *Journal of Nervous Mental Disorders, 192,* 573–575.

Pearlin, L. I. (1989). The sociological study of stress. *Journal of Health and Social Behavior, 30,* 241–256.

Pearlman, L. A. (2005). Self care for trauma therapists: Ameliorating vicarious traumatization. In B. Hudnall Stamm (Ed.), *Secondary traumatic stress* (2nd ed., pp. 51–64). Baltimore: Sidran.

Pearlman, L. A., & Maclan, P. S. (1995). Vicarious traumatization: An empirical study of the effects of trauma work on therapists. *Professional Psychology, 26*(6), 558–565.

Pearlman, L. A., & Saakvitne, K. W. (1995). Treating therapists with vicarious traumatization and secondary traumatic stress disorders. In C. R. Figley (Ed.), *Compassion fatigue: Coping with secondary traumatic stress disorder in those who treat the traumatized* (pp. 150–177). Bristol, PA: Brunner/Mazel.

Perrin, M. A., DiGrande, L., Wheeler, K., Thorpe, L., Farfel, M., & Brackbill, R. (2007). Differences in PTSD prevalence and associated risk factors among World Trade Center disaster rescue and recovery workers. *American Journal of Psychiatry, 164*(9), 1385–1394.

Post, S. G. (2005). Altruism, happiness, and health: It's good to be good. *International Journal of Behavioral Medicine, 12,* 66–77.

Saakvitne, K. W. (2003). Holding hope and humanity in the face of trauma's legacy: The daunting challenge for group therapists. *International Journal of Group Psychotherapy, 55*(1), 137–148.

Savicki, V., & Cooley, E. (1987). The relationship of work environment and client contact to burnout in mental health professionals. *Journal of Counseling & Development, 65*(5), 249–252.

Schauben, L. J., & Frazier, P. A. (1995). Vicarious trauma: The effects on female counselors of working with sexual violence survivors. *Psychology of Women Quarterly, 19,* 49–64.

Schwartz, C., Meisenhelder, J. B., Ma, Y., & Reed, G. (2003). Altruistic social interest behaviors are associated with better mental health. *Psychosomatic Medicine, 65,* 778–785.

Smith, R. P., Katz, C. L., Holmes, A., Herbert, R., Levin, S., Moline, J., et al. (2004). Mental health status of World Trade Center rescue and recovery workers and volunteers—New York City, July 2002–August 2004. *MMWR Weekly, 53,* 812–815.

Stamm, H. (Ed.). (1999). *Secondary traumatic stress: Self-care issues for clinicians, researchers, and educators.* Baltimore: Sidran.

Thoits, P. A. (1995). Stress, coping, and social support processes: Where are we? What next? *Journal of Health and Social Behavior, 35,* 53–79.

Ting, L., Sanders, S., Jacobson, J. M., & Power, J. R. (2006). Dealing with the aftermath: A qualitative analysis of mental health social workers' reactions after a client suicide. *Social Work, 51,* 329–341.

Tosone, C., Bialkin, L., Campbell, M., Charters, M., Gieri, K., Gross, S., et al. (2003). Shared trauma: Group reflections on the September 11th disaster. *Psychoanalytic Social Work, 1091,* 57–77.

Tripanny, R. L., White Kress, V. E., & Wicoxon, S. A. (2004). Preventing vicarious trauma: What counselors should know when working with trauma survivors. *Journal of Counseling and Development, 82,* 31–37.

CHAPTER 15

Summary and Conclusion

Priscilla Dass-Brailsford

On August 29, 2005, when Hurricane Katrina made landfall near the Louisiana–Mississippi border, it exposed a large number of people to extraordinary loss and suffering. The enormous swath of physical devastation that was wreaked across the marshes of Louisiana's Plaquemines Parish to the urban communities of New Orleans and the coastal landscape of Mississippi and Alabama caused a notable change to the demographics of the Gulf Coast region.

Unlike man-made disasters such as the Oklahoma City bombing and September 11, 2001, terrorist attacks on the Pentagon and the World Trade Center, natural disasters significantly impact the infrastructure of affected communities and hamper their ability to respond effectively. Besides being one of the most expensive natural disasters in U.S. history to date, Hurricane Katrina is also considered one of the worst natural disasters in terms of the area affected and the number of people killed, injured, and displaced. The storm affected 90,000 square miles in the Gulf Coast, an area geographically the size of Great Britain (U.S. House of Representatives, 2006). Electrical service was still unavailable for large parts of New Orleans even 16 months after the storm. More than 1 million people were displaced, making the aftermath of the hurricane one of the greatest humanitarian crises within the United States since the Great Depression. This final chapter summarizes and provides a commentary on each of the chapters of this book.

Chapter 1 introduced the reader to the disaster field by providing an overview of several disasters that have occurred nationally and globally. The disasters were selected for the special lessons they have offered and for their contribution to the disaster field. However, we should bear in mind that just because society has been offered a lesson after a disaster occurs that the lesson will be heeded. In the aftermath of every disaster, an assessment is made of successes and failures and interventions are examined; however, many of the findings are soon forgotten, only to be relearned by another community (and sometimes the same community) in the aftermath of the next disaster.

Volunteer efforts have grown tremendously in recent years as service learning programs at universities have increased. This chapter reviewed the development and growth of several disaster relief organizations in the United States. The widespread involvement of volunteers in disaster relief is in keeping with the nation's historical spirit of benevolence. Since the 1800s, volunteer agencies have helped individuals, families, and communities get back on their feet after the devastating effects of disasters. Without these agencies, local, state, and federal disaster relief organizations would be unable to meet all the unique needs of disaster victims.

Chapter 2 looked at what went wrong after Hurricane Katrina. Several explanations have surfaced, and each is explored. Explanations ranged from it being a natural disaster and therefore unavoidable to it being a man-made disaster caused by poorly constructed levees. An environmental perspective that examined the neglect of the marshlands and the rapid growth of the casino industry in the Gulf Coast appears to be another plausible reason. The conclusion reached is that the consequences of disasters must be understood in the context of socially produced conditions of vulnerability that place some individuals at far greater risk than others; the elderly, the poor, and the isolated are disproportionately at greatest risk.

Ecological vulnerability bears important consideration. Beyond individual characteristics, structurally disadvantaged neighborhoods are less capable of sustaining viable social networks in the aftermath of a disaster and may suffer from deficits in local social interaction and support. For example, in a study on the effects of the Chicago heat wave of 1995, Browning, Wallace, Feinberg, and Cagney (2006) found that more extensive social ties, including non-kin exchange networks and kinship-based affiliations, are likely to have benefited elderly urban residents. Areas that have communal efficacy are likely to enhance a community's capacity to attract and maintain high-quality services and amenities. The researchers concluded that elderly residents may have felt more comfortable using streets with more vibrant social ecologies during the heat wave and thus could have avoided isolating themselves from potential sources of support.

The way we take care of our dead is symbolic of the contributions they have made to society; it is an honoring of their role in our lives. Chapter 3, "Ignore the Dead: We Want the Living," critiqued the insensitivity and disregard federal and state authorities had for those who lost their lives in Hurricane Katrina. Many survivors at local shelters were preoccupied with the dead they had left behind in the torrid waters of the storm. The chapter outlined the cultural importance of the funeral ceremony, including the jazz funeral, a distinguishing aspect of New Orleans culture.

The jazz funeral is usually conducted in style and can last a week, feature jazz bands and parades, and draw bigger crowds than weddings. The jazz funeral offers a catharsis through music and a positive coping mechanism for communities in the city's poorest neighborhoods (Raeburn, 2007). New Orleans is a city steeped in ritual, in which public displays of mourning are valued and where ritual becomes an important tool of healing. In fact, celebration of one's death may well be the grandest celebration in one's life (Holliday, 2005). The brass band music of the jazz funeral generates dancing in the street, inviting the entire city's residents to join in. This tradition enables communities beset by institutionalized racism, poverty, high crime, and mortality rates to maintain a positive attitude in the midst of loss and oppressive daily realities. It is estimated that only 250 musicians, less than 10% of the pre-Katrina music population, have returned (Raeburn, 2007). This is a precarious testament in terms of cultural loss for the residents of New Orleans and may have far-reaching consequences for the future of New Orleans.

Chapter 4, which discussed effective interventions in the aftermath of disasters, offered the reader practical skills on disaster response. Mental health professionals require specialized skills and training to appropriately respond in the aftermath of a disaster. A lack of this training can be detrimental for both the helper and those who need help. Faust, Black, Abrahams, Warner, and Bellando (2008), based on their personal experience and recognizing that they were not trauma psychologists but psychologists providing trauma services after the storm of Hurricane Katrina, strongly urge mental health professionals to seek specialized training in this area. Mental health providers have a professional and ethical obligation to seek this training because they usually interact with individuals who are in their most vulnerable state. To provide effective interventions, they should be adequately trained and prepared to do the work efficiently and skillfully. The empowering model of crisis intervention is offered as an appropriate and effective intervention that acknowledges clients' strength, restores control, and empowers them to take charge of their lives.

In Chapter 5, "Families Affected by Hurricane Katrina and Other Disasters: Learning From the Experiences of African American Survivors," Boyd-Franklin examined how African American families were affected by Hurricane Katrina and other disasters. She indicated that African American families generally subscribe to a collective worldview that places greater importance on the community and the interrelatedness and interconnectedness of all things, including nature and physical place. The ecosystem that surrounds individuals influences their functioning. Survivors of Hurricane Katrina, who were forced to make new homes in distant U.S. towns and cities, have experienced a rupture in their ecological framework; in addition to their physical losses, they have lost all that was familiar.

Research has found that survivors of a natural disaster who remain in familiar surroundings are able to maintain family cohesion and preserve psychological community; such survivors are also able to contribute to the recovery and reconstruction of their community (Galante & Foa, 1986; Najarian, Goenjian, Pelcovitz, Mandel, & Najarian, 2001). In contrast, those who relocate to distant areas experience a loss of connection and a weakening of communal ties. In addition, an ecological consideration of an individual's political, cultural, environmental, and social realities has the additional benefit of helping responders identify their support networks (Kaniasty & Norris, 1999).

Both formal and informal community support networks are equally important in helping survivors recover (Beaver & Miller, 1992). Formal support networks are usually those services provided by governmental and other nongovernmental organizations. A community's history with these institutions determines how the support is viewed. Family, friends, and community members provide informal networks and can become a primary source of support, ameliorating the negative effects of stress for some survivors. For example, research shows that adults who are 65 years and older received more than 80% of their assistance after a disaster from informal support networks (Bowie, 2003). Time will shed greater light on the long-term psychological consequences of forced distant relocation on the lives of Hurricane Katrina survivors.

Children are members of a vulnerable group who are prone to experiencing a disaster and its sequalae as traumatic. In Chapter 6, "Children and Crises," Knapp provided information on working with children affected by disasters and other crises. The protective factors that enhance recovery and support resiliency in children were outlined. This chapter prepares the reader to recognize the crisis reactions, methods of treatment, and particular developmental concerns as they relate to children.

In a significant study conducted after the Indian Ocean tsunami, Vijayakumar, Kannan, and Daniel (2006) evaluated the effect of exposure to the tsunami on the mental health of children. They found that pre-existing vulnerability worsened affective and somatic symptoms but both severity of exposure and pre-existing vulnerability correlated significantly with symptoms of PTSD. The implications of the findings are that children who experienced death or injury to parents or siblings due to a disaster are more likely to develop anxiety disorders.

Similarly, two studies conducted among children who were initially evacuated and later returned to their former neighborhoods found that more than half were in need of mental health services and about a third reported clinically significant symptoms indicative of PTSD and depression. These symptoms were most prevalent among those who had experienced a previous loss or trauma (Osofsky & Osofsky, 2006). Thus, attending to the mental health needs of children immediately after a disaster is critical to ensure future well-being.

In Chapter 7, "Provider Perspectives on Serving the Needs of Displaced Disaster Survivors Following Hurricane Katrina," Houston, Reyes, Pfefferbaum, and Wyche reported on an empirical study conducted among providers who worked with Hurricane Katrina survivors. The study presented important findings on the psychosocial needs and difficulties faced by disaster survivors, the adequacy of community services, survivor integration in the host community, and the role of the media in supporting or delaying recovery. The authors recommended that providers and organizations in the host community collaborate with each other to coordinate response efforts and foster the integration of survivors by orienting them to the new community.

Chapter 8, "Older Adults and Natural Disasters: Lessons Learned From Hurricanes Katrina and Rita," by Cherry, Allen, and Galea, demonstrated that the U.S. disaster management system does not sufficiently meet the needs of the elderly in our society. The death of 70 residents in 13 nursing homes during Hurricane Katrina underscores the need for nursing homes to better address the medical needs of older individuals during disasters and to make improvements in developing more efficacious evacuation plans and crisis protocols. In general, nursing home residents have substantial medical needs that are exacerbated following a disaster; it may come as no surprise that their mental health needs may also grow considerably as the physical environment becomes increasingly unstable.

Appropriately supporting the acute and long-term care facilities under disaster conditions is essential. We should not lose sight of the fact that staff members are also local residents who often experience their own personal and property losses in disasters. It is likely that nursing homes that become sheltering facilities after a disaster may have to deal with the challenges of staff shortages. Reduced productivity as a result of fatigue, emotional health, and the ongoing need of staff members to attend to their own housing, transportation, and family issues is predictable; dealing with this issue is a priority in disaster management (Laditka et al., 2008).

Religion, an organized system of beliefs, practices, and rituals designed to facilitate closeness to God (Koenig, McCullough, & Larson, 2001), is embraced as a way to understand and cope with personal suffering and loss (Taylor, Chatters, & Levin, 2004). For African Americans in particular, a belief in a divine force that intervenes in one's life is consistent with an African cultural worldview (Grills, 2004), and individuals living in the South display a strong religious faith (Taylor, Thornton, & Chatters, 1987) by using prayer as an integral source of coping in the aftermath of personal tragedy or adversity.

In Chapter 9, "The Spiritual Dimensions of Caring for People Affected by Disasters," McCombs discussed how African American survivors are likely to struggle with a spiritual explanation of why a tragedy has befallen them. They may display fluctuations between intense emotions of loss and gratitude for survivorship. Disaster responders should be adept at recognizing the values, practices, and spiritual orientations that support a community's psychological and spiritual well-being (Peregoy, 2005; Zhang & Snowden, 1999).

Encouraging coping behaviors consistent with indigenous beliefs and customs helps ethnic minority clients to heal rapidly; the first responder may have to suspend his or her spiritual beliefs in order to support clients. Ministers and other clergy are highly regarded in African American communities and can potentially serve as first responders. In fact, some survivors may prefer to seek psychological comfort from religious ministers rather than mental health professionals. Finally, to promote the effective healing of African American people, attention to the mind, body, and spirit is important (Holliday, 2005).

Poor disaster preparedness, a lack of resources for rebuilding, and a legacy of historic trauma and collective grief makes recovery from disasters a challenging enterprise for some vulnerable people. In Chapter 10, "Working With Rural and Diverse Communities After Disasters," Boyd, Quevillon, and Engdahl discussed community approaches in working with rural and Native American communities after a disaster. The authors focused on understanding the cultural background of disaster-affected communities. For example, it is important to bear in mind that many Native American communities possess collective and historical grief stemming from the inception of this country that may make them distrusting of outsiders.

Thus, seeking an invitation from the tribal government before offering any help to Native American communities is a good way to gain acceptance. Personal introductions are highly valued and preferred to institutional introductions because Native American communities care more about who you are rather than who you represent. In addition, Native American communities value knowing the commitment level of outsiders, especially in terms of the length of time they will spend in the community; making a long term commitment to working with a community and collaborating with staff from local mental health or disaster relief organizations is viewed positively.

In Chapter 11, "Voices of Hope: A Commentary on Dislocation and Relocation," Marotta commented on how mental health professionals and government policy makers can incorporate lessons learned from survivors and responders into the design and delivery of mental health services for future disasters. Using case examples and the voices of survivors, she outlined 10 important lessons that should be borne in mind by disaster management and recovery groups. The lessons include the importance of safety in the immediate aftermath of a disaster, the resiliency of the human spirit, a caution not to pathologize survivors of disasters, and recommendations that mental health professionals prepare appropriately for the stress of disaster work.

In Chapter 12, "The Federal Government in Disaster Mental Health Response: An Ever-Evolving Role," Dodgen and Meed discussed the complexity of the federal role in addressing the psychological aspects of disaster preparedness and response. They addressed both the underlying principles behind the design of federal disaster policy in behavioral health and the legislation that authorizes federal agencies to respond to the behavioral health needs of survivors. In addition, they reviewed current federal support mechanisms and the future directions of federal behavioral health responses.

The many reports on responding to disasters and disaster services that have emerged since the September 11th terrorist attacks in 2001 and Hurricane Katrina in 2005 attest to an increased understanding and a wealth of knowledge about disasters. Of special note is the maturation of federal mental health services in recognizing the needs of affected populations by offering enhanced services, interventions for complicated grief, and increased accountability by assessing the delivery and outcome of services.

Historically, federally funded crisis counseling programs have not supported traditional treatment but focused instead on short-term counseling and the needs of persons whose reactions do not reach the level of psychiatric care usually delivered in traditional mental health settings (Pfefferbaum, 2006). However, after a disaster, the potential for serious and enduring pathology increases dramatically. A change in federal help has been recently noted as providing more support toward overburdened state and local mental health programs. This change indicates a positive evolution in disaster mental health care, and its growth is reflected in the ability to respond to subsequent disasters of increased dimensions in the context of more complex and devastated environments.

Likewise, research has also benefited from increased federal funding that was rapidly offered in the aftermath of both disasters (September 11th and Hurricane Katrina). The concern, strongly voiced after the 1995 Oklahoma City bombing, that conducting evaluation and services research was antithetical to providing high-quality care and an exploitation of vulnerable communities has diminished (Pfefferbaum, 2006). Instead, a partnership of providers, administrators, and researchers has been shown to greatly enhance what we know about disaster mental health services in terms of their efficacy and outcomes. Incorporating such collaborations in future disaster responses will continue to improve services while enriching the evidence-based literature on best approaches. It is also important that research and other disaster literature highlight the successes and failures of the disaster mental health system so that both the larger professional audience and policy makers can make informed choices about needs and priorities after disasters.

In Chapter 13, "A Community-Based Approach to Coping With Crises in Africa," Carr discussed the experience of working internationally as a cross-cultural worker in Africa. She identified the protective factors that help cross-cultural workers cope and reviewed a specific community-based approach that proactively addressed the skills and strengths needed to adapt in an international setting. The challenges and benefits of doing international crisis work were also discussed in this chapter.

It is well established that individuals who work with traumatized clients can be profoundly affected by the experience (McCann & Pearlman, 1990; Yassen, 1995). This impact has been referred to as "compassion fatigue" and "secondary traumatic stress" (STS; Figley, 1995). Figley defines STS as "the natural, consequent behaviors and emotions resulting from knowing about a traumatizing event experienced by a significant other— the stress resulting from helping or wanting to help a traumatized or suffering person" (p. 2). STS can affect mental health professionals in many ways, cognitively (reduced concentration), emotionally (depression), or spiritually (anger at God; Yassen, 1995). Finally, Chapter 14, "Secondary Trauma Among Disaster Responders," emphasized the need for self-care, because disaster responders are apt to experience vicarious trauma in the aftermath of disasters.

RECOMMENDATIONS FOR DISASTER READINESS

This book has provided an overview of the disaster field, and in each chapter, the authors have provided some insight into the lessons learned after major crises and disasters. In summary, the following recommendations serve to ensure disaster readiness. As a first step and at a basic policy level, the public can be educated in disaster preparedness. For example, many residents in California know what to do in the event of an earthquake. The same precautions can be taken for those who live in the Midwest, which is prone to tornadoes, and those living in the coastal regions, which are vulnerable to floods and hurricanes.

In addition, it is imperative to have workable evacuation plans and advanced warning systems as well as appropriate disaster protocols that reduce chaos; maintain security; protect human dignity; and take care of the medical, mental health, and other needs of all disaster affected people. The benefits of conducting disaster drills on a regular basis cannot be minimized. More important, the insights provided by such practices should not be taken lightly. Ironically, a disaster drill was executed in New Orleans a few months before Hurricane Katrina occurred in 2005. Questions of what to do with those who could not evacuate during the practice period were ignored, with calamitous results when Hurricane Katrina struck.

Open communication and effective collaboration among those in leadership positions is always necessary before a disaster occurs but especially needed when a disaster is predicted. Better communication and coordination at all levels of government is crucial; cooperation between civilian and governmental agencies swiftly reduces anarchy and a breakdown in the social order. Good leaders must be able to exude calmness, take charge, and maintain control at all times; in this way, they represent role models to the people they serve. Senior officials and those in leadership positions must be prepared for the most disastrous eventualities so that they can instill hope among survivors who feel overwhelmed and anxious.

It is imperative that the local population participate in recovery efforts as much as possible. Local residents know their community best, and their involvement improves coping and reduces their grieving. Financial aid to survivors is always beneficial but should be done in a way that does not set into motion a cycle of dependency that later becomes problematic. Shelters should be set up as close as safely possible to disaster-affected areas so that survivors can participate in recovery and reconstruction efforts. Uprooting and relocating communities is not psychologically supportive; it extends their recovery time and may exacerbate their trauma reactions. Holliday (2005) advises that if minority communities want to play a significant role in their community's disaster response and recovery, they should have a pre-existing relationship with emergency planning and response agencies.

Even though survivors may no longer live in their original communities, they carry with them their cultural values and practices; in times of crisis and tragedy, cultural and racial affinity is often strengthened. Relief organizations should thus make a concerted effort to either include responders who are reflective of survivors' ethnic, racial, and social background, or include individuals who are culturally competent; this will reduce the stress of cross-cultural interactions and will likely be experienced as supportive by survivors. People in the helping profession who understand a survivor's traumatic experience in the context of the cultural and socio-historical factors they hold as important are viewed as supportive by survivors, whereas familiarity with the unique traumatic reactions of ethnic minority groups facilitates cross-cultural interventions.

However, establishing racial and ethnic affinity is not always possible; in its absence, the racial attitude of first responders becomes an important consideration. Open, accepting, and empowering responders dissolve the initial barriers of racial differences. Training in multicultural competence and experience in working with diverse clients hones this skill. A disaster site should not be the arena in which to test multicultural competence skills for the first time.

Most people are able to display resiliency in the aftermath of trauma. For example, Kessler et al. (2006) in an early study conducted soon after Hurricane Katrina found that many survivors reported developing a sense of purpose and deriving meaning and inner strength from the disaster experience. On the other hand, for most people, the psychological interventions they receive soon after a disaster may be the only mental health services they receive. Such services should therefore be of a high quality and at the same time strive to adequately meet the diverse needs of survivors. Mental health professionals should be appropriately trained in the provision of crisis and disaster services, and academic programs and professional organizations have a responsibility to make sure that this occurs.

Notwithstanding the tendency for most people to display resiliency in the aftermath of crises and disasters, there are some vulnerable groups that may need more long-term mental health care (women, children, and those with pre-existing mental health concerns). For example, a study by Yang, Xirasagar, Chung, Huang, and Lin (2005) indicates the need for effective policies to address the long-term mental health care of communities affected by disasters. The researchers emphasize that the serious disruption of life and social networks places some individuals at high risk for suicide; mental health care mobilization should therefore be extended for a sufficient period of time to support the full recovery of survivors.

Disasters reveal the values that a society holds as important and the level of caring expressed toward those who are less fortunate. It is to be expected that governmental bureaucracy may sometimes hamper relief efforts, but in a country such as the United States—the leader of the industrialized world—more was expected after Hurricane Katrina. As support poured in from European and Asian countries, the storm raised questions about America's capabilities to protect its citizens. What we saw in September 2005 in New Orleans had the appearance of a struggling developing nation; the institutional response was in many ways a catastrophe unto itself. We should not allow this to happen again.

REFERENCES

Beaver, M. L., & Miller, D. A. (1992). *Clinical social work practice with the elderly: Primary, secondary and tertiary intervention* (2nd ed.). Belmont, CA: Wadsworth.

Bowie, S. L. (2003). Post-disaster crisis intervention with older adults in public housing communities. *Crisis Intervention and Time Limited Treatment, 6*(3), 171–184.

Browning, C. R., Wallace, D., Feinberg, S. L., & Cagney, K. A. (2006). Neighborhood social processes, physical conditions, and disaster-related mortality: The case of the 1995 heat wave. *American Sociological Review, 71*(4), 665–682.

Faust, D. S., Black, F. W., Abrahams, J. P., Warner, M. S., & Bellando, B. J. (2008). After the storm: Katrina's impact on psychological practice in New Orleans. *Professional Psychology Research and Practice, 39*(1), 1–6.

Figley, C. R. (1995). Compassion fatigue: Toward a new understanding of the costs of caring. In B. H. Stamm (Ed.), *Secondary traumatic stress: Self care issues for clinician researchers and educators* (2nd ed., pp. 3–28). Lutherville, MD: Sidran.

Galante, R., & Foa, A. (1986). An epidemiological study of psychic trauma and treatment effectiveness for children after a natural disaster. *Journal of the American Academy of Child and Adolescent Psychiatry, 25,* 357–363.

Grills, C. (2004). African-centered psychology: Basic principles. In T. Parham (Ed.), *Counseling persons of African descent: Raising the bar of practitioner competence* (pp. 10–24). Thousand Oaks, CA: Sage.

Holliday, B. (2005, October). *An anatomy of a disaster: The cultural, psychological and spiritual lessons of Hurricane Katrina.* Paper presented at the 2nd annual conference of the African American Mental Health Summit, Memphis, TN.

Kaniasty, K., & Norris, F. (1999). The experience of disaster: Individuals and communities sharing trauma. In R. Grist & B. Lubin (Eds.), *Response to disaster: Psychosocial, community and ecological approaches* (pp. 25–62). Philadelphia: Brunner/Mazel.

Kessler, R. C., Galea, S., Jones, R. T., & Parker, H. A. (2006). Mental illness and suicidality after Hurricane Katrina. *Bulletin of the World Health Organization, 84*(12), 930–939.

Koenig, H. G., McCullough, M. E., & Larson, D. B. (2001). *Handbook of religion and health.* New York: Oxford University Press.

Laditka, S. B., Laditka, J. N., Xirasagar, S., Cornman, C. B., Davis, C. B., & Richter, J. E. V. (2008). Providing shelter to nursing home evacuees in disasters: Lessons from Hurricane Katrina. *American Journal of Public Health, 98*(7), 1288–1293.

McCann, I. L., & Pearlman, L. A. (1990). Vicarious traumatization: A framework for understanding the psychological effects of working with victims. *Journal of Traumatic Stress, 3,* 131–149.

Najarian, L. M., Goenjian, A. K., Pelcovitz, D., Mandel, F., & Najarian, B. (2001). The effect of relocation after a natural disaster. *Journal of Traumatic Stress, 14,* 511–526.

Osofsky, J., & Osofsky, H. (2006, August). *In the eye of the storm: Resilience in Katrina's wake.* Paper presented at the annual convention of the American Psychological Association, New Orleans, LA.

Peregoy, J. J. (2005). Working with diverse cultures: Revisiting issues in prevention and intervention. In P. Stevens & R. Smith (Eds.), *Substance abuse prevention and intervention* (3rd ed., pp. 266–270). New York: Prentiss.

Pfefferbaum, B. (2006). Disasters in the 21st century: Lessons from Project Liberty. *Psychiatric Services, 57*(9), 1251.

Raeburn, B. B. (2007, December). They're trying to wash us away: New Orleans musicians surviving Katrina. *Journal of American History, 94,* 812–819.

Taylor, R. J., Chatters, L. M., & Levin, J. (2004). *Religion in the lives of African Americans: Social, psychological, and health perspectives.* Thousand Oaks, CA: Sage.

Taylor, R. J., Thornton, M. C., & Chatters, L. M. (1987). Black Americans' perceptions of the socio-historical role of the church. *Journal of Black Studies, 18,* 123–138.

U.S. House of Representatives. (2006). *A failure of initiative* (Final report of the Select Bipartisan Committee). Washington, DC: Government Printing Office.

Vijayakumar, L., Kannan, G. K., & Daniel, S. J. (2006). Mental health status in children exposed to tsunami. *International Review of Psychiatry, 18*(6), 507–513.

Yang, C. H., Xirasagar, S., Chung, H. C., Huang, Y. T., & Lin, H. C. (2005). Suicide trends following the Taiwan earthquake of 1999: Empirical evidence and policy implications. *Acta Psychiatrica Scandinavica, 112,* 442–448.

Yassen, J. (1995). Preventing secondary traumatic stress disorder. In C. Figley (Ed.), *Compassion fatigue: Secondary traumatic stress disorder from treating the traumatized* (pp. 178–208). New York: Brunner/Mazel.

Zhang, A. Y., & Snowden, L. R. (1999). Ethnic characteristics of mental disorders in five U.S. communities. *Cultural Diversity and Ethnic Minority Psychology, 5,* 134–141.

Index

Abrahams, J. P., 230
Acute Stress Disorder, 84
Africa
    Bakonga African burial traditions and, 41
    funeral traditions, processions in, 41
    U.S. Embassy in Kenya bombing (1998) and,
        140–141
    See also Crisis coping in Africa
African American elderly (Hurricane Katrina
        survivors)
    elderly refusal to evacuate and, 74
    family systems intervention and, 74–75, 81
    Hurricane Katrina and, 7
    kinship care tradition and, 74
    role and care of elderly importance and,
        73–74, 232
    Texas Tornado (1987) and, 7
    See also African Americans, African American
        families (Hurricane Katrina survivors);
        Older adults and natural disasters
African Americans, African American families
        (Hurricane Katrina survivors)
    African American church and, 78–79,
        232, 233
    anger as positive coping mechanism and, 69
    anniversary of death remembrances of, 45
    Bakonga African burial traditions and, 42
    biblical quotations and, 79
    Black *vs.* White racism perceptions and, 68
    children and adolescents trauma and, 72–73
    church homes, church families destruction
        and, 77–78, 231
    conclusions regarding, 81, 231
    cultural mistrust and suspicion, treatment
        resistance and, 29, 69–70, 156–167
    double psychological trauma of, 68
    evacuation, rescue, media, and displacement
        inequities and, 155, 156
    extended families, informal kinship networks
        and, 70–72, 81, 231

family systems disaster interventions and,
        74–75, 81
family therapist guidelines and, 75–76
funeral traditions, Black church and,
        40, 79–80, 81, 230
grief groups and, 40
"healthy cultural paranoia" of, 29, 69
institutional prejudice and cultural mistrust
        of, 21–22, 30, 69–70, 156–167
institutional racism and, 69, 70
multiple treatment modalities and, 76
multisystems intervention model and,
        76–77, 81
"Oh Freedom" spiritual and, 79–80
"parental children" role and, 72–73
power of prayer and, 79
practical implications regarding, 81
psychological trauma of perceived racism
        and, 69, 81
PTSD onset, racial factors in, 7–8
race and income segregation in, 24
racism denial and, 68
reaching out and, 76
relocation and dislocation traumas and,
        73, 231
socioeconomic inequities and, 23
spiritual and religious diversity of, 77–78
spirituality and religion elements of, 77–80,
        177, 233
spiritual metaphors and, 79, 80
strength-based intervention focus
        and, 75–76
"Testimony Therapy" concept and, 80
"the power of praise" and, 75–76
therapeutic rapport and, 69–70
therapy stigma and, 70
treatment resistance and, 78
See also African American elderly
        (Hurricane Katrina survivors);
        Children and crises; Jazz funeral

239

Farfel, M., 223

Faust, D. S., 230

Fawcett, J., 204

Federal Emergency Management Agency
  mental health emergency declaredness
      authority and, 186
  See also FEMA (Federal Emergency
      Management Agency)

Federal government in disaster mental health
      response
  Assistant Secretary for Preparedness and
      Response (ASPR) and, 186–187, 189, 192
  behavioral health services definition and
      focus of, 183, 185, 187, 193, 233–234
  best practices development and, 189, 234
  conclusions regarding, 193, 234
  Crisis Counseling Program Grant,
      FEMA and, 182
  deployable assets and, 188–189
  disaster behavioral health support programs
      and, 185–189
  disaster knowledge accumulation and, 234
  Disaster Mental Health Subcommittee,
      of National Biodefense Science Board
      and, 193
  documentation requirement waivers and, 182
  emergency response, federal government
      support, 183–185
  Emergency Response Team, of HHS and, 181
  Emergency System for the Advance
      Registration of Volunteer Health
      Professionals (ESAR-VHP) program and,
      188, 189
  Employee Assistance Program, of HHS
      and, 188
  Federal Occupational Health and, 188
  federal program funding process and, 185
  *The Federal Response to Hurricane Katrina:
      Lessons Learned* (White House) and, 192
  Health Resources and Services Administration
      (HRSA) and, 181, 185, 191
  Homeland Security Presidential Directive-21
      and, 192–193
  Hurricane Katrina Community Advisory
      Group study and, 192
  Hurricanes Katrina and Rita, aftermath of,
      192–193
  Hurricanes Katrina and Rita, federal programs
      responses and, 190–192

Indian Health Service and, 181

long-term community recovery focus of, 184

Louisiana Spirit Program and, 181

Medicaid systems and, 172, 175–176, 191

Medical Reserve Corp (MRC) and, 188, 189

National Center for Posttraumatic Stress
      Disorder (NCPTSD) and, 182, 190

National Disaster Medical System (NDMS)
      and, 188, 189

National Institute of Mental Health (NIMH)
      and, 182, 189

National Response Framework and, 182

National Summit to Address the Nation's
      Disaster Behavioral Health Preparedness
      and Response (by SAMHSA), 192

Pandemic and All-Hazards Preparedness Act
      (PAHPA, 2006) and, 186–187

practical implications regarding, 193

preexisting psychosocial problems and,
      184–185

Project Recovery of Mississippi Department
      of Health and, 191

psychosocial needs and, 184–185

public health and mental health preparedness
      and response focus of, 187

public health infrastructure and, 182

public health system's state
      control and, 184

Rapid Assessment Post Impact of Disaster
      (RAPID) grants and, 182

resilience as disaster preparedness element
      and, 187

SAMHSA Emergency Response Grants (SERG)
      program and, 186, 191

SAMHSA (Substance Abuse and
      Mental Health Services Administration)
      and, 181, 191

Stafford Act/Crisis Counseling Program
      and, 186

state and local rights respected by,
      184, 187, 190

Strategic National Stockpile of medical
      supplies and, 191

trauma and disaster mental health research
      and, 189–190

traumatic stress services for the military
      and, 189

U.S. Public Health Service and, 188, 189,
      190–191

About the Editor

Priscilla Dass-Brailsford is an associate professor in the Division of Counseling and Psychology at Lesley University. She has more than 20 years of clinical experience working with underserved and chronically traumatized populations in addition to working in child advocacy and conducting court-ordered sexual abuse evaluations. For several years, she has coordinated a statewide crisis team, the first of its kind at its inception. In this role, she responded to high-profile incidents of violence by supporting affected communities in their healing and recovery.

Her research projects are multiple: resiliency in the aftermath of political trauma and socioeconomic stress, the effects of community violence, multicultural research on institutional trust and racial identity, the effects of secondary trauma on first responders and other volunteers, and the benefits of walk-in mental health services for disaster survivors. She was a first responder in New York after the terrorist attacks in 2001 and was deployed to New Orleans immediately after Hurricane Katrina devastated the Gulf Coast in 2005. She has returned to New Orleans several times to work with mental health providers. This edited book was inspired by her work with the survivors of Hurricane Katrina and is written as an acknowledgment of their resiliency despite the challenges of loss, dislocation, recovery, and reconstruction.

About the Contributors

Priscilla D. Allen, PhD, is an associate professor of social work and the associate director of the Life Course and Aging Center at Louisiana State University (LSU). Prior to her appointment at LSU, she worked as a social worker in the nursing home setting and later as a long-term care ombudsman. During Hurricanes Katrina, Rita, Gustav, and Ike, she provided social work services in the Special Needs Shelter on the LSU campus. Her research interests include long-term care and psychosocial intervention with older persons, culture change in the nursing home, and societal influence of ageism.

Beth Boyd, PhD, is an enrolled member of the Seneca Nation of Indians. Since completing her PhD in 1992, she has taught in the clinical psychology graduate program at the University of South Dakota. She is involved in a number of projects seeking to train culturally competent clinical psychologists and to develop culturally responsive mental health services for Native American communities. She is a faculty member in the University of South Dakota Disaster Mental Health Institute and has responded to a number of disaster and crisis situations, particularly in Native communities. Her work with tribes has focused on crisis response team development, effects of trauma, youth suicide, and community empowerment following crisis.

Nancy Boyd-Franklin, PhD, is a professor at Rutgers University in the Graduate School of Applied and Professional Psychology. She is the author of five books, including *Black Families in Therapy: A Multisystems Approach* (Guilford, 1989), and an editor of *Children, Families and HIV/AIDS* (Guilford, 1995). Her more recent books are *Reaching Out in Family Therapy: Home-based, School and Community Interventions* with Brenna Bry (Guilford, 2000); *Boys Into Men: Raising Our African American Teenage Sons* with A. J. Franklin (Plume, 2001); and the second edition of *Black Families in Therapy: Understanding the African American Experience* (Guilford, 2003).

Karen F. Carr, PhD, is a licensed clinical psychologist living in Accra, Ghana, and working as the clinical director of Mobile Member Care Team–West Africa, which is a nonprofit organization providing training, consultation, crisis response, and counseling for cross-cultural workers in Africa. She received her PhD in clinical psychology from Virginia Commonwealth University in 1989. She then worked in forensic and community mental health crisis work for 8 years at Henrico Mental Health Services in Virginia. She began full-time overseas work in Africa in 2000.

Katie E. Cherry, PhD, is a professor of psychology and director of the Life Course and Aging Center at Louisiana State University. In 2002, she was awarded the Emogene Pliner Distinguished Professor of Aging Studies professorship for her contributions to the field of adult development and aging. She is currently a co-investigator in the Louisiana Health Aging

Study, a multidisciplinary research project funded by the National Institute on Aging to examine the determinants of longevity and healthy aging in the oldest-old. Her research interests include the psychosocial and cognitive consequences of Hurricanes Katrina and Rita.

Daniel Dodgen, PhD, is a director for At-Risk Individuals and Behavioral Health Coordination in the Office of the Assistant Secretary for Preparedness and Response at the U.S. Department of Health and Human Services. He is also executive director of the White House–directed national advisory group on disaster mental health. He previously was emergency coordinator for the Substance Abuse and Mental Health Services Administration, serving as the national mental health lead during Hurricane Katrina. He responded to the 1992 Los Angeles riots, 1994 Los Angeles earthquakes, 1995 Oklahoma City bombings, and the September 11th Pentagon attack in 2001. He is a licensed clinical psychologist in Washington, DC.

Ryan M. Engdahl is a graduate student in the University of South Dakota's Clinical Psychology PhD program. He is a graduate assistant in the Disaster Mental Health Institute. His research interests include posttraumatic stress disorder and the assessment of post-trauma reactions. He received a master's degree in 2008 and continues to work toward the completion of his doctoral degree with a specialization in disaster psychology.

Sandro Galea, MD, is a professor of epidemiology at the School of Public Health, research professor at the Institute of Social Research, and director of the Center for Global Health at the University of Michigan. He did his graduate training at the University of Toronto Medical School, at the Harvard University School of Public Health, and at the Columbia University Mailman School of Public Health. He is primarily interested in the social and economic production of health, particularly mental health and behavior in urban settings. He has an abiding interest in the health consequences of collectively experienced traumatic events.

J. Brian Houston, PhD, is an assistant professor of research in the Department of Psychiatry and Behavioral Sciences at the University of Oklahoma Health Sciences Center (OUHSC) and is Program Director for the Terrorism and Disaster Center at OUHSC, which is a member of the National Child Traumatic Stress Network. His research interests focus on disasters and the media, risk and crisis communication, and disaster mental health.

Kenyon C. Knapp, PhD, LPC, NBCC, is an associate professor of counseling and psychology at Troy University, Montgomery Campus, where he also teaches all the school counseling courses. He has worked as a school counselor, as a youth court counselor, and in many other positions with children and adolescents. He has worked with numerous crisis situations, such as suicides, physical and sexual abuse cases, and natural disasters such as Hurricane Katrina, and continues to develop this specialty. He also has an active private practice with the Alabama Baptist Children's Homes counseling division. However, his greatest joy and accomplishments come in the form of his wife and four children, who keep him practical, multitasking, and very grateful.

Sylvia A. Marotta, PhD, ABPP, is a professor of counseling at the George Washington University in Washington, DC. As a board-certified counseling psychologist trained in the scientist-practitioner model, she focuses her research on the stress continuum, from the daily hassles of human living to complex posttraumatic stress disorders at the pathology end of the continuum. She writes and presents nationally and internationally on the spectrum of stress disorders, family systems, diversity, and attachment-related trauma. She received her PhD in counseling psychology from the University of Houston in 1992.

Harriet G. McCombs, PhD, is an ordained minister in the African Methodist Episcopal (AME) Church. She received her PhD in psychology from the University of Nebraska and a master's certificate in Global Mental Health: Refugee Trauma from Harvard University. She has served on the faculties of three major universities and as a public health advisor in the federal government. She has pioneered work in integrating the mental health services within disaster responses, faith communities, and primary health care settings. She serves on the Health Commission of the AME Church as emotional wellness coordinator.

Jessica Meed is a PhD student at the University of North Carolina at Chapel Hill's Gillings School of Public Health. She has a master's of public administration from Baruch College–School of Public Affairs (2005). She has done graduate training in the areas of refugee management and disaster response and traumatic stress.

Betty Pfefferbaum, MD, JD, is a board-certified general and child psychiatrist and professor and chairman of the Department of Psychiatry and Behavioral Sciences at the University of Oklahoma College of Medicine where she holds the Paul and Ruth Jonas Chair. She is the director of the Terrorism and Disaster Center of the National Child Traumatic Stress Network and Head of the Child Research Section of the National Center for Disaster Mental Health Research.

Randal P. Quevillon, PhD, is a professor and the chair of the Psychology Department at the University of South Dakota. He is also a teaching faculty member of the Disaster Mental Health Institute. He specializes in rural community mental health, stress and social support, community interventions, extending psychological services to underserved groups, and community issues in recovery from disasters. He has published in the areas of disaster management, behavioral self-control, rural community mental health, interventions in disasters, and aviation disasters.

Gilbert Reyes, PhD, is a licensed clinical psychologist and an associate dean in the School of Psychology at Fielding Graduate University. He consults with the Terrorism and Disaster Center of the National Child Traumatic Stress Network and chairs the Disaster Relief Committee for the American Psychological Association's Division of Trauma Psychology. He is the lead editor of both the *Handbook of International Disaster Psychology* and *The Encyclopedia of Psychological Trauma*.

Karen Fraser Wyche, MSW, PhD, is a professor in the Department of Psychiatry and Behavioral Sciences at the University of Oklahoma Health Sciences Center (OUHSC) and a project director at the Terrorism and Disaster Center at OUHSC, which is a member of the National Child Traumatic Stress Network. Her research and publications focus on the role of sociocultural and socioeconomic factors in a variety of outcomes including mental and physical health, ethnic identity, and community resilience.